Ryszard Kapuściński

Ryszard Kapuściński

A Life

◆

ARTUR DOMOSŁAWSKI

Translated by Antonia Lloyd-Jones

VERSO

London • New York

This English-language edition first published by Verso 2012
© Verso 2012
Translation © Antonia Lloyd-Jones 2012
First published as *Kapuściński non-fiction*
© Świat Książki 2010

1 3 5 7 9 10 8 6 4 2

Verso
UK: 6 Meard Street, London W1F 0EG
US: 20 Jay Street, Suite 1010, Brooklyn, NY 11201
www.versobooks.com

Verso is the imprint of New Left Books

ISBN-13: 978-1-84467-858-7

British Library Cataloguing in Publication Data
A catalogue record for this book is available from the British Library

Library of Congress Cataloging-in-Publication Data
Domoslawski, Artur, 1967-
[Kapuscinski non-fiction. English]
Ryszard Kapuscinski : a life / Artur Domoslawski ; translated by Antonia Lloyd-Jones.
   p. cm.
Includes bibliographical references and index.
ISBN 978-1-84467-858-7 (hardback) -- ISBN 978-1-84467-918-8 (ebook)
1. Kapuscinski, Ryszard. 2. Journalists--Poland--Biography. I. Lloyd-Jones, Antonia. II. Title.
PN5355.P62K36313 2012
070.92--dc23
[B]

2012012437

Typeset in Bembo by Hewer UK Ltd, Edinburgh
Printed in the US by Maple Vail

Everyone has three lives: a public life, a private life, and a secret life.
Gabriel García Márquez to his biographer, Gerald Martin

All sorts of biographies enjoy great popularity (every bookshop has a large, separate biographical section). It implies a sort of self-defence reaction against the advancing anonymity of the world. People still have a need to commune (if only through reading) with someone specific, an individual who has a name, a face, habits and desires. The appeal of biography also comes from the fact that people would like to see how this great person achieved greatness, they'd like to get an inside look at his style.
Ryszard Kapuściński, *Lapidarium*

The merit of writers' biographies continues to be disputed. For some, the work is all we need to know. Others say they love the books, so they want to know more about the people who wrote them. Then there is always the possibility that the life will throw light on the books and deepen our understanding of them.
Ian Buruma, writer and journalist

The lives of writers are a legitimate subject of inquiry; and the truth should not be skimped. It may well be, in fact, that a full account of a writer's life might in the end be more a work of literature and more illuminating – of a cultural or historical moment – than the writer's books.
V. S. Naipaul, writer, Nobel Prize winner, 2001

A biography can never fully reveal the source of its subject. The commonplace that a biographer has found the 'key' to a person's life is implausible. People are too complicated and inconsistent for this to be true. The best a biographer can hope for is to illuminate aspects of a life and seek to give glimpses of the subject, and that way tell a story.
Patrick French, biographer of V. S. Naipaul

Contents

The Smile

More than anything, one is struck by the smile. Always the same smile, everywhere, as if that face were never sad, worried or angry. And if it wasn't smiling, it was pensive or focused instead. Or sheepish. 'I'm not disturbing you, am I?' he would ask whenever, whether unheralded or even if expected, he dropped in at the newspaper office and stopped by someone's desk or room. And there was that smile again: apologetic, very slightly embarrassed. It was a defensive smile that kept the door open for retreat.

How many times did I hear him effusively greet a friend he had known for half a century, a female acquaintance he saw from time to time, an editor with whom he needed to negotiate, or a student he'd never met before who had come to show him her dissertation on his work – and always with that same smile on his face?

'Oh, how modest he is.'

'He always listens so carefully to what you have to say.'

'Oh yes, we're friends.'

Everyone who ever talked to him had the same impression.

And so at the start of this journey through his life I am surprised when some of his old friends struggle to fish the anecdotes and situations from their memories, and finish their story before the story I am expecting to hear has even begun.

'Oh God, we knew each other for decades, but I know so little about him – nothing really. How sad!'

They came away from every encounter feeling that they had had a fascinating, unforgettable conversation. Now they are realising that they did all the talking. He said nothing – he just listened.

'The smile you mentioned was a mask that became natural to him over the years,' says an old friend who really did know him well. 'Modesty? That was a mask too,' she says. 'There are various things you could say about him, but not that he was modest. He had a high opinion of himself – he believed he had things to say that other people have no idea about.'

We agree that his mild manner and friendliness, the fact that he was not full of himself, were taken for modesty.

I say I don't know where to start my account of him; perhaps it will begin with some impressions on the theme of his smile. Because when someone has the same smile for everyone, it cannot be just friendliness – there has to be more to it, doesn't she think?

'He used that smile to disarm the world when it could have done him harm. Those soldiers, who let him pass through prohibited zones in Africa, but who could have shot him. The Communist Party decision-makers who sent him out into the world. The potentially jealous people, who are all too common in the journalist's profession. Why not try to find out if he learned that smile during a war? Did that smile ever save his life?'

'Right,' says one of his closest male friends, to whom I recount this conversation, 'but is that all there is to it? I always felt that he lived in a world of mystery, that he was hiding a lot of secrets – from his friends, his loved ones and from himself; yes, yes, you can also have secrets from your-self. What sort of secrets did he have? Personal ones, political ones, writer's ones. Despite his world fame, which should have given him self-confidence and peace of mind, there was something weighing him down. I could see it in his eyes, in his step; that smile, that softness, that way of giving the impression that you like everyone and are listening, even when they're talk-ing nonsense.'

The secrets of Ryszard Kapuściński. Is that what I should call my book about the man known as the 'reporter of the twentieth century', my mentor and special friend, close and not so close, whom – I often find myself think-ing – I will come to know better now?

Yes, we did a lot of talking throughout the last ten years of his life, always in the private loft-kingdom of his house on Prokuratorska Street in the Warsaw district of Ochota. I must have been there a hundred times, but as I see with hindsight, I got to know a smaller part of Mr Kapuściński – who with closer acquaintance became Ryszard, then Rysiek – than I thought I had. We talked about recent journeys we had made and ones we were planning; about intelligent books and stupid governments; about what was happening in politics and what we'd read in the papers; about how we should never, ever give up our passions, even if someone tried to beat them out of us. And we talked a lot about people: Maestro Kapuściński loved to gossip.

But I never questioned him about how a career was made in People's Poland; what strings had to be pulled, to what uses he had put his smile, and what price had to be paid. I sensed that he didn't like questions about his past, and whenever the conversation headed in that direction, he would deftly change the subject. Sometimes he commented that, democracy or no democracy, conformism and the herd mentality are alike, even though times change. I never asked questions about which side he was on during Poland's various political turning points of the past half-century, about what he had done and thought. Or what he had been looking for as he eagerly set off for Congo after Lumumba's assassination, as he drove into the middle of a revolution begun in the name of Allah, or toured a rebellious Poland in the carnival era of 1980–81. His ideas and motivations seemed perfectly clear back then, though now perhaps I understand them better. I never inquired whether he might occasionally have embellished or invented anything, as some foreign critics claimed. Did he feel fulfilled? I think he did.

Now as I spend my time in libraries and other archives, among the books and documents he kept at home, as I travel in his footsteps through Africa and Latin America, and above all as I talk to his close friends, acquaintances, and people who shared episodes in his life, I am discovering a Kapuściński who almost seems a stranger. Would anyone who ever saw, heard, or met him believe that this mild-mannered man with the permanent smile once seized an official by the lapels, pinned him to the wall, and grappled with him, yelling, 'How dare you, you bastard!' (I will return to this story later.)

We often discover him through a joint effort, as we swap observations and try to put names to things we can only just discern. To some degree, all my interlocutors are co-authors of this book, even if they do not agree with all of it or with its conclusion.

Some of the people who know some of Kapuściński's secrets ask, 'So, will this be a biography or the portrait of a saint?'

A woman who was once in love with him says, 'I hope you aren't writing a hagiography. Rysiek was a wonderful, colourful guy: a reporter, traveller, writer, husband, father. And lover. He was a complex man, living in tangled times, in several eras, in various worlds.'

'Don't worry,' I answer. 'I owe him a great deal, but I won't take part in the "beatification process".'

We're both smiling. Do admiration and friendship have to kill off inquiry?

They probably don't help. I won't pretend – I do have a problem with this, and writing this book has been a struggle between competing loyalties.

I'm still looking for a tone for my account, trying to devise its architecture. Will the master's narrative inventions come to the rescue?

> The worst chaos is on the big round table: photos of various sizes, cassettes . . . And more posters and albums, records and books acquired or given by people, the collected remnants of an era just ended . . . Now, at the very thought of trying to put everything in order . . . I am overcome by both aversion and profound fatigue.[1]

As a way of sorting things out, I have put several cardboard binders on the windowsill and labelled them: 'Pińsk and the war', 'High school, college, first poems', 'ZMP (Union of Polish Youth), PZPR (Polish United Workers' Party), Stalinism, revisionism', 'African controversies', 'Fiction – non-fiction'. Before making my final selection of notes, cuttings and books, I review the photographs – I almost always do this before sitting down to write a major piece. A photograph stirs a chord that words cannot set in motion. (I'm falling into a trap, because I'm sure the photograph of Kapuściński's smile will seduce me as easily as the original did, leaving me incapable of pursuing a proper investigation.)

I'm sitting alone looking through notes and pictures on the table, listening to taped conversations.[2]

I'll try to start like this . . .

I

Daguerreotypes

In one of the last photographs, Kapuściński, smiling of course, is surrounded by a group of young people. These are boys and girls from the Leonardo da Vinci Lycée and the University of Trento, on 17 October 2006 at a mountain inn not far from the city of Bolzano in Italy. One of the participants, Anna, asked if he would be willing to answer a personal question. Kapuściński coyly replied that there was nothing that hadn't already been written about him, that no secrets remained. (Now, after an almost three-year journey through his life, I know that a great deal has been written about his work, but almost nothing about the man himself.) The girl is well prepared and quotes one of Kapuściński's own poems to him:

> Only those clad in sackcloth
> are able to take upon themselves
> the suffering of another
> to share his pain[1]

Then she asks why he has devoted his life to writing about poor people. Kapuściński replies that 20 percent of the people in the world are wealthy, and the rest are poor. And that if you belong to the chosen few, you are extremely privileged. You live in a paradise beyond the reach of most people on the planet. He shares some discoveries about life: a man can be impoverished not because he is hungry or has no possessions, but because he is ignored and despised: 'Poverty is a state of inability to express your opinion.'[2] That is why he speaks in their name. Someone has to.

This Promethean manifesto is his last public statement in that vein. By this point, Kapuściński is feeling overwhelmed by pessimism and a presentiment of the approaching end. A few days later, he refuses to meet a friend for coffee. Some interesting, but unfamiliar, people were to be joining them. 'There comes a moment in life when we can no longer take in new faces,' he notes afterwards. To meet with strangers he would have to 'furnish his face', stick on the smile, but he no longer has the desire or the strength to do so.[3]

Here's a picture taken a few years earlier, in Oviedo in 2003, when Kapuściński is still in good shape. He is receiving the Prince of Asturias Award for Communications and Humanities, regarded as the Nobel Prize of the Latin American world (and how proud he was of it!). He is stunned. Fulfilled and appreciated. As he thanks Prince Felipe, he finds it hard to hide his emotion. In justification of its choice, the jury wrote that he embodied the independence of the reporter; and that for half a century, at risk of life and health, he monitored wars and conflicts on several continents. Nor did the jury fail to acknowledge that he was on the side of the disadvantaged.

Kapuściński was filled with pride at receiving the award jointly with the Peruvian priest Gustavo Gutiérrez, father of liberation theology, defender of the excluded and critic of social inequality. As a thirty-something correspondent working in Latin America for the Polish Press Agency, Kapuściński had been fascinated by the rebel movement. But he never met Father Gutiérrez at the time. For a reporter from poor, socialist Poland, with limited funds, gaining access to an intellectual star such as Gutiérrez would have been difficult. More than three decades later, he stood next to his hero as joint winner of a coveted award.

And here are some photographs with great writers, including a series with the Nobel Prize–winner Gabriel García Márquez during journalism workshops in Mexico City. García Márquez invited Kapuściński, as a master of the craft, to run workshops for reporters from Latin America. I remember his being adamant that *Gazeta Wyborcza* use one of these photos to illustrate an interview with him about the transformations in Latin America, and that he almost withdrew the text shortly before the deadline, when it turned out that the picture wouldn't fit on the page. ('This interview is worthless! It should go in the bin if no one knows the reason I was in Mexico!' he cried in boyish pique. He calmed down when I told him that alongside our conversation would be a short piece about his workshops with García Márquez and a picture of them together.)

Another photo shows him having dinner with Salman Rushdie in the 1980s, in New York or perhaps London. After reading Kapuściński's book about the war in Angola, and fascinated by his descriptions of the wooden city floating away, Rushdie wrote that numerous reporters had seen the wooden city, but Kapuściński was the only one to have noticed it. He called him a 'codebreaker' of the encrypted dark century.

One photograph attracts my attention, not because of what it depicts, but because of something written later in connection with the moment immortalized in it. It shows an open air café in San Sebastian in 1996. Here is Kapuściński with the Polish philosopher Father Józef Tischner, the Polish editor-in-chief of *Gazeta Wyborcza* Adam Michnik and Jorge Ruiz, Warsaw correspondent for the Spanish news agency, EFE. All four were taking part in seminars at a summer university in the Basque country. After Kapuściński's death, Michnik wrote that he had asked him that summer when he'd stopped believing in communism. Kapuściński had replied that 1956 was decisive, though he had remained permanently on the side of the poor and the disadvantaged.

This picture has no date. Nor is Kapuściński in it – he took it himself, but it says more than many of the portraits. It shows a small table, with several necessities for his next journey lying on it: books (one of the titles, surprisingly, is *Africa for Beginners*), notebooks, folders, several small wallets, a camera, some pills, little bottles of heart drops and Amol (a herbal tonic). I call this picture 'life on the road'.

The pills and bottles remind me of another photograph, which I saw at the home of Kapuściński's friends Agnieszka and Andrzej Krzysztof Wróblewski. In it, he seems thinner than in all the other photos from that era – or is that just auto-suggestion? It's September 1964, Paris. As they walk past one of the many cafés, his friends notice a book in Polish lying on a table. Shortly after, Kapuściński appears; he has just briefly stepped away. He is there with his wife, Alicja, gathering his strength after suffering from cerebral malaria and tuberculosis in Africa. One of his rare holidays, because he doesn't know how to relax – he gets bored, and doing nothing makes him twitchy. On their way home that night from the café, they lose their way. Kapuściński remembers a petrol station next to the campsite where they are to spend the night. Because he had no sense of direction, they wander till dawn. ('How on earth did he manage in Africa?' say his friends, clutching their heads.)

Only now does it occur to me that the photographs are arranged in reverse chronology, but I need to tell – and I want to understand – from what sort of place, in what way and by what road he reached the students at Bolzano, Gabriel García Márquez and Salman Rushdie, how he came to his faith and lack of faith in socialism, and a hundred other things besides.

So, before the reporter sets off on a journey, climbing rocky paths and fighting his way through hostile bush, before he comes to Africans who mistrust whites, or discovers the confused world of the conquerors and the conquered, before he investigates the mysteries of rebellions and revolutions, gets to know a hundred other places and sees a thousand mind-boggling things, there is Pińsk, a house on Błotna Street, and a wooden rocking horse on which little Rysio sits, putting on a smile, making an impatient face, or squinting because of the sunlight shining in his eyes.

Pińsk: The Beginning

This is one of the earliest photographs. It differs from the one on the balcony of the house on Błotna Street, but again features the rocking horse, now in the yard. Little Rysio's hair is combed slightly to the right and he wears a warm jacket but no hat, so it must be spring or autumn. He may be three or four years old. It is the essence of childhood, nothing more.

A few later photographs have survived: showing him wrapped up as he walks along a street in winter, holding his father's hand. A shop window in the background is inscribed 'Józef Izaak'. In a similar photo of him with his mother, on the same street, he wears shorts; it is a sunny day in the summer of 1937, when he was five years old.

These photographs were taken in Pińsk, a city then in eastern Poland and now in Belarus. His parents, Maria and Józef, were from elsewhere. His mother, whose maiden name was Bobkowa, was the granddaughter of a baker known locally as 'the Magyar'. (Because of a dark complexion? because he was an immigrant?) Maria came to Pińsk from Bochnia, near Kraków; Józef, the son of a local civil servant, was from the Kielce region. The government of the new Polish state, which came into existence after the First World War, wanted Poles to resettle along the eastern border, where they could disseminate Polish education, but few were keen to uproot themselves and go to a distant, culturally alien region.

Polish was the minority language in Pińsk. Two-thirds of the citizens were Jews and the rest were Belarusians, Ukrainians and Russians, plus a handful of Germans. Shortly before the outbreak of the Second World War, following the influx of settlers from the heart of Poland, almost one in four of Pińsk's 35,000 citizens was an ethnic Pole.

Going to Pińsk (or Polesie, as the surrounding region is called) from central or southern Poland was a cross between exile and missionary work. Kapuściński used to say that his parents were told, in effect, 'If you want

jobs, go to teacher training college, and when you graduate, go to Polesie.'
And that is just what Maria and Józef did.

The two young teachers arrived in Pińsk on the eve of the Great
Depression. 'I was born the child of settlers,' said Kapuściński. It was 1932.
Just over a year later, his sister, Basia (short for Barbara), was born.

Thirty years after the war, Kapuściński goes to visit the city of his childhood
for the first time. It is the mid-1970s, and Pińsk now lies within the Soviet
Union.

Standing in Kościuszko Street (then, as today, Lenin Street), he immediately recognizes his surroundings. That is Gregorowicz's restaurant, where
Mama used to take him for ice cream. Over there is 3 May Square and
there, Bernardyńska Street. Some images from his childhood, 'though they
are covered up by other ones, still exist'. Later he will say, 'I feel that if I
don't write about it, the world of pre-war Pińsk will cease to exist, because
it probably remains only in my head.'[1]

Does the seven-year-old boy from the remote province dream of the
journeys inspired by Pińsk's location or by the landscape beyond the
window? Does the sight of the Riverine Flotilla of the Polish Navy stationed
there stir his imagination? Knowing who the boy would become, one
would like to conjure up a story of this kind.

'Polesie was truly exotic,' he told an interviewer. 'Lots of rivers and
canals, great floodplains. If you boarded a boat, you could sail the seas without disembarking. Pińsk was connected by water to all the oceans.'[2] How
do you sail to the oceans from Pińsk? Along rivers to the Baltic Sea, then
via the Baltic Sea to the Atlantic; or along the River Dnieper to the Black
Sea, and from there via the Bosporus, the Mediterranean and the Suez
Canal to the Indian Ocean . . .

The folk beliefs of Polesie say more about the world Kapuściński came from
than all the historical stories about dukes, wars and sacred relics. Country
people tell stories about the suicide, whose soul wanders the local woods,
still wearing his body:

> People regard a dead man remaining on earth and wandering as a punish-
> ment imposed on his soul by the Lord God. This soul cannot get into
> heaven. According to folk belief, there is always a penitent soul of this
> kind inside a whirlwind, and if one were to throw a knife at it, blood
> would be shed. But naturally it is hard to hit![3]

This is like an Eastern European version of Macondo, the mythical land
invented by Gabriel García Márquez in One Hundred Years of Solitude. In
Macondo people fly around the village on carpets, or rise and hover in the

air after drinking a cup of chocolate; they also have epidemic outbreaks of insomnia and memory loss.

Kapuściński sees associations with Africa. Among his handwritten notes I find a comparison, titled *Polesie found in Africa*, of the land of his childhood years with the continent he described as a reporter. Apart from poverty, hunger and disease, he lists belief in a spirit world, a cult of ancestors, and consciousness of tribal identity. Also, like Africa, Polesie is 'colonized terrain'. There is, moreover, a handful of tangible similarities: no electricity, no surfaced roads, no shoes.

In other words, a description of the city where Kapuściński's parents came to live in the early 1930s.

Kapuściński's enduring memories of his family home are meagre. He remembers little from before the war. His account contains more intuition, more impressions bordering on poetry and fantasy, than specific information.

In sketches for a book about Pińsk (which he planned to write but never did), he says his father was good to him, and that this was important, sacred. He admits to having had no sense of his mother as a separate being; his parents were a single entity.

The only other person able to dredge up memories of the family home before the war is his sister, Barbara. As a student of English, she emigrated in the 1960s to Great Britain and later to Canada. Kapuściński was so angry at her departure that their relationship initially cooled. He believed it was necessary to stay in Poland and help build the country's future after the destruction of the Second World War. Then a loyal member of the Communist Party, he felt that leaving for the West was a betrayal. But he and his sister had other causes of conflict. In People's Poland the political authorities disapproved of anyone who had relatives in the West. Remaining abroad, in a capitalist country, was regarded as a form of running away and of renouncing one's socialist fatherland. Kapuściński, who at the time had recently started working at the state press agency, was afraid that his sister's emigration to the West might damage his reputation, undermine the trust of the decision-makers, and ruin his developing career.

'We weren't rich, but we weren't deprived in any way. Both our parents worked at a school,' recalls Barbara, whose married name is Wiśniewska, when I spend three days talking to her in Vancouver in June 2008.

Her testimony differs from that in certain of Kapuściński's accounts which suggest he came from an impoverished background in Pińsk. It is true that teachers earned little in those days, but they belonged to a social stratum corresponding to the modern middle class; they were the cultural élite, especially in a provincial town like Pińsk. Photographs of their several-storey house also reveal that the Kapuścińskis did not live in a shack.

Yet the memories of poverty in Pińsk are a partly justified piece of literary self-creation. Little Rysio really did see poverty all around him. Although the Kapuścińskis themselves were not indigent, poverty dominated the local landscape; it was a ubiquitous element of his childhood. ('This year's spring,' we read in a 1936 issue of *Nowe Echo Pińskie* (Pińsk New Echo), 'fortunately quite an early one, has stirred new hopes among the unemployed masses that the tough winter is over, when frequently there were no potatoes in the house for dinner, and when gaunt, hungry children huddled together in cold, unheated hovels').

Over the years, Kapuściński relates pieces from the book he planned to (but never did) write about Pińsk in the 1930s in interviews and chats, such as:

I think that era and Pińsk's pleasant climate of co-existing, cooperating multiculturalism is worth salvaging in the modern, stressed-out world . . .

I was shaped by everything that shapes so-called borderlands man. Borderlands man is always and everywhere an intercultural person – someone 'in between'. He is a person who learns from childhood, from playing in the yard, that people are different, and that otherness is simply a feature of mankind . . . In Pińsk one kid would bring a herring from home, another a piece of koulibiac, and a third a chop . . . Being from the borderlands means being open to other cultures, or more than that – borderlands people do not regard other cultures as different, but as part of their own culture . . .

It was a town full of friendly people and friendly streets. Until the outbreak of war, I never saw any conflict there. It was a place without pomp or show, a place full of modest, ordinary people. As teachers, my parents were those sorts of people too. Maybe that's why I always felt all right later on in the so-called Third World, where people are distinguished not by wealth but hospitality, not by ostentation but cooperation.[4]

Was there really such an idyllic world on the borders where several nations, religions and cultures met? In that part of the world, during the 1930s, when the entire region seethed with ethnic, religious and class hatred?

It is 1930, and parliamentary elections are approaching. *Piński Przegląd Diecezjalny* – the 'Pińsk Diocesan Review', a periodical issued by the church – asks

whether the non-Christian, or unfaithful, indifferent Christian will make sure that only laws which are in accordance with the teachings of the Gospels will emerge from the Sejm and the Senate? Of course not. And if the majority of members of parliament are non-Christian or not very Christian, one can always expect non-Christian laws. Hence the final conclusion: to vote only for righteous, sincere Christians.[5]

And in another issue of the same journal: 'From the pulpit one should clearly give the congregation the following instructions: . . . not to vote for the candidate lists of other denominations (Jewish, Orthodox, etc.)'.[6]

The Polish press issued in Pińsk and Polesie in the 1930s never stops warning of threats – from communists, Jews, Belarusians and Ukrainians.

Dwutygodnik Kresowy – the *Borderlands Bi-Weekly* – calls for a battle against 'Jewishness' and for 'the establishment of full Polishness'. It warns that 'despite its best intentions', society 'will not cope with Jewishness' on its own; 'the municipal authorities must insist on legislation that recognizes the precedence of Poles in Poland'.[7]

The overwhelming majority of citizens in Pińsk are Jews, yet the pro-government *Echo Pińskie* (Pińsk Echo) demands that Poles should hold the majority on the city council and should have their own mayor – and that is what happens.

Unlike cities in the Białystok region, as well as Wilno (now Vilnius) or Lwów (now Lviv), Pińsk in the 1930s never goes so far as to institute pogroms against the Jewish population, and the influence of the nationalist camp is small. However, according to the Jewish historian of Pińsk, Azriel Shohat, the city's political landscape is far from idyllic:

> This discrimination was strongly felt in Pinsk. Despite the fact that it was a Jewish city for the most part, the city's mayor was a Pole and, until 1927, the city was run by an administrative body appointed by the Polish authorities. The city council included only two Jews and they, too, were appointed by the Polish authorities.[8]

In the 1930s, Polish nationalists are often heard proclaiming 'each to one's own for one's own', which serves as a form of incitement to boycott Jewish shops. This campaign, and the accompanying rise in anti-Semitism, does not bypass Pińsk. People talk about it at home, on the street, at work and in church.

Years later, the same Jewish historian will write,

> Anti-Semitic students who came from outside the city plotted attacks against the Jews. However neither of these attempts succeeded. The Polish businesses could not compete with the Jewish ones and the Jewish youth knew how to silence the Polish hooligans and caused them to flee the city.[9]

In interviews and conversations, Kapuściński idealized the land of his childhood, depicting Pińsk as a perfect, harmonious place, where tolerance reigned and people regarded mutual dissimilarity as a treasure. Yet in his notes for the book on Pińsk, that image becomes complicated, full of stains and flaws. Here, for instance, is an extract titled 'Good Manners for Christian Children':

> [W]hen I look into the depths of time towards my childhood, the first thing I see is the dog catcher's wagon coming down our bumpy road, Błotna Street, later called Perets Street and now Suvorov . . . when the dog catchers see a dog, they rush towards it and surround it, emitting wild shrieks, and then you hear the swish of a lasso and the terrified animal howling as they drag it away and throw it in a cage. Soon after, the wagon moves on.
>
> Why these nasty, scruffy men are catching the poor dogs is something every Christian child will discover if he gets up to any mischief. Be good, he or she will then hear Mama or Grandma warn, or the dog catchers will take you away to make matzos! And so thanks to the constant presence of the dog catchers on the streets of our town, the Christian children are well brought up — not one of them wants to be eaten as an anonymous piece of brittle kosher flatbread.[10]

Are tales about Jews performing the ritual murder of Christian children so as to extract their blood and add it to their matzos — a monstrous myth, repeated in churches and Catholic homes, which for centuries was at the root of intolerance, pogroms and crimes against Jews — something little Rysio hears on the street, from neighbours, from his relatives?

His sister, Basia, a year younger, remembers stories of this kind. Here is one she told me: 'An old Jew with a long beard once accosted me in the street. "Wait here," he said, "I'll go indoors and fetch you some sweets." So I stand outside his house, waiting. A neighbour appears, and she says: "What are you doing here, Basia?" "I'm waiting for him," I say, pointing at the Jew's house. "He promised to bring me some sweets." "Run away from here at once, child! He wants to kidnap you for his matzos!"'

She then added, 'In those days people used to say the Jews needed children's blood for their rituals.'

In the summer of 1942, the army of the Third Reich attacked the Soviet Union, taking Pińsk in the process. Eleven thousand of the city's Jews were killed at once in two mass executions. The rest were driven into a ghetto, where a year later a resistance movement formed and a revolt occurred. A few of the Jews managed to escape and hide in the forest. Some joined partisan groups; others were finished off by the locals.

Years later, Nahum Boneh, a witness to that place and time who, after the war, headed the association of Pińsk Jews in Israel, wrote that

> it was very dangerous for a Jew to be a member of a partisan group. In those days any Gentile who encountered a lone Jew could murder him or hand him over to the Germans. Among the partisans too there were

anti-Semites who exploited every occasion (and there were many) to kill Jews, even though they were partisans.[11]

Among the accounts gathered by Boneh, there is also evidence that some Poles from Pińsk helped their Jewish neighbours, but Boneh's verdict leaves no room for illusion: 'the entire Gentile population waited passively and even happily for the extermination of the Jews and the opportunity to steal their possessions.'[12]

Kapuściński's Pińsk, 'a town full of friendly people and friendly streets', was a wonderful Arcadia, the harmonious world that in adult life he desired for Africa, Latin America and all the inhabitants of the poor South. Was it also an element of his literary self-creation? A bit of myth-making to under-pin the biography of an 'interpreter of cultures', as he wished to be seen at the end of his life? It would usefully point to the roots of this predisposition: here is a man of dialogue and many encounters with the Other, who has lived and breathed multiculturalism since childhood and has it in his blood.

Between the Pińsk of the home archive – the Pińsk of the dog catchers, where Poles murder Jews themselves or turn them over to the Germans to be murdered – and the idyllic Arcadia of Kapuściński's casual talk and inter-views lies a yawning chasm. Indeed, the chasm is so broad that it is hard not to wonder whether these two images of the city never came together in the long-heralded book simply because they were so contradictory and so mutually repellent.

Their father taught practical technology; Barbara cannot remember what their mother taught. She may have given lessons on everything – reading, writing and arithmetic for the youngest schoolchildren.

During the day, Rysieczek (the diminutive name his mother gives him) and Żabcia ('Froggie', as she calls little Basia) are looked after by a nanny, the hunchbacked Masia. Following her own mother's death, Maria Kapuścińska takes over the care of her teenage sister, Oleńka. Barbara's glimmers of childhood memory indicate that her parents had a large circle of friends and acquaintances, and that social life flourished in their home.

To say that Rysieczek is the apple of his mother's eye says nothing about their feelings or relationship. She loves her daughter, but she worships her son. He is the loveliest, the cleverest, the most intelligent. Maria Kapuścińska's faith in her son's genius – according to family friends who knew her after the war – goes much further than the average mother's idolizing of a talented son. 'My son, my son' – she spoke of him adoringly, in a sort of elation, as Kapuściński's widow, Alicja, described it.

His mother's youth coincided with the period between the wars, an era when patriotism was often associated with a uniform. For Pińsk's Polish minority, the main centre for parties and gatherings was the officers' casino.

There the Kapuścińskis attended elegant balls, with Maria – her hair styled like the film star Jadwiga Smosarska – wearing a little hat and looking proud of belonging to the élite. When twenty-something Rysiek, as a student at Warsaw University, came home from military training in a field uniform, he clicked his heels together and cried, 'Second Lieutenant Ryszard Kapuściński reporting at home!' whereupon his mother burst into tears and declared, 'My son is an officer!'

Maria found it hard to bear her son's long absences when, as a correspondent for the Polish Press Agency (PAP), he would disappear for months on end, sometimes spending more than a year at a time in Africa or Latin America and occasionally offering no signs of life for several weeks. Whenever he went away, he asked his friends to 'keep an eye on my parents'. From afar he wrote loving letters to 'Maminka', as he started calling his mother when he returned from one of his first trips abroad, to Czechoslovakia.

To know at least where he was, what was occupying his thoughts, and what he was witnessing, his mother would go to the PAP's head office on the corner of Jerozolimskie Avenue and Nowy Świat Street to ask for her son's reports. Often she received his articles before they were issued in PAP bulletins. Only once was she deliberately not given a report to read. It was from Nigeria, in 1966, just after a coup d'état:

> I was waiting for them to set me on fire . . . I felt an animal fear, a fear that struck me with paralysis; I stood rooted to the ground, as if I was buried up to the neck . . . My life was going to end in inhuman torment. My life was going to go out in flames . . . They waved a knife before my eyes. They pointed it at my heart.[13]

The editor, Wiesława Bolimowska, went to the head of the department, Michał Hoffman, and insisted: 'We can't let this go out, because Mrs Kapuścińska will die of a heart attack if she reads it.' In order to stop the newspapers from reprinting the article, they blocked its publication in all the agency's bulletins, which was a frequent practice. A decade later, it appeared as 'The Burning Roadblocks' in Kapuściński's collection of reports titled *The Soccer War*. Maria Kapuścińska was no longer alive; she died in 1974 at the age of sixty-three.

The father, by contrast, enjoyed making fun of his son. Whenever Rysiek was keenly studying something, he always underlined important sentences in books – a habit he continued throughout life, initially as a renowned reporter and then as a world-famous writer – and his father would provoke him by saying: 'Go to bed, Rysio. I'll have the whole book underlined for you by morning.'

He also used to joke that Rysiek was of medium height, causing Maria to burst out, 'What do you mean, medium? Rysio is tall!' His father would laugh and say, 'Rysio is medium taller and I'm medium smaller', at which point his mother would end the debate by shouting, 'What are you on about, old man? You're small, and my son is tall!'

Rysiek could not look to his father for inspiring conversation about culture, books, politics or the world. For years he suffered from feeling he was a poorly educated provincial who had been given little at home and had had to achieve everything through hard work. Once he told me that as a young reporter, whenever he used to meet his fellow writers Kazimierz Dziewanowski and Wojciech Giełżyński, both of whom came from truly intellectual homes, he was ashamed to speak up. 'They knew all about everything; they used to exchange names and book titles I had never even heard of,' he said, perhaps with a note of pride at having outdistanced these colleagues. Yet many years earlier, as he sat with them not knowing what and how to contribute to the conversation, he must have felt pain rather than pride.

Józef Kapuściński only dimly understood his son's occupation. He was outraged to see newspapers featuring the name 'Kapuściński' spread across the floor to be trodden on or used to line the waste bin. A conscientious and dutiful man, he claimed to have never once been late for a lesson. He found it irritating that his son shut himself in his room for hours at a stretch doing goodness knows what (in other words, writing) instead of going to work and earning a living for his family. In Józef's mind, someone who went to work was working, while someone who sat at home for days on end was not.

Once when he came to visit his son and daughter-in-law, he inquired, 'Were you at work today, Rysio?'

'Yes, Dad, I was.'

'What time did you have to be there?'

'At eight, Dad, eight o'clock,' lied his son, to avoid a pointless argument.

Another time, Józef Kapuściński waxed indignant when a female friend of his son and daughter-in-law mentioned that her double surname consisted of her maiden name combined with her husband's. 'Where is your respect for your husband?' he bristled.

As Kapuściński's sister told me, to the end of his days their father, who died in 1977, never fully understoond what Rysiek did or who he was.

3

War

I am seven years old, I am standing in a meadow (when the war began we were in the countryside in eastern Poland), and I am staring at some dots moving ever so slightly in the sky. Suddenly nearby, at the edge of the forest, there is a terrible boom, and I can hear bombs exploding with a hellish bang (only later will I discover that they are bombs, because at that moment I still don't know such a thing as a bomb exists – the very idea is alien to me, a child from a remote province, who isn't yet familiar with the radio or the cinema, doesn't know how to read or write, and has never heard that wars or deadly weapons exist), and I see gigantic fountains of earth flying into the air. I want to run towards this extraordinary show, it stuns and fascinates me, and as I haven't yet had any experience of war I cannot connect into a single chain of causes and effects the shining silver aeroplanes, the boom of the bombs, the plumes of earth flying up as high as the trees and death threatening me. So I start to run towards the forest, towards the bombs falling and exploding, but a hand grabs my arm from behind and pulls me over onto the meadow. 'Lie down,' I hear my mother's trembling voice say, 'Don't move' . . .

It is night, and I want to sleep, but I'm not allowed to sleep, we have to go, we have to escape. Where to, I do not know, but I understand that escape has become an absolute necessity, a new form of life, because everyone is escaping; all the highways, roads and even the field tracks are full of wagons, carts and bicycles, full of bundles, cases, bags and buckets, full of terrified people wandering helplessly. Some are escaping to the east, others to the west . . .

We pass battlefields strewn with abandoned equipment, bombed-out railway stations, and cars turned on their sides. There is a smell of gunpowder, a smell of burning, and a smell of rotting meat. Everywhere we come upon the dead bodies of horses. A horse – a large, defenceless animal – doesn't know how to hide; during a bomb attack it stands still, waiting for death. At every step there are dead horses, either lying in the road, or in the ditch next to it, or somewhere further off in a field. They lie with their legs in the air, shaking their hooves at the world. I do not see any dead people anywhere, because they are buried quickly, just endless corpses of horses, black, bay, piebald, chestnut, as if it wasn't a war between people, but horses.[1]

Fifty years later, on reading this description of the scene, the American author John Updike writes in a letter to Kapuściński that only now does he understand the significance of the figure of the horse in Picasso's *Guernica*.

After days of wandering we are near Pińsk, and in the distance we can already see the town's houses, the trees of its beautiful park, and the towers of its churches, when suddenly sailors materialize on the road right by the bridge. They have long rifles and sharp, barbed bayonets and, on their round caps, red stars . . . they don't want to let us into town. They keep us at a distance – 'Don't move!' they shout, and take aim with their rifles. My mother, as well as other women and children – for they have already rounded up a group of us – is crying and begging for mercy. 'Plead for mercy,' the mothers, beside themselves with fear, implore us, but what more can we, the children, do – we have already been kneeling on the road, sobbing and stretching out our arms, for a long time.

Shouting, crying, rifles and bayonets, the enraged faces of the sweaty and angry sailors, some sort of fury, something dreadful and incomprehensible, it is all there by the bridge over the river Pina, in this world that I enter at seven years of age.[2]

In Pińsk there is nothing to eat. Maria Kapuścińska stands in the window for hours, watching. In the neighbours' windows Rysiek sees people gazing at the street in the same way as his mother. Are they waiting for something? But what?

Rysiek spends hours roaming the streets and courtyards with his friends. They play a few games, but in fact they're hoping to find something to eat.

Sometimes the smell of soup comes wafting through a door. Whenever this happens, one of my friends, Waldek, thrusts his nose into the gap in the door and starts urgently, feverishly inhaling the smell, rubbing his stomach with relish, as if he were sitting at a table full of food, but moments later he loses heart and sinks into apathy again.[3]

He will constantly return to the admission that the war – as for everyone who lived through it – was a decisive experience; for the growing boy, the period which shaped his view of humanity and the world came between the ages of seven and thirteen.

Those who lived through the war will never be free of it. It has remained in them like a mental burden, like a painful growth that even as excellent a surgeon as time will never be able to remove. Listen to a gathering of people who lived through the war when they get together and sit down at table one evening. It doesn't matter what they start to talk about. There may be a thousand topics, but there will be only one ending, and it will be remembering the war . . .

For a long time I thought this was the only world, that this is how it looks, and this is what life is like. That is understandable – the war years were the period of my childhood, then of my early adolescence, my first understanding, the birth of my consciousness. So it seemed to me that not peace, but war is the natural state, or even the only one, the only form of existence, that wandering, hunger and fear, air raids and fires, round-ups and executions, lies and screaming, contempt and hatred were the natural, eternal state of affairs, the meaning of life, the essence of existence.[4]

What do these words mean? That fear is a principle of the world and the most basic human emotion? That danger is another one? Instincts like these – maybe not yet thoughts, not so fully formulated – must have been aroused in the seven-, eight- or thirteen-year-old by 'the natural state of war'.

Now, as I look through various texts by Kapuściński – whether spoken abroad, when he was already famous, or written – I find that the war continually recurs; if only as a brief memory, a reference, a starting or finishing point, it always finds room for itself. Somewhere he wrote that war reduces the world to black and white, to 'the most primitive battle between two forces – good and evil'. How, then, do we emerge from it? How do we recover?

I'm trying to do some bookkeeping: what, where, when. As far as possible, I want to do it item by item. The only person who can help me with this is Barbara. In the course of our conversations I establish, unsurprisingly, that the siblings remembered certain events in the same or a similar way, and others in an entirely different way. Many Kapuściński never mentioned. Did he not remember them? Did he think them unimportant, or too traumatic?

I compare their accounts, even the ones about trivial events, and am often unable to determine which is closer to the truth – these are the truths of two children's memories. Below I alternate Barbara's story with fragments taken from Rysiek's published accounts.

'When war broke out, we were in the countryside near Rejowiec, which is not far from Chełm in southeastern Poland. We were on holiday there at our uncle's place. I can't remember much of the journey home. In Pińsk, which was under Soviet occupation, Rysiek went to school, and I was still too small.'

> In school, starting in the first grade, we learn the Russian alphabet. We begin with the letter *s*. 'What do you mean by *s*?', someone asks from the back of the classroom. 'It should begin with *a*!' 'Children,' says the teacher (who is a Pole) in a despondent voice, 'look at the cover of our book. What is the first letter on this cover? *S*!' Petrus, who is Belorussian, can read the whole title: 'Stalin, *Voprosy Leninizma*' (Studies in Leninism). It is the only book from which we learn Russian, and our only copy of this book . . .
>
> All the children will be members of the Pioneers! One day a car pulls into the schoolyard . . . Someone says that it's the NKVD . . . The NKVD people brought us white shirts and red scarves. 'On important holidays,' says our teacher . . . 'every child will come to school in this shirt and scarf'.[5]

'Soon people start talking about deportations to Siberia. The Polish teachers and policemen are going to be deported. Our father, who was a teacher and a reserve officer, decides to escape, which means illegally cross-ing the border into the General Government – the part of Poland under German occupation. He sets off at dusk, first to the house of his friend Olek Onichimowski, also a teacher, who lives near the railway station; they are going to escape together.

'That same night the NKVD comes for my father. They are armed with rifles fitted with bayonets. They shout at Mama, Where's your husband? Every five minutes Rysiek runs into the bathroom – he must have under-stood what was happening better than I did, and was more afraid; I was six and he was seven. Finally, perhaps out of spite at not finding my father there, the NKVD men stick their bayonets through a reproduction of Matejko's painting *Batory at the Battle of Pskov*, which is hanging on the wall. They leave Mama in peace. Next day we discover that my father was in Pińsk that night, because he and Olek missed the train. Luckily he spent the night at his friend's place.'

> Several of them burst in, Red Army men and civilians, they barge in nervously and with such lightning speed, as if enraged wolves were chas-ing them. Rifles immediately leveled at us. A great fear: What if they fire? And what if they kill? . . . And to Mother: *Muz kuda*? (Where's your husband?) And Mother, pale as a sheet, spreads her trembling arms and says that she doesn't know . . . What are they searching for? They say that it's weapons. But what kind of weapons could we have? My toy gun,

which I used to fight the Indians with? . . . They want to take Mother away. Why, as a punishment?

[O]ne of the Red Army men, probably the eldest, probably the commander, hesitates for a moment, then puts on his cap, fastens the holster of his pistol, and says to his people: '*Pashli!*' ('Let's go!')[6]

'For the next few nights we didn't sleep – we were waiting for the NKVD to come back again.

'Deportations of entire families began. That fate befell the family of my friend from next door, Sabina, whose father was a policeman. At five in the morning a wagon full of soldiers drove up to their house. The soldiers loaded their things onto the wagon, and allowed Sabina's mother to cook a little buckwheat for the journey. I heard the noise and asked Mama if I could go to their place. Mama probably didn't realize the danger I was in, and said yes.

'The train they were using to deport them consisted of at least a dozen coaches, and loading them with people took several days. With our nanny Masia, Rysiek and I managed to smuggle in cooked buckwheat several times. It was winter and terribly cold, about thirty degrees below. Before the train set off, Sabina's younger sister froze to death.'

In school, during breaks, or when we are returning home in a group, the talk is of deportations. There is now no subject more interesting.[7]

'I remember that the whole time people talked about food, that something had to be obtained, or when would something be brought. One night it was my turn, and I had to stand in a queue for broken eggs. People pushed me out of the crowd, I didn't get anything, and on top of that I broke the clay pot.'

Once, hungry and desperate, we approached the soldiers guarding the entrance to the barracks. *Tovarishch*, said Hubert, *day pokushat*, and mimed putting a piece of bread into his mouth . . . Finally one of the sentries reached into his pocket and instead of bread pulled out a little linen sack and handed it to us without a word. Inside were dark brown, almost black, finely chopped stems of tobacco leaves. The Red Army man also gave us a piece of newspaper, showed us how to twist it into a cone and pour into it the damp, foul-smelling tobacco gruel . . .

We began to smoke. The smoke scratched our throats and stung our eyes. The world started to swirl, rock, and was turned upside down. I vomited, and my skull was splitting from pain. But the all-consuming, gnawing sensation of hunger eased, weakened.[8]

'Our Mama was lovely, we were never spanked, but just one time when she came back from the broken egg queue she hit us. Maybe she was feeling desperate and frustrated because she hadn't got anything? It was about cigarettes. While she was out, Rysiek and I had found a box and smoked them all – about a hundred of them. We threw the dog ends and ash behind the bed, thinking Mama wouldn't notice. She was really angry with us – I can't remember her ever being like that again.'

'It was warmer by then, probably the start of spring 1940, and we left Pińsk for good. They announced that anyone who wanted could go across to the German side, taking thirty kilos of luggage with them. Mama didn't hesitate for a moment, despite the fact that she was leaving a fully furnished house, surely realizing she would never return to it. She put me and Rysiek on the wagon and we set off on our way. I remember a train ride after that. Before we crossed the border, first we went to Przemyśl, where my father's parents lived. My grandfather was fairly fit, but for years my grandmother had suffered from paralysis in both arms and needed to be looked after on the arduous journey.

'On the Soviet–German border we had to hand over money, jewellery and any valuables. On the German side they shaved our heads, because the Germans thought everyone coming from the East had lice. First they smeared some white paste on our heads, then they cut our hair. The boys were shaved bald, and the girls had their hair cut short.

'I cannot remember how we met up with my father, but in any case we all went to live together in Sieraków outside Warsaw. It was a two-storey house, with one room downstairs, where my father ran a one-class school; he was the only teacher. Up thirteen stairs, there were two rooms with sloping walls under the roof. My grandparents, Rysiek and I slept in one, and my parents in the other.

'My father was a strict teacher, and used to whack the pupils on the hands with a ruler; he told me to write a word out twenty times which I had written wrongly.

'Did we suffer from hunger? Not at that point, but it was tough, and we were all pretty thin. At home there was a large cast-iron pot in which Mama used to make soup. There was soup every day – after all, we were living in the countryside. The children used to bring something as "payment" for school, a litre of milk, or some potatoes . . . Sometimes there wasn't enough soup for everyone, and then Mama would say she wasn't hungry.'

Hunger followed us here from Pińsk, and I was always looking for something to eat, a crust of bread, a carrot, anything at all. Once my father, having no alternative, said in class: 'Children, anyone who wants to come to school tomorrow must bring one potato' . . . The next day half the class did not come at all. Some of the children brought half, others a quarter of a potato. A whole potato was a great treasure.[9]

'Rysiek and his friends invented a game which involved sprinkling gunpowder into a small metal pipe, and then throwing the pipe as hard as you could at the ceiling – that's how I remembered it. There was a fiery explosion – luckily it didn't burn our faces, or our eyes; there could have been a tragedy.

'After about a year living in Sieraków we moved to Izabelin, where we had fabulous conditions for those days: a house with two rooms, a kitchen, hall and veranda. We also had a garden, where we grew vegetables, a few fruit trees – apples and plums – and in a wooden outbuilding there were rabbits and hens, which meant we had eggs on a daily basis. Dad rode a bike to the school in Sieraków, and Mama babysat the local children, for which she got jam and honey. Rysiek and I went to school in Izabelin.'

'There were often at least a dozen bikes "parked" outside our house. Underground meetings were held there – my father was in the Home Army [Armia Krajowa, or AK – the Polish resistance] – which unfortunately was evident to all. And dangerous. Our neighbour Grothe, the shop owner, was *Volksdeutsch* [an ethnic German]. He had a wife and three daughters, one of whom, Iza, I befriended. One day, when I had come home from seeing her, an operation began at Grothe's house. The AK had passed a death sentence on him, though luckily they hadn't appointed my father to carry it out. We heard shouting and cries for help. There was nothing we could do. Later we found out that in trying to defend himself, Grothe had thrown acid at one of his attackers and barricaded himself into the shop. They had shot him through the door.

'The next day a nightmare began. A lorry full of gendarmes drove into the village. There were cars, motorbikes, dogs – a general uproar. They dragged out our neighbour Wojtek Borzęcki, who was someone in the area, a handsome man who went about in jodhpurs and knee-high riding boots; I think he was a count. They started torturing him in full view of everyone. They stuck nails under his fingernails, and he howled so loud I can still hear that howling now. Rysiek and I are watching this, glued to the window. Then they drag out the teacher, Franciszek Pięta. They drive him about the village by car, strip the skin off his face and sprinkle salt on it. Mama and I kneel down and pray at an accelerated rate, as if a rapid prayer were going to bring him aid faster.

'We were afraid for my father. He had gone to Sieraków that morning and he wasn't back. It turned out the Germans had launched a crackdown throughout the district. In Sieraków, as he was closing the school, they were already waiting for him. From what he told us afterwards, somewhere by a roadside cross they divided the men they had rounded up into two groups. They took some with them, but luckily our father was in the group of men they let go. During the selection he had managed to throw to the ground some small pieces of paper containing secret information and bury them with his foot.

'By the time he came home, it was night. We hadn't slept a wink; we were terrified. That night my parents made the decision to run away. In the morning our father went to work in Sieraków, but didn't come back – afterwards he went straight to Warsaw. He spent the next few nights in various places, staying with friends. Every night he had a problem, because he had to organize a different place to stay.'

> At night the partisans come . . . One time they came, as usual, at night. It was autumn and it was raining. They talked to my mother about something in a whisper (I hadn't seen my father for a month and I would not see him until the end of the war, as he was in hiding). We had to get dressed quickly and leave: there was a round-up in the district, they were transporting whole villages to the camps. We escaped to Warsaw, to a designated safe house. It was the first time I had been in the big city, the first time I ever saw a tram, high multi-story tenements, and rows of big shops.[10]

'Rysiek, Mama and I spent several months living with a friend of my parents from Warsaw, Jadwiga Skupiewska. My father occasionally dropped in for the night, but he was not usually there. Where exactly the flat was, I don't know; I remember a tenement with a central well. We weren't allowed to go up to the windows, because staying with someone without being registered was strictly forbidden. So both we and the friends who gave us shelter were taking a risk.'

> We were living in Warsaw then [as the winter of 1942 approached], on Krochmalna Street, near the gate to the ghetto, in the apartment of the Skupiewskis. Mr Skupiewski had a little cottage industry making bars of green bathroom soap. 'I will give you some bars on consignment,' he said. 'When you sell four hundred, you will have enough for your shoes, and you can pay me back after the war.' People then still believed that the war would end soon. He advised me to work along the route of the Warsaw–Otwock railway line, frequented by holiday travellers; vacationers will want to pamper themselves a little, he counselled, by buying a bar of soap. I listened to him. I was ten years old, and I cried half the tears of a lifetime then, because in fact no one wanted to buy the little soaps. In a whole day of walking I would sell none – or maybe a single bar. Once I sold three and returned home bright red with happiness.

After pressing the buzzer I would start to pray fervently: God, please have them buy something, have them buy at least one! I was actually engaged in a form of begging, trying to arouse pity. I would enter an apartment and say: 'Please, madam, buy a soap from me. It costs only one zloty, winter is coming and I have no shoes.' This worked sometimes, but not always, because there were many other children also trying to get over somehow – by stealing something, swindling someone, trafficking in this or that.

Cold autumn weather arrived, the cold nipped at the soles of my feet, and because of the pain I had to stop selling. I had three hundred zloty, but Mr Skupiewski generously threw in another hundred. I went with my mother to buy the shoes. If one wrapped one's leg with a piece of flannel and tied newspaper on top of that, one could wear them even in the worst frosts of winter.[11]

'We moved to Świder, outside Warsaw, on the other side of the Vistula [River]. It was a house with four flats, and we occupied one of them. Rysiek and I went to school in Otwock, seven kilometres one way, on an almost empty stomach; in the morning we barely drank a mug of chicory coffee. At school our dinner snack was a bowl of hot soup. After coming home and doing our homework, Mama usually said: "Children, go to bed, there won't be any supper today". So it went on almost until the war ended.

'Our father was then working as a tax collector in Karczew – about a dozen or more kilometres from Świder – under a false name. He visited us once a week and sometimes brought a bit of sausage. These were the presents people with no money had given him to buy themselves off; they had asked him to come back some time later for their dues.

'Then our father tried to work as a handyman. He advertised that he could solder pots, for instance, but no one wanted to employ him. People had no money, or even food to pay him for the work. My father sewed me dresses and made us shoes.'

> Throughout the war my big dream was about shoes. To have shoes. But how could I get them? What could I do to have some shoes? . . . A strong shoe was a symbol of prestige and power, a symbol of command; a wretched, worn-out shoe was a sign of humiliation, the stigma of a man stripped of all dignity and condemned to an inhuman existence. To have strong shoes meant to be strong, or even simply to be.[12]

'Other memories? I remember the tragic story of a Jewish woman who was hiding in one of the four flats in our house. She gave me maths coaching. I don't think she taught Rysiek, because he didn't have any problem with maths. We used to share our soup with her. She had a beautiful fur coat and a woman she knew wanted to . . . get it from her? Buy it? The Jewish woman refused. One day she went to see that other woman, wearing the fur, and never came back. Did the other woman betray her for the fur? That was what was said afterwards . . .

'The Warsaw Uprising meant little bits of burned paper blowing our way from Warsaw, and the death of our uncle in the fighting.

'The Soviets were getting nearer, and the Germans were taking all boys over the age of sixteen to dig trenches. Those taken away for this work never came back . . . That fate befell Janek, whose own father, our janitor, bundled him off because he himself was afraid to go. Thank God, Rysiek was barely twelve, and didn't look too solid, so they left him alone.

'We were living near the front line and we could hear the noises of fighting. We often went down to the cellar, which served as our shelter. Everyone prayed that no bomb would hit the house, and God heard us . . .

'At that time Rysiek was very religious; he would stay like that to the end of the war, and perhaps a year or two after it as well. In Izabelin he also served at mass as an altar boy. One time I noticed a pool of saliva by our bed. "That's so I'll be on an empty stomach for Holy Communion," he explained to me very earnestly.'

In 1944 I became an altar boy. My priest was the chaplain for a field hospital. There were rows of camouflaged tents hidden in a pine forest on the left bank of the Vistula. During the Warsaw Uprising, before the January offensive was launched, there was feverish, exhausting activity here. Ambulance cars kept rushing in from the front, which roared and smoked nearby. They brought the wounded, often semi-conscious, hurriedly and chaotically piled one on top of another, as if they were sacks of corn (but sacks dripping with blood). The orderlies, themselves only half alive from exhaustion by now, fetched out the wounded and laid them on the grass, then took a rubber hose and doused them in a strong jet of cold water. Any of the wounded who started to show signs of life were carried into the tent housing an operating theatre (on the ground outside the tent, every day there lay a fresh pile of amputated arms and legs), but anyone who wasn't moving anymore was taken to a large grave situated at the rear of the hospital. It was there, over the never-ending grave, that I stood for hours next to the priest, holding the breviary and the stoup for him, repeating the prayer for the dead after him. To each person killed in action we said: Amen, dozens of times a day, Amen, in a hurry, because somewhere nearby, beyond the forest, the machine of death was working away relentlessly. Until finally one day it was silent and empty – the ambulances stopped coming and the tents were gone (the hospital went west), and the crosses were left in the forest.[13]

According to one hypothesis about the 'psychological inheritance of war', war has created the conviction that those who stick their necks out – the brave ones – are the first to come to grief.

In notes from a conversation I had with Wiktor Osiatyński, one of Kapuściński's closest friends, I see that he echoes this thought: 'The brave children in war were killed, the less brave had a better chance of surviving. It's that simple. The experience of war, the sight of death and suffering, the poverty, hunger and terror – all this changes a person's attitude for ever, his approach to life.'

In talking about brave and less brave children, Osiatyński is not directly referring to his friend, but rather suggesting a possible key. 'I never judge anyone whose youth coincided with the war and then Stalinism,' my notes read. 'I don't know how I would have got through that time myself, or how I would have behaved.'

Later in the conversation, Osiatyński says: 'He wasn't a man of great courage, though several times he managed to say no. For example, following the introduction of martial law on 13 December 1981, when he gave up his PZPR [Polish United Workers' Party] membership card – that must have been hard for him. I have no reason to challenge his stories of how he was going to be shot several times when he was a correspondent in Africa and Latin America, or rather I have no solid proof to the contrary. But nor could I ever resist the impression that he created his courage in literature. He knew he was different.'

To have experienced the privations, suffering and danger of war has a paradoxical flip side: it facilitates adaptation to the tough conditions of work as a foreign correspondent during wars, revolutions and unrest on various continents, when there is nothing to eat and you sleep anywhere you can. The point is not that it was easier for Kapuściński than for other reporters, or that he suffered less, but that he probably had a different 'internal limit' of resilience, a greater capacity to adapt, perhaps also to cope with fear, than those journalists who had not had a taste of war in childhood and grew up in relative peace and prosperity.

'Rysiek never openly admitted it, but he was fascinated by images of war. I feel exactly the same,' says Mirosław Ikonowicz, a friend from the same generation. They met as students in the history faculty at Warsaw University and spent many years working for the same press agency. Like Kapuściński, Ikonowicz was a PAP correspondent during the civil war in Angola. 'War, revolution, dangerous places were necessary to him for "life on the edge,"' he told me. 'I would compare this need of his – and of mine as well – to the needs of people who go in for extreme sports. Though he used to say he wasn't looking for extra adrenalin, I think this need lay deep inside him – we talked about it a number of times.'

Another note from my conversation with Ikonowicz reads, 'Rysiek didn't like being confronted.' To what extent can his war experiences be involved in this dislike of confrontation? Is it that when it comes to conflict, a squabble or a clash, a person can get hit? And yet throughout his professional life he was eager to go to dangerous places.

I shall answer these questions later, and also return to the question of personal courage. I note in the margin: 'Establish everything possible on Kapuściński's several near-executions by firing squad' – extreme confrontations which he described in books and interviews.

But in response to the question 'How did the war shape Kapuściński?' I offer Hanna Krall's short answer: 'He was a child of the war, and like many people of his generation the war made him eager for life.'

When *Imperium* was published, readers from Pińsk corrected and sometimes challenged some details of Kapuściński's account of their city under Soviet occupation. One wrote that only Russians, and not even all Russians, were accepted in the Pioneers' organization; apparently Polish children could belong to the Pioneers as long as their parents immediately took out USSR citizenship. Another correction was that the Pioneers received the white shirts and red scarves from that organization, not from the NKVD at school.

Memory, especially a child's memory, affected by knowledge gained years later, is always subjective. Inevitably it blurs the borders between hard facts and impressions, family stories and gossip. But can there be another truth which a person is capable of telling about himself?

Kapuściński may have got some details wrong. Perhaps his memory encoded the same events differently than did the memories of his Pińsk reviewers. In the CVs he attached to applications for college, and later to join the PZPR, Kapuściński wrote that he belonged to the Pioneers – a detail in his memoirs that has been challenged. By now, his membership is impossible to verify.

Yes, the question of whether Kapuściński embellished his own life story is legitimate. As I read, converse with Barbara, friends, and colleagues, compile facts and dates, and do the biographical bookkeeping, I come upon clues that make it impossible not to have doubts. As he told stories about his life, was he 'writing' yet another book? Is Ryszard Kapuściński – the hero of Ryszard Kapuściński's books (and he is the hero of almost all his own books) – a real person? To what extent is he also a literary character? Did Kapuściński create his own legend? How? Why?

4

Legends 1: His Father and Katyń

'My father, a reserve officer, escaped from a transport to Katyń.'

In the spring of 1940, on Stalin's orders, the Soviet NKVD (People's Commisariat for Internal Affairs – the secret police) murdered thousands of Polish officers at Katyń. They were soldiers who were taken prisoner at the beginning of the Second World War when the Soviet Union occupied eastern Poland.

In *Imperium*, there is a section about the early stages of the Soviet occupation in Pińsk. Presenting his account in the manner of a child, Kapuściński describes his father's return from the first conflict that occurred in 1939:

> I see my father entering the room, but I barely recognize him. We had said good-bye in the summer. He was in an officer's uniform; he had on tall boots, a yellow belt, and leather gloves. I walked down the street with him and listened with pride to how everything on him creaked and clattered. Now he stands before us in the clothes of a Polish peasant, thin, unshaven. He is wearing a cotton knee-length shirt tied with burlap string and straw shoes on his feet. From what my mother is saying, I understand that he fell into Soviet captivity and that he was being driven east. He says that he escaped when they were walking in a column through the forest, and in a village he exchanged his uniform with a peasant for the shirt and straw shoes.[1]

Kapuściński's school friend, the writer and translator Andrzej Czcibor-Piotrowski, expresses his doubts about the father's escape from Soviet captivity (not to mention his escape 'from a transport to Katyń'). 'Many writers have a tendency to self-create, to supplement their own life stories with made-up, or partly made-up, embellished events,' he says. 'There's nothing sensational about that. Rysiek, as I remember him, liked to confabulate.'

In an interview not quite four years before his death, Kapuściński talks about his 'father's escape from a transport to Katyń'.[2]

I ask his sister whether she knows the details of Józef's escape from Soviet captivity. She is surprised by the question and says categorically that their father was never in Soviet captivity, and that Divine Providence was watching over them. So he didn't escape from a transport to Katyń, I ask? No, he didn't escape from a transport to Katyń, nor any of the camps for Polish soldiers and officers. Their father was never a prisoner, and if he was, she would certainly have known about it. He did come home dressed in civilian clothes when the fighting stopped, and shortly after that he and his friend Olek Onichimowski, who was also a teacher, got across into the General Government. He had to escape because, as a teacher, under Soviet occupation he was in danger of being deported to the East.

A letter from Kapuściński's paternal uncle, Marian, which I find in the master's study, confirms his sister's version. A month before the outbreak of war, Marian Kapuściński began working at the forestry commission in Sobibór. In September 1939, before the Germans had reached Sobibór, Józef Kapuściński turned up at his workplace in army uniform. The forestry district manager, the uncle's boss, gave him civilian clothing so that he wouldn't be recognized as an officer and taken to a German Oflag (officers' prison camp). Józef Kapuściński journeyed to Pińsk in civvies.

Why did Kapuściński add this martyrological feature to his father's biography? The first thing that comes to mind is that in this way he settled some scores with part of his own life story, in which he had given his heart and mind to the idea of communism. Was a father who 'escaped from a transport to Katyń' meant to 'counterbalance' something? To deter attacks by those who, after the collapse of real socialism, tracked down examples of approval for that system and of co-operation with the secret services – examples from the lives of famous political and cultural figures, including Kapuściński?

In post-1989 Poland, the parties and circles of the anti-communist right presented many people active in the spheres of politics and culture who in their youth had believed that communism was the future of the world as in fact traitors to the nation, cowards, careerists and villains. Kapuściński saw this drama affecting friends and acquaintances of his own generation, who were being verbally manhandled. He was afraid that he, too, would be pilloried by the press and subjected to public humiliation.

Kapuściński took criticism badly, and personal attacks made him almost ill. Shortly before his death a rumour was going around Warsaw that one of the commentary programmes on public television was going to examine his co-operation with the secret services in People's Poland (also known as the Polish People's Republic, or PRL for short). Stricken with terror, he called his friends and asked if anyone knew what on earth they wanted to bring up about him and what rod they intended to beat him with.

'Dreadful chaps,' he would say about right-wing politicians and commentators, lowering his voice. 'Dreadful chaps.'

He had been expecting an attack on himself since the early 1990s. In the second half of that decade, the right-wing journals had begun to suggest that he owed his literary success to good connections with the communist government and co-operation with the PRL's intelligence service. It was then that, in talking about his late father, Kapuściński would say that he escaped from Soviet captivity. Katyń was also mentioned.

In the history of Polish twentieth-century martyrology, Katyń is sacred. It is harder to throw stones at Katyń. If the father 'escaped from a transport to Katyń', the son must have known from the start that communism was a criminal system. And if he served that system, he did it without faith – like most Poles, he simply came to terms with communism and devised a way of surviving the best way he could. That, I think, must have been the underlying message of the legend of his father's escape from being sent to Katyń.

I search for another hypothesis as well: the psychoanalytical one (for a short while I forget my own scepticism about this school of thought). In New York I meet Renata Salecl, an interpreter of the ideas of Lacan, and speak with her about Kapuściński's Katyń confabulation. 'In a son's life, the father can be a figure prompting strong anxiety,' she tells me. 'The father's absence, or his weakness, do not quell this anxiety at all. On the contrary, they can stir or provoke him into seeking a father substitute, who may for example be a cult political leader with whom he can identify.'

Salecl knows nothing about Kapuściński's relationship with his father. Only after hearing her theoretical explanations do I tell her that the father was not an inspiration for Kapuściński. No doubt unconsciously and with no ill intent, Józef belittled his son's efforts and achievements; truth be told, he did not fully comprehend either what his son did or who he was.

'It is possible that in adding this strong element of Poland's heroic, martyrological history to his father's biography,' Salecl then speculates, 'Kapuściński as it were created him over again, built an authority which never existed, but which he so greatly needed.' In fact, these comments harmonize quite well with what I have managed to establish about the son's relationship with his father.

5

Inspired by Poetry, Storming Heaven

Although this photograph is undated, it was certainly taken no earlier than September 1948 and no later than the spring of 1950, outside the Polytechnic building in central Warsaw. It shows four friends from the Staszic High School: the one with the biggest shock of hair is Andrzej Czcibor-Piotrowski, and the one on the right, standing up straight and smiling, is Rysiek Kapuściński.

September 1948 was their first encounter. The pre-war Staszic High School building on Noakowski Street had not yet been reconstructed following war damage, so the Staszic boys are being put up at the Słowacki High School for girls on Wawelska Street. Here the window panes have already been replaced, but not all the floors are finished. In the gym, the pupils exercise on compressed clay.

For those of us born circa 1930 in the deep, poor Polish provinces, in the countryside or in small towns, in peasant or impoverished gentry families, the period immediately following the war was characterized above all by a very low level of knowledge, a complete lack of wide reading or familiarity with literature, history and the world, a complete lack of good manners (my pitifully miserable reading matter in those years: *A History of the Yellow Poulaine*, by Antonina Domańska, published in 1913, or *Memoirs of a Sky-Blue Uniform*, by Wiktor Gomulicki, published in 1906). Earlier, during the occupation years, either we were not allowed to read or there simply wasn't anything to read.

In our class at the Staszic High School we had one old, torn copy of a pre-war history textbook. At the start of the lesson the teacher, Mr Markowski, would tell our classmate, a boy called Kubiak, to read out an extract from this book, and then he would ask us questions. The point was for us to retell in our own words what had just been read out . . .

So we were still victims of the war, even though its sinister noises had long since fallen silent, and grass had grown over the trenches. Because limiting the concept of a 'war victim' to those killed and wounded does not exhaust the actual list of losses that society incurs. For how much destruction there is in culture, how badly our consciousness is devastated, how impoverished and wasted our intellectual life! And that affects a series of generations for long years afterwards.[1]

Andrzej Czcibor-Piotrowski reads this extract from his school friend's memoirs and shakes his head.

'Is there something wrong?' I ask.

'This is literary self-creation.'

'Meaning?'

'Rysiek was very well read, but towards the end of his life he emphasized the things he lacked in those days purely to show what a long road he had travelled. It was long, that's a fact. But the story about the only two books he had read makes it much longer, doesn't it?' says his friend from high-school days, smiling.

In the renovated Staszic High School building, boys and girls studied together for the first time − co-education.

'Oh, what a lovely, chocolaty boy he was, with dark eyes and thick, dark hair,' his classmate Teresa Lechowska (years later a translator of Chinese literature) says of Rysiek.

The 'chocolaty boy' sits at a desk right behind Piotrowski. They soon find a common language: poetry. Two other fellow lovers of the arts, Janek Mazur and Krzysiek Dębowski, later to graduate from the Academy of Fine Arts as a graphic designer, complete the gang.

They are teenagers − hungry for each other's company, conversations, antics, and just being together. To spend as much time with each other as they can, they meet up half an hour before classes. They sit on the desk tops, smoke cigarettes and chat about everything, most of all about poetry. They sing. Kapuściński taps out the beat on the teacher's chair and, with the ardour he later applied to everything he did in life, sings Lermontov's poem about Queen Tamara, set to a tune:

> In that tower tall and narrow,
> Tsarina Tamara did dwell:
> As fair as an angel in heaven,
> As sly as the devil in hell.

His friends sing along, and when they lose the thread, Rysiek prompts them with the first lines of the verses they have forgotten. They go on wailing until the bell rings for the first lesson. At the end of the school day, they drop in at the Finnish cottage on Wawelska Street where the Kapuścińskis live, very nearby.

Just after the liberation, the family had to cram into one small room next to the construction materials warehouse which Józef Kapuściński was running. When the rebuilding of Warsaw got underway, and the Finns started sending prefabricated cottages for the capital's builders, the Kapuścińskis were allotted one. Barbara recalls that after the misery of living in a virtual rabbit hutch, the two-family Finnish cottage seemed palatial: there was a small living room with an alcove, a kitchen, and a lavatory, as well as a little garden where their father planted vegetables, flowers and fruit trees.

When Rysiek's parents are out, the Finnish cottage is a fine place for the high school boys' first carousals. They crack open a bottle of vodka – a quarter litre of 'red label' (the cheapest kind, as they haven't the money for anything better) – and play bridge. The empty bottles end up in a small attic space above the lavatory. Rysiek's friends are all the more willing to come by because several of them have taken a fancy to his younger sister ('Oh, that Basia, what a beauty she was!').

Rysiek is popular with the girls. One of his schoolmates is madly in love with him, but he is in love with her younger sister. This is the time of first loves and conquests. The boys show off in front of each other. One has the following experience:

One day the boy turns up at a friend's house, slightly embarrassed, but at the same time proud of a conquest. 'Listen,' he says, 'she's in the family way. Could you possibly help?' The friend's aunt is a gynaecologist with a private surgery on Słupecka Street. The friend writes her a note: 'Dearest Auntie Niusia, I'm sending a girlfriend of mine to see you.' The aunt doesn't actually know who got the girl into trouble but feels certain it was her nephew.

Meanwhile, the real troublemaker is not at all perturbed by what has happened. He has been boyishly reckless. The others rather envy him – not for what has happened, but for the fact that he has already experienced something that still lies ahead for them. As for Rysiek, one school friend remembers that he loved boasting about girls.

Unlike the high times at the Kapuścińskis', at Czcibor-Piotrowski's home on Filtrowa Street there is no drinking. The friends sit politely at table, listening to the maths coaching given them by the host's brother, Ireneusz. But they have no passion for maths – their thoughts and imaginations have flown to a very different realm. All thanks to the Polish teacher, Witold Berezecki. He has infected them with a love of literature, poetry. He's given them the weekly *Odrodzenie* (Renaissance) and other cultural periodicals to read at home. Czcibor-Piotrowski remembers one occasion when the homework was to write a sonnet.

Staszic is a remarkable school; until 1950, when they take their school-leaving exams, the most highly qualified pre-war teachers will still be teaching here. Lectures on Latin are given by a female professor from Warsaw

University. 'In the humanities class', notes Andrzej Wyrobisz, who was at
the top of the class then and is now a retired professor of history at Warsaw
University, 'we were taught to "think mathematically"; in history lessons
no one ever asked about dates, but about why and where from. You won't
find any dates in Kapuściński's books either.'

A telling story from Teresa Lechowska: 'The Polish teacher was discussing our homework and called on Kapusta [cabbage], as we used to call
Rysiek, to read his aloud. It turned out to be a poem! A bit socialist–realist,
a bit lyrical. I remember there was something about a mason who builds a
window, which is a frame for the sky. I was surprised Kapusta had revealed
a talent for poetry, because I associated him with nothing but football,
which he was totally mad about.'

With Berezecki, the pupils discuss books they have discovered outside
the classroom. Each one wants to show off how much he has read beyond
the required minimum – that is how they impress each other. Many book
collections were destroyed during the war, but a fair number have survived
– the library on Koszykowa Street, for example. The Staszic pupils make
use of lending libraries which are spontaneously appearing on the streets
and in private flats. The young men with literary aspirations organize a
school literary circle, run by Czcibor-Piotrowski. They invite well-known
writers and critics to discuss literature.

Kapuściński and Czcibor-Piotrowski are crazy about the French poets.
They manage to get hold of *An Anthology of Modern French Verse*, translated
by Adam Ważyk. They know most of the poems by heart and recite them
aloud. Rysiek declaims the first verse, Andrzej adds the second, and so on.

'Once we were chatting about Paris in the 1870s and someone mentioned
the "revolt of Parisians storming heaven,"' recalls Czcibor-Piotrowski.
'Rysiek was planning to write a story about Rimbaud and Verlaine, about
their journey from the countryside to the city to stand on the barricades of
the Commune.'

The two boys also recite Pushkin and Lermontov, Yesenin and Mayakovsky.
Both being from the eastern borderlands, they can read Russian in the original. As Czcibor-Piotrowski tells me: 'I remember how one day Rysiek came
to see me, clearly excited. At the Czechoslovak Information Centre he had
got hold of a volume of poems by František Halas. This poet's verse, though
actually he didn't understand much, almost nothing, made a huge impression on him – the metre, the richness of the language . . . He quoted me
something from memory and suddenly stopped on the word *koralka*, which
he associated with the Polish word *koralik*, a coral bead. Years later, when I
became a Czech scholar and translator of Halas's poetry, I found out that
koralka simply means the same as our Polish *gorzalka* – homemade hooch.'

Rysiek, predictably, makes his own first attempts at poetry and sends his
work to *Odrodzenie* and also to *Dziś i Jutro* (Today and Tomorrow), a

journal issued by PAX, the Catholic association licensed by the PZPR. In August 1949 this journal publishes two of his poems, 'Written by Speed' and 'The Healing'. His friends, the high school literati, are secretly jealous that Rysiek is the first to enter the literary world. Years later he will say, 'I sent them off half-heartedly, just as an experiment.'

> Into the city, where joy lay buried under bricks,
> Feeling thorn-sharp sorrow came
> a man.
> His eyes saw tortured ruins burned to sticks,
> His hands shot through with pain were portents of
> a plan . . .
> And now the streets are paved in sunshine bright
> And high among the trees rise red-tiled roofs.
> As stars roam through the shallow dark
> of night,
> People are taller than houses. For in them grows
> the Truth.[2]

Does the sixteen- or seventeen-year-old high school student fully understand what is happening in the country? He knows there was a different political system before the war, and that now Poland is to be socialist; that the former enemy – the Soviet Union – is now a 'fraternal country'. Does he grasp what it all means?

At the beginning of Rysiek's high school days, the socialist revolution which is starting to occur in Poland still lies beyond the horizon of interests of the boy from 'the deep and indigent Polish provinces', from the 'impoverished gentry'. It is also doubtful whether he perceives a connection between the new order and his own chances in life.

Indeed, he does join the communist youth organization, the Union of Polish Youth (ZMP), but this is not a conscious ideological choice. Whole classes and schools were enrolled in the union collectively, without asking the young people if they wanted to join. Religious instruction was still given at state schools, and sometimes the pupils went straight from a lesson in religion to a ZMP meeting.

Kapuściński has described the atmosphere within the school organization several years later when, by now conscious and politically committed, he applies for acceptance into the Communist Party: 'The attitude of group members at the time when I took on the presidency was for the most part alien to our organization. Many people had joined it for careerist reasons. At the meetings they used to play cards or do their homework, or else they didn't turn up at all. Wanting to eradicate this behaviour, I threatened them with expulsion from the organization. That gave them a shock.' For this reason, he submits a self-critical report, declaring that he should have been attracting his fellow pupils to the ZMP, encouraging them rather than scaring them with expulsion. Regrettably, as he admits in his hand-written curriculum vitae, he used 'leftist methods of managing the organization'.

Deep in his soul, the recent altar boy and now freshly baked ZMP member is still experiencing his 'religious and mystical' phase. He offers a friend a small collection of his own poetic and prose miniatures, *God Wounds with Love*, the title of which he took from Verlaine. He bangs out the text on a typewriter and signs it with the publisher's name 'Leo', in honour of Lwów, his friend's hometown. An extract reads:

> On Golgotha stand three crosses. The centuries weigh down on them, yet they remain strong, invincible to the power of time. Strong as the Word of God, powerful as the Will of Christ, mighty as the Truth of the Holy Spirit.[3]

'We had deep metaphysical anxieties,' recalls Czcibor-Piotrowski, to whom the religious stanzas were addressed. 'We used to wonder what happens to us after death.'

But not for long. The spirit of the times is starting to change radically the questions posed by literature, and 'the Truth of the Holy Spirit' is turning into an entirely different truth, as is evident in the following extracts from a debate about poetry held at Staszic High School. These were introduced as 'the most typical statements made by the young debaters'.[4]

> Krzysztof Dębowski: Mayakovsky's and Kapuściński's poems contain a defined ideology: Marxist-Leninist ideology. That is why they are simple, understandable and conscious.
>
> Eugeniusz Czapliński: The poetry of the twentieth century is burdened by the chaos of the capitalist world. Works that seem to talk about life are the negation of life. That is not the case in the poems cited by V. Mayakovsky and R. Kapuściński. These poems were written in the context of building socialism. A conscious ideology speaks through each poem; they address the issues of the worker and the education of socialist youth, and illustrate problems that lie within the reader's sphere of interests.
>
> Andrzej Piotrowski: I would like to conduct an experiment, involving the comparison of two pieces of writing: an extract from *Good!*, the epic poem by the great poet Vladimir Mayakovsky, and extracts from a poem called *Winter Scenes – Pink Apples,* by the novice poet Ryszard Kapuściński.
>
> In Mayakovsky the theme of the poem is work, work, which is a basic element of life in socialist society. In Kapuściński we are dealing with another element – rest (children on holiday).
>
> Kapuściński does not strongly stress his political affiliation, as Mayakovsky has done . . .

The author of *Winter Scenes* takes the position of an observer, a commentator. And here lies a basic error.

A second error, which highlights this comparison best of all, is Kapuściński's use of a symbol which comes, as we know, from a totally different era, which erases the simplicity of the poem, creates appearances of insincerity and avoids calling things by their proper names. I say appearances, as I have no doubt that Kapuściński is sincerely dedicated to our common cause and knows that poetry should have a truly ideological countenance.

It is hard to judge a poet on the basis of only one of his poems. Kapuściński's future work will give us the opportunity to examine the matter again . . . Each of us keeps repeating the comment that every creative artist learns from his mistakes. We say it all the more sincerely, as Kapuściński is our friend, and we ourselves will help him to overcome his errors through criticism of his poems.

At the end, colleague Ryszard Kapuściński read out his new poem, closer, in his view, to the correct poetic traditions.

ON OBLIGATIONS

Well, my comrades and poets,
let me say a few words to you.
For us the need is vital
to outpace the tortoise in poetry too.
. . .
Let's not mince our words,
the matter is simple and clear:
we cannot let poetry's cause
be left to trail in the rear.

We are lagging far behind.
But after the miners let us race.
Perhaps you can easily guess
What Mayakovsky would say in our place?
. . .
Many a man will outdo me, I know,
Outshine me with his talent's flame,
I am not swapping the song of the lyre
for labour's whirring just for fame.

They question Markiewka,
Poręcki, Michałek, and Markow.
They're questioned by the workers led
by the Party.[5]

The socialist realist verses are Kapuściński's first conscious ideological declaration.

Up the 'staircase' of Mayakovsky's stanzas, the eighteen-year-old Rysiek enters two worlds: that of literature, and the kingdom of the New Faith.

6

Lapidarium 1: The Poet

'I was a victim of Mayakovsky,' he said years later in a conversation with a younger colleague, the poet Jarosław Mikołajewski. 'My attempts at the time, my "Mayakovsky period", was disappointing for me too. I wanted to shake it off, but I no longer had the time to look for other paths to take. I started working as a journalist and moved over to prose. To reportage.'

Kapuściński never fully confronted his youthful choices, and never mentioned the circumstances of the era in which he went through his 'Mayakovsky period'. What cause did it serve? Years later, how did he judge that time and his involvement in it as a poet writing propaganda poems?

After his adventure with 'Mayakovsky-ism', he parts ways with poetry for almost thirty years. He reads and collects books by Polish and foreign poets but does not return to writing poetry himself. He will not publish his collection of poems entitled *Notebook* until 1986; his second and last, *The Laws of Nature*, will come out shortly before his death. He says he does not feel like a 'professional poet', that what he values in poets is their attention to language itself (whereas prose writers pay the most attention to the plot, and essayists to actual thought):

> Writing poetry allows you to touch the living language, explore its limits, and appreciate the value of the actual word and metaphor stripped of secondary reinforcement.
>
> Some states and moods cannot be expressed in any other way. Only through poetry.[1]

Kapuściński's poems arouse greater interest abroad than in Poland. The Italian writer Claudio Magris calls him 'an original poet of intense and sparing expression',[2] and compares him with the greatest Polish poets of the twentieth century – Czesław Miłosz, Wisława Szymborska and Tadeusz Różewicz.

I ask another eminent Polish poet, Julia Hartwig, who was a friend of Kapuściński's, about their conversations concerning poetry. I also ask what she thinks of her late friend's poems. 'He was a poet manqué,' she replies. 'He said that if he could have chosen who he would like to be, he would have chosen to be a poet. He read poetry and was interested in new work, and sought out opportunities to meet poets. He did his best to encourage young, unknown and underrated poets. I don't think his poetic talent was a patch on his talent as a reporter. And I think he had a complex about it. His poems are certainly genuine, some are truly well "made", but they don't have what I would call a "grand scale", they don't move anything inside me.'

Didn't he have a great talent for poetry?

'Maybe he didn't, or maybe he did, but was never able to develop it, because he spent his whole life doing something else. Writing reportage means being "in action", "in motion". Poetry demands a different kind of focus; it develops different qualities in a writer. As Baudelaire said, poetry requires "doing nothing". Kapuściński was sometimes a superb poet in prose.'

Andrzej Czcibor-Piotrowski remembers how, with some sorrow and a little envy, Kapuściński once said to him: 'You are a poet in the Polish Writers Union, but I'm just a journalist.'

7

On the Construction Site of Socialism

In the first year of history there are more than a hundred students. They sit on long benches, several of them on each one. There is not enough room, and it is terribly crowded. Post-war poverty.

Ewa Wipszycka, years later a professor of ancient history, remembers it like this: 'From the start it was a known fact that the shock-headed boy with the flirtatious look was a poet who wrote for the newspaper *Sztandar Młodych* (The Banner of Youth). Talking to him, you could feel at once that he had more experience of life than many of his peers.'

To my left was Z. – a taciturn peasant from a village near Radomsko, the kind of place where, as he once told me, a household would keep a piece of dried kielbasa as medicine: if an infant fell ill, it would be given the kielbasa to suck. 'Did that help?' I asked, skeptically. 'Of course,' he replied with conviction and fell into gloomy silence again. To my right sat skinny W., with his emaciated, pockmarked face. He moaned with pain whenever the weather changed; he said he had taken a bullet in the knee during a forest battle. But who was fighting against whom, and exactly who shot him, this he would not say. There were also several students from better families among us. They were neatly attired, had nicer clothes, and the girls wore high heels. Yet they were striking exceptions, rare occurrences – the poor, uncouth countryside predominated: wrinkled coats from army surplus, patched sweaters, percale dresses.[1]

Autumn 1951. President of the ZMP in the history faculty, colleague Kapuściński, summons colleague Wipszycka for a chat. Wipszycka, who like him has belonged to the organization since high school days, serves as deputy president of the students' union in their faculty. She is not the activist type, and her colleagues have been muttering in the corridors that she is not coping very well. Kapuściński has an instructive chat with her.

'It was like going to confession!'

During the 'confession', Kapuściński encourages Wipszycka to make a self-critical report at a meeting of the faculty's ZMP. Self-criticism is a form of ritual, a public admission of one's sins and negligence with regard to the Party, the ZMP, and the ideals of socialism.

'I cannot remember the details of the conversation, only that just as Kapuściński wished, I made the self-critical report. In fact, my work as an activist for the student union really wasn't going well. However, Kapuściński's persuasion and insistence were so embarrassing that for a long time after-wards I retained the image of him as a fanatic who had played the leading role in some regrettable proceedings.'

Another time Kapuściński and a few other ZMP members from the faculty give two female students a public grilling. They knock out of their heads the young women's faith in God and the idea of going to church on Sundays. 'He was furious that the girls dared to stick to their guns. I myself was a non-believer, but I thought it disgraceful to force someone to drop their faith. I don't think he understood that,' Wipszycka relates.

In the second or third year, one of the women students edits a newsletter consisting of satirical epitaphs for the male students and lecturers who were giving others a hard time. The epitaph for Kapuściński reads thus: 'Here Kapuściński was put to rest, / but not long had he lain / Before he was suddenly summoned / to rush off to work again'. (A decade later, in his reportage *The Junk Room*, Kapuściński makes use of this couplet to describe the hero of his text: 'Here lay Grzegorz Stępik / But not long had he lain / When they pulled him from his grave / To rush off to work again'[2]).

'That epitaph describes Kapuściński perfectly in those days,' says Wipszycka. 'An activist who is always being summoned somewhere, and then comes back with the task of mobilizing us into action. I must clarify that he was basically liked. Even though he had something of the zeal of an inquisitor in him, you never felt any malice in anything he did, and he never acted in a way meant to harm or upset anyone. What mattered to him was the cause, and he believed in it deeply.'

> . . . fighting the counterrevolution. Yes, they knew at last what to do and what to say. You don't have anything to eat? You have nowhere to live? We will show you who is to blame. It's that counterrevolutionary. Destroy him, and you can start living like a human being.[3]

Years later, this quotation from *Shah of Shahs*, one of Kapuściński's most famous books, sounds like a self-ironical comment . He understood what he was writing about — and not just because of the observations he made in Iran.

The years 1949 and 1950, when Kapuściński is completing his high school studies and starting at Warsaw University, are the beginning of several of the grimmest years in Poland's post-war history. After the Second World War, Eastern Europe has ended up in the Soviet Union's sphere of influence. Under the protection of Stalin's troops, homegrown communists assume power in Poland. Initially they tolerate pluralism and a political and cultural opposition, but after a few years they establish the dictatorship of the Polish United Workers' Party (PZPR). Thousands of opponents of the new system are put in prison; even the most moderate criticism in the press, in literature or on the theatrical stage is quashed.

However, millions of Poles alive in that era would not agree to only this memory of the earliest post-war years. Their account might sound like this: We emerged from the war as a destroyed, damaged society – everyone had lost someone close to them – and at the same time we were full of hope and enthusiasm that the end of the war meant the end of hell on earth. For the small number of people who took up the fight against the new regime, hell did not end – they went to prison or were deported to Siberia. Yet the majority entered 'life's new stream', as the poet wrote;[4] they dreamed of a normal life, of finding their loved ones, of settling down, founding or rebuilding their families, and devoting themselves to the joys of life in peacetime and to reconstructing Poland out of the ruins.

These circumstances, plus the communists' appealing social slogans – a fairer Poland than before the war, agricultural reform, social advancement for peasants and workers – make it easier for the new regime to gain support and to strengthen its initially weak position within society. The communists take repressive measures against their political opponents, but at the same time they introduce reforms that are met with wide-spread enthusiasm. They overturn the old social structure and improve the social status of the masses of peasants and proletarians.

> There may have been talk about terror, the camps and the UB [the secret police], but every debate led to the conclusion that regardless of the darker aspects of this reality, socialization would entail social cleansing, and everything bad would disappear. It was assumed that we would manage to make Poland socialist, but not Soviet.[5]

This is how Jacek Kuroń – a man of Kapuściński's generation, then a young communist and later a prominent dissident – reconstructs the atmosphere of the years immediately following the war.

From the beginning of the 1950s there is increasing fear and, gradually, less enthusiasm for the regime, which stifles criticism, centralizes decisions and ever more frequently applies instruments of repression. This turn in communist policy can be plainly seen in the countryside. During the first few years after the war, by giving the peasants land of their own, the communists win their gratitude. However, in the 1950s they start to oppose these very same peasants, whom they gifted with land, as private owners and producers. They force them to provide compulsory supplies of food; those who refuse are subjected to torture, arrest, fines and imprisonment.

The Party's policy towards young people undergoes a similar shift. Until the end of the 1940s, reasonably free debates are held within youth organizations, but in the 1950s fear starts to dominate, and even those who are most loyal to the regime are afraid to express critical views. In 1950 almost half the young people arrested are ZMP members; they usually end up in custody cells and prisons because they dare to have their own opinion, different from official directives.

To end up in prison, you do not have to plan an armed rebellion – it is enough to tell jokes about the Party rank and file, the Soviet Union, or Stalin. The authorities find out about these jokes from denunciations – Poland's Stalinist era is the heyday of the informer. As Kuroń recalls years later:

> Out of fear, sometimes even school friends who sat at the same desk would start to inform on each other. The Soviet pioneer Pavel Morozov, the boy who informed on his own parents, was promoted by the propaganda as a positive hero. The authorities not only rewarded denunciations, but expected and demanded them. The social education was geared towards creating the conviction that socialist man must be loyal to nothing but the socialist state and the Party or the ZMP.[6]

As the 1940s turn into the 1950s, the Party starts to muzzle people in the world of culture. It establishes a compulsory trend for creative artists: socialist realism. Immediately after the war, reasonably free discussions are still being held about the paths and styles that may be chosen by creative artists. However, in the 1950s the Party completely subjugates culture and art to its propaganda aims. Writers, poets, composers, painters and architects are to work according to 'the only legitimate' rules and principles. The aim of creative art is to support the building of socialism in Poland and to generate the new socialist man. The regime sets the mass media exactly the same objectives: they are to promote the Party's policies, and in international affairs, those of the socialist camp. The press, radio and then newly developing television are subject to preventive censorship and the control of the Central Committee's Press Office.

It is the academic year 1950–51. The regime launches a campaign to convert the universities into a breeding ground for cadres loyal to the Party. Part of it involves denouncing 'reactionary' lecturers. This task is usually performed by the students – fervent young activists gathered within the ZMP.

The history faculty at Warsaw University, where Kapuściński starts his studies in 1951, emerges from this campaign unscathed, at least considering the climate of the times and in comparison with other faculties. By some miracle, Tadeusz Manteuffel, head of the Institute of History, as well as dean and deputy vice-chancellor of the university, 'gained the consent of the "appropriate authorities" to let control of historical studies remain in the hands of the old teaching staff, as recognized experts who had declared their intention to apply Marxist methodology', remembers Professor Stefan Kieniewicz.

'The history faculty was an exceptional place,' says Andrzej Werblan, a historian who was then starting out as a lecturer and would later be a Party dignitary, one of its intellectual pillars in the 1970s. 'Half the faculty board were pre-war celebrities, and the other half were post-war lecturers. Both the former and the latter were excellent historians and teachers. It was in those years that the history faculty educated the later élite of historians.'[7]

History studies shine, and not only compared with other faculties at Warsaw University. When Ewa Wipszycka goes to Paris on an internship, she soon realizes that her academic skills and general knowledge far exceed the capacities of her French contemporaries. 'However grim that era was and whatever ideological imperatives were in force, at the history faculty the profession of historian was superbly taught,' she says to me. 'In our classes most of the professors said by and large what they wanted. The ruling principle was that the student learns just as much from the lecturer as from the other students in the course of debate. This atmosphere of free-dom was not even destroyed by the fact that among the students there were many functionaries from the Ministry of Public Security, sent to college by their department. The security agents did not merely study; they also sat on the committees at entrance exams and co-decided whom to accept and whom not. Their other duties are obvious.'

'Did the students know who was who?' I ask.

'It was often a "known fact" − the security agents even had a different way of moving than the rest of us.' She laughs. 'What was striking was not their presence, but the limited influence they had on the atmosphere prevailing within the faculty.'

I am looking through Kapuściński's student file from the Warsaw University archive.[8] First, his marks for the *matura* (high school graduation exams): not bad, but not highly impressive. The highest marks are for Polish, military training, religion and physical education; history and the study of Poland and the modern world are good; mathematics, chemistry, Latin, English and geography are satisfactory.

A note from 1950 entitled 'Pupil Profile', drawn up by some school committee, says: 'Distinct humanities skills. Poetic talent. Very widely read, especially contemporary literature. Very active as president of the ZMP Writers' Circle. Ideological attitude − very good. Graduate of the city administration's political school'. The note bears the stamp of the district authorities and a comment that the authorities 'see no obstacle to the candidate taking university studies.'

Kapuściński studies history but spends his first year in the Polish faculty. The file contains an essay he wrote at that time (it is not clear whether he wrote it for his entrance exam or while already a student): 'The Duties of Youth Organizations in the Six-Year Plan Period'. Announced by the government in 1950, this plan established Poland's rapid industrialization, the centralization of economic management, and the eradication of the remains of the capitalist economy.

The student (or candidate) Kapuściński writes:

> The Six-Year Plan period is a particularly difficult stage in the historical development of People's Poland. In this period, still-existing forms of the capitalist system will be removed, while at the same time the new, better life represented by socialism is being developed.

And so on, in the same lyrical tone.

The file also contains two versions of his curriculum vitae, which Kapuściński wrote out by hand (one is affixed to his application for acceptance into Polish studies; the other is from when he moved to the history faculty). In both, he relates his war experiences in a dry, colourless tone – where he lived, where he went to school, and so on.

At the end of one version of the CV is a notable sentence: 'Differences in our political opinions have led me to maintain casual contact with my family and I am supporting myself.' In fact, Kapuściński was living with his parents and sister at the time. How should we understand an admission of this kind, written by an eighteen-year-old in an era of repression and imprisonment, of not only opposition activists but also 'bar-room' critics who told jokes about the regime? I am reading this document more than half a century later, in the light of everything that is known about that era, so I cannot avoid asking questions. How should we understand the disclosure by a candidate for university in Poland in 1950 about loosening ties with his family for political reasons?

For an answer, I turn to witnesses of the era, people who played a part in the drama.

In Professor Wipszycka's view, 'it is absolutely not a denunciation, but a sign of the times.'

She says: 'This sort of confession resulted from an inner need for sincerity. As young ZMP activists, we reasoned like this: if I don't tell the people in my organization about the political differences between me and my family, it will be as if I'm hiding something. And that would mean I don't have trust in the institutions which should know rather a lot about me, whether the college or the Party organization. Many of us had clashed with our parents over our world outlook, and we used to talk about these conflicts at ZMP meetings. We were terribly worried about generational and ideological differences in those days.'

(One day Kapuściński will tell one of his friends that after he joined the Party his parents cursed him.)

Kuroń, a student in the history faculty two years behind Kapuściński, remembers that 'loyalty to the collective was admissible only within the scope of organizational loyalty,' and that although 'loyalty to a close friend or relative could appear on the most distant horizon', 'you always had to remember that everyone, even your nearest and dearest, could turn out to be a cunningly concealed enemy, a covert ally of America or a disguised fideist who should be denounced without delay.'[9]

In a conversation with Andrzej Werblan, I find further confirmation that this was how the young communists (or 'pimplies', as they were known in those days) thought:

'Writing and speaking badly about your family was the norm among young ZMP and Party activists in those days, almost a ritual. They spoke about their families more or less the way the first Christians spoke about the pagans.'

'So the definition of communism as the New Faith is not just a metaphor?'

'It is literal. The point of having the young activists make frank confessions was to cut them off from the past, and to emphasize that they were aware of the difference between the old and new times. Of course, some of them did it for their careers, but not Kapuściński. He was sincere, genuine in his faith at the time, just as later on he was able to change his views under the pressure of reality.'

> Some cars stop outside a large barracks decorated with flags and portraits of the hero workers. Lads in SP uniforms and red ties jump out [the SP was the 'Service for Poland', a youth organization connected to the Party and the army]. In a short while, the first district ZMP conference at Nowa Huta will begin. At it, the young people of Nowa Huta will talk about their successes, analyse their mistakes and shortcomings, share experiences and jointly draw conclusions from them, then elect the new Board.[10]

Such articles – reports from meetings and rallies attended by youth and Party activists – by Kapuściński perfectly illustrate the mood of the ZMP revolution of the 1940s and 1950s. Continuing in the same vein, he writes:

> There is huge enthusiasm in the hall. The welcome speech . . . is interrupted by warm applause and cheers. The words 'Nowa Huta – Peace – Stalin – Bierut – ZMP' are chanted non-stop . . .

Long live the PZPR and its leader, Comrade Bierut.

Long live the Leader of the World Camp for Progress and Peace, the great friend of youth, Joseph Stalin . . .

All the delegates join in with the applause and for a long time the hall roars with clapping and enthusiastic cries of 'Long may they live'.[11]

As a mature writer, Ryszard Kapuściński has a sense of déjà vu when, thousands of miles from Poland and a quarter century later, he sees similar scenes:

Now I visited the committee headquarters. Committees – that's what they called the organs of the new power. Unshaven men were sitting around tables in cramped, littered rooms . . . What should we do? Do you know what to do? Me? Not me. Maybe you know? Are you talking to me? I'd go whole hog. But how? How do you go whole hog? Ah, yes, that's the problem. Everyone agrees: That is indeed a problem worth discussing. Cigarette smoke clouds the stuffy rooms. There are some good speeches, some not-so-good, a few downright brilliant. After a truly good speech, everyone feels satisfied; they have taken part in something that was a genuine success.[12]

Before the farcical elections of 1952, Kapuściński runs about town with Andrzej Wyrobisz, a friend from high school, now also in the history faculty; together they encourage people to get out and vote. The agitation is pointless, because everyone knows who will win and that there is no real choice. However, the authorities want to boast of a 99 percent turn-out. The fervent ZMP members are helping them.

'Rysiek yelled so enthusiastically that he lost his voice,' says Professor Wyrobisz with a smile.

He really did know what it meant to go the whole way.

In the autobiographical section of *Travels with Herodotus,* in which he writes about this period in his life, Kapuściński says not a word about his ZMP activities, or his later ones in the Party.

8

Lapidarium 2: Lance Corporal Kapuściński

'He was a pretty annoying career NCO.'

At military training for Warsaw University students, history of art student Krzysztof Teodor Toeplitz, many years later one of Poland's best-known columnists, gets to know history student Kapuściński. They meet at military science lectures as well as every Saturday at exercises in drill, crawling, and shooting.

'Rysiek was our star student. He cared about physical fitness, in spite of having a rather small physique. This fitness later helped him survive tough conditions in Africa, when he was working as a Polish Press Agency correspondent. Even before cadet camp, which took place towards the end of our training, they promoted Rysiek to lance corporal, and Lance Corporal Kapuściński gave us common privates a really hard time. Running harder, more press-ups . . . Most of us took military studies with a pinch of salt, but Rysiek took it deadly seriously.'

9

On the Construction Site
of Socialism, *Continued*

In 1952 Kapuściński writes an application requesting to be 'admitted as a candidate for the Polish United Worker's Party'.

> It is my greatest need and desire to join the ranks of our beloved Party. This necessity is on a par with my greatest aspiration, which is to serve the cause of our Party with all my strength and my entire being. Throughout my life, ever since I understood to whom I should devote it, I have felt how every victory brings me closer to the Party, and how every defeat or mistake demands that I make an even greater effort not to turn back on the road I have taken – the road to the Party.
>
> Being admitted as a candidate for our Party will be a very great reward and honour for me, and also a very high obligation. I want even more and even better to live the Party life, to work and fight to fulfil the tasks set by the Party for the best Party comrades. I pledge to safeguard the recommendations which Comrade Stalin has vowed to protect and fortify in the name of all 'people of a special cut'.
>
> My guiding light shall be total dedication to becoming worthy of that title, and to remaining so for the rest of my life.[1]

On the next few pages of his application to join the Party, Kapuściński provides a self-critical report, saying that the young communist in him did not awaken quickly enough: 'My world outlook was still burdened by remnants of petty bourgeois ideology, there were many things I did not understand, and I did not feel the need to get involved.'

Among his mentors at this time he mentions Wiktor Woroszylski, a young socialist-realist poet and the editor of the culture section of the ZMP newspaper *Sztandar Młodych*, as well as several other poets and writers, above all Władysław Broniewski. (Someone later tells me that as president of the Young Writers' Circle affiliated with the Polish Writers' Union, Kapuściński made sure that the notoriously drunken Broniewski drank a bit less.)

In support of his application, Bronisław Geremek, Kapuściński's fellow student in the year above, writes him a letter of recommendation: 'I have known Comrade Ryszard Kapuściński since October 1951 from work within the ZMP organization at our college.' As well as praising his 'dedication and devotion, youthful enthusiasm and eagerness, militant attitude', and also his 'political sophistication' and 'exemplary moral attitude', Geremek informs the Party of the candidate's 'serious mistakes and shortcomings':

1) failure to understand the role of the Party organization within the faculty, an inappropriate, ill-considered attitude to his Party comrades in Year One,

2) an immature attitude to his studies, continuing from the previous year, which recently Comrade Kapuściński has managed to overcome, as evidenced by his good results in the summer session,

3) a not fully collective style for his work in managing the faculty organization, originating mainly from a lack of confidence in people and in the collective,

4) reluctance to accept criticism, and also too little self-criticism,

5) immaturity of decisions often involving youthful bluster and leftism.2

'That was the lyrical style required for recommending candidates to join the Party,' explains the famous historian. 'It wasn't appropriate to give nothing but praise.'

Despite his critical words, Geremek supports Kapuściński's request, 'in the belief that our Party will gain a member worthy of it'.

On 30 June 1952 a meeting of the PZPR executive at the history faculty is held to discuss admitting Kapuściński to the Party. The participants include Bronisław Geremek, Adam Kersten, Jerzy Holzer and a few other activists. The candidate is present too.

Comrade Kersten takes the floor:

'Comrade Kapuściński shows evidence of a certain failure to appreciate the value of academic studies. For Comrade Kapuściński, the chief measure of an activist is social work.'

Another comrade polemicizes:

'Comrade Kersten is somewhat overcritical of Comrade Kapuściński's academic situation. This issue came up in the winter session. Comrade Kapuściński's attitude to his studies has now changed for the better.'

Comrade Geremek stipulates:

'Comrade Kapuściński should be cut off from organizational work so that he can put more emphasis on his studies. Comrade Kapuściński does not always know how to work with colleagues who are not committed.'

Comrade Kapuściński defends himself:

'What has been said in the discussion is fair, but I am sorry it has been limited to academic issues. I did indeed have a non-Party attitude to my studies, and I have not yet fully overcome that attitude.'

Comrade Holzer rushes to Comrade Kapuściński's rescue.

'He has done good work on the ZMP Faculty Board. He has a strong emotional attachment to the Party. He is highly enthusiastic and eager to work. He has not entirely overcome the following defects: an insufficiently serious attitude to his studies, not always fully considered decisions, and a not always self-critical approach. Being admitted as a candidate for the Party will help Comrade Kapuściński to overcome these faults.'

From the stenographic record: 'Comrade Kapuściński was unanimously accepted as a candidate for the PZPR'; he becomes a Party member on 11 April 1953.

Professor Wipszycka explains this eagerness to vet the CVs and attitudes of candidates for the Party as follows: 'Within the Party élite in the history faculty, the cult of knowledge was paramount, and that is why Kapuściński was so harshly treated for his 'non-Party attitude to his studies'. We wanted – and I do not exclude myself – to show that we were the best in terms of quality, especially to those professors and students who were "non-believers" in socialism. That is why we demanded the highest standards from each other, the best academic results.'

Why did a person become a communist in those days? Why did so many young, and not just young, talented people voluntarily – enthusiastically even, with religious zeal and fanaticism – declare their intention of taking part in a system which limited freedom and applied repression?

> For us, still children, the reasoning was simple: if Hitler fought against Bolshevism, it must be a good thing, worth supporting. That was how identifying with Bolshevism came about, which someone born later might no longer be able to understand.[3]

Kapuściński never made any other significant statement about the origins of his post-war choices. There are a few perfunctory remarks in interviews, such as 'everything I did, I did with immense conviction'.[4]

There was a sort of religious element in all this, an attempt at a sort of faith.

Other writers of that generation were more talkative on this topic. From the vast literature squaring accounts with their involvement in building socialism in the 1940s and early 1950s, I have chosen the voices of two of Kapuściński's colleagues as representative of the mind-set of the part of their generation that believed communism was the start of a new world, the future of mankind.

This is how Wiktor Woroszylski remembered it:

We hated the world order in which we had lived through that bad period between childhood and youth. We despised the older generation for failing to prevent that world, and we longed for some sort of major compensation, for a new world built on the ruins, a world that was not only good and fair, but strong, attacking, suppressing evil, merciless. We were hungry for a great division, in which we could stand on the side of good.[5]

Tadeusz Konwicki remembered it this way:

When I was seventeen or eighteen, the nation was being massacred all around me. Right next to me there were boys with machine guns, for whom killing someone was no big deal. I did not belong to the generation of businessmen involved in scams, but to the generation of people exhausted by a terrible war. At that point people climbed to the zenith of humanity. I was living in a moral ecosphere, in a tense atmosphere. That is why it was easy for me to accept such a proposal for a better way to run the world. While also convinced that the stupid world had led to a hecatomb. Nowadays if I were to tell a Polish businessman that the world needs improving, he'd laugh at me, but in those days it wasn't funny . . .

I confess to being totally incapable of even attempting to describe to you, or to anyone who did not live through it, the time at the end of the war, the moment when we entered a new life. Sunshine, orchards in blossom, the hopes that something would be built, something would be done, that life would be different, better. Of course you can say: 'You were terribly naive, gentlemen'. Yes, we were naive, that was to do with our age, with our very painful war experience, not so long, but intense, and with our civic upbringing in the convention of Polish Romanticism. My generation lived on an entirely different level from yours. We lived in a world of moral necessities, dramatic situations.[6]

What did the young people know about Stalin's crimes? About the Katyń massacre, about repression and disappearances, or about the transports to Siberia? What did the young Rysiek Kapuściński, history student, ZMP and Party activist, know about all that? How did everyone cope with it?

A note in the margin: 'Ask RK's close friends if anyone ever talked to him about it.'

Once again I come upon a clue implying that Kapuściński wove a slightly distorted autobiography in his books. In *Travels with Herodotus*, after recalling the strict political censorship of the Stalin era of 1949–55, he writes:

Two years had passed since Stalin's death. The atmosphere became more relaxed, people breathed more freely. Ilya Ehrenburg's novel *The Thaw* had just appeared, its title lending itself to the new epoch just beginning. Literature seemed to be everything then. People looked to it for the strength to live, for guidance, for revelation.

I completed my studies and began working at a newspaper. It was called *Sztandar Młodych* (The Banner of Youth). I was a novice reporter and my beat was to follow the trail of letters sent to the editor back to their points of origin.[7]

I quote this extract from *Travels with Herodotus* to Professor Wipszycka, and before I have a chance to ask a question, she waves her hand and says: '1955? Oh, that's too late. From the start of college we all knew him as a reporter and poet for *Sztandar Młodych*.'

Why, in a book written at the end of his life, does he not mention his work for *Sztandar Młodych* during the years when Polish Stalinism was at its height? For an answer, I go to the library.

No one now remembers who offered the high school pupil Kapuściński the opportunity to work for *Sztandar Młodych* in 1950, nor is it of any significance. Someone must have taken notice of the young poet, who has just published several poems in *Odrodzenie* and *Dziś i Jutro* ('I owe the fact that I became a journalist to poetry – not the best, but it was mine,' he would say years later). The fledgling poet belongs to the Youth Circle attached to the Polish Writers' Union, and there he meets Woroszylski.

Sztandar Młodych, the newspaper for young communists in the ZMP, is produced by people of various temperaments and, above all, various experiences in life. One has been through exile in Siberia, another has fought in the Warsaw Uprising, another has survived the Holocaust. 'We were ready to move mountains, climb to the peaks, often demolishing things along the way that you weren't supposed to demolish,' one veteran of the paper will recall.[8]

Their later fortunes will vary. One will remain faithful to socialism to the end; another will be a famous figure in the opposition. One will take part in the anti-Semitic witch-hunt of 1968; another will be its target. And one will end up as the world's most famous Polish reporter.

To the offer to work for the newspaper, the high school poet Kapuściński replies: 'First let me pass my high school graduation exams.'

Straight after these exams, in 1950, he turns up at the *Sztandar Młodych* editorial office, which occupies three floors of a tenement house on Wilcza Street in the centre of Warsaw. There are stacks of paper, lots of cigarette smoke, some lively minds and interesting discussions. The young poet finds the atmosphere of the place thrilling. At once, his pieces start to appear regularly in the newspaper. He reviews books and theatre, writes poems, and is a fully involved reporter and commentator – a participant in the ZMP revolution.

On 12 August, there appears a poem entitled 'Our Days' (an extract from a long poem called 'The Road Leads Forward'):

> And whenever
> in statistics you see
> the picture of days to come,
> whenever
> through hard work and ambition
> you pour the concrete of socialism
> whenever
> your heart starts beating impatiently
> like the piston in a machine
> at once you are
> a worker of victories
> and a poet of powerful plans.[9]

An article dated 31 August about a socialist labour competition includes the following passage:

'Yes, Comrades, more can be produced,' says worker Czesław Naziębło, 'but only once our norms are changed. Right now they are still old and unsuitable, and prevent us from raising our productivity' ... 'I believe that by breaking the old, unsuitable norms we will build the foundations of socialism in People's Poland faster'.[10]

And on 18 November there is a poem called 'Second Defenders of Peace Congress':

> Let us ignite in our hearts
> the flame of our will
> The arm of Peace
> flexes
> more forcefully.
> We –
> stronger by a billion hands,
> mightier
> by force of Stalin's mind.[11]

At a private party in the 1970s, as often happens over a glass of vodka, some Poles are chatting the night away. Wiktor Osiatyński is teasing Kapuściński:

'How could you write those things in the 1950s? How could you support all that? After all, it was a repressive system, people were in prison.'

'We didn't know anything about the prisons.'

'What didn't you know? I'm twelve years younger than you and I knew about them in primary school.'

'What did you know?'

'That some of my friends' fathers were in prison. How could you not have known?'

'Because there was no one like that in my environment. "Class enemies" and their children weren't admitted to college in those days.'

Maybe that's true, says Osiatyński, but on the other hand he'd have had to be a moron not to know.

Among Kapuściński's acquaintances in the 1950s, a classmate from Staszic High School, Teresa Lechowska, was sent to prison for political reasons. At the time she was a student at Warsaw University and a member of the ZMP. She was arrested in 1953 on a charge of telling political jokes and sentenced to two and a half years in prison for, as the verdict stated, 'disseminating false information about economic and political relations within Poland and the friendly relationship between Poland and the USSR, and information heard on radio broadcasts by imperialist states capable of causing harm to the interests of the Polish People's Republic'. She served a year, first in the Mostowski Palace (militia headquarters), then with female convicts sentenced for common crimes at a penal institution in Warsaw's Gęsiówka Prison.

'They had a thick file on me – I was denounced by a close female friend,' says Lechowska. 'There were jokes about Soviet science, for instance. Ivan Michurin was experimenting with genetic hybrids, and one of the jokes went: "Why is it a good idea to cross an apple tree with a dog? Because it waters itself, and if anyone tries to steal the apples, it barks." You can understand what a threat that was to the Polish–Soviet alliance and the interests of People's Poland,' says Lechowska ironically.

She remembers Kapuściński from high school and university as an ardent idealist. 'He wasn't some sort of awful swine – he just believed in it, that's all.'

'Did you ever see each other at college?'

'We bumped into each other from time to time. The university wasn't as big as it is now, and old friends from high school knew about each other, where they were and what they were doing.'

'Perhaps he didn't know about your arrest and sentence?'

'That's pretty much out of the question. When I came out of prison, I was told that at ZMP and Party meetings at the university I was pointed out as an example of a concealed "class enemy" who had cunningly wormed her way into college. He might not have remembered someone else's case, but I was one of his classmates and we did see each other sometimes. He must have known.'

Many years later, the only time he will ever do so in such an open way, Kapuściński will admit:

> One of the basic features of a totalitarian system is to block information right from the level of the individual: people keep quiet, they see and they know, but they keep quiet. A father is afraid to tell his son, a husband is afraid to tell his wife. This silence is either demanded of them, or they choose it themselves as a survival strategy.[12]

When he mentioned silence, did he have his classmate in mind?

Teresa Torańska, who conducted in-depth interviews with Party dignitaries from every stage of the PRL's history, offers a possible key. 'Remember General Jaruzelski's biography,' she says. 'He and his family were transported to the Soviet Union, so he knew all about Soviet Stalinism and its crimes, in spite of which he built communism in Poland. Years later he became the Party leader. Human memory is selective; it rejects the things that hurt and retains the things that make life easier. Kapuściński's family came from eastern Poland, where "everyone knew" who the Soviets were and what they did after 17 September 1939. The Kapuścińskis escaped to the General Government to avoid the Soviet transports to the East – how could Rysiek not have known what that system was like? He knew it all. But as Comrade Gomułka used to say, "A man only knows as much as he wants to know".'

I lay this key beside 'Konwicki's key': that it was not so hard for young people to accept the communist proposal for a better way to run the world, especially as the old one had 'led to a hecatomb'. There was exhaustion following the war, then there was agricultural reform, the enthusiastic drive to build Nowa Huta – the forerunner of a better world, and efforts to eradicate illiteracy, in which the young ZMP activists played a leading role.

To understand why so many young, talented and sensitive people felt 'mightier by force of Stalin's mind' requires exercising the imagination, especially when the privilege of being born later comes into it. Osiatyński's words come to mind: 'I never judge anyone who lived through the war and Stalinism.' How would any of us, who were born much later, have behaved? Which side would we have been on? At the same time, it is harder to understand, and to walk in someone else's shoes, when years later the people of that era – like Kapuściński – so desperately want to forget, to wipe out and erase all traces of the past, because that suggests they cannot find any positive explanation for their earlier commitment.

When Kazimierz Wolny-Zmorzyński, now a Jagiellonian University professor specializing in literature and the mass media, tells Kapuściński towards the end of his life that one of the books about him includes biographical elements concerning, inter alia, the evolution of his political views, he erupts:

'You're not going to go rummaging about in my life story!'

Kapuściński threatens to take him to court, even though the man is an expert on his work.

Stalinism in Poland is the first revolution Kapuściński witnesses – he experiences it at first hand as an active participant, a youth activist, a propagandistic reporter, and a committed poet. The revolutionary cause, an obsession with great social change and with the collapse of the old world and the emergence of the new – the attitudes of people in such times and in extreme situations will become the leitmotifs of Kapuściński's life; they will stir his passion to discover the world and will be the driving force behind his entire future literary output.

In a way, the romantic reporter running about the world in pursuit of revolutions, rebellions and liberation movements is born in the Stalinist era in Poland – a sinister one in view of the terror, and yet for many people a time full of hope that they will succeed in building a just world free of hunger, wars and poverty. This paradox of revolution, the internal rupture of great political shocks, will become an intrinsic part of the reporter's life story and of the attitudes of the man who made his intellectual, professional and practical choices in the Cold War era, amid conditions under which his own country's sovereignty was limited.

Alicja, Maminek, Zojka

He looks at her once, then a second time. He invites her to the cinema, perhaps the Stolica in Mokotów; she can't remember which film it was. It is autumn 1951, the start of the academic year.

At ZMP meetings she sits in the corner with her girlfriends, chatting and laughing. Colleague Kapuściński, a very important ZMP activist, sits at the presidium table, sermonizing about class enemies and increased vigilance, and occasionally he hushes the giggling girl: 'Colleague Mielczarek, stop talking!'

'He had a naughty look in his eyes,' she says. 'That was how he let me know he was watching me.'

They meet at university parties. She waits for him because, after all, he's an activist. A revolutionary is always having to rush off and see to something or advise about something – a revolution is no joke, it's hard work from dawn to dusk. He is late for their dates, and when he finally turns up, they start to tango. Their male and female friends form a circle around them, but as they gaze at each other, they don't even notice.

They made friends at once in the first year of history. She was totally fascinated by him. He was so handsome, with thick, dark hair, fit and athletic, with a good physique, she remembers. He used to kick a ball about – he loved playing soccer.

'You've picked up the best-looking guy in the year,' her girlfriends say enviously.

She has come to Warsaw from Szczecin for her university studies, and she feels very liberated in the big city. One time, several girls are sitting in a café with their legs crossed, each smoking a cigarette. She is laughing and gesticulating. He sits down opposite. He looks at her, staring and staring, and shakes his head in disapproval. She pretends she hasn't seen him and goes on chatting, but she swiftly stubs out her cigarette. She never smokes again.

Teresa Torańska, with whom I conduct a joint interview with Alicja Kapuścińska for *Gazeta Wyborcza*,[1] says to her: 'He only had to nod his head?'

'No, he shook it . . . He didn't want the girl who had caught his eye to be a smoker. In those days, young girls like me didn't smoke.'

'But he smoked, didn't he?'

'For over thirty years. Too long. He only gave it up in 1980, when Professor Noszczyk got him scared about it. You have clogged arteries, he told him, so either give up smoking or I'll have to chop your legs off.'

Alicja's parents, Mr and Mrs Mielczarek, came from Łódź. They had been to teacher training college and met as village teachers. They taught at one-class schools, and before the war had always lived in accommodation adjoining their workplace. Not knowing what else to do with her small daughter, Alicja's mother used to take her into the classroom. With a very serious look on her face, the child would sit among the first-year pupils in the front row – and at barely three years old she started to read. Afterwards she was always very proud of being better at parsing the grammar and logic of a sentence than her brother, who was three years older.

The war caught up with them in the village of Józefów, where her parents taught, in territory which the Germans annexed to the Reich. The Mielczareks headed for the General Government, managed to get across the border and found a place to live in the Lublin area. Alicja spent the four years of German occupation in a small village with not much more than twenty houses and two wells a few dozen metres deep. She remembers a small barrel on a chain tied to the well shaft, with two buckets fixed inside it. The water was poured into the buckets and carried on a special yoke across the shoulders, as in Africa, carefully, to avoid spilling a single drop.

In the 1960s when she visits her gravely ill husband in Africa, where he is a PAP correspondent, their close friend Jerzy Nowak, a diplomat, will say: 'Look how they carry the water here, Ala.' She will reply, 'I've seen that before, during the war, in the countryside near Lublin.'

After the war, Alicja's parents left for western Poland, to settle in the so-called Recovered Territories. First they lived in Koszalin, and then Szczecin. Alicja went to a girl's high school, where pre-war discipline prevailed and the girls wore a compulsory uniform.

Alicja was a star pupil – she had top marks and was president of the student council. She was even a *przodownik nauki* – 'the number one student', in communist terminology – yet another sign of the new times.

The year before her high school graduation exams, the headmistress calls her in to her office.

'Now then, Miss Mielczarek, you are president of the council and you're a good student. I have received a directive from the authorities to create an education class. There is a lack of teachers in this country, so we need to train new staff. I'd like you to join this class, and then I'll have an argument to persuade others – when you have joined, the other girls will follow your lead and willingly agree.'

Like it or not, she cannot say no.

She is already in the ZMP, which displeases her mother. 'Why did you sign up for that?' she complains. 'Why shouldn't I?' answers the daughter.

Her father, on the other hand, is pleased. Even before the PZPR came into being, he belonged to its wartime predecessor, the PPR, or Polish Worker's Party. He and his wife were always quarrelling about it, but there was no domestic war in the Mielczarek home as a result.

Alicja's mother had dreamed of a career in medicine, but before the war she had no chance of achieving it. She tells her daughter: 'I'd love you to become a doctor.' And Alicja is convinced that one day she will do just that. When at school the girls are assigned the essay title 'Who Do You Want to Be?', she writes: 'I am going to be a doctor.'

Along with her high school graduation diploma, Alicja receives a state order to work at one of the schools in Szczecin. It looks as if medicine, or any other studies, will forever remain a dream. But she wants to study – very much, at any cost. She goes to see the local superintendent of schools. She is told: 'There's nothing we can do, you'll have to go to the Ministry.' She goes to Warsaw. There they tell her: 'You can go to college, but only the kind that prepares you for school teaching.'

So Alicja chooses to study history at Warsaw University. She isn't obsessed with the subject, but she likes her school history teacher. In Warsaw she lives in a four-person room in the so-called New Dziekanka – a university residence hall on Krakowskie Przedmieście in central Warsaw, near the statue of Adam Mickiewicz. It is attached to the old Dziekanka, which belonged to the art college.

Rysiek is now living with his parents and sister in the two-family Finnish cottage on Pole Mokotowskie (Mokotów Field, a large park in Warsaw); the Kapuścińskis occupy one half of it. At the entrance, several steps lead into a tiny vestibule, with a small toilet and kitchenette with a metal sink to one side, and a living room with an alcove to the other. In the living room there is a sofa bed for the parents, a wardrobe, a table, and a couple of chairs. In the alcove, divided from the room by a curtain, are two iron beds. Rysiek sleeps against one wall, and his sister Basia against the other.

Rysiek's father has finally returned to work, as a teacher of handicrafts, while their mother works for the time being at the Central Statistical Office. While his parents are at work and his sister is at college, Rysiek brings Alicja to the cottage.

When Teresa Torańska and I question her about these meetings, Alicja Kapuścińska is reluctant to answer.

'Don't write about that,' she says.

'What mustn't we write about?'

'That when they were out, Rysiek and I used to meet at the Finnish cottage.'

'What's wrong with that?'

'I don't like talking about private matters in public.'

'Are we asking?'

'Don't you think anyone will guess, Teresa?'

'The Finnish cottage has to be in there, Ala.'

'With restraint, then, please.'

The Finnish cottage still stands in the same spot. In 1988 Rysiek and Alicja go for a walk to Pole Mokotowskie during the time when the National Library is being built there. They see that of the original fifteen or so cottages, two are still there, transformed into storerooms for workmen. One is the Kapuścińskis'. They peep through the window. The round, black table made by Rysiek's father still stands in the middle of the room, with papers spread out on it. When Józef moved in the 1970s, he didn't take it with him, because it wouldn't fit into his new flat.

Maria Kapuścińska is not thrilled by her son's relationship with Alicja, especially as a wedding and a child are soon on the way. She thinks they are too young to get married – he is twenty and she is nineteen. Maria dreams of an unusual future for her son, though she is not entirely sure what kind. She is afraid that too early a marriage will obstruct him in his career, whatever that may be. And she bears a grudge against Alicja for falling pregnant – in those days, the girl was always to blame.

Once Alicja starts coming to the Kapuścińskis' cottage as the official fiancée, Mrs Kapuścińska gives her her son's socks to darn. Alicja darns, launders and irons Rysiek's shirts. Under Mrs Kapuścińska's tutelage, without a word of protest, she learns the duties expected of her beloved Rysieczek's wife. She is to be meek, industrious and supportive to her husband. Alicja tries to mollify her future mother-in-law and to show her that her son has not made a bad choice. She is grateful to be allowed into the house at all.

At Alicja's family home in Szczecin, Rysiek quickly makes a good impression. He immediately announces that they are planning to get married, but don't know when because they do not have a place to live. Alicja asks her mother if she would be surprised if they soon had a child. Her mother is neither surprised nor shocked; she knows what's going on.

On 6 October 1952, at Ryszard and Alicja's registry office wedding, besides the witnesses and a few friends, the only close relatives present are Józef Kapuściński and Rysiek's sister, Basia. Maria Kapuścińska boycotts the ceremony. She invites them to dinner afterwards, but Rysiek wriggles out of it. Of everyone involved, his beloved Maminek is the least willing to accept his marriage. Only when she was dying would Maria Kapuścińska admit to her daughter-in-law: 'Ala, you have been a daughter to me.' Alicja reckons this is the highest distinction she could possibly have received from her mother-in-law. After more than twenty years of marriage, she deserved it.

Alicja's parents did not come to the wedding either. The young couple deliberately decided to tell them about it too late – they sent a telegram the day before the wedding – so there would be no confrontation between the parents. They were afraid that an altercation or an exchange of sour looks on that particular day would affect relations between the families for years to come. After that, there was an appropriate relationship between the two sets of parents.

As a result, when Alicja, in a modest navy blue dress with a white collar, and Rysiek, in the black suit from his high school graduation ceremony (the only suit he had at the time), take their seats before the registrar, several of the most important people in their lives thus far are not present.

The registrar recites the dull official formulae about the family as 'the basic social cell', while Rysiek takes the rings from his pocket, nudges Alicja and says: 'Put it on my finger.' Later they do not wear the rings. Alicja explains that while working at a hospital she had to keep washing her hands, and the ring got in the way; Rysiek simply loses his.

Soon after the wedding, Alicja takes dean's leave from college and goes to Szczecin. While waiting for the baby to be born, she works in the library at Szczecin's Palace of Youth. On 2 May 1953 Alicja's mother sends her son-in-law a telegram saying: 'You have a daughter.' Rysiek would have preferred a son.

As Alicja recalls: 'People used to think a real man should produce a son who would inherit his father's duties, running the family, building a house and planting trees. Rysiek was wondering what to call our daughter when he bumped into a friend of ours. "Zocha", he announced, "I've had a daughter." Later she told me he looked pleased. "So call her Zofia," she suggested [Zocha is a diminutive of Zofia]. He liked that idea.'

But there's another name he likes even more than Zofia – Zojka. A girl named Zojka is the heroine of the era, a role model for young communists in the ZMP, and a sacred figure in the communist revolution. When Germany attacked the Soviet Union, a Soviet schoolgirl named Zoya Kosmodemyanskaya joined a special unit in the Red Army. This unit performed acts of sabotage behind enemy lines. After blowing up a German ammunitions store, Zoya was caught and hanged.

If the child had been a boy, he would have been called Wowka (Polish spelling of the Russian 'Vovka'), short for Włodzimierz, in honour of the leader of the October Revolution, Vladimir Lenin. According to a different version of the story, 'Wowka' would have been a tribute not to Lenin but to Vladimir Mayakovsky, which is what Kapuściński told his translator Agata Orzeszek.

'In those days he was captivated by Mayakovsky's talent and the power of his voice,' she says. 'He was sorry Broniewski was called Władysław, and not Włodzimierz, because then his son's name would have paid homage to both his favourite poets.'

But his dream of having a son had not come true.

Rysiek boards a train and goes straight to Szczecin. However, for the first year of their marriage they live apart. Alicja takes care of Zojka in Szczecin and wonders whether to return to her studies, while Rysiek goes on study-ing and running the ZMP revolution in Warsaw. He comes to visit, but he is a husband and father 'at arm's length'. When he comes, he sometimes goes out for a walk with the pram, but rather reluctantly. So young, and already a father. He is the eternal bachelor type and likes appealing to the girls. A baby in a pram is not well suited to this pursuit.

One time, he turns up in Szczecin in an anxious state: his mother has had a stroke. It is either a haemorrhage or a cerebral embolism. It seems truly life-threatening. There are no telephones in the Finnish cottages where the Kapuścińskis live. Rysiek runs to the hospital on Hoża Street to call an ambulance, and the doctor offers this advice: 'The best thing to do is apply leeches to draw blood from the carotid artery.' So he races to the market on Polna Street and buys a jar of leeches. Alicja reckons those leeches saved her mother-in-law's life. After the stroke, Maria Kapuścińska never went back to work. She functioned fairly normally and did not need to be cared for like a disabled person, but her strength was seriously impaired.

After this incident, Rysiek tells Alicja to drop her studies in the history faculty. He says that, after graduating, he plans to become a journalist. But what about her? If she graduates in history, she will have to teach rowdy little brats. 'Go and study medicine,' he suggests.

Alicja passes the exams for medicine in Szczecin and gets credits for her first year of studies there. Meanwhile Rysiek finishes his history degree in Warsaw. He writes a dissertation, on the education system within the Russian partition in the early twentieth century, under the supervision of Henryk Jabłoński, later chairman of the Council of State (the PRL equiva-lent of a national president without any real power). Rysiek goes back to work at *Sztandar Młodych* and is soon allotted an employee's flat.

After her year in Szczecin, Alicja returns to Warsaw and continues her medical studies there. Zojka stays behind in Szczecin with her grandpar-ents. She is too small to go to nursery school. A year later her parents take her to Warsaw.

The young family is assigned a room with a kitchen and a bathroom in a block on the corner of Nowolipki Street and Marchlewski (now Jan Paweł

II) Avenue. The kitchen is quite large, with a window. There they put a desk – this will be Rysiek's workroom.

Alicja gets up early in the morning, quickly makes something to eat, then hurriedly irons her husband's shirts, takes Zojka to nursery school – luckily, in the house next door – and rushes to lectures or practical studies at the hospital. In the evening when she comes home, the laundry is waiting for her in the bathtub, because they have no washing machine.

The constant noise coming from the other side of the walls is a daily nightmare. Their flat is sandwiched between a lift and a rubbish chute: on one side the lift doors keep crashing shut, and then the lift thunders up or down; on the other is the chute, producing yet more clatter. On top of that, the chute is connected to the kitchen by a ventilator, in order to provide ventilation for the kitchen, but usually it is the stink from the chute that invades the kitchen. Alicja seals up the ventilator, but it doesn't help.

Rysiek is infuriated. He can't bear being disturbed while he's writing. He needs peace and quiet. If he doesn't have it, everything irritates him.

So when Alicja sees Rysiek starting to twitch and pace nervously, she and Zojka sit quietly in the corner to avoid further antagonizing the lion. She knows him well enough to understand when to keep out of the way and not respond to provocation. Never does she strike her fist against the table; never does she say she's had enough. ('Of course not! That was my Rysio! Whatever do you mean?')

Once the writing starts to go smoothly, he solemnly announces that now he's making progress, that now he has the wind in his sails. He reads out the first sentence, and Alicja jumps for joy. And so on . . . to the next paragraph. He always writes slowly and barely meets the standard editorial quotas. His concern is with the quality of his writing, not the quantity, and so he earns a pittance.

Alicja's father helps them. Both her parents are working, and although teachers' salaries are not high, they offer to assist. Only in 1959, when Alicja finishes her medical studies and receives her first salary, does she write to her father to say that they are grateful for his support but from now on will manage on their own.

II

'56: Revolution All Over Again

Every revolution is preceded by a state of general exhaustion, and takes place against a background of unleashed aggressiveness. Authority cannot put up with a nation that gets on its nerves; the nation cannot tolerate an authority it has come to hate . . . A climate of tension and increasing oppressiveness prevails. We start to fall into a psychosis of terror. The discharge is coming. We feel it.

Ryszard Kapuściński, *Shah of Shahs*[1]

'This will never get through,' snaps the editor-in-chief of *Sztandar Młodych*. She can tell that the report about Nowa Huta that has just landed on her desk will get the newspaper into trouble.

Irena Tarłowska is not a timid boss. At thirty-seven, she is quite a bit older than the twenty-somethings who form the main core of her staff. ('Irena Tarłowska was a strapping, handsome woman with thick blond hair parted to one side', Kapuściński would write about her years later.[2]) A left-wing woman who radiated French culture, she had been in the communist youth movement during the inter-war years and in the PPR (Polish Worker's Party) and the underground People's Army during the war. She had personal connections with high-ranking officials of the post-war regime. Her appointment in 1954 as the editor-in-chief at *Sztandar Młodych* was interpreted by the journalists as a harbinger of approaching change.

'There's no question – the censor won't let this through,' she repeats firmly, leaving no hope for the poet and history graduate upon his return to work.

For the past three years, Kapuściński has been writing for *Sztandar Młodych* sporadically – an occasional review, a short report or a poem in praise of socialism, but no more than a few items a year. He has been fully occupied by his studies and his ZMP activities at college, and a revolution has occurred in his family life as well.

Now he returns to the newspaper, where the ice of Stalinism is starting to melt. 'Ilya Ehrenburg's novel *The Thaw* had just appeared, its title lending itself to the new epoch just beginning',[3] he will write half a century from now.

Ehrenburg's novel is the subject of heated debate at gatherings in smoke-filled cafés and in newspaper columns. Men of letters, critics and students are all discussing it.[4] Some see the book as 'a superb moral polemic with the image of man tailored to meet the demands of ideology'. Others criticize it for 'losing the pathos of the struggle to build socialism' and falsely contrasting these ideas with 'an apology for everyday life'. Both the former and the latter can feel that something is changing, that something new is coming.

The writers have been noticing something which earlier they could not, or would not, see. In a thaw-era poem, Mieczysław Jastrun, who is the bard of socialism, describes looking through one window at prisoners building garages for the security service, and through another at free bricklayers no longer building the bright future of socialism, but now rather 'the wall of a lunatic asylum, or House of the Dead'.[5]

Tone and language, aesthetics and subject matter are changing.

The main characters in stories by emerging novelist Marek Hłasko, cult writer of the thaw and of October '56, are still workers, but they are not heroes erecting the great edifice of socialism; instead they are frustrated individuals who cannot see the future, sometimes ordinary down-and-outs whose dreams go no further than a bottle of vodka after the end of the day's work. A lyrical note appears – alien to the spirit of socialism.

From the West comes 'putrid imperialist literature' – the weekly *Życie Literackie* (Literary Life) publishes *The Old Man and the Sea*, by Ernest Hemingway.

An exhibition entitled 'Arsenal' overturns Stalinist notions of aesthetics and the aims of the fine arts; abstraction makes its appearance, having previously been abhorred as 'the degenerate art of the bourgeoisie'. The same sort of revolution is triggered in the world of music by the Warsaw Autumn festival, whose inception coincides with the peak of the political watershed of October '56. The idea for the event is born a year earlier, on the rising tide of the thaw. Jazz, too, is rehabilitated – after formerly being banned as 'the music of American imperialism'.

From its distant place of exile, there is also a comeback for laughter. At last people are allowed to laugh at the 'distortions of socialism': shows performed at the Student Satirical Theatre, which opens in Warsaw, attract crowds of intellectuals and prompt fiery debates in the youth press.

One daring bard of the era wrote:

> Comrades, you may find this question
> much too bold and even rude:
> Comrades, is it my impression
> you lack red cells in your blood?[6]

One of the most profound changes brought about by the thaw is, in the words of Jacek Kuroń, 'the rehabilitation of private life'. Only a year or two earlier, a public debate at the university on the subject of sex was unimaginable. 'A public meeting on the topic "May One Have Sex Before Marriage?" broke all the conventions, because until then there had only ever been meetings about the war in Korea, the Colorado beetle and German militarists, but the gradually advancing political changes were also overtaken at lightning speed by a revolution in the arts. The young people who played jazz tracks were dressing in "gear" that more distinctly and plainly rebelled against official life.'[7]

Thanks to the youth and student festival, in which almost two hundred thousand young people take part, including thirty thousand from abroad, including the West, smiling faces and bright colours pervade the streets of Warsaw, fresh air wafts in, and a different kind of music is heard. Originally conceived as a propaganda event on behalf of the socialist cause, the festival becomes an opportunity for Polish youth to encounter the Western culture abhorred by propaganda, and also to meet some of their contemporaries from behind the Iron Curtain. The festival, said Kuroń, 'exposed the entire hypocrisy and falsehood of a lifestyle which had been promoted as progressive. It turned out that you could be progressive, but at the same time enjoy life, wear colourful clothes, listen to jazz, have fun and make love.'[8]

The young people of 1955 want to mend socialism, because there is no returning to pre-war Poland, to exploitation and inequality. Socialism is the future, justice, equal opportunities for all! We made some mistakes, yes, but they can be fixed, and lack of integrity can be avoided in future.

The Party is losing control on the cultural front. Blasphemous voices are saying the political authorities should not interfere in culture at all: this is a coup against the most sacred dogma concerning 'ideological–political and Party management in the arts'. The Politburo advises and orders: Resist! The obedient writers rush to the counter-offensive. They decry 'the recidivism of the bourgeois concept of art', 'nihilism', 'showing off', 'revolutionary tendencies', and 'the emptiness of petty bourgeois radicalism'.

As Kapuściński wrote a quarter-century later in his book about the workings of revolution, *Shah of Shahs*:

More than petards or stilettos, therefore, words – uncontrolled words, circulating freely, underground, rebelliously, not gotten up in dress uniforms, uncertified – frighten tyrants. But sometimes it is the official, uniformed, certified words that bring about the revolution.[9]

The snowball of youth opposition and unleashed imagination can no longer be stopped.

★ ★ ★

'We still believed in socialism. We believed it was possible to go back to the ideals, and that it was just a matter of eliminating lack of integrity. We were under the irresistible influence of the debate about new literature and art . . . We were longing for an open window onto the world.'

Historian and Holocaust survivor Marian Turski is Tarłowska's deputy and Kapuściński's line manager at *Sztandar Młodych*. He often runs the paper when Tarłowska is busy smoothing out its relationship with the authorities.

Whenever an article appears in *Sztandar Młodych* that the Party top brass find indigestible, Tarłowska applies the crafty strategy of pretending to be feather-brained: she fibs that she wasn't at the office, she had gone out, and her young colleagues printed something without her knowledge. She saves her own neck and makes it look as if she is going to take measures against her subordinates, but she never does.

Step by step, *Sztandar Młodych* is becoming one of the tribunes of thaw-era criticism, but the role model for how to haul the authorities over the coals is provided by the editors of another journal. *Po Prostu* (Quite Simply), a weekly for students and young intellectuals and until recently an organ of the ZMP, is the first to point out the 'mistakes and distortions' at enterprises and manufacturing co-operatives. This happens at the start of the thaw, but as the months go by, *Po Prostu* demands democratization of the system, free debate within the Party and the ZMP, and even an equal partnership with the Soviet Union. It reaches out to social groups which until now have been anathematized by the authorities in the PRL – people with origins in the non-communist resistance movement during the Second World War (members of the underground Home Army and people who took part in the 1944 Warsaw Uprising). Every week, queues form at the newspaper kiosks to buy the journal that speaks a different language and covers previously banned topics.

Meanwhile, *Sztandar Młodych* is still the official newspaper of the ZMP, although an extremely heated debate about the youth movement is being conducted on its pages. 'The paper was a forum for debate,' says Turski, 'a tool for criticism and at the same time a focal point around which young people wanting to do something within society were gathering. For the first time we have wider access to the Western press.'

It is a moment of social ferment, and no one yet knows what will emerge from it.

During stormy conferences about the youth movement and the distortions of socialism, the editor-in-chief of *Sztandar Młodych* speaks for the Party 'liberals': 'It is undoubtedly true that the Party has a better view of the historical interests of the working class. However, if this does not occur by way of full openness in political life, some very harmful rifts are bound to appear between the Party and the masses, and these rifts could result in power becoming a tool of oppression in the hands of the Party. Then the criticism will be stifled.'

Only a year or two earlier, people went to prison for such heresies.

Since early 1955 – before bringing Tarłowska his report on Nowa Huta, which she is convinced has no chance of slipping through the censor's net – Kapuściński has been travelling around Poland. He visits workplaces, talks to workers, listens in on ZMP debates about why things are not as colourful as they should be, what mistakes we have made, and what should be done.

He is often away from home and also from the newspaper office. During these business trips, he stays at workers hotels. He argues with his ZMP comrades. He passes many nights in hoarse, drunken discussion, listening until daybreak to stories about the lives of ordinary people. He catches up on his sleep in trains.

For *Sztandar Młodych* he writes a series of reports from the provinces, which provide a voice in the debate about the apathy and hopelessness that are eroding the ZMP, about the degeneration of the Party bureaucracy and the mistakes made by those in power.

On returning from a ZMP conference in Kraków, Kapuściński reports: 'What is bothering the Kraków activists? Among other things, the escalating activity of the reactionary part of the clergy . . . Some priests do not admit them to meetings, do not let children wear scouts' scarves, and are instilling passivity in the young . . . At the Kraków conference, ten speakers have claimed that the training is "bunk", and that the young people often go to the priest to learn things. Why?' asks Kapuściński, and from a cool reporter he transforms himself into an ardent participant in the debate:

There is no miraculous force pushing them into the presbytery. What is it about the atmosphere of meetings, about the temperature of debate that means the young people are bored during training? No one has yet uttered a word about it.[10]

At another time in his life, in another part of the world, when he witnesses the Iranian people's rejection of the Shah's version of modernization and their return to their religious roots, Kapuściński will find one answer to the question, Why did the young reject the ZMP revolution? Surely his experience of the failure of the Stalinist revolution in Poland will give him inspiration a quarter of a century later:

The Shah's Great Civilization lay in ruins. What had it been in essence? A rejected transplant. It had been an attempt to impose a certain model of life on a community attached to entirely different traditions and values. It was forced, an operation that had more to do with surgical success in itself than with the question of whether the patient remained alive or – equally important – remained himself.

And yet there were noble intentions and lofty ideals behind the Great Civilization. But the people saw them only as caricatures, that is, in the guise that ideals are given when translated into practice. In this way even sublime ideas become subject to doubt.[11]

I look through a large file of his articles from that era: they contain a good deal of the propaganda typical of the time they were written. There is plenty of naive enthusiasm – Kapuściński was only twenty-three – sometimes the language is pompous or full of pathos, and sometimes strait-jacketed by Party newspeak. There are many clumsy or banal statements: 'Human experience bids us be prudent', one of the longer articles begins.

Among the streams of 'hot air', as he himself refers to Party prattle somewhere, there are pearls of wit and irony: 'I took part in a ZMP conference at which the chairman said: "Comrades, there is a proposal to open the window. Let the comrades express their opinion." '[12]

The articles belong to the tenor of the thaw and of score-settling with the failures of the Stalinist years. With the eagerness of a boy scout and the principled approach of an A student, Kapuściński cautions his comrades that self-flagellation is not in fact the only thing to do: 'Let's get down to work on a positive programme.'[13]

In this and a few other articles one can sense a fear that thaw-era criticism could change into hostility towards socialism and the Party regime. Can the ardent ZMP activist still not see what the years of Stalinist revolution really were? Can he see, and yet still not come to terms with it? Can he see, but only write as much as he is able to? Or does he write what he is told to?

Kapuściński is not one of the Party 'counter-reformers', but he does not yet feel comfortable on the side of the rebels. However, from week to week he is becoming radicalized. He writes, for instance, 'We needed to reprimand the bureaucrats, all those lovers of bits of paper'.

The whole thing began to intrigue me, so I sat down in one of the committee headquarters (pretending to wait for someone who was not there) and watched how they settled the simplest of problems. After all, life consists of settling problems, and progress is settling them deftly and to the general satisfaction. After a while a woman came in to ask for a certificate. The man who could issue it was tied up in a discussion at the moment. The woman waited. People here have a fantastic talent for waiting – they can turn to stone and remain motionless forever. Eventually the man turned up, and they began talking. The woman spoke, he asked a question, the woman asked a question, he said something. After some haggling, they agreed. They began looking for a piece of paper. Various pieces of paper lay on the table, but none of them looked right. The man disappeared – he must have gone to look for paper, but he might just as well have gone across the street to drink some tea (it was a hot day). The woman waited in silence. The man returned, wiping his mouth with satisfaction (so he'd gone for tea after all), but he also had paper. Now began the most dramatic part of all – the search for a pencil. Nowhere was there a pencil, not on the table, nor in the drawer, nor on the floor. I lent him my pen. He smiled, and the woman sighed with relief. Then he sat down to write. As he began writing, he realized he was not quite sure what he was supposed to be certifying. They began talking, and the man nodded. Finally, the document was ready. Now it had to be signed by someone higher up. But the higher-up was unavailable. He was debating in another committee, and there was no way to get in touch with him because the telephone was not answering. Wait. The woman turned back into stone, the man disappeared, and I left to have some tea.[14]

This is not Poland in the 1950s, but Iran following Khomeini's revolution, during the period when one bureaucracy was replacing another. For ordinary people, too much stayed the same as before.

As I play this game of mixing texts from different times and places, I am thinking of a conversation I had with Mark Danner. This 'major league' American journalist, reporter and essayist, Berkeley professor and friend of Kapuściński's has left me with this reminder:

'If you asked me what I'd like to learn from a biography of Kapuściński, I suppose it would be to have an answer to this question: What were the experiences Ryszard had in his life that allowed him to attain such a perfect understanding of the workings of power and revolution – in Iran, Ethiopia, and Latin America, among so many other places.'

Exactly these.

Marian Turski no longer remembers who sent Kapuściński to Nowa Huta late in the summer of 1955.

'It was many a journalist's ambition to be sent there – it was a prestige topic. Those who were sent thought of themselves as privileged.'

Nowa Huta is not just any old conglomerate – it is the flagship, the symbol of Polish socialism. Meanwhile, here and there people are hearing rumours that all is not well aboard ship. Somebody at the PZPR Central Committee comes up with the idea of sending someone there on a special mission. The job is entrusted to Remigiusz Szczęsnowicz, manager of the cultural centre in the Warsaw district of Targówek, who works with 'difficult' young people. He is to look around and write a report for the Central Committee. As he recalls years later, at the time there was a story doing the rounds at Nowa Huta about some newborn babies found in lime pits there.

Kapuściński is given a different task: to take a stand against Adam Ważyk's 'Poem for Adults'. '[W]ithin the Party management they were ready to flip – "What shall we do about Ważyk's lampoon? Let's prove it's all lies!" '[15] recalled the late Wojciech Adamiecki, then a journalist for *Sztandar Młodych*.

'Poem for Adults' is emblematic of the time, a landmark text from which the beginning of the thaw in Poland is often dated. In fact, the Stalinist ice has been melting for over a year when the poem appears on 21 September 1955 in the weekly *Nowa Kultura* (New Culture). But as a composition reflecting the spirit of the times, this, and no earlier or later literary text, is the one that passes into history. Its author is a poet who in past years has dedicated his entire soul and creative art to the cause of socialism. ('I destroyed the mythology that I myself had believed in until then,' he will admit years later.)

The 'Poem for Adults' is about Nowa Huta, the construction of which was extolled by the socialist–realist poets. Ważyk does not embellish; he sees the naked truth about socialism in Nowa Huta.

> From villages and towns they come by the cartload
> to build a steelworks, conjure up a city,
> dig a new Eldorado out of the earth,
> an army of pioneers, the assembled rabble,
> they crowd into shacks, barracks and hotels,
> they whistle as they trudge down the muddy streets:
> a great migration, dishevelled ambition,
> a string round the neck with a cross from Częstochowa,
> three storeys of curses, a small down pillow,
> a gallon of vodka and a yen for the whores,
> a mistrustful soul, torn from near the border,
> half aroused and half deranged,
> reticent with words, singing folk songs,
> suddenly ejected from medieval darkness,
> the wandering mass, inhuman Poland,
> howling with boredom on the long December nights . . .
>
> The great migration building industry,
> unknown to Poland, but known to history,
> fed on the emptiness of great big words, living
> wild, from day to day and in defiance of the preachers –
> in a cloud of carbon monoxide, in a gradual torment,
> from it the working class is being smelted.
> There's a lot of debris. But so far it's a shambles.[16]

Five years earlier, in his 'Poem about Nowa Huta', Kapuściński had praised this showpiece construction project of People's Poland. He went there with Wiktor Woroszylski in the summer of 1950, where Woroszylski had read his poems to the men building Nowa Huta, and the eighteen-year-old Kapuściński had listened, looked around, and become acquainted with some people. Later he wrote many critical comments about the authorities' negligence 'in the cultural sphere', including that the travelling cinemas did not come to Nowa Huta often enough, that the libraries for workers were inferior, and that there was a lack of quality entertainment.

Now his job is to go there and see that everything is in the best possible order.

Kapuściński and Szczęsnowicz share a rented room in one of Nowa Huta's small hotels. They expect to have a boring time trudging about the building site and having cliché conversations with the workers. And suddenly they discover an unknown world whose existence they have never imagined.

In his report to the Central Committee, Szczęsnowicz writes that 'you won't be able to educate the young people building Nowa Huta with the help of a church and a wretched pub selling vodka'.[17] The image that Kapuściński paints in his report, entitled 'This Is Also the Truth about Nowa Huta', prompts the editor-in-chief of Sztandar Młodych to say, 'This will never get through.'

What won't get through?

The story about the pimping mother, who sits in one room collecting money for services provided by her daughter in the next room. Or the one about the fourteen-year-old girl who has infected eight boys and 'described her exploits in such a vulgar way that one felt like vomiting'. Or the young married couples who spend their wedding nights in gateways and ditches ('whoever thought up the brilliant idea that married couples can only stay together in a hotel room until eight p.m.?').

A worker friend tells Kapuściński that he will never marry, because in these conditions he would be bound to 'have no respect for his wife'.

[A]t Huta the bureaucracy reaches a degree of barbarity. For example, a woman living in a workers' hotel is going to give birth. There are six other girls living in the same room. After three months she is supposed to go back to work. She doesn't: she works at Huta, several kilometres from the hotel, but she has to feed her baby four times a day. Nevertheless, they tell her to bring a certificate proving that she is working. Yes, but she cannot get one. Then along comes the hotel man, takes away her bedding, takes away everything that is not her property, and the woman and her baby are left on the bare floor-boards.[18]

Kapuściński hears about the fortunes of his friends from a few years earlier who have had enough and refuse to put up with 'all these obscenities'. One has written complaints and petitions, for which he has been punished by having his accommodation allotment withheld, despite the fact that he has a sick mother and his wife lives out in the countryside because they have no home of their own in the town. Another critic has been sacked from his job. Still another has been stymied by lethal rumours that 'he is a shirker and troublemaker. Not the worst method either!' he writes. 'People can see what's going on. It is as if some monstrous bureaucratic fungus has sprung up here, which is proliferating and crushing everything, but no one seems at all concerned.' In his report, Kapuściński reveals that complaints about what is going on at Nowa Huta have reached the ZMP authorities in Warsaw, but no one cares and they have gone unanswered.

Instead of painting the world of Ważyk's poem in rosy colours, Kapuściński adds even more black to it. He is on the side of the workers, who feel hurt by the poet's words: 'rabble', 'semi-deranged soul', 'inhuman Poland', 'a shambles'. 'To them these expressions,' writes Kapuściński, 'are wrongful, untrue and insulting'; they feel as if 'they are of no use to anyone, as if they are invisible'. 'But they admit that many of the images in the poem are true, all the more since they all too rarely read the whole truth about themselves.'

Kapuściński ends with a challenge to the Party and the ZMP: 'At Nowa Huta they must see that we are on the side of the working man every day of the week . . . The people at Nowa Huta are waiting for justice. They cannot wait for long. We have to go there and dig up everything that has been carefully hidden from human sight, and respond to a very large number of different questions.'

'There's no point even going to the censor with this,' says Tarłowska.

There's a fuss in the corridors at the newspaper office. Kapuściński has given the article to his colleagues to read, and now they are asking the editor-in-chief to call a meeting.

'The article should be printed!'

Tarłowska resists. Kapuściński takes it upon himself to sort the matter out at the censor's office. He has a friend there from his student days, Mietek Adamczyk, and with the report in hand he goes straight to him.

'If you stop this article, I will never shake your hand again.'

With what is left of her instinct for self-preservation, Tarłowska prevents her younger colleagues from posting the article on the front page – it ends up on the second page, on 30 September 1955. It is Kapuściński's first article to have repercussions.

A scandal erupts, on a scale that probably only Tarłowska was expecting. The Central Committee Press Office makes a decision to fire her, and the generous censor is also given notice. The board of *Sztandar Młodych* is to be taken to task by Jakub Berman in person, the Party's number two, and he is gearing up for a meeting with the journalists. Meanwhile, Kapuściński's colleagues are urging him to disappear and sit it out somewhere.

So he goes to Nowa Huta, and skulks at a workers' hotel. A man called Jakus – the activist whose criticism was silenced by rumours that 'he is a shirker and troublemaker' – takes him under his wing.

Now the Party reformers go on the counter-offensive. Jerzy Morawski, one of the leading lights of the thaw (and soon to become Tarłowska's second husband), devises a Central Committee commission to investigate the situation at Nowa Huta. The commission goes to the site and sees . . . the same things as Kapuściński. The 'commissars' try to get in touch with the reporter, but the ZMP members at Nowa Huta, who have given him shelter, say they won't give up their colleague until the Party provides a guarantee that nothing bad will happen to him. The Party not only provides the guarantee but gives him a national decoration – the Gold Cross of Merit. Tarłowska and the friendly censor return to their jobs. Soon *Trybuna Ludu* (The People's Tribune), the organ of the Central Committee, is writing about the social ills at Nowa Huta. The paper brands the local Party organization as the culprits, the board of the conglomerate is replaced, and the local Party authorities offer their resignation.

Kapuściński learns three lessons from this story. He discovers that writing is a risky business and that written words carry consequences. He also becomes convinced that the written word can change reality. Finally, as he learns from the story with the censor, success in the public sphere also depends on taking care of things through informal channels, and on building a network of personal contacts with people in power. If you have friends here and there, they will help you in times of need.

Adam Daniel Rotfeld, a good friend of Kapuściński's, believes that to the end of his life Rysiek carried the conviction that honesty and competence are not enough. When in 2005 the poet, journalist and expert on Italian culture Jarosław Mikołajewski applied for the post of director of the Polish Institute in Rome, his friend Kapuściński called Rotfeld, who was then head of the diplomatic service, and said: 'Listen, my friend Jarek . . .' He had decided to help in the certainty that he was supporting an undoubtedly excellent candidate. Rotfeld insists that he did not intervene; Mikołajewski did get the job, because he really was the best applicant.

'But till the end, Rysiek was certain, even proud of the fact, that he had "fixed" the dream job for his friend.'

When did the cultural dissent, later known as revisionism, cease to be partly fashion and become front-line politics?

It starts with a secret speech by Khrushchev, given in February 1956 in Moscow at the Twentieth Congress of the Soviet Communist Party. Its content creates a sensation in Poland: here is the Soviet Party admitting to murder, to the destruction of its political opponents, to fabricated trials. Knowledge of similar methods used by the authorities in People's Poland has already reached certain segments of public opinion: almost two years earlier, Józef Światło, deputy director of Department X at the Ministry of Public Security, defected to the West and exposed crimes committed by the Polish apparatus of repression (his department was involved in eradicating ideological deviations within the Party). The Poles hear these revelations on Radio Free Europe; those who are glued to their wireless sets manage to catch bits of these nightmarish stories despite the jamming devices working at full steam.

Khrushchev's speech initiates a political earthquake throughout the socialist bloc, most of all in Poland and Hungary. It is discussed at Party meetings, in cultural circles and on the streets. Duplicated using crude methods, the key points of the speech can be bought for an astronomical sum at flea markets and bazaars. At exactly the same time, Polish Party leader Bolesław Bierut dies in mysterious circumstances, prompting a wave of speculation: Was he murdered? Soon there's a popular saying: 'He went out in a fur overcoat and came home in a wooden overcoat.' Straight after that the Party's number two, Jakub Berman, is thrown out of his job. The Party is bursting from the inside.

There is a clash between two tendencies, later called fractions. One group is known as the 'Puławians' – people who seek more civic freedom, relative autonomy in cultural life, more democracy within the Party, less central planning within the economy, and more independence for enterprises. They have the sympathy of opinion-forming circles and of many people in the press and the cultural world. (It is interesting to note that they meet at the flat of Ignacy Loga-Sowiński, secretary of the Central Council of Trade Unions, and Irena Tarłowska, still editor-in-chief of *Sztandar Młodych*). The other group is called the 'Natolinians'. They are believed to have connections with the Soviet embassy; they're not keen on democratization, but they're not against sacrificing a few scapegoats, preferably of Jewish origin, on the altar of squaring accounts with Stalinism.

The political prisoners are released, including people from the post-war anti-communist underground as well as followers of the 'new faith', who were locked up for being critical or as a result of internal power struggles. Functionaries within the apparatus of repression who have been particularly cruel to the prisoners lose their jobs and are accused of abusing their power. The Stalinist system is collapsing . . .

In June the workers' rebellion in Poznań occurs. After several days of strikes and street demonstrations, the army and the secret police fire on the protestors. Several dozen people are killed, and many are wounded. A Party plenum calls the Poznań revolt 'counter-revolutionary' and a campaign by 'imperialist circles'. Prime Minister Józef Cyrankiewicz warns that any hand raised against the people's power will be cut off. The entire movement for renewal finds itself under threat.

A day after the massacre, on the orders of the Party leadership, *Sztandar Młodych* – like other papers – writes about the tragedy in a tone ringing with Stalinist propaganda:

> For some time, imperialist agencies and the reactionary underground have been trying to exploit economic difficulties and weak points at certain production plants in Poznań in order to provoke unrest against the people's power ... The enemy agents succeeded in provoking street riots. There were attacks on several public buildings, which resulted in human casualties ... The provocation in Poznań was organized by enemies of our homeland ... The government and the PZPR Central Committee are convinced that any attempt to provoke riots and protests against the people's power will be met with the appropriate rebuff from all working people, all citizens who care about the good of the country.[19]

The Poznań tragedy is a shock, especially for those who still believe in socialism but want it to be thoroughly reformed. As a result, the workers' protest, the massacre and the Party leadership's conservative attitude to the tragedy accelerate the impetus for change. At the production plants, workers councils are established, and pro-democratization rallies are held at schools and colleges. The culmination of the political turmoil is a Party plenum held in October. Comrades from Moscow fly to Warsaw, headed by Soviet Communist Party First Secretary Khrushchev, and Soviet troops move towards the capital. There is a fear that their tanks will run down the Polish movement for the renewal of socialism.

The crisis ends with the election of a new Party chief, Władysław Gomułka, who led the communists during the war and who has recently been released from prison. He was sent to jail in the early 1950s for so-called rightist–nationalist leanings. Gomułka – who installed the Stalinist system in post-war Poland, took part in the elimination of the opposition, and agreed to Poland's becoming subordinate to the Soviet Union – did, however, want Polish socialism to retain some specific national features. He was not a fan of collectivization; he was in no rush to condemn the 'Yugoslav path to socialism', which was independent of Stalin; and he was fond of the national features of Polish Socialist Party tradition. As Jacek Kuroń wrote about him years later:

> No leader of the Polish People's Republic ever gained such popularity or was as loved by the crowds as Władysław Gomułka was in autumn 1956.

Few people remembered the role he had played in the late 1940s. The crowds saw him as the man of the moment, the saviour of the fatherland, the one just man. The years he had spent in prison had built him a legend as a defender of democracy and an advocate of liberty.

Many of his initial moves appeared to confirm that legend. A few days after Gomułka was brought in, Cardinal Wyszyński was released from house arrest in Komańcza. Polish debt relief was soon negotiated in the USSR, as were the rules for stationing Soviet troops in Poland, and Soviet officers were withdrawn from the Polish army.[20]

So Gomułka sails forth on the wave of the thaw and starts off by making a powerful anti-Stalinist speech, but soon shifts to pacifying the movement for renewal. Many of those involved in the October 1956 movement for change imagine that his election marks the start of reforms and the building of democratized socialism. During a historic rally outside the Palace of Culture and Science in Warsaw, however, Gomułka plainly states that he has no desire to make radical changes. He says there's been enough rallying and calls on the people to go home and get down to work.

After the fuss about Nowa Huta, Kapuściński becomes a bolder promoter of the movement for the renewal of socialism.

He visits a chemical plant in Kędzierzyn. During the day he tours the production halls, and in the evenings he goes to a workers' hotel. He wants to find out what ordinary people think. Later he writes that during his conversations, 'tongues loosen, and people who were passive shortly before, turn out to be thoughtful, astute and intelligent.'[21]

He tells the story of a female worker named Cela Wehner, who had some curious adventures. One time, she saved a colleague's life when he was electrocuted, then found a grenade among the lumps of coal on a production line that almost blew up in her hands. She also exposed 'the engine scandal' – discovering an engine that someone had removed from the factory floor and hidden in a burned-out building under a pile of rags. But instead of giving her a reward, a bonus, or praise, the management cut her pay. Cela Wehner's problem is that although she belongs to the ZMP, she isn't an activist ('although she is capable of talking about the organization more thoroughly, wisely and truthfully than several of its official activists').

'I'd like to find a caricature of one of the many stiflers of criticism, an article branding a specific oppressor, a call for joint management of the department, or condemnation of a specific bureaucrat. But there's none of that.' The local ZMP is not aware that something is changing in the country, and that even the Party in Warsaw is now allowing limited reforms. Meanwhile, the enterprise in Kędzierzyn is being strangled by bureaucracy, and the people are feeling increasing rage.

One current of the October renewal is the workers councils that are spontaneously being formed at major industrial plants. According to people such as Lechosław Goździk, then the workers' leader at Żerań (site of the FSO car factory), as well as Jacek Kuroń and Karol Modzelewski, the future authors of a famous letter to the Party, this is the only way to remove the authorities' bureaucratic hold on society – by taking the path of democratization and of limiting central control of the economy. This current arises from the conviction that socialism is a good thing, but that it has been stifled by the bureaucrats.

Kapuściński shares this belief. In *Sztandar Młodych* he publishes one of the few articles he ever wrote that had the tone of a theoretical treatise, almost a political manifesto: 'On Workers' Democracy'. In it he writes that in a centralized system, there is no room for workers' democracy, and that the system prevents the workers from making even the most minor decisions concerning their own enterprise.

Kapuściński is a fan of the movement to create workers' councils and encourage the independence of enterprises. 'This movement is extremely valuable, because it speaks the language of practical proof and tangible example . . . The Party's best forces are interested in strengthening this movement.'[22]

Why do the poets, writers and commentators – people like Woroszylski, Ważyk, and the then still greenhorn Kapuściński – who were the most passionate in the Stalinist era, form the vanguard of the anti-Stalinist movement? What causes them first to build a Stalinist order and then, a few years later, dismantle it with the same ardour?

In the account-settling literature written after the fall of communism, various explanations are offered, including that the years of stabilized Stalinism were a period of frustration for them, because the spontaneous movement for building a new order had been curbed by the iron fist of the Party, the secret police and the bureaucracy. To the dictatorship, anything spontaneous, grass-roots or outside their control – including these people – represented a threat.

Sociology professor Hanna Świda-Ziemba comments ironically that during the thaw and the events of October '56, the former young Stalinists could once again stand at the head of the procession, leading the movement for change, once again believe in a utopia, once again experience their youthful enthusiasm and enjoy being on the side of dissent. She adds that the 'Octobrists' – both earlier as Stalinists and later as anti-Stalinists – are full of altruism; during the thaw and October they 'return to being their real selves, with force and anger at those who have enslaved them, while at the same time wiping from memory the fact that they were co-creators of those times'.[23]

Adam Michnik, the legendary oppositionist who in the 1960s began as a young communist revisionist, calls the dissent of October 1956 'a furious reaction' and 'the shame of people' who 'had taken part in totalitarian destruction'. 'Revisionism rejected totalitarian doctrine and practice, by citing Marxist language and the communist system of values,' he writes. 'In formulating its criticism, it took both domestic and international realities into consideration. In this way, it caused pain to deluded people who had followed the path of self-delusion.'[24]

Is it possible to explain this more simply, and without stern judgements? For young people like Kapuściński, who after the Second World War believed that communism was a new beginning for the world that would produce the just system of their dreams, the natural reaction to the newly discovered tragedy and deception of Stalinism was to attempt to right the wrongs, go back to their ideals, and oust those who had lied to them. They did not have to wipe anything from memory – they genuinely felt deceived.

October '56 was a consequence of their earlier involvement, idealism and altruism. They had committed no crimes, although crimes were committed in their names. They had not necessarily deceived themselves; they quite simply believed that this time it was for real, that now at last . . . They were neither the first nor the last people in history who would attempt, invoking noble ideals, to repair a social order founded on crimes and injustice.

It is the end of 1957. Almost a year has gone by since Gomułka's speech outside the Palace of Culture. On 14 September 1957 *Sztandar Młodych* is put on trial at the Central Committee Press Office.

Press Office chief Artur Starewicz takes the floor:

> While *Sztandar* takes no political line within the youth movement, it does take a harmful political line in international affairs. A campaign of opposition to our Party, our line and People's Poland as a whole, and to other socialist countries too is being conducted on the pages of *Sztandar Młodych*. This line involves an emphasis on everything that divides us, and on [writing] nothing about what unites us. For example, on Hungary it always writes about sentences and arrests . . . This is harmful activity . . .
>
> It is no accident that in the USSR *Sztandar* is regarded as a harmful newspaper. For us it is painful and significant that *Sztandar* is seen there as an anti-Soviet publication . . .
>
> The Party makes harsh demands on the press. It must be explained that our political line is the only right and appropriate one. This newspaper does not have a political line of this kind . . .
>
> People who have departed from socialism cannot hold editorial positions. Comrades who are implementing the Party's political line need to

stamp their mark on the paper. There has to be an outward unanimity of views. That is a condition for Party discipline.[25]

Once Starewicz has finished his speech, a debate begins. Grzegorz Lasota from *Sztandar* says: 'Showing anti-Stalinist changes in the Soviet Union is a way of getting through to the young. It's a pity it is regarded as anti-Soviet activity.' Comrade Stanisław Brodzki, president of the Polish Journalists Association, says: 'I believe a debate is needed here on the optimal limits of freedom of speech. What has been said here about anti-socialist tendencies is slander, but *Sztandar* has to know the range of what is viable and what is not.' During the debate, Mirosław Kluźniak from *Sztandar* points to a polemical dialogue between Ryszard Kapuściński and Krzysztof Kąkolewski, entitled 'Our Birth Certificate',[26] as an example of the paper's vitality. Kąkolewski has praised privacy in post-October Poland, and Kapuściński has called for this generation to become involved in fixing the world, 'even if it falls over dozens of times along the way'.

But storm clouds are gathering over the newspaper; there is increasing trouble with the censors, and more and more phone calls from the Central Committee Press Office.

'The interference usually involved allusions to the Soviet Union and our sympathies for the Italian and French communists,' says Marian Turski.

At the newspaper office, everyone is seething – and the younger they are, the more they seethe. Everyone sees designs everywhere on the ideals of October. The journalists keep an eye on Turski (who is officially acting editor-in-chief at the time): Isn't he going too far in his compromises with the authorities? Turski can usually guess which articles the censor will not let through, but he avoids preventive editorial interference. He wants to show the journalists that he's with them.

Meanwhile Gomułka, the new Party leader, has his own plans for *Sztandar Młodych*: the paper is to be subordinated to a new organization, the Union of Socialist Youth (ZMS), which is replacing the ZMP. The Union is 'a transmission belt' to convey the will of the Party to youth groups. The *Sztandar* journalists can only dream of independence and moderately free criticism.

Yet it is *Po Prostu* that is first in the firing line. A bastion of revisionism, this weekly continually urges Gomułka to democratize socialism. However, for Gomułka attaining power is not the start but rather the end of the changes. He regards revisionism as 'a set of false views' which 'put strain on Party unity'. It is an intellectual invention, and he doesn't like intellectuals; it is a dangerous, infectious virus outside Party discipline and control.

At a meeting convened by the Central Committee Press Office, Jerzy Morawski, a member of the Party Politburo, announces that the weekly *Po Prostu* will have to be disbanded or suspended.

'I was the only person in that circle who defended *Po Prostu*,' says Turski, who was at the meeting. 'I fudged, I said that inappropriate views had appeared in the weekly but that it shouldn't be terminated, because it had a lot of prestige.' However, the Party decides that *Po Prostu* must go. The closing of the weekly and a brutally dispersed student demonstration against the decision are regarded as the symbolic end of October '56.

Now Gomułka and Morawski order all the newspapers to publish an editorial approving the closure of *Po Prostu*. ' "Jurek", I said to Morawski, "if I print that, you will never shake my hand again," ' Turski recalls. ' "I defended *Po Prostu* at the meeting, and I can't behave like a weathercock." '

Sztandar Młodych is the only paper that refuses to publish Gomułka's statement. Soon Morawski informs Turski that the Party leadership have decided to dismiss him from the post of acting editor-in-chief. In an act of solidarity, most of the journalists working for the paper hand in their resignations.

At the time, Kapuściński is *Sztandar's* correspondent in China. As soon as he hears what has happened at the newspaper office, he leaves the paper.

Shortly before leaving for China, Kapuściński writes a series of reports on ZMP members who have been set adrift since October '56, and about the hopes that have been dashed for the second time in their short lives.

At the Dymitrow mine in Bytom he goes to see a newly founded club for former ZMP members, who are now frustrated. 'The students come and shout: drive him out, he's a Stalinist', confides a former activist. Nowadays the most common attitude is: don't stick your neck out, don't be active, because, as another interviewee says, 'There are plenty of active people among the Stalinists'. Yes, the former activists are disillusioned at the way they have been repaid for all their enterprise and dedication.

Until recently a ZMP activist just like them, and president of the faculty organization at college, Kapuściński shows open solidarity with the spurned ZMP members. He contrasts them with the masses, who 'go straight to bed after work, go out chasing girls, or sometimes go to the cinema'.

For who can still be counted on? Who is going to change our world? The *końcowi* ('enders') aren't going to do it, are they?

The *końcowi*, who are also young people, are the opposite of the ZMP members. Kapuściński encounters them in the Warsaw districts of Wola and Ochota. These are people from another world; a few years earlier, he would have described them as 'the enemy'. For the *końcowi*, good looks, strength and money are what matter. They don't like intellectuals or smart alecs – 'squares' – because they reek of school, and school is the worst thing of all. Under Stalinism, they rebelled against the ZMP's prim-and-proper manner, and among themselves they said what they thought about socialism. There was a bit of risk and cynicism in their behaviour. But now? Now anything's allowed. You can even laugh at a ZMP president to his face, and what happens? Nothing.

Stories about the *końcowi* contain a hint of nostalgia for the grand years of building socialism, even if the mirror image of the solemnity of those years are now people who don't give a hoot about socialism. In his pieces about the *końcowi*, Kapuściński records the climate of apathy and post-October decadence, portraying a Poland he hardly knew – as a young ZMP activist, he never paid attention to it. But the moment is coming that will mark the end of rebellion, the exhaustion of strength, a collision with the pervasive presence of those who hated socialism. By the same token, his stories about ZMP members describe the atrophied hopes of those who wanted to repair socialism.

And afterward? What happened afterward? What should I write about now? About the way that a great experience comes to an end? A melancholy topic, for a revolt is a great experience, an adventure of the heart. Look at people who are taking part in a revolt. They are stimulated, excited, ready to make sacrifices . . . But there comes a moment when the mood burns out and everything ends. As a matter of reflex, out of custom, we go on repeating the gestures and the words and want everything to be the way it was yesterday, but we know already – and the discovery appals us – that this yesterday will never again return. We look around and make another discovery: those who were with us have also changed – something has burned out in them, as well, something has been extinguished. Our community falls suddenly to pieces and everyone returns to his everyday I, which pinches at first like ill-fitting shoes – but we know that they are our shoes and we are not going to get any others. We look uncomfortably into each other's eyes, we shy away from conversation, we stop being any use to one another.

This fall in temperature, this change of climate, belongs among the most unsettling and depressing of experiences. A day begins in which something should happen. And nothing happens. Nobody comes to call, nobody is waiting for us, we are superfluous. We begin to feel a great fatigue, apathy gradually engulfs us.[27]

So he will write many years later, in his book about the Iranian revolution. (Can we be certain it is just about Iran?)

And so begins the period in Polish history known as the 'minor stabilization'.

But Kapuściński, the romantic, cannot come to terms with what he sees and describes in his reports: 'We should continue to take up the task of liberating the world anew, even if it means falling over dozens of times along the way.'[28] Were it not for a certain journey, from which he has recently returned, he would not have written this manifesto.

12

The Third World: A Clash and a Beginning

[W]hen I saw that in India millions of people have no shoes, a sense of community responded in me, a sense of fraternity with these people, and at times I was even overcome by the mood we feel when we go back to our childhood.
Ryszard Kapuściński, *Travels with Herodotus*[1]

An Indian face smiles out of the poster. It's a girl, standing in the shade of the palm trees, and in the distance is the dark silhouette of an ancient temple. Underneath runs the inscription: 'VISIT INDIA!' The Indian girl is beautiful, and you can't say no to beautiful people.[2]

Before he reaches the point of delighting in the beautiful Indian girl, the palm trees and the ancient temples in the poster, there is major panic. The newspaper wants him to go to India – but he doesn't know a single thing about India. How can he write about a country of which he's completely ignorant? He doesn't even speak English. How is he going to communicate? In Polish? In Russian? How? With whom? A quick dash to the bookshop, the second-hand one, to buy something about India. Do they even have anything? Perhaps at least a dictionary, or a map.

When in the summer of 1956 the editor-in-chief of *Sztandar Młodych* calls him in and announces, 'You're flying to India,' Kapuściński is twenty-four years old. He has plenty of experience as a journalist fighting for socialism, as a reporter covering ZMP conferences, writing about the lot of the workers at major industrial plants. He's made a few trips abroad – to Prague and to youth festivals in Moscow and Berlin – but he knows nothing about the work of a foreign correspondent and even less about the place where he is to go. Rysiek is a provincial boy from a modest family of teachers – a novice reporter and activist whom they are sending off to a distant, alien world without preparation, without the language, and without refinement.

Why India? Because it's the thaw. In the Soviet Union they are settling accounts with Stalinism, Moscow's international policy is changing, and the rulers in the Kremlin are beginning to open up some of their doors and windows. The socialist camp is looking outwards towards the countries of the so-called Third World which are escaping from colonial dependence on the West. In the era of the Cold War divide, even if they are not Red, liberation movements struggling against colonialism are frequently engaging in some form of co-operation with Moscow as a rival to the West – and later also with Peking. The emerging countries offer large markets for goods from countries in the Soviet orbit, above all for major industrial products such as machinery, fertilizer and weapons. Leaders from the socialist bloc are paying official visits, while the leaders of those newborn countries are coming to see how progress and socialism are doing in Eastern Europe.

Exactly one year earlier, Kapuściński covers Indian leader Jawaharlal Nehru's visit to Poland for *Sztandar Młodych*. 'Prime Minister Nehru is a politician fighting for important issues for humanity: for the peaceful coexistence of nations, co-operation and friendship', he writes in a predictable welcoming article.[3] (Meanwhile, the following joke is doing the rounds: 'Why did Nehru come to Poland in his long johns?' – a reference to the tight white trousers he wore – 'To show that India is building socialism too.') Kapuściński is the paper's natural candidate when someone from the Central Committee Press Office decides that, in the spirit of friendship between the socialist camp and the Third World, Polish reporters will go abroad and write about the countries of the far South. The future star journalists of their generation set off on their way. One will go to Egypt, Syria, Lebanon and Iraq; another to Indonesia; someone else to Morocco. Kapuściński is to go to India.

As a result, he misses the era of greatest revolutionary fever in Poland – he is not there in October 1956, when Soviet intervention is a whisker away, or in the period afterwards, when amid cheering crowds Gomułka assumes the post of Party leader. Indeed, during the coming quarter-century he will not witness any of the major political breakthroughs in Poland – right up to the strikes on the Baltic coast in the summer of 1980, when the Solidarity trade union is born. He will not be there in 1957, when Gomułka closes the weekly paper *Po Prostu* and cracks down on the movement for the renewal of socialism – instead he will be travelling in China and Japan. During the student protests of March 1968 and two years later, when the Party ruthlessly suppresses the workers' protests on the coast, he will be working as a PAP correspondent in Latin America. In 1976, when once again the Party deploys force against the working class, in whose name it has supposedly been governing, he will be writing a weekly account of the war in Angola, and will be in Africa for months on end.

For the young reporter whose horizons are tedious Party confabs, factories in small provincial towns, or possibly youth festivals where he can communicate in Polish or in Russian, the trip to Asia is frightening but, to a greater degree, thrilling. Everything on the journey is large and amazing. The aeroplane is massive: a four-engine giant Super-Constellation that flies from Rome to New Delhi and Bombay. The distance to be covered is incredible – eight thousand kilometres! And so many hours in the air – twenty!

Also incredible is the lake of lights that stuns the fledgling globetrotter when the plane stops to refuel in Cairo. With some surprise, he finds that the Egyptians are black and that they dress in white – as he writes – 'cassocks'. With childlike satisfaction, he notes that he has now set foot in Africa. These are the comments and emotional responses of a greenhorn traveller.

His associations and thoughts on landing in India are amusingly gauche too, including his mention of the fact that Columbus tried to reach India and failed, whereas he, Kapuściński, has succeeded. He makes the conventional first observations: the traffic moves on the left, following the British example; and of course he must mention the sacred cows, which do not obey the rules of the road and walk about the streets with impunity, now with the flow of traffic, now against it – and nothing can be done to them because they are sacred.

Kapuściński gets his first lesson on India in the plane, sitting between an elderly Englishman and an elderly Indian. The Englishman complains that ever since the Indians broke free of colonial dependence they have been limiting the rights of British companies, and by doing so they are making a rope for their own necks.

'Do you know what India's economy will be like without the British?' asks the Englishman.

'But we do know what India's economy was like with the British: universal poverty. The Middle Ages,' the Indian explains to his fellow passenger from Poland. (At least, this is what the reporter who hardly knew any English understood him to be saying.)

The New Delhi airport building is small and dark. It is night – and he is alone in the Indian darkness. He looks around, he is completely lost, he doesn't know where to go or whom to ask for help. Unprepared for the journey, he can't speak English, and he has no names or addresses in his notebook. Despair! Described this way in *Travels with Herodotus*, it sounds like an adventure.

The fact is, Kapuściński stands alone at the airport only until PAP correspondent Ryszard Frelek arrives by car to fetch him. They have met just once before – at a labour camp for prisoners: Kapuściński was going to write a report on it for *Sztandar Młodych* (he never did), and Frelek was there to research an account for the PAP.

After one day in New Delhi, Kapuściński has just one wish: to go home. He is oppressed by the tropical heat and humidity, tormented by a feeling of loneliness, and horrified by the sight of people suffering en masse.

The city, and the entire area of the country that is situated along the Ganges, have just experienced the predictable annual cataclysm: a flood. The fields beyond the city are filled with people, and in the city there are campsites in the streets. Children lie on the baking-hot ground, and old men warm their bones in the sunshine. Anyone who has managed to spread a small piece of matting on the road has a home; anyone who has failed to do so is roaming about, still searching. All of life is concentrated in the streets. If there's a bowl above some embers, a stink, and some flies, it's a restaurant. If there's a man squatting and another man flourishing a pair of scissors about his head, it's a barber's shop.

'Life here is not life, food is not food, only poverty really is poverty,' he will write immediately after returning home.[4]

For the next two weeks, Frelek shows Kapuściński New Delhi. In this apocalyptic setting they strike up a friendship, an understanding that will last for the next thirty years. Frelek will be a guardian angel, a protector and a co-architect of Kapuściński's career – first as one of the PAP's decision-makers, and later as a senior Party dignitary, able to help when needed, to protect, push matters forwards, press the right buttons.

After two weeks as a tourist in the capital, Kapuściński starts to worry. He doesn't know what to write about and has no material to form the basis of his reports for *Sztandar*. But how can he get any, when he's losing his battle with English? ('Language struck me at that moment as something material, something with a physical dimension, a wall rising up in the middle of the road and preventing my going further,'[5] he will say years later in his final book.) To teach himself English, he buys Hemingway's *For Whom the Bell Tolls* from a street stall, but the language of the novel is too difficult – he'd be better off with *English for Beginners*.

He decides to leave the city and see the provinces, the sites of religious worship and deepest India. 'You haven't any clothes – the weather could vary on the journey: winter's coming,' says Frelek astutely, and takes his colleague to the bazaar. They buy a warm hat and coat made of multi-coloured wool. Kapuściński sets off on a rickety, crowded bus. Frelek notices that his new friend is the only white man among the passengers.

Four weeks later, the watchman comes running into the building where Frelek's office is located and cries out, 'There's a dirty, ragged Indian trying to get in here, and he's given your name!'

Kapuściński had dark eyes and a swarthy complexion, so once he was dirty and ragged, he could well have looked like a local vagrant. On the journey he bought a quilted blanket that he rolled up during the day and unrolled at night, sleeping in sheds with the locals. Years later Frelek will say, 'He identified with the Indians.'

From New Delhi:

> A large gang of children are lying in the dust, idly gazing around them.
> They aren't playing: they are hungry. There's nothing happening here . . .
> A couple of kilometres away is the army. Dinghies are doing the rounds,
> and the soldiers are picking up whatever they can – people out of trees,
> drowning cattle, the wreckage of tools . . .
>
> It's the same everywhere. There is no end to the people, the water and
> the tragedy.[6]

From Bengal:

> India is so unlike Poland! The same concepts do not mean the same
> things here as there. 'I have no home,' says my friend from Warsaw, 'I'm
> literally living in the street.' Of course he wasn't telling the truth, he was
> using a metaphor. Not a single person in Poland lives in the street. But if
> a homeless Indian gives me his address as 'The Mutra Street roadway,
> somewhere between the bridge and the cinema', I can boldly go and
> look for him in that spot – he is sure to 'live' there.
>
> In our life we have no equivalents for various Indian phenomena, and
> that's why it's so easy for all sorts of eyewash to be believed . . .
>
> The exotic? I've been looking for it in the streets of Calcutta, the
> villages of Bengal and the towns of Andhra. I can't find it, and I'm not in
> the least bit concerned. India is not an exotic country, but if you insist,
> then the only thing that's exotic there is the scenery . . . [India] is living
> at the bottom of utter poverty, among plagues of disease and under ruth-
> less, alien authority. This was a 'shameful topic' and it had to be replaced
> with something more palatable and more enticing. And so the popularly
> distributed literature about India is limited to the Mysterious Exotic –
> jungles and fakirs, sacred monkeys and snake charmers. That is what our
> imagination has been fed on; hungry as it is for knowledge of faraway
> countries, it cannot tell that instead of facts it is absorbing myths.[7]

Thoughts on the road from Bangalore to Hyderabad:

> The crime of colonization arrested development a very long time ago . . .
> Machinery and industry reached India not as an element of progress or
> the liberation of man, but as an oppressive weapon, a yoke. Higher tech-
> nology made it possible to plunder and starve, enslave and destroy. This
> injury has not yet healed today.[8]

At the end of his journey, Kapuściński has a curious adventure. He is due
to go home on a ship called the *Stefan Batory*, which sails between Gdańsk

and Bombay. But conflict erupts over the Suez Canal, whose nationaliza-
tion has been announced by the Egyptian president Gamal Abdel Nasser;
the British and the French dispatch troops, and traffic through the canal is
halted. Kapuściński has to go home by plane, via Karachi, Kabul and
Tashkent to Warsaw.

On landing in Kabul he has a nasty surprise. He hands his passport to the
immigration official. He waits. The airport is a small barracks, surrounded
by desert. The policeman comes back with his passport, places one arm
over the other to form a cross and spreads out his fingers: he's in detention.
An official summoned from the airport explains that a transit visa is obliga-
tory in Afghanistan; Kapuściński doesn't have one.

The Soviet embassy rescues Kapuściński from this predicament. A diplomatic courier whom he met on the plane realizes that he has been detained
at the airport; someone from the Soviet embassy finds a Polish salesman,
who accompanies the Soviet attaché to the Afghan Ministry for External
Affairs, where they sort out a visa, probably by bribing an official. Together
they come and fetch the 'prisoner' from detention. But now Kapuściński
has to extend his visa, because the one issued at the Afghan ministry is valid
for only a single day.

At the police station he receives one of his first lessons about the Third
World during the Cold War. As the official hands him back his passport, he
says in broken English: 'You are lucky to be under the protection of the
Soviet embassy. If you were British, you'd get to know our cellars.'

Part two of Kapuściński's first encounter with Asia comes a year later – in
China. He also visits Japan, and it is this brief visit of a mere few days,
rather than the longer one to China, that generates a series of reports.
However, it is China that makes the deeper impression on Kapuściński, in
the same way as he was struck by India's unfathomable, fascinating
dissimilarity.

In China he is to arrange co-operation with the communist youth wing
and a newspaper called *Chungkuo*, which is the equivalent of *Sztandar
Młodych*. At a certain point the Polish October and Mao Zedong's Hundred
Flowers Campaign seem to involve similar ideas about re-energizing socialism and making room for greater freedom, but when Kapuściński arrives in
Peking, both parties are changing course and the reversal of reforms has
begun. Gomułka closes down *Po Prostu*, while Chairman Mao tightens the
screws and gears up for the Great Leap Forward.

One day in Peking, an employee of the Polish foreign trade centre brings
Kapuściński a letter from his colleagues at *Sztandar Młodych*. They inform
him that they have refused to support the closure of the weekly *Po Prostu*
and, following the dismissal of Marian Turski from the post of acting editor-
in-chief, they have decided to leave the newspaper. Some are hesitating,

and want to know what Kapuściński will do. He decides to return home earlier than planned, not by plane but by the Trans-Siberian Railway. He joins the protestors and quits his job at *Sztandar*.

The journalists who have resigned agree that he should publish the reports from his recent journey in *Sztandar*. They promise not to regard it as a breach of solidarity or an act of disloyalty towards his colleagues who have left the paper. They understand that if they were to set excessive moral demands, and Kapuściński were to accept them, he would be in trouble: he flew to China as a correspondent for *Sztandar*, using state money raised by the editors, and so it is appropriate that he fulfil his assignment.

Within a few years the Third World, though not India and not China, will become Kapuściński's professional passion. 'Passion, passion, you've got to have a passion!' he repeats to his friends, acquaintances and the young reporters he meets. Years later, he writes in a poem that 'whosoever creates his own world will live on'.[9] The world of Kapuściński the writer and reporter began being created during his journey to India. So, too, did the fate of the ever-absent husband, father, friend and co-worker. Neither in the winter of 1956 nor even a year later, however, does he yet know that he has already picked up the scent of his own tone, his own independent voice, his own original topic.

In his series of reports from India one can see many of the themes that recur in his writing and his world outlook till the end: empathy for the poor, a moral objection to the colonial powers, a certain reserve towards the whole of the capitalist West, a critical attitude to Eurocentric modes of thinking about the world, a basic interest in dissimilarity. In India he also hones his craft as a reporter who prefers to speak with ordinary people in the street, in the desert, or in a godforsaken village than to seek out interviewees in the corridors of power; he would rather blend into the background and try to live like the locals, although he does have a return ticket in his pocket. In a way, from the very start, beginning with his first journey to India, he works towards being an 'interpreter of cultures' – a reporter who describes other countries and cultures with respect and without the taint of Western condescension – though of course he has no idea that in thirty years' time he will be world-famous and, from those heights, teaching that the role of a journalist is to explain faraway cultures to the reader.

Is he really so mature at just twenty-four? Yes and no. On returning from India, he has no idea what he wants. He is experimenting, looking around, searching. India is an accidentally sown seed, from which in a few years' time something will grow. Apart from some mature reflections on the wealth of Indian culture, all he can write about Afghanistan is that it is 'a wild country', and about Sudan that it is 'a place called Sudan'.

Professor Wipszycka, his college friend, remembers that after Kapuściński's first return from Africa, in 1958, the history faculty held a meeting at which he said 'some dreadful things': 'The auditorium is packed, and Kapuściński announces that the British should send their Gurkhas to Ghana to deal with internecine conflicts among the tribes. I was horrified. "What is he saying?" I remarked to someone next to me. It was a mixture of colonial thinking and probably criticism of his own views from the previous, i.e., Stalinist phase. I remember that what he said offended me as a historian. He had graduated from the same faculty as I, but at that moment it was as if five years of study had flowed off him like water off a duck's back. He gave the impression of being naive and downright crude in his thinking. The "wising up" came later.'

Does Kapuściński in fact notice in India that what really fascinates him is large-scale social change? And does it occur to him that he can witness major changes not just in Poland but in other countries as well? At home, Gomułka is just putting an end to the rebellion of the young people who want to reform Stalinist socialism – and yet hope remains that the ideals of socialism, authentic and not distorted, will be successfully implemented in the politically awakening Third World. That is where History is now happening.

In his personal manifesto, 'Our Birth Certificate', written shortly before the final suppression of the October renewal in Poland, Kapuściński declares:

> Asia, home to more than half of humanity, Asia, downtrodden and despised, decimated by plague and hunger, for the first time in centuries is starting to eat three times a day, to wear shoes and learn to read. Has there ever been an era when an equally humanitarian task has been achieved? What about the total liberation of man from the plough, the mud hut, the tallow lamp, or bast footwear? . . . The twentieth century is the world's century, and to measure it against the experience of a single country (and one that has been browbeaten throughout history) is like trying to drain the sea with a spoon . . . We should keep taking up the task of liberating the world anew, even if it means falling over dozens of times along the way, and even if everything good always seems to be so infinitely far away.[10]

The romantic fascinated by revolution – Major Change – will soon be seeking it out on other continents. ('The revolution at home was over, and he went in pursuit of it elsewhere,' one of his PAP colleagues told me.) But before he races abroad for good, an exceptional reporter will be born in Poland, who will break free of the strait jacket of Party newspeak – also a man who will learn how to move nimbly within the corridors of power, a skill that will enable his career in the sort of conditions prevailing in Gomułka's, and later Gierek's, Poland. Ryszard Frelek, the new friend Kapuściński has gained in India, will soon be his political patron and will play a key role in building his career.

13

In 'Rakowski's Gang'

'I'm not the same person anymore,' he replies . . . 'I haven't got that spark, that vigour. But in those days! Do you remember how we held that meeting at night, how we started the campaign, how it collapsed, and how we got people out afterwards . . .'

Those years have burned him out; he's worn to a frazzle. He expended a lot and acquired a lot. He has a whole store of experiences and wisdom. He can no longer summon up the energy to start all over again.[1]

What is a young intellectual to do when he has been battered by the storms of the 1950s and 'those years have burned him out'? An intellectual who started off by building socialism with neophyte eagerness, then noticed the distortions, and with equal zeal tried to fix socialism but found that the authorities would only allow a limited adjustment. This is someone who has never stopped believing in socialism, and who believed that if the system was to be changed, it must be done with the Party, within the Party, and by the Party. He was on the side of the October '56 reforms but did not fully identify with the revisionists, because they took the path towards 'liquidating socialism', as the Party put it; perhaps he was also motivated by realism, by seeing how the radical reform movement in Hungary was drowned in blood. He was even further removed from the opponents of the system who shut themselves inside either the Catholic Church or the privacy of their own homes. Nor could he summon up the energy to start all over again . . .

The place on the political and cultural map of People's Poland where this intellectual can find a safe haven is the newly founded weekly *Polityka* (Politics). Sacked from his job as managing editor of *Sztandar Młodych*, Marian Turski has moved to *Polityka*, bringing with him the group of journalists who resigned in a gesture of solidarity against his dismissal. Among them is Kapuściński.

Polityka had a terrible start. It was established in January 1957 by the Central Committee secretariat. Stefan Żółkiewski – Marxist scholar of the humanities, and minister of higher education (years later, to show solidarity, he would support the Warsaw University students demonstrating against the authorities) – was put in charge. This happened before the closure of the revisionist weekly *Po Prostu* – *Polityka* was meant to be a whip to beat the revisionists, an anti–*Po Prostu* publication. It was seen as heralding the departure of First Secretary Gomułka from the ideals of October '56, and as a desire to exercise full control over intellectual life and thought, which had been relatively free during the years of the thaw and the October movement.

The revisionists from *Po Prostu* – 'the rabid', as their opponents call them – regard *Polityka* as a 'despot's organ', a paper that on Gomułka's orders is to determine the political line for the entire press. Both editorial offices are located within the Palace of Culture and Science, *Po Prostu* on the fifth floor and *Polityka* on the eleventh. The *Po Prostu* people are so allergic to the *Polityka* people that when they don't have enough glasses in their office, and the head of administration amicably wants to borrow some from *Polityka* six floors above, the *Po Prostu* staff have a meeting, debate the idea, hold a vote and reject it.

When Gomułka closes down *Po Prostu* in the autumn of 1957, the editors of *Polityka* welcome the move. Many people assume that once the revisionists' weekly has been eliminated, *Polityka* will have carried out Party orders and may leave the press scene. Meanwhile, under the management of its new chief, Mieczysław Rakowski, a former political officer and Party apparatus man, *Polityka* is changing from a dull, sermonizing newspaper into the most interesting weekly with a Party stamp. It will train the journalistic stars of the generation, create the Polish school of reportage and become a notorious thorn in the side of the government, a disparaging and sometimes ironic internal critic of the Party and the realities of People's Poland. Marian Turski will say that *Polityka* began by being branded anti–*Po Prostu* but ended up becoming a sequel to its revisionist predecessor.

> The young editors at *Polityka* knew their generation, and could sense its needs. They had been through October with it, and started their first jobs with it. They knew that the time for rallying was over, and now the time had come to establish families, wait for accommodation, and confront theory with actual life. But life was putting up resistance to their ambitions. Because life, as it turned out, also meant stagnant systems, stupid bosses defending their own jobs, regulations that block initiative, provincialism and backwardness.[2]

So wrote Wiesław Władyka, a historian of the PRL and beginning in the 1980s a features writer for *Polityka*, many years later in a book about the newspaper.

Polityka intuitively seeks contact with the engineers who have packed up their books and left the student hostel to go out into the country, with the teachers who once founded the Young Intellectuals' Clubs, with the managers who believed in reforms, and with the artists who – as at Warsaw's Student Satirical Theatre – made fun of the absurdities of life and of themselves, as well as of politics.[3]

These are the people who will be the heroes of the reportage and also the readers of the weekly created by 'Rakowski's gang' (no one can remember who gave the *Polityka* team this name). On returning from a brief period of exile behind a desk, Kapuściński quickly earns himself a prestigious place in this 'gang'.

'Gomułka's departure from the ideals of October was a disappointment for Rysiek; he believed that an original form of socialism would come into being in Poland, another path, different from the Soviet one.'

Jerzy Nowak, his closest friend for forty-six years, is trying to reconstruct Kapuściński's state of mind and spirit at that time. They will meet a few years after the withdrawal from the new thinking of October '56, in 1961, when Nowak is getting ready to leave for his first diplomatic posting in Dar es Salaam. Kapuściński has already made his first two journeys to Africa when they arrange to meet at a café in central Warsaw. Kapuściński is keen to meet someone who apparently shares his interest in Africa, and who is going to Tanganyika as a diplomat. The time for serious conversations about Poland and socialism, about their hopes and disappointments, will come much later.

'At that time Rysiek believed that only within the Party, through acting from the inside, would it be possible to have a reasonable effect on Polish reality. That meant we should muster as many intelligent, sensitive people from the October generation as possible and encourage them to join the Party ranks, because without it we would never accomplish a thing and our efforts would be in vain.'

This is a good explanation for why the recent 'thaw supporter' and denouncer of the abuses of Stalinist bureaucracy would find a safe haven at *Polityka* – the weekly branded an ideological destroyer of the deeper reform of socialism. But there is another one as well.

On returning from his journey to the Far East and uniting with his colleagues who have left *Sztandar Młodych* in protest, Kapuściński does not know where to go. Some of the protestors find work at an evening paper, others at a magazine covering international affairs; one is banned from appearing in print. They set up a welfare fund to help anyone left without work; each of them pays a small sum into it. Officially it is a collection for a sailing boat, in case the Party should accuse them of forming an illegal professional union or an anti-government conspiracy.

Kapuściński's new friend from India, the PAP correspondent Ryszard Frelek, now comes in handy. Frelek recommends Kapuściński to his boss, Michał Hoffman. A communist from the inter-war years, Hoffman takes Kapuściński into his team.

> Because I had arrived from China, my new boss, Michał Hoffman, concluded my expertise must lie in matters of the Far East and decided that this would now be my beat – specifically, the part of Asia to the east of India and extending to the innumerable islands of the Pacific.
>
> We all know a little about everything, but I knew nothing about the countries I had been assigned, and so I burned the midnight oil studying up on guerrilla warfare in the jungles of Burma and Malaysia, the revolts in Sumatra and Sulawesi, the rebellions of the Moro tribe in the Philippines. The world once again presented itself to me as something impossible to even begin to comprehend, let alone master. And all the more so because, given my work, I had so little time to devote to it. All day long, dispatches arrived in my office from various countries, which I had to read, translate, condense, edit, and send on to newspapers and radio stations.[4]

He hates working at a desk. Only once again in his life, and only for a short while in the late 1960s, will he be exiled behind a desk again – by the same Hoffman – at the agency's Warsaw headquarters. Kapuściński thinks a man who works behind a desk is like 'an invalid in an orthopaedic corset': while the desk is his instrument of power, it is also his prison, fencing him off from life and from people, and making him into a slave. The world of the man behind the desk undergoes radical transformation as other values become important, and his career becomes a journey from a smaller to a bigger desk. That is not what Kapuściński wants.

He has a flair for reporting, he is 'stoked up' – as he puts it – by talking to ordinary people in Poland, India, Japan, and, later, other continents too. Not only would he have been incapable of working at a desk for long, he couldn't have been a reporter in any Western country either. A few years before his death, he said in earnest that he would have died of boredom as a correspondent reporting from Brussels on the European Union, or serving the American establishment in Washington, because in those places life takes place in offices, behind closed doors, behind piles of documents – behind desks. He preferred to wade into the River Ganges with the pilgrims, to contract malaria in Uganda, and to shoot a gun during the civil war in Angola.

And so when, in the second half of 1958, Marian Turski comes along with an offer to join 'Rakowski's gang', Kapuściński feels as if life is returning.

Daniel Passent, *Polityka* columnist: 'He didn't join in with social life at the newspaper office. We were always getting together somewhere, going out together, having a drink or a party, but Rysiek didn't take part in all that. I ascribe this not so much to his reserve towards people from the office, as to his personal plans and his lack of any social, political or environmental needs. He was self-contained, and no one knew much about him. He never talked about his family life.'

Mieczysław Rakowski, for many years chief of *Polityka*: 'He was quiet, always on the sidelines, unaggressive.'

Passent: 'His weak spot was the girls. He used to spend hours sitting at the table for the office gofers. There was an extremely pretty girl working there, and everyone used to sigh over her, but she only had eyes for Rysiek. Sometimes I even used to wonder what he talked to her about for hours and hours on end.'

Rakowski: 'He made my secretary fall in love with him – a very beautiful girl! He broke her heart. One day she didn't turn up at work. She left a note on the desk saying she was leaving.'

At *Polityka* Kapuściński conquers two summits. With several other reporters he cofounds the trend in post-war journalism that will come to be known as the Polish school of reportage. Here, too, he will discover his life's subject. Witnessing decolonization in Ghana and the civil war in Congo, he earns a reputation as a reporter on African affairs and catches the African bug for the rest of his life.

Polityka sends him out to Ghana almost immediately. When I questioned Rakowski about Kapuściński more than a year before his death in November 2008, he could not remember how the idea arose that the journalist who didn't know Africa (in Poland, who did in those days?) should be sent to Ghana straight after being taken on staff. 'Probably,' he said, trying to remember, 'Rysiek himself had been following the foreign press and the agency dispatches when he was still working at the PAP, and had noticed that this was a watershed moment in African history. He came to me with this and persuaded me that the topic was worth an expedition. I arranged the consent of the Central Committee Press Office and some hard currency from RSW 'Prasa' [the Workers' Publishing Co-operative], because weeklies had no funds of their own for trips of that kind. There was a great hunger for news from the Third World, and we felt History was happening there.'

Kapuściński himself writes about it as follows:

In those days, the 1960s, the world was very interested in Africa. Africa was a puzzle, a mystery. Nobody knew what would happen when 300 million people stood up and demanded the right to be heard. States began to be established there, and the states bought armaments, and there was speculation in foreign newspapers that Africa might set out to conquer Europe. Today it is impossible to contemplate such a prospect, but at that time, it was a concern, an anxiety. It was serious. People wanted to know what was happening on the continent: where it was headed, what were its intentions?[5]

Little is known about Kapuściński's first trip to Africa except what he himself writes in his reports and books. It lasted for about two months.

But before he writes one of the most famous sentences in Polish reportage, 'I am living on a raft, in a side street in the merchant district of Accra . . .'; before he is dazzled by the bright sunlight described several decades later in *The Shadow of the Sun*; before he is struck by the odours of hot bodies, dried fish, rotting meat and roasted cassava, on the plane from London to Accra he meets Nadir Khouri, an Arab, who will take him from the airport to the Hotel Metropol (the one that resembles a raft).

In Accra he goes to a rally led by the most iconic figure in the African liberation movements of that era, Kwame Nkrumah. A year earlier, as the first leader of a self-governing African country, Nkrumah declared Ghana's independence and took over from the British colonial authorities. At the time, people were struck by Nkrumah's confession in his autobiography that he did not know the date of his own birth.

'The crowd is standing in West End Square. The crowd is standing in the sunshine, under a white African sky. The crowd is standing and waiting for Nkrumah, the patient black crowd, the sweating crowd.'[6] Thus begins the first of Kapuściński's series of reports for *Polityka*, 'Ghana Close Up'.

There is no evidence that Kapuściński meets Nkrumah in person. Certainly he very much wants to, and goes to see one of his ministers. He is fascinated by the Ghanaian leader and his pan-African aspirations, and he likes the references to the ideas of Marx and Lenin. But Nkrumah is also a Christian and says that these two sources of inspiration are not mutually exclusive, and that he is interested in African socialism, which will not use violence either to fight for power or to exercise it.

A few months before Kapuściński's death, at a reading of his poetry in Rome, a woman comes up to him and introduces herself as Samia Nkrumah, daughter of Ghana's former leader. Soon afterwards, she will write him a letter in which, without implying that he ever met Nkrumah in person, she invites him to a celebration of the fiftieth anniversary of Ghanaian independence. Kapuściński does not live to attend it.

It is in Accra's West End that the seeds sown in India begin to flourish, producing a reporter and writer with an anti-colonial world outlook, critical of the West and of capitalism. This world outlook – despite subtle changes – remains with him for the rest of his life.

So Kapuściński stands on the square in Accra and listens as Kwame Nkrumah says:

We must be vigilant, because imperialism and colonialism might arrive in Africa in a new guise. The imperialists are ready to grant political independence, but at the same time they still want to rule over Africa in the economic sphere by keeping control of economic life in the newly liberated countries. There is no difference between political and economic imperialism.[7]

The people shout 'Imperialists Out!', and 'Lead us, Kwame!' After three-quarters of an hour, Nkrumah ends his speech with a cry of 'Long live the unity and independence of Africa!', whereupon a jazz band starts to play and the crowd starts to boogie.

In Ghana, Kapuściński discovers something else as well: himself from a few years earlier. He talks to an enthusiastic revolutionary called Ded, who believes that Nkrumah is indeed wonderful but has stopped halfway. That is why, instead of going to America on a scholarship, Ded wants to go to Poland to study revolution. Kapuściński finds that Ded reminds him of someone, and that he envies him something. Another idealist, a young African communist, or 'pimply', tells the journalist, 'We must go further, more boldly to the left. My generation will come to replace Nkrumah, move the country forward and give the people power.[8]

Following his Polish experiences, Kapuściński has no trouble noticing that the African liberation revolution, though full of lofty ideals, is bound to run into trouble soon; and that after the initial period of enthusiasm, bitterness and disappointment will set in. He asks another African acquaintance why he didn't go to Nkrumah's rally. What did Nkrumah say about wages? Nothing. So why should he have gone?

On returning from Ghana but before setting off on his next trip, Kapuściński engages in a small but important skirmish about Africa in the pages of the press. He also gathers wind in his sails – it seems the theme of Africa has caught on.

Polityka's journalists go out and circulate, meeting their readers at schools, student clubs, youth clubs and cultural centres. In the course of barely eighteen months, Kapuściński attends almost fifty such meetings. He is staggered by the interest in the 'exotic' continent. The people who come to the meetings do not especially want to hear about elephants and African dances; above all, they want to know what is happening in politics and society; how the Africans are liberating themselves from colonial bondage, how they are ruling themselves, and what problems they are facing.

At public meetings Kapuściński grapples with the racist, distorted image of Africa which popular literature has created in the readers' minds. For instance, the Polish Nobel Prize winner Henryk Sienkiewicz, who wrote: 'As one observes this human swarm, one feels as if one were observing teeming maggots'. Or a Catholic missionary from the 1930s: 'Wherever the blacks enjoy liberty, where the eye of the white man's authority is not watching over them, old pagan practices firmly prevail, hideous rituals at which human flesh is the major and favourite dish'.

At one of these meetings Kapuściński comments ironically: 'Africa was a mystery, wild and primitive, its peoples were passive cavemen and, topped up with palm trees, the shadow of the jungle, the roar of lions, and the hiss of snakes, the whole thing presented a scene where the white saviour could play his historic role as the Messiah in a pith helmet.'

People ask questions such as, 'Do they slaughter each other there?' and 'Are the Negroes like children?' One lady is embarrassed to ask out loud, so after the meeting she comes up to Kapuściński and says, 'Please tell me the truth, do those black people stink? Because they are actually very handsome!'

So Kapuściński patiently explains. He looks for analogies, for points of contact in the history of the Poles and the Africans. In a personal account after a series of meetings, he writes:

> We have a clear conscience with regard to Africa: we never had a colony there, and we had our own experience of life under the colonial boot. Thus in our history there is something that brings us particularly close to the drama that the Dark Continent is going through, to the fortunes of its citizens, their struggle and their opportunity. The year 1960 is Africa's year. So people are saying, and it is true. In this unexpected, unorganized way the African question, one of the biggest problems of the modern world, has come into our field of vision and become the object of our fascination.[9]

He is irritated by articles that play on fascination with 'the exotic'. Years later, eliminating 'the exotic' when writing about the Third World and guarding against this pitfall will be the subject of Kapuściński's lectures, interviews and workshops.

> The so-called exotic has never fascinated me, even though I came to spend more than a dozen years in a world that is exotic by defini- tion. I did not write about hunting crocodiles or head-hunters,

although I admit they are interesting subjects. I discovered instead a different reality, one that attracted me more than expeditions to the villages of witch doctors or wild animal reserves. A new Africa was being born – and this was not a figure of speech or a platitude from an editorial. The hour of its birth was sometimes dramatic and painful, sometimes enjoyable and jubilant; it was always different (from our point of view) from anything we had known, and it was exactly this difference that struck me as new, as the previously undescribed, as the exotic.[10]

After writing his reports from Ghana, Kapuściński cannot sit still, and he seeks excuses to return to Africa. Rakowski, however, sends him into the field to report on the Polish provinces. Meanwhile, that summer – it is 1960 – Congo declares independence. The army rebels, Belgian paratroopers intervene, and there is civil war and anarchy. Kapuściński rushes back to Warsaw by train and begs Rakowski to send him to Congo. Although Rakowski is in favour of this plan, it turns out that all the journalists from socialist countries have been thrown out of Congo.

'Then maybe go to Nigeria,' Rakowski suggests.

'Nigeria will have to do.'

Rakowski supports his efforts to raise money for the trip, and the RSW's travel committee assigns Kapuściński some funding for an expedition to Nigeria. Almost twenty years later, Kapuściński recalls in *The Soccer War*:

But what's Nigeria to me? Nothing's going on there (at the moment). I walk around depressed and heart-broken. Suddenly a glimmer of hope – somebody claims that in Cairo there's a Czech journalist who wants to force his way into the Congo by the jungle route. Officially I leave for Nigeria, but secretly have the airline ticket rewritten for Cairo and fly out of Warsaw. Only a few colleagues are in on my plan.[11]

The 'secret plan' is presumably one of the legends that are to form the reporter's adventurous biography, filled with amazing events. But it wasn't baseless legend. Indeed, in Cairo, Kapuściński meets up with two Czech journalists, Jarda Bouček and Dušan Provazník (who later translated his books into Czech); together they fly to Sudan and then daringly make their way across into Congo. Also taking part in the expedition are Miloslav Vaclavik, from Department I of the Czechoslovak Ministry of Internal Affairs, posing as Mirek Vesely, a journalist for Czechoslovak Radio, and a reporter named Fedyashin, from the Soviet press agency, TASS, who joins the group in the Congolese city of Brazzaville. However, the expedition by no means takes place in secret from his colleagues at the office: Kapuściński sends a letter home, which is published in *Polityka*:

Dear Friends,

I'm writing on my knee, shortly before leaving Khartoum. Tomorrow night (on 27 January) I will cross the Congolese border. The road from the border to Stanleyville runs through the thickest jungle in Africa. This 900-kilometre road leads through terrain inhabited by entirely primitive tribes whose only understanding of white men is as Belgian colonialists. In Cairo people from Congo told us: even if they don't take you for Belgians, they will take you as brothers of the Belgians.

Hell knows what's better . . . For the time being, I'm not afraid somehow. I think the fear will come later. You know, it's going to be a 900-kilometre drive through dense jungle, in full awareness that at any moment someone could fire a volley of shots at the car from the bushes. I'm very curious about this journey.

I have left a list of documents, some money and other things at the diplomatic post in Cairo, just in case I go missing. Some friends in Khartoum have supplied me with food, cigarettes, bandages and other small items.

The most intriguing fact is that we're going there totally in the dark. We don't know a thing – neither how to get there, nor where to live, nor what to pay with, nor whom to talk to. NOTHING. The situation means that we could immediately fall into the hands of Mobutu, and that'll be the end. There are too many fronts in Congo for us to be able to get our bearings. Casual groups from both sides are moving about the entire country, and only pot luck will decide whose wing I first come under.

. . . It is very hot here, and it will be even hotter there. Literally and metaphorically. But I'm feeling well and I believe in my lucky star . . . My God, how far it is from here to Poland. I envy you the snow. But I must stop writing now, the engines are starting up. Goodbye until spring. Keep your fingers crossed for me. I'll do my best not to disappoint you.

All the best,
RYSIEK
Khartoum, 26 January 1961[12]

When they finally cross the border into Congo, the beauty of the country takes his breath away:

This is a fairytale place, like a wonderful dream. The landscapes of the eastern province and Kiwu, the roads through the jungle, the riverbanks, Garamba Park, the waterfalls and bridges – at last after driving across the barren Sahara and the burned-out Sudanese savannahs, we are entering the enchanted kingdom of Africa. I never want to leave this place.[13]

The political situation, however, is not in the least like a fairytale or a dream, more like a nightmare. The group of reporters reaches Congo at the moment when the divided country has, in effect, four governments, each of which has its own army. The government of Colonel Mobutu, supported by the West, is exercising power in Leopoldville; the government of Antoine Gizenga, supported by the socialist bloc and some African and Asian governments, has its headquarters in Stanleyville; Moise Tshombe and Albert Kalonji, the leaders supported by the Belgians, control the richest province, Katanga, and the 'diamond state' of Kasai; on top of which, with Belgian support, Tshombe has earlier announced the separation of Katanga from the rest of the country. The culminating point of the crisis is the kidnap by Mobutu's men – with the support of the US and Belgian governments – of Patrice Lumumba (a colleague of Gizenga's), hero of the Congolese anti-colonial movement, who has recently (in September 1960) been dismissed from the post of prime minister. In January 1961, shortly after being imprisoned and subjected to torture, Lumumba is brutally murdered; his family flees to Cairo (where Bouček's wife, PAP correspondent Aniela Krupińska, will visit them).

In Stanleyville, at the Résidence Equateur hotel, the reporters find out about the murder of Lumumba. It is February, and Lumumba was killed a month earlier, but news of his death has been covered up. Now it is circulating in a version propagated by Mobutu's people – a version which implies that after escaping from prison, Lumumba was battered to death by enraged villagers. No one in Stanleyville believes this story. There is a general conviction – to be confirmed in the coming years – that Lumumba's death is the result of a plot by the Belgians and the Americans, in short the West, the white man, never mind whether the sentence was carried out by his African compatriots, sent by Mobutu, or by Western agents.

According to Kapuściński's account, the reporters are afraid to leave the hotel, because Lumumba's supporters are – absolutely correctly, in fact – blaming the Western powers for their leader's death. In practice, the hatred of the street is turning against anyone with white skin.

> The Stanleyville station was giving government communiqués appealing to all the whites still in the city to stay off the streets and not to appear in public because of the behaviour of isolated elements and certain military groups which the government 'is not able to control fully'.[14]

Not for the first time – though for the first time in such a way as to make him fear for his life – Kapuściński realizes what the stigma of skin colour can mean. Later he writes that once, in Accra, he was walking with an African female student, who was being hounded by curses and derision for associating with a white man.

'I had five people and twenty blacks with me,' an Englishman told me. It's the ones like him who help build the myth. The total, absolute myth of the colour of skin, still alive and powerful.

People ask why the blacks beat the whites in the Congo. Why, indeed. Because the whites used to beat the blacks. It's a closed circle of revenge.[15]

Then come days when Kapuściński and his travelling companions are able to leave the hotel and go out into the streets. They go to the post office to send their reports. They run away from gendarmes. So Kapuściński tells it. Not without perturbation and reluctance on the part of the UN mission staff, he recalls years later, the pack of reporters succeeds in leaving Stanleyville. They are to fly by UN freight plane to Juba, in the north-east, but instead they land at Usumbura (later Bujumbura, the capital of Burundi), where Belgian soldiers are permanently stationed.

In a dramatic account in *The Soccer War*, Kapuściński describes the entire group's brutal treatment by Belgian paratroopers, their imprisonment for several days in a barred room at the airport, and the fear that they would be murdered and their bodies would disappear without trace.

I once heard a comment to the effect that Dušan Provazník only found out what happened to the group in Congo years later, when he read *The Soccer War*.

Is there an unintentional hint of irony in that remark?

14

Legends 2: Sentenced to Death by Firing Squad

Bożena Dudko, author of a book of conversations with Kapuściński's translators, asked Dušan Provazník about dangerous moments on the Congolese expedition:

> So I question Mr Provazník about all these dangers: the encounters with gendarmes while crossing the jungle to Stanleyville and with vengeance squads . . .; the trip to the post office at the other end of the terrorized city to send agency dispatches; escaping from Stanleyville with the help of the UN commissioner; avoiding being shot in Usumbura . . .
>
> But in vain.
>
> 'Ryszard has described it all splendidly in *The Soccer War* – I have nothing to add' – that is the reply I hear several times more.[1]

Paradoxically, this way of confirming Kapuściński's version sounds to me like a staunch denial.

Why are the dangers of the expedition the only thing Provazník refused to talk about, despite Dudko's repeated questions? He has no qualms about discussing other aspects of the journey to Congo, despite the fact that 'Ryszard has described it all splendidly'; on the contrary, often he had interesting details to add.

His reluctance to answer the question and his adamant confirmation of Kapuściński's version (which no one had actually challenged) stirred my interest and inspired me to investigate Jarda Bouček's account. I turned to a reporter friend who writes about the Czech Republic to ask how and where to look, and whether such an account did actually exist. He helped me get in touch with Jaroslav Bouček, son of the late 'commander' of the Congolese expedition, and this led me to a radically different story from the one presented in *The Soccer War*.

It turned out that Bouček Jr had written an essay titled 'In Deepest Congo'. In it, he compares Kapuściński's account with his father's, which he found in the National Archive in Prague, along with his Cairo diary, his letters and dispatches.

Jaroslav Bouček wonders if Kapuściński's expressive depiction of the dangerous journey to Congo, compared with the 'civilian' mood of Bouček's account, arose from the fact that it was the first time Kapuściński had ever found himself in the dramatic situation of civil war in an African country, and so he took the verbal threats addressed to the 'suspicious foreigners' quite literally. As a reporter, Jarda Bouček, on the other hand, was a veteran of several armed conflicts, and 'verbal threats did not throw him off balance to that extent'.

From Bouček's account it emerges that the journalists certainly did not have to leave Stanleyville for fear of losing their lives because of impetuous mob law imposed by Africans on whites. The Czechoslovak reporter's son writes:

> Before leaving for Congo, Bouček wrote to his editors that he would be able to stay in Stanleyville for about a month, and then he would have to come back to buy medicine, which in view of some chronic ailments he could not do without. His exit visa from Congo was signed by Louis Lumumba, brother of the murdered prime minister; before his departure, Bouček had arranged a return visa, as he foresaw that he would go back to Congo again.[2]

According to Bouček's account, the reporters left Congo because their money had run out, they weren't sure if their dispatches were getting through, and an opportunity had presented itself in the form of a UN plane flying to Burundi. Bouček challenges Kapuściński's account of the UN staff's alleged reluctance to help their group; unlike Kapuściński, he claims they knew from the start that they were flying to Usumbura. Bouček Jr again:

> Writing further about how the Belgians were determined to kill them all, [Kapuściński] probably let himself be excessively frightened by the bravado-filled utterances of some young Belgian officers who cast swaggering remarks in their direction, such as, 'Best shoot these journalists right away!'
>
> In no instance did Bouček feel fear that the Belgians were planning to kill them. Usumbura was a civilian airport; in addition to the soldiers, the civilian airport staff was there too, as well as some customs officers, pilots and stewardesses from Sabena airlines, and passengers who would have involuntarily been witnesses to such a crime.
>
> But above all – what sense would it have made for the Belgians to put to death five journalists who were officially accredited by the UN?[3]

The younger Bouček sums up the situation by saying that 'the expedition to Congo did not shake' his father 'in the least'.

Many of Kapuściński's friends and acquaintances think he was a catastrophist, in the sense that he could blow up small incidents to unimaginable proportions and present ordinary fears as the end of the world.

'I divided everything he said by at least two,' says Adam Daniel Rotfeld, smiling.

The words of one of his friends come back to me – Kapuściński created his own courage in literature; he knew he was different.

Part of the legend of Kapuściński the reporter is based on the several times he avoided execution by firing squad. We know about all those incidents from him alone. In Bolivia, as he tells us, he was saved by a chauffeur who managed to intoxicate the officer who apparently wanted to shoot Kapuściński as a communist spy. In another of his accounts, after a coup in Ghana they wanted to shoot him as a spy working for Kwame Nkrumah, who had just been deposed.

He was also reportedly sentenced to be shot dead in Usumbura at the end of the Congolese expedition, after being locked up in a barred room at the airport along with the Czechoslovak and Soviet journalists. In a 1978 interview with Wojciech Giełżyński, he refers to 'when I was in prison in Usumbura sentenced to be shot'.[4] 'I had a death sentence, I escaped shooting by a miracle,' he says of this incident in another interview, also from the 1970s.[5]

People react variously to stress and danger, especially when away from home and in an alien world. However, such profound differences between Kapuściński's and Bouček's accounts place a question mark not only over the threat of being shot in Usumbura, but all the other near-executions as well. There is rather a large difference between stating that 'it could have been dangerous' and claiming that 'several times I escaped being shot'.

For many years Kapuściński created his own legend: the macho reporter who is unafraid of war, starvation, wild animals, tropical insects and diseases, even of death staring him in the eye. There is no doubt that for a quarter of a century he did push his way into some dangerous places; often he ended up in situations that would make anyone feel panic and fear.

The British journalist William Pike, who has been living in East Africa for several decades, told me how in 1988 he and Kapuściński fell into an ambush set by guerrillas in Uganda (Kapuściński described this in *The Shadow of the Sun*). 'He behaved calmly and with dignity, he didn't panic,' says Pike, whom I meet in Kampala. He does, however, have reservations about the accuracy of Kapuściński's descriptions. For example, some grasses that were less than a metre high grew in his account to three metres, and a broad, even road became a potholed, dangerous track.

The differences between Bouček's and Kapuściński's reports from the expedition to Congo, in particular the parts about being detained in Usumbura, are more serious. They suggest that Kapuściński exaggerated, created a sensational account based on situations that were not in fact as sensational as his descriptions of them. He created the literary figure of Ryszard Kapuściński, the hero of Ryszard Kapuściński's books, and by this means his own legend.

Friends mention that he frequently picked up women on the strength of his stories about poverty, starvation and the dangers of war. He seduced the public, his readers, with his heroism and the image of the macho reporter. He understood superbly that one of the ingredients of good literature is the aura that surrounds it – the legend of the writer. So he devised an ideal life story for the reporter who goes to war zones, covers revolutions and coups d'état in the Third World, of which only a small part needed to be 'embellished', because most of the elements in the legend were true.

My hypothesis is indirectly supported by a comment from Jerzy Nowak: 'He always used to tell us, his friends, about those "executions" with a pinch of salt. We knew it was Rysiek's poetic licence. With time, however, he started taking those stories seriously. He allowed his readers and listeners to believe he really had experienced all those dangerous adventures, and whenever other people spoke or wrote about them, he didn't deny them.'

15

In 'Rakowski's Gang', *Continued*

We will never know which comrade from the Polish Ministry for Foreign Affairs (MSZ) tells Kapuściński that he should not make any more trips abroad as a correspondent because he doesn't understand 'the Marxist–Leninist processes happening in that world'. On his return from Congo, Kapuściński writes a note for the MSZ in which he outlines the Congolese conflict, the prevalent anarchy, and the coming collapse of the newly arising state. He prophesies the defeat of Gizenga, whose sympathies lie with the socialist camp, and the victory of the pro-Western Mobutu. His dissenting prophecies do not please the comrade from the MSZ.

The assassination of Lumumba, a romantic leader who broke free of Congo's colonial authorities, reinforces Kapuściński's convictions about the sinister role of the West in the Third World – not just the former colonial powers but also the United States, which during the ongoing Cold War is playing the leading role among the Western superpowers. (Years later, it will come to light that the CIA did prepare the plan to assassinate Lumumba.)

> Any aggression is a crime, but in the case of Congo the colonialist invasion has an extra feature of cynical mockery . . . The fight is uneven, like five tough thugs picking on a small boy . . .
>
> The Belgians have isolated Congo from the world . . . The drama of Congo, as one European there told me, lies in the fact that the most backward country in Africa came under the control of the most worthless, insignificant people in Europe.[1]

The expedition to Congo is a crucial element in the formation of Kapuściński's world outlook, his view of the Cold War conflict and of the dilemmas and dramas of the times from the perspective of the Third World countries attempting to gain their liberty.

In an entry in his *Political Diaries* dated 23 June 1961, *Polityka*'s editor-in-chief, Mieczysław Rakowski notes: 'Rysiek has finished a series entitled "Congo Close Up". We published twelve reports. Rysiek is a fantastic reporter. This is no ordinary journalism. This is political literature produced by a devilishly talented writer. We collected 2,687,138 zloty for the Lumumba Fund.'[2]

A year later, in a popularity contest for *Polityka's* writers, Kapuściński comes first. His reports from Ghana and Congo play their role in gaining him fame and public recognition, but this is not the only way he displays his talents. In less than two years of working at *Polityka*, Kapuściński has created his own language, a new literary style, with a poetic rhythm to his sentences and an original way of depicting things – free of the wooden, propagandistic phraseology of his early years as a journalist at *Sztandar Młodych*. It is this new language and new tone that make the then cub reporter Małgorzata Szejnert (later co-founder of *Gazeta Wyborcza* and head of its reportage department for fifteen years) think on reading one of his reports: 'He writes as he wants to.'

'He flourished at *Polityka*,' says Daniel Passent. 'He wrote articles that showed what was really happening in Poland, warts and all.'

Between the African trips, Kapuściński travels to the Polish provinces, but he is not yet aware that his current visits will be his farewell – as a reporter – to Poland. A curious farewell, because he had just begun to shine as an incisive observer of the Poles during the 'minor stabilization' when he went off on a completely different path.

'He deserted,' some people would say.

Kapuściński refutes the charges: 'Africa and the Third World were a continuation of the heroic period of reportage in Poland.'

As the 1950s turn into the 1960s – the years of the 'minor stabilization' – people are no longer marching romantically, storming the great edifices of socialism, holding ideological debates and awakening dreams. It is a time of positivism for the PRL, of work at the foundations, doing whatever possible within the conditions of the plebeian, puritanical socialism of Władysław Gomułka. People earn money for new flats, dream of owning a car, or try to settle down; few minds are occupied by the struggle for or against socialism. The majority shut themselves up in the privacy of their domestic, family and social life.

Polityka looks for its own way of thinking about society, the economy and culture. It is sometimes sceptical or ironical, and poses awkward questions – within bounds that concur with the fundamental Party line. It sets fashions and initiates beneficial vogues. 'For example,' writes Władyka, 'the paper's campaign entitled "Citizen, Don't Stutter" is to do with the first global experiences of the generation of then thirty-year-olds who, unfortunately, don't know any foreign languages; the "Let's Look at Our Watches" campaign is essentially a fight for work and life to be sensibly organized, a fight against bureaucracy and lack of respect towards people.'[3]

Kapuściński travels about the country, portraying the provincial Poland of the late 1950s and early 1960s. He compiles most of these reports into his first book, *The Polish Bush*. He still writes the occasional positive, semi–socialist–realist story. A 'Positive Report' (the phrase already sounded ironic) is the kind of article that describes the rosy aspects of life under socialism, has an optimistic tone, and shows that with hard work and persistence you can conquer mountains – just like the 'hero of labour' from Nowa Huta, who used to be a cowherd but has become a university professor ('More Than You Can Chew'). In another 'positive report' Kapuściński describes a visit to the tenants in a newly completed apartment block and is delighted by the efficiency of socialist construction ('The House').

However, in most of his Polish stories, the topics and his take on them are original and surprising. He describes, for instance:

• how two German women ran away from an old people's home in Szczytno ('The Fifth Column Marches Out', a report that years later was accused of having anti-German overtones);

• how a number of down-and-outs rescued a ruined state agricultural farm ('Wydma'); and

• the society in a small town where several women tortured a beautiful girl because an artist had used her face for a sculpture of the Madonna outside a local church ('Danka').

In 'No Address', he writes about footloose, drunken students expelled from college. In 'Ground Floors', he describes workers who roam from factory to factory, lack ambition, and have no desire to build a career – the complete opposite of the socialist–realist heroes who erected the great constructions of socialism in the 1950s. Taken together, the reports make up a broad picture of B-grade, and even C-grade, Poland – places little known in Warsaw.

Polityka's scathing spirit informs the reporter's comments in 'Toothpaste Advertisement', his story about girls from a village called Pratki: 'I went on dreaming that the district instructor, who runs successive Party gatherings, once the decisive issues for the further flourishing of our fatherland had been discussed, would involuntarily and entirely incidentally want to ask: "And how are the teeth, Comrades? Are you brushing your teeth, or not?" '[4]

Some of the reports have a moral, such as the one about a discus thrower named Piątkowski ('The Big Throw'). Kapuściński, who loves sport, especially soccer, perceives a quality in the champion discus thrower that drives his own aspirations, too – passion.

Kapuściński contrasts the discus thrower's passion with widespread 'scheming?', and as a result, the feature about the sportsman carries a broader social message. He somewhat sarcastically proposes, 'Maybe all it takes is a little scheming, worming your way in somewhere and it'll be OK.

Why slog your guts out? A song, maybe the right face, or some bows aimed in the right direction – isn't that enough?'[5]

The sentences have a wonderful rhythm and the language is relaxed, with none of the stiffness in which Kapuściński voluntarily imprisoned himself in the days of socialist realism. Many of these texts eventually enter the canon of Polish literary reportage; they will be the starting point for successive generations of reporters.

> It was Trofim who discovered Wydma. In 1959 a bigwig from the district administration asked him: 'Are you any good at guarding things?' Trofim thought about it. 'Why not?' he replied. At which the bigwig said: 'Take him along.' They took him to the place by car. He stood in the yard and looked around him.
>
> He was standing in the middle of a world gone to waste.[6]

'When I read *Wydma*, I stopped in my tracks – it felt as if something vital had happened to me. I was stunned by the language and the rhythm of the sentences. I read that article over and over again, until I knew it by heart.' Many years on, Małgorzata Szejnert still finds it hard to contain the thrill that this report gave her. After 1989, she decides to run a reporter's workshop for young trainees in the art of reportage for *Gazeta Wyborcza*, based on Kapuściński's old articles, among others. 'No one wrote like that in Poland before him,' she tells me. 'Certainly no one in our generation. There was a freedom of depiction in his articles, there was artistic language, and what verve! As if there were nothing restraining him: no censorship, no political loyalties, it was pure, unrestricted creativity. I was sorry he'd become a foreign correspondent, because I'd love to have read his reports on Poland.'

Two of Kapuściński's reports from that era are under a shadow for having been written to political order. One of them, 'The Abduction of Elżbieta', is about a teacher from the Kalisz area who decides to become a nun and shuts herself away in a convent, leaving her ailing parents without any help. On their behalf, as it were, Kapuściński goes to the convent and tries to talk to their daughter.

> Through the bars I could see the nun's eyes, large brown eyes with fever in them. She remained silent, staring to one side. People who stare to one side have something to say, but they are choked by fear. Then I heard her voice:
>> 'What have you brought me?'
> But I had nothing. I had no words or things at all . . .
>> 'I don't really know. Maybe just your mother's cry.'[7]

It is not known whether Kapuściński came up with this topic himself or Rakowski commissioned him to cover it (in our conversation, Rakowski denied doing so). The article prompted doubt and disgust. About fifteen years later, Szejnert would write of it: 'The author intervenes in an issue that is difficult to judge, and takes an over-impassioned approach. He must know that the article is grist for the mill of official prejudice against the Church, and yet he acts in the best faith, he is convinced that he is helping the sick, abandoned parents of the central character, who chose a convent that was indifferent to the fate of her relatives.'[8]

A report is always rooted in the realities of the time and place when it was written – read after the fall of real socialism, in an era when the state authorities and the Church get on well together, sometimes even too well, 'The Abduction of Elżbieta' holds its own as a story about one woman's choice and the soullessness of an institution.

In the second article that adheres to a political demand – that of Party leader Gomułka himself – Kapuściński artfully hid behind literary form and a witty idea. 'Gomułka', says Janusz Rolicki, then a cub reporter for *Polityka*, 'demanded a report on the front page to celebrate the 550th anniversary of the Battle of Grunwald, the Polish troops' great victory over the Order of Teutonic Knights. He was probably expecting anti-German overtones – he was a politician for whom the issue of the Recovered Territories restored to Poland after the Second World War, and also standing up to the Germans in international politics, was almost an obsession.'

So Rakowski commissions Kapuściński for the 'prestigious' order. The reporter finds himself in a trap: preserving his independence of outlook, or succumbing to the beck and call of politicians? How is he to deal with it?

His solution is to describe a farmer named Piątek, who farms near the village of Grunwald. Piątek has a smallholding and a few hectares of land. He sends his children to school and can afford a washing machine for his wife. He has never heard of the battle against the Teutonic knights in 1410. When they talk about the war, Piątek is thinking of the world war against Hitler, while the reporter means the feudal war, the jingoistic image of which was created in the collective imagination by the writer Henryk Sienkiewicz and the artist Jan Matejko. Piątek is pleased to hear that the young people are coming down to Grunwald and that the village has become famous, though he can't understand why. However, he 'is worried in case all those hundreds of feet will trample the field of corn that has grown so promisingly'. Kapuściński concludes that 'Piątek isn't interested in history. What matters to him is the land ... The land will yield a crop anyway. Piątek will harvest it anyway.'[9]

Devoid of patriotic bombast or political overtones, the mildly humorous report is not suitable as an anniversary article for the front page. Rakowski, who gets the occasional carpeting from Gomułka, does not want to antagonize the First Secretary yet again, and so 'Piątek of Grunwald' ends up in the middle pages.

Kapuściński proves to be a master dodger. Many friends and acquaintances tell me about his ability to avoid head-on collisions and confrontations. He doesn't refuse to write a report that fulfils a political order, but he writes it in such a way that it doesn't meet the demands of the commissioner. Saying no was not in his nature – neither earlier nor later was he the dissident type, the protestor type, nor did he regard it as his mission to bear moral witness. Yet he also wanted to avoid being labelled a propagandist, a reporter at the disposal of others, and so he would write an article to order but it would be one he didn't have to be ashamed of.

The situation in which he found himself is a good illustration of one of the dilemmas faced by reputable journalists in People's Poland, the PRL. They wanted to write and operate within the official distribution of news, and many, including Kapuściński himself, despite their disappointments, still regarded socialism as their system. At the same time, they wanted to preserve relative independence of views and judgements, and felt bad in the role of Party drudges, scribes to order, plenty of whom surrounded them at the same or other papers. Moreover, Kapuściński had already done his share of propaganda work.

Rakowski says to me: 'Gomułka told me off for one of Kapuściński's reports. The problem was a conversation between two young ladies, in which one advises the other how to have it off with someone, using the phrase "Do it standing up". "In a Party organ, on the front page, you're describing a guy screwing a girl!" screamed Gomułka. Then, after a pause, he asked pensively: "Standing up? Is that actually possible?" ' (The reference is to a 1959 report titled 'The Peaceful Mind of the Gawker'; the relevant passage is: 'He happens to overhear a conversation between two of his pupils: "You idiot, do it standing up. You won't fall pregnant." '[10])

Artur Starewicz, head of the Central Committee Press Office: 'Kapuściński was highly rated at the Central Committee, Gomułka himself valued him. Of course he never voiced any in-depth views about him, but I remember some favourable comments and expressions of recognition for his writing talent and the quality of his analyses.'

Janusz Rolicki: 'Kapuściński had respect for Gomułka. He said that Gomułka was a politician for whom only two Polish embassies could possibly exist: in Moscow and in Bonn. In Moscow, for obvious reasons; and in Bonn, because Gomułka's hobby-horse was the Recovered Territories. He aspired at any price to having West Germany recognize that those lands belonged to Poland. Kapuściński respected that. He saw Gomułka as a good farmer who takes care of every sack of grain.'

*   *   *

Shortly before parting with *Polityka*, Kapuściński finds himself at the centre of a scandal. What happens is that a writer called Bohdan Drozdowski publishes a play called *The Cortège*, which Kapuściński regards as plagiarism of his own piece entitled 'The Stiff'.

Here is a summary, written by Kapuściński himself:

A group of people is transporting a coffin by lorry. Inside the coffin is the corpse of a miner who has been killed in an accident, crushed under a pile of coal. The group are on their way to the miner's hometown, where he is to be buried. However, on the way the vehicle breaks down. It's impossible to repair the damage, so the question arises, What are they to do? Night is approaching, and it is not far to their destination. Some think they should find some means of transport. Others think they can pick up the coffin and carry it to the place themselves. The latter view prevails. So the group of people carry the coffin in the darkness, through a forest. After a while they are tired, so they stop, put the coffin down, and light a bonfire. In the nervous atmosphere of the night they come to blows and fits of hysteria. Meanwhile, some girls pass by and some flirtation follows, though not everyone takes part in it. Finally the envoys from the mine continue their procession, carrying the coffin on their shoulders.[11]

The plotline of Drozdowski's play is almost identical.

In a letter to *Polityka*, Kapuściński reveals that before he left for Congo Drozdowski had approached him, asking him not to publicize the matter. (Drozdowski later claimed that he found out about Kapuściński's grievances only through friends, and that he himself had never read 'The Stiff' before.) Kapuściński claims they made a gentleman's agreement: Drozdowski would write a letter to the theatrical monthly *Dialog* (where *The Cortège* had been published), in which he would admit to being inspired by Kapuściński's article, and would not let the play be staged; in turn, Kapuściński would not take him to court and would not publicize the matter. In the course of a further meeting at a book fair, Drozdowski writes a dedication to Kapuściński in his collection of poems: 'To dear Rysiek Kapuściński, the secret co-author of my best (so far, as it's my only) play *The Cortège*, with warm wishes, the totally "Stiff" with cold Drozdowski. 14 V 61.'

On his return from Congo, Kapuściński explodes with rage when he finds out that not only has Drozdowski failed to publish any explanation, but *The Cortège* is now going to be staged at several provincial theatres. In a furious letter published in *Polityka* he lays into all Drozdowski's defenders: the critics who have praised *The Cortège* and defended the author's integrity, the editors-in-chief of the journals who have published their articles, the theatres that are prepared to put on a play by a plagiarist, and even the silent people who prefer to say nothing so as to avoid losing good connections.

> I do not really want more of the sort of pleasure afforded by reading my own ideas signed with someone else's name, I do not want yet another fan of 'reportage as inspiration' to raise what I or my colleagues on the paper write to the heights of real literature. Our profession as reporters is difficult, and – strange as it might seem to some – we put blood, sweat and tears into our writing. I never imagined that the fact that we lack the wings and the greatness that are only bestowed on those who produce so-called real literature justified depriving us of what is ours. That was what I imagined, but how wrong I have proved to be![12]

The quarrel about plagiarism revolves around the literary form of 'The Stiff'. In his letter attacking Drozdowski, Kapuściński calls his article a fictional story. Drozdowski defends himself thus:

> [T]his piece could have been read as a report, a genuine report to boot . . . The facts presented in news reports are nobody's property and may be regarded as public property, just like anonymous agency news items, which quite often contain ready-made dramatic plots . . .[13]

Drozdowski is defended by the Polish Writers' Union. Meanwhile, the editors of *Polityka* stand solidly behind Kapuściński:

> Drozdowski is trying to suggest that plagiarism would be involved only if the words and sentences in 'The Stiff' and *The Cortège* were exactly the same. Let's not be so naive! No one is trying to hide the fact that *The Cortège* does have some different features too, slightly different characters and some slightly different details, especially in the background. But the fact remains: not only is the idea the same, but also the plotline and, crucially, the psychological and philosophical atmosphere . . .[14]

Famous writers join the debate. In the satirical weekly *Szpilki* (Pins), Antoni Słonimski writes that Drozdowski has committed plagiarism. In turn, Julian Przyboś attacks *Polityka*, mocking the artistic quality of Kapuściński's reportage-story: 'the cry of alleged plagiarism has rashly drawn attention to "The Stiff", which can only bring harm to Kapuściński's reputation as an author of fiction..[15]

Rakowski told me that he did not rule out the possibility that such a big fuss in the press on this matter was inspired by the Central Committee itself. It could have been done by people who didn't like *Polityka* – there was no lack of them – taking advantage of an excuse to attack the weekly's 'belligerence' and managing to drag some writers into their intrigue. But when asked for names, Rakowski fell silent.

The quarrel about plagiarism has another, totally non-political significance in Kapuściński's biography. It focuses attention on both the principles for, and the limits of, introducing elements of fiction into journalism. To what extent may one distort reality in order to reach the deeper truth that reflects the 'heart of the matter'? Where are the lines that mark the borders between fiction and non-fiction? By introducing elements of invention, by processing reality, do we shift our text from the 'journalism' shelf to the one marked 'literature'? Is literary reportage – as Kapuściński himself thought – independent artistic work, a legitimate literary genre (hence, above all, his rage at Drozdowski)?

Years later, by now a world-famous reporter and writer, Kapuściński quite often comes in for stern criticism because of his nonchalant treatment of the facts as the raw material for his texts – his inaccuracies, ignorance or even plain old fabrications.

His declaration that 'The Stiff' is a story will prove rich in revolutionary consequences for his future work and for his journalism's tendency towards a non-fiction which does not hold fiction in contempt. Fiction will make its way into the world described in his work as much as it does into his autobiographical themes, which are sometimes one and the same: after all, Kapuściński is the hero of most of his own books.

Early in 1962, Ryszard Frelek, his new friend from India, reappears in Kapuściński's life. On returning from his posting as a correspondent in New Delhi, he becomes a decision-maker at the PAP and offers Kapuściński the job of opening the agency's first bureau in Africa. The location is Dar es Salaam in Tanganyika – the very same city where the young diplomat Jerzy Nowak, whom Kapuściński met at a café in central Warsaw, has been posted.

For Kapuściński this is an opportunity to develop his new passion for the Third World. No daily or weekly has the same financial possibilities as the PAP; they are able periodically to send the reporter abroad. Moreover, in Africa Kapuściński has his beloved revolution, Major Change. In Gomułka's Poland 'there's none of that spark, that ardour', and he is missing the years that 'fired him up' so much in the days when he 'wore himself out, got washed away'. He rediscovers these feelings in Africa. Now it is all happening there. He doesn't want to continue being one of the characters in his own reports – the ones who went through a great deal at the time of the ZMP revolution, then during the thaw and October '56, and now haven't the energy for anything new. He does not identify with the people from the 'minor stabilization' period whom he so incisively describes, nor with the gawkers – Hamletizing humanists, dreamers overcome by inertia, ill-fitted for life, incapable of pressing ahead despite obstacles – nor with the rationalizing engineers who are set on success, money and consumerism, and are obsessed with 'the world of four wheels', as he puts it in 'The Peaceful Mind of the Gawker'.[16]

During the first few years of his work as a correspondent in Africa, he will occasionally submit longer articles to *Polityka*, but he and the weekly will gradually part ways. On returning from his postings in Africa and then Latin America, he will choose other workplaces. Never again will he write for *Polityka*, either in the PRL era or after the fall of real socialism.

Rakowski bore a grudge against Kapuściński for having sailed out from *Polityka* onto broader waters and then turning his back on the journal: 'After the fall of socialism, in one of his biographical notes he left out the fact that he had spent more than four years at *Polityka*. I never mentioned it to him, but it was upsetting.'

'Maybe he thought his connections with *Polityka* were compromising?' suggests Passent. 'It must have been because his own image was at stake, his position within the establishment.'

Perhaps Passent's idea has some merit. In the 1970s *Polityka*, a Party paper of course, was more critical of the realities of the PRL and stood slightly further away from the regime than did the weekly *Kultura*, with which Kapuściński was later connected. He was also distanced from *Polityka* by his political and social connections at the top levels of power. Kapuściński's Party patrons, above all Frelek, spent the whole of the 1960s waging interclique battles against Rakowski and his weekly.

Agnieszka Wróblewska, a journalist from the *Polityka* circle, points out that regardless of political motives Kapuściński did not fit comfortably with 'Rakowski's gang'. Among its members, scepticism and a sense of irony had always prevailed, whereas Kapuściński was the enthusiastic type, an idealist, a zealot. He might not have felt at his best among sceptics and scoffers.

Another element that may have played a role was that he was an individualist, while *Polityka* was a team enterprise.

After the fall of real socialism, *Polityka* bore the stigma of the *ancien régime*. At that point, Kapuściński preferred to be associated with the new era, the democratic movement in favour of change, and he decided that *Gazeta Wyborcza* was the right place for him. He often dropped in at the *Polityka* office for gossip and for visits with old friends, but despite several colleagues' strenuous efforts to try and persuade him otherwise, he never wrote another article for *Polityka*.

16

Life in Africa

This used to be a four-storey clapboard building with a large roof terrace, a bar counter, and a few small tables. The terrace is still there but is now even bigger, with windows added – and it has moved up a few floors. Now it offers a dazzling view of the bay and the Indian Ocean.

This is the Hotel New Africa, right in the centre of Dar es Salaam. Nowadays its main attraction is the view and a locally popular casino. In 1962, when Kapuściński drops in there in the evenings, the attractions are different: the terrace is a meeting place for the African freedom fighters who are here taking advantage of the hospitality of Julius Nyerere, president of Tanganyika, the first independent state in East Africa. This is the place where – as Kapuściński wrote years later – Africa does its plotting. He sits down at the tables where Mugabe from (then) Rhodesia, Mondlane from Mozambique and Karume from Zanzibar are conspiring. He buys them cheap beer and listens. He absorbs the news and the atmosphere.

Africa is on the boil. The colonial system is crumbling, and state after state is declaring independence; Kapuściński witnesses the start of this process in Ghana. In some countries there is armed combat underway. He has met it head-on in Congo; he has seen the chaos, anarchy, divisions and victims.

Into these liberation wars and conflicts, another war is forcing its way – the Cold one being waged by the countries of the Northern hemisphere. On the southern continents, in Africa, Asia and Latin America, Washington and Moscow are setting up training grounds for themselves, competing for influence and raw materials, testing their deadly weapons. In the South, the Cold War has a high temperature.

The socialist countries, including Poland, support the anti-colonial movements. The Polish government opens a diplomatic post in Dar es Salaam, with a staff of three. Tanganyika is the right place: it has declared independence, it is hosting freedom fighters from all over the continent and acts as an informal centre for the conspirators, and its leader, Julius Nyerere, calls himself the first African socialist. It is a superb observation point from which to view the process of decolonization. The socialist camp wants to pave the way for good relations with the continent as it awakens to political life. It is a potential ally in the battle against the capitalist West and a source of valuable raw materials.

Clearly there is a need for news from the region, and so the Central Committee Press Office takes the decision to open a PAP bureau in Dar es Salaam. The task is assigned to a reporter who has proved he has a feeling for Africa, as well as the credentials of a comrade who is devoted to the cause of socialism.

'Oh, they've sent us a Yid,' comments the chargé d'affaires waiting for him at the airport as soon as he sees Kapuściński descending from the plane. Attaché Jerzy Nowak is struck dumb by this remark ('It was meant as an allusion to Rysiek's dark complexion,' he explains).

Kapuściński first heads for the embassy, located in the Indian district of Upanga. For a short time he rents a small flat not far from the diplomatic post, then settles for a longer period in a white-painted multi-family house amid coconut palms and large banana trees, with a view of the ocean. He has a flat upstairs with two rooms, a kitchen and a bathroom. In one room there is a bed with a mosquito net spread above it like a bridal veil; in the other there is a table and some chairs, nothing else.

Upanga is occupied by Indians, predominantly from the Ishmaelite sect; whites are rarely encountered here. Next to Upanga is the luxury district of Oyster Bay:

> magnificent villas, gardens exploding with flowers, thick lawns, smooth, gravel-strewn avenues. Yes, you can live truly luxuriously here, especially since you don't have to do anything yourself; everything is taken care of by quiet, vigilant, discreetly moving servants. Here, a man ambles along as he probably would do in paradise: slowly, loosely, content that he is here, enchanted by the beauty of the world.[1]

Naturally, this is the kingdom of the whites.

Kapuściński finds himself in a cage of apartheid, a golden cage that makes contact with the locals difficult. For them he is just a white man, just like the British who are packing up to leave Tanganyika. He belongs to the race of oppressors – so what if he comes from a country that has nothing to do with the wrongs done to the Africans. He notices the perversity of apartheid: a black cannot enter a white district (except for the servants), but by the same token a white cannot feel safe in the African districts.

There is no one to talk to, at least not at the beginning. He makes his way to the local newspaper, the *Tanganyika Standard* – nothing but whites, from

Oyster Bay. They are sitting on suitcases and don't give a damn about anything.

Every day Kapuściński drops in on Jerzy and Izabella Nowak at their home within the embassy grounds; he becomes part of the household, and they make friends for life. He sets the style in which they will spend time together. He buys a Land Rover, thanks to which they do a lot of touring, and later a second car, a Morris Mini, which he will sell to his new friends at the end of his mission in Dar. Together they discover evidence of the German empire: solid oak furniture at the town hall, and post boxes. They also follow the trail of the Polish writer Henryk Sienkiewicz and visit the former slave market at Bagamoyo, once the German capital of East Africa, famous for its attractive beaches.

Kapuściński enjoys going to the African markets and tries to take photographs, but he finds that the Africans shout at him angrily. First he's amazed, then realizes you have to ask permission if you want to take a photo. He is learning the ABC of travel.

Wanting to get close to the Africans, he complains to Nowak in a friendly way that the Polish diplomats shut themselves within the circle of the other whites. 'Do you ever go and see Tanganyikans?' he inquires. Nowak explains that it isn't easy, and that the Africans never invite them to their homes. Once he and his wife did manage to get invited to a local home, and they went, but their African hosts felt ashamed of their poverty – and whenever the Poles invited Africans to their home, the guests never turned up.

During a trip outside town, Kapuściński and Nowak meet some Germans and Africans at a hostel. Kapuściński admits that there is nothing to talk to the Africans about, and that getting close to them seems almost impossible. However, he doesn't hide his antipathy towards the whites in Africa. In a report from Ghana he describes one of them:

> I look at that fat little man, at his sweaty face and his hangdog expression. What could I tell him? I think to myself: he's a petty capitalist, not a financial shark, another little man in the ranks of the army of little shopkeepers.[2]

Nowak explains that the whites they meet in Tanganyika 'are ghastly, even in terms of facial appearance', whatever the nationality: Germans, Britons, Belgians, Poles . . . Abominable types, losers who flocked to Africa because things hadn't worked out for them anywhere else; upstarts, exploiters of the local population, and, without exception, racists. They run bars and hotels – they are 'petty businessmen'. One of the people they encounter goes about with a monkey, because 'he'd rather drink with a chimp than a black'. These are the typical remnants of the colonial class whom

Kapuściński encounters in Africa: the face of Europe, which came to Africa 'to spread civilization among the savages'.

Many years later, as Poland's ambassador to NATO in Brussels, Nowak will take his friend to Belgium's African museum, where, in the 1920s, Africans were still being brought to live in a summer village built in the museum's courtyard. You could look at them in their huts, above which was a sign: 'Please don't feed them, we feed them very well'. Forty years later, in *The Shadow of the Sun*, the summary of his African experiences, Kapuściński will write:

> The philosophy that inspired the construction of Kolyma and Auschwitz, one of obsessive contempt and hatred, vileness and brutality, was formulated and set down centuries earlier by the captains of the *Martha* and the *Progresso*, the *Mary Ann* and the *Rainbow*, as they sat in their cabins gazing out the portholes at groves of palm trees and sun-warmed beaches, waiting aboard their ships anchored off the islands of Sherbro, [Kwale] or Zanzibar, for the next batch of black slaves to be loaded.[3]

The two men learn French together, attending a course at the French cultural centre three times a week. There they flirt with Ishmaelite women of heavenly beauty. Kapuściński also studies Swahili and reaches a level that will allow him to have a simple conversation and to figure out what the local papers are writing about.

They take long walks and go to the beach at Oyster Bay or further – an hour and a half by car, along a bumpy road – to Bagamoyo. During one of their walks by the sea, Kapuściński says to Nowak: 'I know we're always going to be friends.'

'Our relationship was always more sisterly than brotherly,' says Nowak, laughing, 'by which I mean to say that we confided in each other about everything, like sisters. It was like that right to the end.'

They have similar sensitivity and similar fortunes. Both are from the Borderlands. Both are modest in their social relationships, and they do not overwhelm each other. Each is making his way in a different sphere professionally, so there are no grounds for competition, and this provides a sense of security and helps create the loyalty of true friends. Neither has a brother, and both always longed for one; they have an idealistic notion of fulfilling that dream.

During one conversation by the sea, Kapuściński encourages Nowak in his plan to join the Party. Although far from home, they are still living within the framework of the recent revolt of October 1956. Kapuściński believes it is possible to reconcile Polish interests with participation in the socialist camp. Despite Gomułka's mistakes, one should not withdraw into a private niche; there is a need to attract honest, idealistic people into the

Party and to change socialism for the better from the inside. The condition for active involvement in socialism should be to do no one any harm. Despite violent objections from his wife, resulting in an actual domestic row, Nowak does decide to join the Party. Kapuściński writes his friend a letter of recommendation.

'As soon as they started praising socialism, I would immediately counter-attack,' Izabella Nowak tells me with some pride. In her traditionally anti-communist family home – her father had fought in the war of 1920 against the Bolsheviks – they trusted Radio Free Europe, not the Party organ, *Trybuna Ludu* (The People's Tribune). 'You're a total reactionary, Izunia!' Kapuściński used to thunder as a joke, but sometimes entirely seriously.

According to her, 'He was dreadfully upset by my remarks, even more since it was a woman uttering them. In time he began to tolerate me, got used to me and grew fond of me. But he never treated any woman as an equal partner in conversation.'

In photos from the beach in Dar (or is it Bagamoyo?), Kapuściński looks slim, fit and athletic. In his flat he has a bar for pull-ups and takes daily exercise despite the heat. He likes showing off his physical fitness. He sunbathes on the beach and goads Mrs Nowak, daring her: 'Izunia, stand on my stomach, see how rock-hard it is, I won't even shudder.'

'He was always the macho type,' she tells me, 'but of a very specific kind: he had warmth, sensitivity and even fragility in him.'

A long, fat caterpillar with a black exoskeleton and red legs crawls onto him as he's lying in bed. The victim must not move, lest the horrid creature stick its legs into his body. He moves! Though the creature isn't poisonous, it leaves a burn on his hand that itches for several weeks.

Life in Africa involves constant vigilance to make sure nothing bites or stings you, including poisonous scorpions, invisible amoebae in the water and food, and giant cockroaches, which are certainly disgusting but at least not dangerous. Above all, there are the omnipresent mosquitoes, carriers of malaria, and the tsetse flies.

> [T]hese small but insistent aggressors establish each evening a battle plan meant to exhaust their victims, because if there are ten of them, say, they do not attack all together – which would allow you to deal with them all at once and have peace for the rest of the night – but one by one. The first to take off is, as it were, the scout, whose reconnaissance mission the rest closely observe. Well rested after a good day's sleep, he torments you with his demonic buzzing, until finally, sleepy and furious, you organize a hunt, kill him; you are just lying down again, confident of returning to sleep, just turning off the light, when the next one begins his loops, spirals, and corkscrews.[4]

Africa is an adventure, and not just on the war front.

One day Kapuściński and Nowak go together to sort something out at an office. In the waiting-room they sit on some solid old benches. Shortly afterwards, red spots appear on their bodies. Soon the spots change into sores. The doctor confirms that insects nesting in the benches have laid their eggs under the men's skin; now the victims will nurture the larvae until maggots emerge from them.

Kapuściński accepts this kind of inconvenience. He explains it to himself thus: 'This is the only way I will get to know the life of the people I'm writing about.' He wants to live like them; he lets himself be bitten by the same insects, falls ill with the same diseases, eats the same food. He is not disgusted when he finds grilled locusts on his plate – fat, whitish abdomens that have been only lightly toasted. Nowak finds this disgusting, but Kapuściński all but leaps on his food. He's in Africa, so he will eat what Africa eats.

In dangerous or uncertain situations he does not panic. Once when they are driving to Lake Nyasa in Kapuściński's Mini, they are attacked by a group of aggressive monkeys, which besiege the car. It's enough to cause hysterics – they haven't any water left, it's baking hot in the car, yet they can't open the windows. Kapuściński keeps his sang-froid – they'll be off eventually. Slowly they drive out of the danger zone and the monkeys give up. Another time, the Mini breaks down far from town. Kapuściński knows how to fix anything; he is manly in the extreme – he talks about engine construction, boasts of his knowledge of car technology, and loves rally-driver's goggles and gloves.

He also seeks adventure at sea. They sail a small boat to a nearby island, catch fish and light a bonfire. Kapuściński pitches the tents, and they go to bed early. He can get to sleep in any circumstances and makes a point of saying that, unlike most intellectuals, he isn't a night owl – he goes to bed early and gets up early. Suddenly some small, twinkling lights appear around the bonfire: it's a pack of rats. Nowak wakes up his friend and they keep the bonfire going all night, staying awake until dawn.

Intent on studying Africa, Kapuściński explores beyond Tanganyika. He goes to Kampala for the Ugandan declaration of independence celebrations; he visits Nairobi, which is still under British rule; and he witnesses the inception of the Organization of African Unity (OAU) in Addis Ababa.

In Addis he sees the great leaders of Africa as its new countries are being born: Ben Bella from Algeria; Gamal Abdel Nasser, then leader of the United Arab Republic; Ugandan premier Milton Obote; Sékou Touré from Guinea; the Ethiopian Emperor Haile Selassie and his old 'friend' from Ghana, Kwame Nkrumah. The latter is calling for the creation of a political union of African states. Obote offers Ugandan territory as a training ground for guerrillas from countries that have not yet gained independence: Angola, Mozambique, South Africa, Southern Rhodesia, and so on.

The fact that the British still rule Kenya is plain to see from the newspapers. Liberation from the colonial powers is just around the corner, and yet on the front page of the *East African Standard*, published in Nairobi, are announcements that the Duke of Gloucester is sick with the flu and that a tea party is being held at Buckingham Palace in honour of Prince Andrew's third birthday. The only newspaper in this part of the continent to be edited by Africans is the *Nakawi News*, issued in Nyasaland (Malawi). Kapuściński studies it from the first page to the last; he sends press reviews to Warsaw that are based on it.

From Malawi: The government issues a directive that all drivers must stop at once whenever Prime Minister Hastings Banda drives past ('a rigid anti-communist,' writes Kapuściński, 'a rich man who maintains his party on his own money'), and 'those who do not carry out the order will incite the rage of the Malawian nation and will be severely punished.'

From Southern Rhodesia: Gangs of young nationalists are hunting down girls who straighten their hair for fashion. The punishment is to be shaved bald: straightening your hair is symbolic of renouncing your race.

From Kampala: A member of the Ugandan parliament is appealing to the Ministry of Health to issue a ban on dancing the twist, because this dance is bad for one's health. The speaker of parliament, owner of three nightclubs, protests: 'This is an attempt to push the government onto a dangerous path of state interference in popular pleasures!'

In November 1962, for the first time, Kapuściński sends in some fifteen in-depth reports for the PAP's Special Bulletin. The articles published there are not just short pieces saying that a particular committee held a session, what a particular leader said, or what a government announced; rather, they are full, sometimes detailed professional analyses, with elements of reportage as well as personal impressions.

The bulletin has a limited audience. At first it is issued only to the highest of the top Party functionaries; in time it also goes to Central Committee members, people from the ministries and other government departments, and newspaper, radio and television editors. As the years go by, the bulletin achieves ever wider distribution, including university libraries, academics and self-governing institutions (the number of copies printed approaches five thousand). Some articles in the bulletin are labelled 'not for publication in the press': they contain information, analyses or opinions that would be undesirable from the viewpoint of state propaganda. Usually these pieces are reprints from the western press that are critical of Moscow and the socialist camp. The bulletin is not censored;

the only censorship is in the mind of the author or the editor responsible for issuing it.

The policy of the agency bosses varies at different periods of the PRL's existence. For example, in the 1970s the agency's editor-in-chief, Janusz Roszkowski, reprimands servile correspondents who 'follow the line' of the Soviet agency, TASS. 'You've got to describe what you see, and not guess how it "ought" to be written; judge it as you feel it to be,' he demands of the journalists. At the editorial office they can of course change the meaning of an article for propaganda purposes, but the chief insists on sincerity from his journalists.

Almost 100 percent of Kapuściński's articles from Africa – and later those from Latin America – contain no news items or analyses that can be considered 'unsuitable' from the socialist perspective. Sometimes they end up in the Special Bulletin merely so that some record of them should remain, or because they do not fit in the agency's daily foreign bulletin. More interestingly, those that provide a broader picture or describe an event of topical importance are reprinted by *Polityka*, and sometimes by other periodicals and dailies, such as *Życie Warszawy* (Warsaw Life) and the Central Committee organ, *Trybuna Ludu*.

Kapuściński is interested in anti-colonial liberation movements, the political awakening of Africa, the United States' struggles to gain influence and access to raw materials on the continent, and also the encroachment of China, which is competing with the Soviet Union for patronage over the anti-colonial revolutionary movements and for natural resources.

To submit his reports, Kapuściński drives to the post office in the city centre. He transmits them to Warsaw by telex via London. When he sends his dispatches by telegram, he combines the shorter words meaning 'of', 'for', 'by' and so on with longer ones to make it come out cheaper. Money is a nightmare for a reporter from a poor country, and the same goes for his agency; Kapuściński earns about $300 a month, and although in the PRL that is a fortune, for a roving reporter in Africa it is peanuts.

'The work of an Africa correspondent is a hard slog.' Like Kapuściński, Wiesława Bolimowska worked on Africa for the PAP, alternately as an editor and as a correspondent. She frequently received and edited dispatches from her friend and, to some extent, rival. 'What an exhausting climate, it gave you the tropical blues,' she remembers. 'And there was constant frustration, because you could make appointments with the Africans, but they wouldn't turn up at the meetings, for no obvious reason.'

Rysiek, she says, did not always perform well as a correspondent. He wrote slowly, was capable of spending all day grinding out a single page, and composed several versions of a single sentence. Working for an agency, however, necessitates the 'mass production' of dispatches. The bosses continually reminded him that he was writing too little.

But that happens later on. At the beginning of his work as a correspondent, Kapuściński floods the PAP bulletins with dispatches, analyses and
thoughts. He soaks up the new and still unfamiliar world. He identifies
with the inhabitants of Africa and their aspirations, walks in their shoes, and
looks through their eyes. He fixates on his new political idols.

17

Objects of Fascination: The African Icons

'In those days Rysiek had various radical objects of fascination,' Nowak tells me. 'Number One was Frantz Fanon. Do you know who he was?'

Fanon wrote the 'bible' of the anti-colonial movements of that era. Born on the French island of Martinique in the Caribbean, he was an Afro-Frenchman who fought in the Second World War and was decorated for bravery. By profession he was a psychiatrist. In protest against the brutality of the French in Algeria, where he was head of a hospital psychiatric ward, he resigned from his job. He joined the Algerian anti-colonial guerrilla movement, the FLN. He died prematurely of leukaemia, but in the last year of his life, 1961, he wrote a book that guaranteed him posthumous fame – *The Wretched of the Earth*.

With Nowak's help, Kapuściński laboriously wades through the original text – they both have rather a poor grasp of French, but the book has not been translated into English yet.

Fanon administers crushing criticism not just to the crimes of the Europeans in the lands they conquered, but also to the governments of allegedly – as he claims – liberated countries. He persuades us that the liberation process being witnessed in Africa is 'false decolonization', which leaves power in the hands of the imperialists and their local puppets. And so he urges the overthrow of these people by way of armed combat; he argues that revolutionary violence is a purgative and liberating force.

> But it so happens that for the colonized this violence is invested with positive, formative features because it constitutes their only work. This violent praxis is totalizing since each individual represents a violent link in the great chain, in the almighty body of violence rearing up in reaction to the primary violence of the colonizer. Factions recognize each other and the future nation is already indivisible. The armed struggle mobilizes the people, i.e. it pitches them in a single direction, from which there is no turning back . . .

At the individual level, violence is a cleansing force. It rids the colonized of their inferiority complex, of their passive and despairing attitude. It emboldens them, and restores their self-confidence . . . When
they have used violence to achieve national liberation, the masses allow
nobody to come forward as 'liberators' . . . Enlightened by violence, the
people's consciousness rebels against any pacification.[1]

Fanon believes in the approaching onset of revolution in Africa. Its chief
motors are to be the lumpenproletariat and the peasantry, because the urban
workers are corrupted by the system and represent an aristocracy within the
poorest social groups. By contrast, the 'formation of the lumpenproletariat
is a phenomenon which is governed by its own logic . . . However hard it
is kicked or stoned it continues to gnaw at the roots of the tree like a pack
of rats.'[2]

Jomo Kenyatta, the leader of liberated Kenya, and one of Kapuściński's
objects of fascination, will soon change into a disappointment.

One morning Kapuściński is woken by the Czechoslovak correspondent
Zdeněk Kubeš.

'Have you seen it?'

'Seen what?'

'Your article, of course!'

Some time earlier, Kapuściński wrote a report about corruption within
Kenyan government circles. He asks the PAP to reserve this material for the
Special Bulletin, not publish it in the press. After moving from Dar es
Salaam, Kapuściński is living in Nairobi, and he has to be careful about
exposing the abuses committed by the rulers of his host country. The PAP
editorial office either does not notice or disregards his proviso; in any case,
Polityka reprints the piece, and then the Kenyan English-language daily
Standard copies it from the Polish weekly.

In the article, titled 'The Ruling Élite', Kapuściński writes:

Over a nine-month period in 1963, Kenya's Prime Minister Kenyatta
acquired three of the most expensive limousines in the world (a Lincoln
Continental, a Mercedes 300 SE and a Rolls Royce – the price of these
cars totals $55,000). Uganda's Prime Minister Obote held a wedding
party in October 1963 for 28,000 people at a cost of $60,000, taken from
the state budget. When asked didn't he think the party was too costly for
Uganda, Obote replied: 'The weddings of the British royal family are no
cheaper. The Ugandan people must bear the costs of maintaining the
high standing of its leaders, who were heroes in the fight' . . .

Today's degeneration of the African élite is a consequence of the fact
that the battle for independence was fought in isolation from social issues,

and that the specific slogan was liberty, but not equality. This was chiefly the result of the political immaturity of the masses, but it also arose from the actual style of fighting for independence, a style imposed by the colonialist, but adopted by many of the groups leading the independence movement, a style that relies on bargaining, compromise, negotiation, constitutional amendments, and guarantees plotted behind the scenes without reference to the masses.[3]

The Kenyan newspaper supplements Kapuściński's text with a commentary in more or less the following tone: 'Look what the communists write about us, while pretending to be Africa's friends.'

Kapuściński is convinced he will soon be deported. He goes to the airlines office to book a return ticket to Poland. Meanwhile, Kenyatta's government is debating the scandal.

'A British man told me afterwards,' recalls Bolimowska, 'that Odinga [vice president at the time, and leader of the left wing of the ruling camp] asked the assembled cabinet members: "Has this Polish journalist written anything that isn't true?" A murmur goes round the room . . . After a pause someone stands up and says: "Unfortunately, it is the truth." Odinga: "So why should we arrest him?" '

Odinga's intervention definitely saves Kapuściński. He is not expelled from Kenya, although three months later he leaves of his own accord. After a short convalescence in Poland, he transfers the PAP post to Nigeria. Soon all journalists from the socialist camp will be thrown out of Kenya; Kapuściński is banned from entering the country for many years.

His fascination with Patrice Lumumba, leader of the fight against Belgian colonialism, comes earlier. Before going to Africa as a permanent correspondent, Kapuściński travels to Congo, arriving just as news of Lumumba's murder is doing the rounds. He succumbs to the cult of Lumumba after the killing, but the portrait he paints of a charismatic leader is essentially realistic:

> Patrice is the son of his people. He will be naive and mystical at times; he will also have a tendency to jump quickly from one extreme to the other, from bursts of happiness to silent despair. Lumumba is a fascinating figure, because he is inexpressibly complicated. Nothing about this man yields to definition. Every formula is too narrow. He is a restless, chaotic zealot, a sentimental poet, an ambitious politician, an impetuous soul, amazingly proud and meek all at once, confident of his truth to the very last, deaf to the words of others, engrossed in his own, wonderful voice.[4]

Nkrumah is not merely an object of fascination; he is virtually a guru, a saviour. A few years earlier, during his first trip to Africa, Kapuściński sees him at a rally in Accra.

With undisguised sympathy, or downright excitement, he writes:

> The fact that we have Kwame is a blessing for Ghana, as it was a blessing for America to have Lincoln, for Russia to have Lenin, and for England to have Nelson . . . He is the Messiah and the organizer, the friend of suffering humanity, who has achieved his eminence by following the path of pain, service and devotion.[5]

Nkrumah's big idea is a large union of African states. He sees himself in the role of leader.

He rejects two of life's temptations and the one force that can overpower him, blind him: women, money and religion. These things might cause him to lose sight of the goal: Ghana's liberation. 'Kwame set himself this goal when he was still a boy,' Kapuściński writes, both enthusiastically and naively. 'Nkrumah is turgid, intent, with the manner retained from his days preaching in the American black churches.'[6]

Kapuściński will have a great deal of trouble when, in 1966, troops supported by the CIA overthrow Nkrumah and it comes to light that Africa's Messiah had given asylum to war criminal Horst Schumann, a doctor from Auschwitz. Schumann, as Kapuściński writes in a report for the Special Bulletin, 'used prisoners as guinea pigs for his experiments'. (During the putsch Nkrumah was on a visit to China. He will never return to his country; he will spend the rest of his life in exile in Guinea, and will die during medical treatment in Romania.)

'If I had to compare him with anyone, then maybe only with Mahatma Gandhi. He was the most genuine idealist. Ever smiling and friendly' – years later, this is how Kapuściński remembers the saint of African socialism, Julius Nyerere, president of Tanganyika (later Tanzania).

Nyerere establishes a one-party system (there is virtually no opposition anyway). He creates political life, which has never existed here before now. His people call him Mwalimu – the Teacher. The Teacher believes that on African land, opposition arises from tribal battles or thoughtless imitation of European models. From the viewpoint of Western democratic thinking these are heresies, but thanks to Nyerere's policies Tanzania is unique in the region in its freedom from tribal divisions and conflict.

The economy, which centres on rural communes (*ujamaa*), is a disaster. On borrowed money Nyerere builds school and hospitals, but the system as a whole is inefficient; people escape from village poverty to the cities. Among the ruling élite, corruption and nepotism are rife, but Nyerere himself is not corrupt – he 'does not help' his family. In the mid 1980s, when Tanzania goes bankrupt, to the amazement of his compatriots and world opinion Nyerere voluntarily resigns. He announces that he has let the country down, and he leaves: an unprecedented occurrence in the history of modern politics. He is a true saint.

18

Life in Africa, *Continued*

In Warsaw, Alicja receives a call from the Nowaks: 'Rysiek is seriously ill. He has contracted malaria, and what's more, it's the nastiest kind – cerebral malaria.'

At this point in time Alicja is on an internship at the Infectious Diseases Clinic. She turns to a tropical diseases specialist, who is horrified. 'Has there been any improvement in his condition?' the specialist asks calmly, not wanting to upset her colleague. Cerebral malaria can lead to fatal complications.

For months Alicja has been learning to live without her husband – that is, her husband is somewhere out there, but far away, sometimes in an unknown place. At home she just about manages to make ends meet. When Kapuściński is in Poland, they borrow money; when he leaves, he lives on his daily allowance, and Alicja uses his salary to pay off their debts. They will live like this for years on end. Before one Christmas holiday, Alicja sells waste paper, because there is no money for Christmas tree decorations, and Zojka must have a decorated tree.

Shortly after the news about the malaria, Maria Rutkiewicz calls from *Polityka* (in private life, she is the partner of Artur Starewicz). She asks Alicja if they might meet, and invites her to the weekly's office.

'We're wondering if you could go and join your husband to take care of him. There's something wrong with his lungs.'

'It's not tuberculosis, is it?'

Rutkiewicz reveals what she knows: they have had news that Rysiek is spitting blood and is completely worn out.

Alicja makes an instant decision: 'I'm going.' She gets a passport and unpaid leave from the hospital. Her husband's cousin will house-sit. She sends Zojka, who is now ten years old, to stay with her mother in Szczecin. For the next year, their daughter goes to school in Szczecin.

Teresa Torańska and I ask:

How did she cope with the year without both parents?
She wasn't thrilled. Many times afterwards she said: 'You went alone, you didn't take me.'

And how did you explain it to her?

I said that no one would have sent me with her in tow, and that I was going to join her sick father, who had tuberculosis in the tropics . . . I wasn't going there on holiday.

The most important thing for him were his trips abroad. And then what?

Working on his books.

And after that? A long, long gap and then . . . ?

I fitted in there somewhere. I think I had my permanent place. So at least it seems to me.

Didn't you bear any grudges?

It's not as if he travelled for tourism, for pleasure. Just for work. And I knew I had to respect his work. I was always absolutely sure this work was the only kind he wanted or had an ambition to perform. I never told him 'maybe you'd better not go', or 'I'd prefer you to stay', or simply 'don't go'.

Did you want to say it?

Perhaps I did. But I understood that every trip – however safe or unsafe – was the fulfilment of his dreams. And the only way in which he would want to fulfil himself. So what was I to say in that situation? You tell me.

Sometimes he was away for half a year at a time, sometimes several months. I used to go to the PAP to ask them to show me what dispatches he had sent. I'd look to see where they were from, thanks to which I knew more or less where he was and what was happening to him. Communication with him was always a nightmare.

He would say: 'I'll be back in six weeks.' And all of a sudden it would turn out something was happening in Mozambique. Or in Congo, or Zanzibar. He'd apply to the PAP for consent, get it and go.[1]

The first illness, malaria, troubles Kapuściński in Kampala. Accompanied by a man called Leonid (probably a correspondent for TASS), he drives his Land Rover from Dar es Salaam to Kampala. The reason for this trip is to attend celebrations for the declaration of independence in Uganda. On the way there, Kapuściński breaks his own life record for driving a car – from six in the morning to eleven at night, 750 kilometres on African roads.

In Kampala, like most of the journalists, he stays at the barracks attached to an old hospital on the edge of the city. There he suddenly loses consciousness.

Unconscious for an unknown length of time, he is found by his travelling companion. There is no way to call for help; the entire city is dancing and singing, because independence has just been declared. All night Leonid nurses Kapuściński, who is delirious. Finally Leonid drives to a hospital and fetches an ambulance. They take Kapuściński away in nothing but his underpants, wrapped in a blanket, with a temperature of 40.6 degrees C (105 degrees F). He ends up in the newly opened Mulago Hospital – a present for the Ugandan people from the British queen, Elizabeth. As Ugandan conditions go, this is luxury.

He opens his eyes and sees a large white screen (it is the ceiling painted white); against the screen he sees an African girl's face. Soon afterwards, he hears a male voice saying, 'Thank God you're alive.'

Worn out by fever, now and then he loses consciousness. The diagnosis is cerebral malaria. From hospital he writes to the Nowaks:

> Today this is heaven, but two days ago I thought I was going to croak.
>
> What rotten luck. I'm surrounded by a colourful city full of light and noise, but I'm lying under six heavy blankets, sweating and wailing with cold. Today I asked my doctor if I'm going to be a loony, and he replied: 'We can't be sure yet.' So there is some hope! Outside I can hear the roar of the stadium, because there's a Ghana [he probably means Uganda] v. London boxing match. I guess whenever the Englishman hits the floor the stadium roars. This is the only evidence of anti-colonialism I've found in Uganda.
>
> The difference between Kampala and Dar is like the one between Paris and Kielce. Kampala = Paris, Dar = Kielce . . . Uganda is a beautiful country, but it's boring . . . I don't think I can last another week here . . . I'm being thrown about the bed again, so I'll end now. I send you my heart [here there is a drawing of a heart with the caption 'my heart'] and best regards, Rysiek[2]

The doctor decrees he must stay in hospital at least a month. 'I thought I'd go mad when I heard that,' says Kapuściński. He is alone, 'hellishly, hellishly lonely', he doesn't know anyone and has no one to talk to; Leonid drops in and brings apples, but quickly disappears. He has nothing to read, and in any case he cannot: he is suffering from fever, hallucinations, drowsiness, and exhaustion.

He can only drink water, and is not eating at all – he cannot, everything comes back up. He starts to dream of broth, chicken and tomatoes. He asks the doctor to feed him glucose intravenously – he is incapable of eating the hospital delicacies and he hasn't any money to send someone to buy better food in the city. He weighs 54.5 kilos (120 lbs); in a letter to Nowak he draws his arm and adds a note to the drawing saying: 'circumference at the fattest point = 1.75 cm'.

On another day he writes again, although writing tires him:

> Something inside me has cracked in the last few days. I'm suffocating, I feel like howling . . . Now I'm like that reed in the gale – thin, fragile and at the mercy of every gust of wind.[3]

In the next letter he is agitated and depressed because he hasn't had news from his friends in Dar:

> My dears! This is my third letter, but no one has written a word to me . . . The sad side of all this is that I'll come out of this hospital a ruined man – with a sick head, a sick liver, a sick stomach, totally worn out and so on. But I won't give in, and maybe everything will be OK.[4]

The PAP and the Ministry of Foreign Affairs co-operate to see that someone from the embassy in Dar flies to Kampala to fetch Kapuściński. It is Izabella Nowak who goes – and when she gets there, she does not recognize her friend, who has become just skin and bones. She removes him from the hospital, and they return together to Dar.

Once Kapuściński is on the mend, during a drunken evening at home ('he had rather a weak head', says Nowak), he announces: 'I had a dream there was a big event in my honour. I made a speech and finished by saying, "Let Iza come up on stage – she's the one who saved my life". Iza came on, and there were resounding cheers.'

After returning to Dar he has no strength for anything, so he leads a quiet life, lying down to rest for whole days on end. One night he finds blood on his pillow. In spite of this, he refuses to go to the doctor. To drag him off for tests, his friends resort to trickery: he must take Iza to hospital, because she is in the early stages of pregnancy and Jerzy is busy at the embassy all day. At the hospital she manages to persuade him to have an X-ray. There are holes in his lungs – it is acute-stage tuberculosis! He is not allowed to travel anywhere by plane or ship.

While being treated he moves closer to the embassy, where the Nowaks live. He lives separately but eats his meals at their house. To avoid infecting anyone, he is given his own wash-basin for cleaning his plates and cutlery. Rysiek knows he should leave Africa and return to Poland. However, he is afraid that if he tells the PAP about the tuberculosis they won't send him here anymore. If you catch diseases in the tropics, they'll say, you're obviously not suited to the climate.

So he stays put. He has fallen in love with Africa – this isn't a job, it's a passion, a truly incurable disease.

He can choose be treated in a hospital for white people, for which the agency would have to pay, or for free in a clinic for Africans. He goes to the clinic for locals. (Afterwards, he will describe how the syringes are boiled in the same pot as the eggs.) He does not want to worry his loved ones; in a letter to his mother, he lies and says he's doing well. He tells her how tanned, strong and healthy he is. He arranges for his mother to receive medicines that are hard to get in Poland, and he sends her money. He asks her not to put the money aside but to buy herself something she's always dreamed of having – let it be a present from him.

Finally, Alicja comes to the rescue. She arrives in Dar, and once Kapuściński begins to recover from his illnesses, they move to Nairobi.

First impressions:

> This place is a dreadful shambles – the British don't give a damn about anything, the Africans haven't yet taken anything on, in short there's an organizational interregnum, so whatever you want to arrange takes three days to-ing and fro-ing . . .
>
> [T]he city is really lovely, enchanting, and it's a dream climate, the Riviera twenty-four hours a day . . .
>
> [I]f anything can be done in this part of Africa, all hopes are pinned on Kenya; it looks as if the Cold War will get here, in fact it already has . . . yet it's a much higher calibre than Dar, at any rate the dynamics here are incomparably greater . . .[5]

Shortly after his arrival in Kenya comes news of the assassination of US president John F. Kennedy. From Kapuściński's dispatch:

> Kennedy's death has stirred deep emotion in Nairobi. The flags are at half mast. The civic committee of the ruling KANU party stresses in its telegram to the US consul in Nairobi that those behind Kennedy's assassination are 'racist and fascist groupings in the southern states of the USA'. Within political circles in both Nairobi and in Dar es Salaam the belief is held that Kennedy's assassination was organized by racists. Here a general fear is being expressed that in the USA racist elements will come to prominence, which will have an effect, among other things, on reducing US aid for Africa, and will make it harder for African countries to operate on UN terrain.[6]

The most exciting event he covers in those months – not counting the scandal prompted by his article about corruption in Kenya and other newly liberated African countries – is the revolt in Zanzibar. In a report published by *Trybuna Ludu*, Kapuściński writes:

> I was the first journalist from the socialist countries to reach Zanzibar five days after the outbreak of the armed revolution, which overthrew the neocolonial government of the Arab bourgeoisie and put the revolutionary government of Sheikh Abeid Karume into power. I gained permission to come here on Wednesday, during a conversation I held by telephone from Dar es Salaam with the president of the new republic, Sheikh

Abeid Karume, and the Minister for Foreign Affairs and Defence, Abdel Rahman Babu. On Thursday I landed in a small tourist plane at Zanzibar's airport, which since the outbreak of the revolution has only been open for planes that have permission to land issued by the HQ of the revolution's field marshal.[7]

When Kapuściński lands on the island, armed patrols of the revolutionary army are touring the narrow little streets of labyrinthine Stone Town. The city resembles a military camp. The shops are closed, and armed civilian rebels are walking about the streets. The units most dedicated to the revolutionary cause are guarding the jail, where members of the deposed government are imprisoned. They are also standing around the headquarters of 'Field Marshal' John Okello. There, the marshal's deputy personally writes out a pass for Kapuściński, allowing him to move about the island.

He goes to the post office to send his correspondence. The post office is especially well-guarded: outside the building are armed men and women, soldiers of the revolution. Each dispatch is read by two men with guns on their chests – they are the censors. Kapuściński goes back to his hotel under revolutionary escort. That evening the streets are empty, martial law is declared, and also a curfew. He sees troops surrounding the American consul's car; President Karume himself and his minister Abdel Rahman Babu take part in the arrest. 'The Republic's intelligence,' reports Kapuściński, 'has uncovered evidence of a counter-revolutionary plot organized by the American embassy. The President announced that on Friday all American journalists will be deported from Zanzibar. At present they are under arrest at a hotel, along with other Western journalists.'

The main controversy of those days is the alleged participation of Cubans in the Zanzibar revolt. Kapuściński denies it:

> The Western press has been trying to sow rumours that Cuban officers led the revolution, and even that you can hear military personnel speaking Spanish in Zanzibar's capital today. This is made-up nonsense – there is not a single Cuban or Algerian in Zanzibar. 'At this point our main task is to establish complete order, to avoid giving the imperialists an excuse for armed intervention,' a member of the Field Marshal's staff told me.[8]

Indeed, during the spontaneous, lumpenproletariat revolt, there are no Cubans in Zanzibar. The left-wing Umma Party (derived from the Zanzibar Nationalist Party) is surprised by the uprising, but it soon takes the helm of the chaotic rebellion. Some twenty-five Umma activists, who are still in the Nationalist Party, underwent military training two years earlier in Cuba, and now their skills are coming in handy.

Is Kapuściński ignorant of their connections with Cuba? Or does he know of it but become, at this moment, a reporter in the service of a revolution with which he sympathizes? It is possible he does not know, because information about the training came to light much later on, though in 1964 the CIA already knew about it. Did the revolutionaries confide such information to the reporter from socialist Poland, either during the revolt or perhaps earlier, on the terrace of the Hotel New Africa in Dar es Salaam?

Fifteen or so years from now, after he has gained more experience, Kapuściński will talk about a reporter's involvement and sympathies, and the dilemmas he faces in wars and revolutions. What is the meaning of journalistic 'objectivity' in a situation where one side is being oppressive and the other side is fighting against the oppression? Or when one group are cannibals and another is fighting for liberation and socialism? In Zanzibar the journalist realizes that certain things might depend on the provision or denial of information – many people's lives, for instance, or the entire fate of a small country.

The most famous *guerrillero* of the twentieth century, Ernesto 'Che' Guevara, number two in the Cuban revolution, will later admit that Cuba did play a role in the success of the revolt on Zanzibar. 'Zanzibar is our friend, and when it was necessary, we provided it with a little assistance, our fraternal assistance, our revolutionary assistance,' he revealed, referring to the training of the corps of Zanzibari nationalists who would later become leftist revolutionaries.

It is in Zanzibar, a little later, that Attaché Nowak meets Che Guevara. Kapuściński is green with envy: What's this Guevara like? What did you talk about?

'You, comrade, are from a socialist country,' says a stranger, accosting the Polish diplomat in the bar at the Hotel Stanley, the name of which had just been changed to Mao Zedong. 'You may have heard of me, I was a minister in Cuba.'

The stranger is Guevara. They spend half the night chatting. Che is lively and full of passion, but when it comes to ideological matters he becomes stiff and doctrinaire. He has come to Zanzibar to see how the revolution is getting on. However, he cannot see a rosy future for socialism on the island: the inheritance of colonialism, of racism . . . The uprising in Zanzibar has, in his opinion, more of the features of a rebellion in the context of race rather than class, and he is a Marxist, after all.

Less than a year after the move to Nairobi, sometime following the scandal involving the article about the corruption and prodigality of Kenyatta's government, Kapuściński and his wife return to Poland. He needs a rest ('he was incapable of resting, he got bored,' say the Nowaks), and he's longing to see his parents, especially his beloved Maminek.

On the way, in West Germany, they buy a Volkswagen Beetle with the first money set aside from his foreign allowance. In those days a Beetle is a piece of good fortune, a luxury, the high life. Kapuściński, however, is not excited by things one can buy, possess or accumulate (with the exception of books). What brightens him up is the thought that after a short rest and some convalescence at home, he will soon be returning to Africa.

Is Kapuściński given orders to transfer the PAP's African post to Nigeria because that's where 'it's all going to be happening', because now that's going to be the main front for superpower rivalry for influence – not just between Moscow and Washington, but also between Moscow and Peking? Nowadays no one can say what the actual reason was. Most likely, after more than two years in East Africa, where decolonization fever is ending, Kapuściński himself suggests it's time to explore West Africa. He writes from Lagos:

> Nigeria is independent Africa's biggest power. It is black Africa's main exporter of products such as crude oil, tin and columbite . . . According to geological estimates, it is one of the richest countries in Africa in terms of mineral assets . . . Nigeria has been treated by Washington as the main base for American influence in Africa . . . Nigeria was among the top seven countries in the world to be receiving US aid. Every other white person you meet in Lagos is an American. The largest Peace Corps team in the entire world operates in Nigeria. For the Americans, losing Nigeria is an enormous blow.[9]

What has happened is the military coup d'état of January 1966, which overthrows a corrupt neocolonial regime incapable of controlling the tribalism that is tearing the country apart at a time of economic crisis. Ten days after the coup, Kapuściński writes an analysis. He predicts 'sabotage, provocation and blackmail on the part of the old reactionaries' and reckons that 'Washington and London will do everything to hold on to Nigeria as their base in Africa,' asserting that 'Nigeria is not Ghana or Tanzania – in Nigeria the West will not let go or give way.' Some of his texts from Nigeria for the PAP's Special Bulletin are marked with the restriction 'Not for publication'. (Nowak reckons the reason for this restriction could have been that the PRL authorities of the time wanted to do business with the corrupt Nigerian politicians, and writing sincerely about them was not in their interest.)

In another report, Kapuściński writes that 'the day of the coup is regarded in popular sentiment as the day of liberation':

> So far there is a lack of proof implying any outside inspiration for the coup. Its main organizer was a group of officers of a decidedly patriotic,

independent attitude. The Nigerian left wants the army to remain in power for as long as possible. The left regards the army as more progressive than any other realistically possible political system.[10]

Kapuściński predicts a series of similar coups d'état in other countries. 'In many cases these coups are the only way out of the decline into which the neocolonial regimes have led the African countries.' Barely two years earlier, he witnessed similar coups in East Africa. Soon the reporter is disappointed by military regimes as 'the only way out of the decline'.

In September 1965, before settling in Lagos, he visits Accra. He is horrified – there is a crisis, and there is literally nothing to eat. In a letter to Nowak he complains that he could only live there if his family came too. While he was at work, his wife could spend all day queuing for bread and margarine (butter is unavailable); however, he's on his own. He complains about the nasty food in the hotels; finally, when someone invites him to their home, he gets something better to eat:

> When you go to someone's house for supper there, and you see e.g. cheese on the table, the done thing is to express surprise and say: 'Oh, where did you get cheese?' I borrowed this writing paper from the embassy because there isn't any paper at all. On the other hand, Ghana is interesting in terms of politics, but so what? If I'd had to spend another month there, it would have been the end of me.[11]

Abruptly he starts to lose weight and fears the tuberculosis has returned because of malnutrition. After ten days, he flees from Accra to Lagos, returning to Ghana for brief periods, for conferences or major occurrences.

As for Lagos, his new abode, he doesn't like it. It is a 'one-storey colossus made of mud, stretching away for miles. Dar was the size of a tiddlywink! So is Nairobi!' Unlike in Accra, here in Lagos you can buy everything ('it's a capitalist country, so the supplies are like in London; they have everything you want, as in Nairobi'), but the prices are unaffordable for a correspondent from a socialist country ('terribly costly'). He likes the bars and the cuisine: Lebanese, Chinese, Italian. He gains weight but is bothered by the climate and the city's situation – on four islands separated by lagoons – because it's a long way to get anywhere ('and for all that, there aren't any good beaches!').

> In terms of heat, Dar was like Siberia! The worst thing here is the humidity – it never stops pouring, there's always hot mist hanging in the air, and it's terribly stuffy day and night. You know how much I hate air conditioning, but here even I have to sit under it non-stop. Horrid. And they

say it's very nice here right now – apparently it only starts to be hell in January.[12]

He battles with the head office in Warsaw to make them send him the money for a car, because he has no way of getting to the post office, where he should be sending off his reports. He sits in the hotel, immobilized because he cannot afford the extremely expensive taxis. He declares a 'strike': he won't write a word until the agency finds funding for a car. And it is doubly necessary, because on top of that there are interesting political events taking place outside the capital, in Ibadan, Enugu and Kano; he has to be on the move all the time. 'The PAP has sent me off without a penny, and these are the results of their economizing,' he complains to his friend.[13] (Finally he buys a Peugeot 403 for £600, using part of the budget earmarked for something else.)

The passionate workaholic makes every effort not to waste time. He reads a lot and has meetings with people, although – as he writes – 'personal contacts are very difficult'. He is pleased that, unlike in Dar and Nairobi, here he lives among the Africans. There are no white districts in Lagos; 'one is right in the middle of Africa'.[14]

The work itself is more boring than in Dar. The local press is 'dreadful', just court chronicles, with no politics and no opinions – 'nothing you could make a report from'. As he confides in Nowak,

> There's literally nothing happening, and I'm not sending any dispatches at all. Everything has already stabilized here [four months later there will be a coup d'état, which Kapuściński cannot yet know], and above all, purely economic and financial matters dominate the whole of the situation, there aren't any other political issues. East Africa was a revolutionary volcano, but West Africa is like Sweden or Switzerland. Deadly boring. In this situation all you can do is travel, explore and tot up countries – nothing more.[15]

But he still doesn't have a car.

Again he falls ill – an infection, or some sort of poisoning. His body is covered in sores and boils. It puffs up. He wants to return to Poland (and, in fact, soon returns on a stretcher). Years later he will admit,

> There is no way out: if you want to enter the most sombre, treacherous and untrodden recesses of this land, you have to be prepared to pay the reckoning with your health, if not your life. Yet every hazardous passion is like this: a Moloch that wants to devour you. In this situation, some opt for a paradoxical state of existence – so that, on arriving in Africa, they disappear into luxurious hotels, never venture outside the pampered

neighbourhoods of the whites, and, in short, despite finding themselves geographically in Africa, they continue to live in Europe – except that it's a substitute Europe, reduced and second-rate. Indeed, such a life-style does not agree with the authentic traveller and lies beyond the means of the reporter, who must experience everything at his own cost.[16]

Apart from illness, he will find it even harder to bear depression, loneliness, sleepless nights, and a morning lack of energy. To defend oneself against them, one has to have 'steely resistance and willpower'. In a letter to Nowak he writes:

> As I sit here in Lagos like this, I realize I'll never have a time in Africa like I had in Dar. That was totally exceptional, because I met you two, and we were there together. Here I feel homesick for Dar, but for Dar with you, I mean the sort of Dar that no longer exists. We only grow fond of a place if there's someone we're fond of in that place. Here I have no one, I spend the evenings howling with boredom in my room, there's nowhere to go and no way to get there. And no one to go and see. My life is awful.[17]

In his next letter, a few months later, Kapuściński writes dramatically:

> Psychologically I'm taking this stay very badly. I'm old, I'm tired, I want to die. I'm in a state of permanent crisis. I'm not writing anything because I don't want to write badly, and I can't write well. It's paralysis, a mental void. I've no energy. Total collapse.[18]

All his optimism has evaporated. So has all the enthusiasm of his first African journey, to Ghana, and his first few years in East Africa.

Independence is turning out to be a 'sham', as is the rule of the Africans. Kapuściński wonders whether decolonization has really taken place at all. Isn't a change of regime merely superficial? It's a fact that African leaders have assumed power, but they have driven straight into the ruts of the colonial governments; they aren't changing the system (with a few rare exceptions), are still dependent on the mother country, and are letting themselves be corrupted by the West.

These questions are posed by the still-committed communist, who at the same time can see why it is hard for the Africans to break free of the old order: their economies are tied to Western markets; they need capital, which only their recent colonialists can supply; they have a common language and personal contacts, inasmuch as the African intelligentsia studied in the European mother countries.

Throughout the continent, independence has become synonymous
with poverty and demagogy. It has improved the situation of the more
or less Europeanized leaders, and also the revolutionaries, as well as the
lackeys of imperialism, but nowhere has it brought improvement for the
masses. Once we used to cry that liberation from the colonial yoke
would be enough to open the road towards progress, but in the mean-
time independence has brought us new difficulties, as well as the old
problems.[19]

Kapuściński takes the words of his Congolese comrade Lumumba as his
own, using them to add a point to an extensive article on African politics.

Here is the analyst, pouring a bucket of cold water over the head of the
revolutionary dreamer.

However, the revolutionary dreamer does have a theory for his own personal
use: self-sacrifice, self-immolation. He expounds it to his friend when they
are still in Dar es Salaam, during one of their long walks by the ocean.

'He was shocked by the poverty and hunger in India, and now in Africa,'
recalls Jerzy Nowak. 'He thinks "salvation via capitalism" has proved a disaster, because the West has done nothing but violate the traditional tribal or
clan structures without solving any of the problems of the world it has
conquered. The socialist camp in its turn, by promising "social salvation",
is beguiling the poor, but is not prepared to make any sacrifices or really
commit itself.

'So what is the alternative, what is the prescription? An individual
programme of self-sacrifice. He is impressed by Saint Francis and the
concept of atoning for one's sins, including sins we ourselves have not
committed. He lives with a sense of mission to save the world. He comes
from a country which did not have any colonies, and yet he feels guilty
about the crimes of Europeans.

' "These people can only be helped by those who are prepared to sacrifice their health and devote their life to them, even at risk of losing it," he
says. He reckons fate has given him a chance to make the affluent world
aware of what is happening in Africa, the tragedy of the situation there, and
that he should speak out to the consciences of the rich. But in order to bear
witness, he must live among the Africans and share their fate as much as
possible: fall ill like them, and go hungry along with them.

'Is he speaking like a shiftless idealist? In our African years I did not think
so. I saw how he turned his ideas into action. And he did it knowing he was
isolated in that idealism, or even naivety of his. In time he started to get
used to his own helplessness. Outwardly he oozed optimism, inside he was
sinking into a pessimistic state, which for my own purposes – maybe rather
unfairly – I called "returning to reality".

'When he starts to fall seriously ill with malaria and tuberculosis, he realizes that self-immolation will not put the world to rights. However, he does not abandon his faith in his mission to inform the world about the tragedy of Africa and other poor countries, his faith in the necessity to save the world.'

Kapuściński will keep returning to Africa for the rest of his life, and will write his most important books about it. He will witness the evacuation of the Portuguese from Angola, the final stage in the country's struggles for liberation and the bloody civil war. In Ethiopia (Abyssinia) he will observe the decline of the rule of Emperor Haile Selassie and the beginnings of the Red despotism of Colonel Mengistu. In Uganda he will feel for himself the shivers down the spine prompted among the locals by the regime of Idi Amin; after the tyrant's fall Kapuściński will go there and collect material for a book about him that he will never complete.

In the early 1990s, while preparing to write the summary of his African experiences, *The Shadow of the Sun*, he sends his old friend a card from Addis Ababa:

Dear Jurek,
  I've been in Africa for two months already – I've been to Uganda, Tanzania (including Zanzibar), Rwanda, Kenya and Eritrea, and now I'm in Ethiopia (for the second time this year). Rather a sentimental journey, in the footsteps of our youth together – heart-breaking. I found our old embassy, where we used to live – it's in ruins.[20]

The ruined embassy reflects the state of mind in which Kapuściński returns from his journey. Everything is going downhill, there is disintegration and moral decay. In Addis Ababa he goes to Africa Hall, a modernist building on one of the city's hills, where in 1963 he attended the first summit of new African leaders. Now children are playing ping-pong there, and a woman is selling leather jackets in the historic building's auditorium.

He tries to find a specific document which supposedly sets out a plan for the development and rescue of Africa. He questions various secretaries and officials about it, naming it by title, but they cannot find it, and most of the people he asks have never even heard of it before. Kapuściński starts to doubt whether such a plan really does exist, and whether Africa can actually be saved.

19

In the Corridors of Power

The phone rings in Artur Starewicz's office.

'Listen, Rysiek Kapuściński is coming to see you – he'll tell you about his African plans.'

Before giving his final consent and arranging a foreign currency allowance for the reporter's trip, PAP editor-in-chief Michał Hoffman calls the man in charge of all journalists and editors, the head of the Central Committee Press Office.

'Hoffman was an intelligent man,' says Starewicz at his flat in Warsaw's Old Town. 'He wanted some back-up in case any of the Party leaders hauled him over the coals for wasting money. Africa wasn't a priority, but Hoffman reckoned it was important and worthwhile, apart from which he valued Kapuściński. And I always gave a positive opinion.'

Starewicz, Gomułka's man, was born in 1917. Close to the Party 'liberals' (the 'Puławians') in the watershed period of October '56, he first meets Kapuściński during his days at *Sztandar Młodych*. Their relations are 'friendly but formal and professional'. They do not meet up in private. They address each other in the formal manner, as 'Comrade', which was regular parlance within the Party apparatus in those days. Kapuściński is on informal terms with Starewicz's wife, who works for *Polityka*.

Rysiek arrives at the Central Committee building on the corner of Jerozolimskie Avenue and Nowy Świat Street in central Warsaw – he has a multiple entry pass – and tells Starewicz where he wants to go and what he is planning to do. On his return from the journey, he returns and tells him what he saw and experienced.

'I heard everything from him that could later be read in his reports, except in a more adventurous version. He told me how he had nothing to eat in Africa or nowhere to spend the night. But he wrote better than he narrated.' Starewicz laughs. 'He wanted to catch my interest so that the door would be open for him to make more trips in the future.'

'Did the Central Committee know who Kapuściński was?'

'Of course, it was known he was a talented man and wrote superb analyses. But to tell the truth, no profound, in-depth view was expressed, because Gomułka was more interested in German affairs – for him Africa was an exotic place.'

'Did you remain in touch later on, when Gierek replaced Gomułka, and you left the Central Committee?'

'No. To be honest, I don't know what Kapuściński thought of me – after all, I represented the Party apparatus which was at loggerheads with the journalists. When I was the Polish ambassador in London in the 1970s, he never visited me, though I know he used to come to London. Maybe he didn't need me any more and chose not to keep up our acquaintance?'

'Did you know that Kapuściński had support within the Party élite that was not entirely sympathetic towards you? His chief protector was Ryszard Frelek.'

'Well, Kapuściński was a journalist; he kept up with various people. In the 1960s Frelek was secretary to Zenon Kliszko [the Party's number two person]. Kliszko took him on because he wasn't a good judge of people. But he knew Frelek was intelligent and could be useful. Frelek could pick up various sorts of rumours for him: who, what, with whom. Kliszko liked to know that sort of thing but had no way of finding it all out.'

In 1968, when the Party starts beating its anti-Semitic drums, Starewicz, who has Jewish roots, will be one of the objects of attack by the Red-nationalist élite, among whom Frelek will play a significant role.

His office is on the first floor, in the wing of the Central Committee building that overlooks the National Museum. The women secretaries' room adjoins at the front, then there is a large study the size of three biggish rooms in an apartment, with a small bedroom at the back. This is where Frelek works. On returning from his posting as a PAP correspondent in India, after a short period co-managing the PAP, Frelek drops journalism and focuses on a political career.

As a thirty-something mapping out a route to the top, he could not have found a better job: his boss, Kliszko, has the deciding vote on the country's most important political issues, with the exception of the economy. Kliszko's authority covers matters of personnel, education, culture, the press, foreign affairs and relations with the Church. In addition, he is quite a cultural snob: he can recite the Polish nineteenth-century romantic poet Cyprian Norwid's verses by heart, and he publishes his own poems under a pseudonym.

They are a perfect match – Frelek, too, will never drop his intellectual ambitions. While working as a Party dignitary, in his spare time he will write stage plays, film scripts and novels of manners; he will also lecture at the journalism faculty and run courses on the history of diplomacy. His friends and comrades describe him as a 'Renaissance man'. His enemies and comrades call him 'a murky character, a schemer'.

Frelek is fond of Kapuściński. It is he, while still one of the decision-makers at the PAP, who brings him into the agency and suggests he take the posting in Africa. He appreciates the talents of his chum from India and finds their friendship flattering. To some extent, he feels like a patron – vicariously satisfying his own dreams, set aside for another day.

While Kapuściński is away for several years on his African posting, unrest within the Party begins. The second and third Party ranks – the thirty- to forty-year-olds – are beginning to grumble about the older ones. This is nothing new: it is the usual rebellion by the younger generation, a revolt by bureaucrats jockeying for position. Meanwhile, their paths to promotion are blocked because the more important posts are occupied by older activists, from the war period and the time immediately afterwards.

The young bureaucrats do not have the ideological zeal of the communists from the heroic era of building socialism. What they are interested in are privileges; they want a comfortable, affluent life. But First Secretary Gomułka is an old-style ascetic, and he has been preventing them from enjoying the fruits of power. It would be worth removing him – but how?

At this same juncture, a group known as 'the partisans' appears on the Party's political horizon. This is a fairly informal faction, whose most prominent figures are people who fought with the communist partisans and are now employed at government ministries. The informal leader of this movement, or ferment, or élite, is a veteran of the Red partisans of the Second World War, Mieczysław Moczar. He holds the post of deputy minister and will soon be minister of internal affairs; he is also the president of an old soldiers union that has several hundred thousand members. His 'partisans' promote a curious ideology: nationalism expressed in the language of communist doctrine.

They rehabilitate the national tradition, which the PRL's official propaganda has perhaps not entirely consigned to the dustbin but regards as a relic, a symbol of bygone days that will never return. The Red nationalists like to talk about the Fatherland, Tradition and the Nation in capital letters, with pomp and pathos. They extol the achievements of the Polish army in centuries past and during the Second World War. Books, films and plays appear in the spirit of Red-nationalist ideology. The main mouthpieces are Catholic journals licensed by the Party and also a few Party publications, including the weekly *Kultura*.

The partisans derive their strength and confidence from the fact that the thirst for their ideology goes beyond the Party ranks. Many people in Poland who keep their distance from the Party and live in a private niche of their own, Catholics who reject the official atheism, and citizens who care about patriotic traditions, view the partisans with a certain degree of sympathy, a touch of incredulity, and some amount of hope. Here a different species of Red has appeared: they talk about the Fatherland and do not abhor the national tradition. Is it possible to attain some sort of patriotic socialism that is common to all of us?

The nationalist–patriotic mythology proves to be the perfect fuel for a revolt by the second ranks, the people within the apparatus who occupy posts at the middle level – on municipal and district Party committees. At the top of the power structure the informal patrons of this new wave are the 'secretaries' secretaries': Walery Namiotkiewicz (Gomułka's secretary), Stanisław Trepczyński (head of the Central Committee secretariat), and Frelek (Kliszko's secretary).

The partisans define their enemies within the Party as nihilists, cosmopolitans, and also, as in the past, revisionists. Gomułka cannot stand revisionists either, which he has demonstrated more than once: however, the partisans think him too lenient, and feel that the poison of revisionism is still destroying the Party. In the eyes of the partisans, the main hotbed of evil includes people involved in culture and the academic world, the eggheads, ever suspicious, who sneer at national tradition – and if they are of Jewish origin, they are sure to be enemies of Poland.

At first the partisans adopt a carrot-and-stick approach to *Polityka* and its editor-in-chief, Rakowski. Before dubbing him an enemy, attempts are made to bring him over to the 'right' side. 'It would happen like this: Frelek would drop in at the editorial office and say to Rakowski: "Listen, why not give Mietek Moczar a call? He's always asking about you. You could meet for dinner and have a chat," ' Marian Turski tells me.

Rakowski, who loathes the nationalist ideology of the partisans, resists all the subterfuge and persuasion. Neither he nor the *Polityka* team give in to the Red-nationalist wave during its apogee in March 1968, when the official language of the nationalist–communists becomes anti-Semitism, and removing people of Jewish origin from Party and public posts becomes Party policy.

Kapuściński, who spends most of this time in Africa, is confused on his return to Poland by the friction within the Party. Rakowski records an anecdote from August 1966:

> Recently Rysiek Kapuściński told the following story. On his return from Africa he was invited in by Trepczyński, head of the First Secretary's office with the rank of CC department manager. Werblan and Olszowski also took part in the conversation. After a while his interlocutors moved from African affairs to domestic ones, and started to criticize Gomułka extremely severely . . . Rysiek was surprised. 'What's going on?' he asked me. 'Can you imagine, his closest associates were bitching about him in the room next door to his. What does it mean?' I tried to explain the situation to him.[1]

Kapuściński is torn by loyalties and friendships. He worked with Rakowski for several years at *Polityka*, and they liked and respected each other; now, however, the editor-in-chief of *Polityka*, as well as the weekly itself, is starting to be frowned on at the summit of power. Occasionally Rakowski gets a dressing-down from Gomułka; he is also being jostled by the partisans and the secretaries' secretaries (most openly by Frelek) – ultimately by friends and colleagues. To be too close to Rakowski and *Polityka* would be politically unwise.

On top of that, Kapuściński has close social connections with Frelek, a history of shared experiences in India, and a chummy relationship. Frelek can do more for him: he can help, fix things – he has already done that anyway. And Frelek can't stand Rakowski; he is waging an underhand war against the editor-in-chief of *Polityka*. Who should be held on to?

According to Marian Turski, his former boss at *Sztandar Młodych* and his colleague from *Polityka*: 'Rysiek always knew how to come to terms with his political bosses. He never fell into disfavour with his superiors, thanks to which he had a free hand in many matters and could put his plans into action.'

Kapuściński showed patience while listening to the high and mighty. He had a friendly expression, a smile, and, whether consciously or not, he did not put on airs or imply that he was better than they. And that flattered the provincials and parvenus in high positions. 'He listens to me,' some of them would think. 'That brilliant reporter, an intellectual who has travelled the world, understands me. So what I say must be clever and interesting.' He knew how to listen to nonsense while showing interest when necessary. He gave the impression of caring about his interlocutors.

Was this opportunism? Possibly. Or maybe just competence, a way of achieving his ends.

'It was a known fact in our environment that whenever Kapuściński came back from his latest journey he gave Kliszko and Frelek a sort of informal briefing.'

Daniel Passent is far from passing censure on Kapuściński. Such were the times, and that was how you functioned if you wanted to work in that profession. To do something positive, to make arrangements or push things onto the right tracks, you had to have connections 'upstairs'. In any case, today's appraisals are often out of historical context: Kapuściński regarded the PRL as his country, a place where he felt comfortable. He was a loyal Party member. Why should he ever have thought of talking to colleagues on the Central Committee as doing something wrong?

'He was more intelligent and better informed than most of our diplomats in the Third World countries. It is to the Party decision-makers' credit that they wanted to hear what he had to tell them about the situation in Africa, and later in Latin America.' This is Frelek's view: that people in power should listen to what Kapuściński has to say about the Third World.

Frelek can fix matters that cannot be fixed. Józef Klasa, who also took part in the 'second ranks' revolt, relates that it was thanks to Frelek that Che Guevara's *Bolivian Diary* was published in Poland – at Kapuściński's request, and in his translation. Being at loggerheads with Moscow, Guevara is regarded within the socialist camp as a shady character, an anti-Soviet lefty. Kapuściński takes the matter to Frelek, Frelek takes it to Kliszko, and the revolutionary's diary is published (it will never been reissued in communist Poland again).

Kapuściński sorts out not just his own affairs through Frelek, but also those of his friends. In a letter to Jerzy Nowak, in which he urges his closest friend to drop the diplomatic service and choose an academic career instead, he writes:

> I had a meeting with a PISM [Polish Institute for International Affairs] seminar on the Third World – the standard was simply desperate. The worst thing is they're all retired people, there are no young ones. They regard anyone who wants to work on the Third World as worth their weight in gold. I have already spoken about you to Ryś Frelek – they'll give you an academic grant and welcome you with open arms. You'll soon get your post-doc done, become an associate professor, and soon after that a Warsaw University professor.[2]

When Kapuściński leaves for his posting as a PAP correspondent in Latin America – the only time he ever takes his wife and daughter along – Frelek looks after his flat in Warsaw's Wola district. When he is in Poland, he often visits Frelek at his summer cottage in Mazuria. Sometimes he hides away there, far from the office, far from Warsaw, and writes.

'I remember those strong, unfiltered cigarettes, those parties. When Rysio used to sing "The magic of Polesie, the wild forests and marshes . . .",' recalled Frelek after his friend's death.

'He had good intuition about people.'

Andrzej Werblan, a prominent Party activist in those days, gets to know Kapuściński through Frelek. Familiar with his African reports issued in the PAP's Special Bulletin, he is delighted by Kapuściński's sense of observation, his analyses and his knowledge of remote and unknown parts of the world.

'He used to come and see us at the Central Committee – I can remember having conversations about the rivalry between the Soviet Union and China on African territory, and of course about decolonization. He was an idealist, always emotionally involved, sometimes a little uncritical. He also had an emotional approach to his leftist convictions and his Party membership, wholly and utterly.'

I ask Werblan for character sketches of Kapuściński's remaining political friends (apart from Frelek) in that era:

Trepczyński: Open-minded, speaks foreign languages, prides himself on having friends in the world of culture. A social charmer. As with Frelek, Kapuściński meets up with Trepczyński socially too, at name-day parties, for dinner, for drinks.

Józef Czesak: Head of the Central Committee Foreign Department. A good deal older than Kapuściński. An émigré who returned from France, from a mining family that left Poland before the war. Western chic, great intelligence. A communist believer, but one who believes 'in the French way', with detachment and self-irony.

Michał Hoffman: Editor-in-chief of the PAP, Kapuściński's direct boss and promoter. Before the war he was a journalist at the Polish Telegraphic Agency, in love with the profession. Indulgent about Kapuściński's extravagances, i.e., disappearing for weeks on end, writing not necessarily in the news style required at the PAP and not always at sufficient length. Someone will mention years later that Kapuściński did not shine for his reports on political and economic events, because he was more interested in fraternizing with ordinary people in each successive African country. Hoffman tolerates his protégé's predilections.

I make the following notes in the margin: Do not forget the most important thing – Kapuściński achieves his success thanks to his talents and some terribly hard work, his wonderful reports, and then his books. His genuine commitment to the Party, friendships and connections at the pinnacle of the power structure facilitate a great deal for him and are extremely helpful; they create the conditions for his talent to develop. Be careful, however, not to imply that Kapuściński's greatness comes from the fact that he knew Frelek and other comrades. This is a significant element of his success, the fascinating know-how necessary to a career in the PRL era, but it is not the essence of why we love and admire Kapuściński. Plenty of writers and reporters had close connections with the authorities, friends in high places, and plenty of them have been forgotten. But we still read Kapuściński, in Poland and worldwide.

Marcin Kula, a historian to whom I talk about Kapuściński's connections within the Central Committee, picks up a surprising lead. He once wrote a book called *Communism Like Religion*, in which he analyses the similarities between church and communist rituals. After reading it, Kapuściński wrote Kula an enthusiastic letter congratulating him.

In our conversation, Kula notes that in communism one can discern a curious vestige left over from feudalism: the relationship between the feudal lord and his vassal. He cites two examples from real life. His father, Witold Kula, was an eminent historian who occasionally benefited from the help of a certain acquaintance, a professor high up in the Party hierarchy. For instance, whenever he had trouble obtaining a passport, he would turn to his 'feudal lord', who would say, 'Go and see so-and-so, he knows who you are, he's sure to help.'

In much the same way, whenever the censors found fault with something in his *History of Brazil*, Marcin Kula would turn for help to an academic he knew at the Jagiellonian University who was a member of the Politburo. He would manage to save the politically incorrect passage, though not in every single case. In tricky situations, Kula used to ask him to intervene two or three more times.

'But please do not write that my father or I, or Kapuściński, were anyone's vassals,' he urges me. 'This imperfect analogy is just meant to illustrate one of the mechanisms of the "progressive" system, one of its paradoxes.'

'In the end Rysiek distanced himself from *Polityka*,' says Janusz Rolicki, a junior colleague from the weekly.

His colleagues can sense that Kapuściński finds his recent connections with *Polityka* uncomfortable.

'Why do you think that was?' I ask.

'He felt tied to people like Frelek, or Trepczyński . . . And apart from that he manoeuvred and calculated.'

Kapuściński publishes his final reports in *Polityka* in 1966. His name appears only a few more times on its pages, for example when it reprints his longer articles from Latin America from the PAP Special Bulletin. After that, the final links are broken.

'Did the "partisans" flirt with Rysiek?'

'I'd be surprised if they didn't try,' Turski tells me.

'He regarded the partisans with sympathy,' recalls a colleague from the PAP, Wiesława Bolimowska, but at once adds a proviso: 'However, you must understand properly what that means.' As she indicates, one cannot regard that conflict within the Party purely in terms of the later anti-Semitic campaign of March 1968. The nationalist–communist wave was a reaction to a lack of motion, to stagnation, and at first it looked like a movement of defiance against the minor stabilization. Moczar was supported not just by nationalists and anti-Semites but also by the 'technical intelligentsia', who wanted to open up the country to modernity. Nowadays it has been forgotten that many people from various parties saw hope for change in nationalist communism.

'And then we were horrified by the face that Moczar-ism revealed to us,' Bolimowska continues. 'Afterwards, Rysiek said something along the lines of "It's a good thing I went abroad, because they wanted me to get more involved; they would have dragged me into it." '

The apogee of the partisans' anti-Semitic campaign coincides with student protests against censorship (concerning a photograph from the National Theatre's poster for Adam Mickiewicz's play *Forefather's Eve*) and in defence of colleagues expelled from academic institutions. Now not just the partisans but also Gomułka, riding on their wave, promote the idea that the youth protests are inspired by former Stalinists of Jewish origin, who want to return to power. This bogus theory serves as justification for the purge that sweeps across the country, removing Poles of Jewish descent from their jobs in offices, on committees and at colleges. The vacated posts are occupied by those who until now have belonged to the second and third ranks of Party bureaucrats. Goal achieved! Gomułka himself, who has no qualms about joining the nationalist campaign, will remain in power for only another two and a half years.

During the apogee of the anti-Semitic witch-hunt, Kapuściński is working as a PAP correspondent in Santiago de Chile, during which time he travels to La Paz, Lima, and elsewhere. Despite being far from home, he has the opportunity to see at close range how Ambassador Jerzy Witold Dudziński is removed from his post on the wave of purges.

Does Kapuściński comment on this event in private conversations? Does he express an opinion about the turmoil in Poland, the anti-Semitic propaganda, the student protests or the repression? A Polish diplomat of the time in Chile says, 'We never got onto "dissident" topics.'

Does Kapuściński know – or will he find out later – that his political patron, Frelek, has a hand in the anti-Semitic campaign?

On 11 March 1968, the front page of *Słowo Powszechne* (The Universal Word) carries an appeal 'To Warsaw University Students', in which the leaders of the student protests are characterized as Zionists and the children of Stalinists. Everything is clear: the 'Judaeo-Stalinists' are raising their heads, so they have to be cut off. The appeal has no signature. Many years later, Rakowski will reveal in his published diaries that this anti-Semitic text was written by Ryszard Frelek.[3]

A friend from the weekly *Kultura* remembers a conversation with Kapuściński sometime after the shock of 1968. Kapuściński said at the time that 'a wave of coups d'état and military dictatorships is rolling across the world', and then predicted that 'the security services are going to take charge in Poland too!' As the friend recalls, 'He announced it with his typical doom and gloom.'

A female fellow journalist remembers a meeting at the *Polityka* office attended by Kapuściński, who at the time was on a short holiday in Poland: 'He clearly didn't want to take a stance on the issue of March 1968, at least within our circle. *Polityka* had behaved decently at the time; it was the only Party newspaper that didn't take part in the anti-Semitic witch-hunt. Rysiek looked down on us a little, from a bird's eye view – for being so excited about our backwoods while in the world outside major things were happening, and so events in Poland should be viewed in a broader perspective. I got the impression that he regarded Moczar-ism as a "refreshing" movement, but after all, lots of people, especially the young ones, let themselves be taken in by it.'

On returning from his short holiday in Poland, Kapuściński writes in a letter to Nowak (who is then working at the embassy in Buenos Aires):

> The situation in a nutshell: the All-Poles have pulled themselves upwards, but not very much, not very much. The old lot have to a large extent managed to restore the balance, to restore the old system. There is stabilization again, and a personnel freeze. This state will continue for ages, several years at least. The year 1968 is now never to be repeated. There will be no great sensations before we go back to Poland. It's a country where nothing is ever done fully.

He continues with a bit of advice for his friend:

> In any case, don't stick your neck out, because it's very unfashionable now. Act according to the principle 'let each within his own circle do as the spirit of the Lord bids him, and the whole thing will fall into place'. A definite individualization of effort has set in, i.e. it's important to do something that aims towards one's own development.[4]

Kapuściński's attitude towards the political turmoil of March is not clear. He writes about the nationalist–communists as 'All-Poles', which sounds mocking and indicates a sense of detachment, implying that he regards them as nationalists rather than as fellow communists. But what does he mean when he says Poland is a country 'where nothing is ever done fully'? Is he saying Poland is a country where even a bad business never manages to be fully carried through? Or even to ruin everything entirely? (Later Nowak remembers his unambiguous view of the anti-Semitic witch-hunt of 1968: 'a disgrace!')

Certainly the advice he gives his friend suggests that the idealist in Kapuściński was at that moment overcome by the realist. If there is no place for socialist ideals, 'let's do our own thing', as a famous bard of the People's Poland era used to sing.

20

Lapidarium 3: The Reporter as Politician

The American journalist Mark Danner, who knew Kapuściński, admits over coffee in New York, 'When it comes to his relationship with the Polish government, I can't obviously say anything from personal knowledge. I have no idea what life was like in Poland in the days of "real socialism", or how much manoeuvring one had to do to write and publish anything that made sense. I imagine that as a top reporter in that world, Ryszard must also have had to be an excellent politician – am I right?'

A good example is provided by his reports from the Soviet Union in 1967. On his return from Africa, Hoffman offers Kapuściński a trip to the Soviet Central Asian republics. He is to write a series of reports for the fiftieth anniversary of the October Revolution. It is a slightly unsettling proposal: he is still a communist believer but has been through a few experiences, even disappointments. By now he can sense what good writing is and what propaganda is, what is genuine and what smacks of insincerity.

Georgia, Armenia, Azerbaijan, Tajikistan, Kyrgyzstan and Turkmenistan – the series of reports is first published by *Życie Warszawy* (Warsaw Life). One of the articles is run with a huge headline: 'ON THE EVE OF THE GREAT ANNIVERSARY: 1917–1967'. Expanded versions of these reports will appear in the book *The Kyrgyz Dismounts*.[1]

'There is vast progress in recent years,' he writes from Armenia. 'Lots of new, stone houses. Lots of cottages being built. Everywhere the old mud ones are being demolished. Women with buckets of water . . .' Elsewhere: 'Please forgive me, but I'm going to speak a bit nationalistically. I'm highly amused by a truculent Azerbaijani woman who knows that nationalism is a forbidden fruit, but on the other hand cannot resist the temptation . . .' And 'Georgia's ancient art with all its splendour and perfection sends a bumpkin like me into a complete daze . . .'

'He writes these stories from the viewpoint of a man who is surprised,' says Janusz Rolicki. 'This permits him to tell us things about the Soviet system that he couldn't say in any other way. It's a masterpiece – to write so much truth without necessarily being critical. The wolf is fed, and the sheep is still in one piece.'

Another of Kapuściński's observations: 'Baku is Azerbaijan's industrial base, a typical colonial enclave, like Katanga in Congo . . .'

'He came back shocked!' says Wiesława Bolimowska. ' "It's impossible," he said, "so many years after the revolution and so much poverty". He found a way to describe it: he looked at the Soviet Union, not from the perspective of Europe but of Africa. That allowed him to show the cultural distance that had been covered in the fifty years since the revolution without having to be ashamed that he was writing propaganda.'

His American friend Danner has good intuition.

21

On the Trail of Che Guevara

PAP correspondent R. Kapuściński reports:

LATIN AMERICA IS UNDERGOING ITS GREATEST POLITICAL SHOCK in the course of the past decade. Right now, a profound internal crisis has hit most of the countries in this region . . .

OVER THE PAST WEEK THERE HAS NOT BEEN A SINGLE DAY IN LATIN AMERICA WHEN PEOPLE HAVE NOT BEEN KILLED OR WOUNDED IN STREET FIGHTING BETWEEN THE POPULATION AND THE ORGANS OF REPRESSION OF THE LATIN-AMERICAN REGIMES.

THE MAIN FEATURE OF THE DISTURBANCES HERE IS THEIR LARGE NUMBERS – on a regional scale, the wave of protest has now involved millions of people.

IN AN EFFORT TO BLOCK THE BLOW, THE DICTATORSHIPS IN SOME COUNTRIES HAVE UNLEASHED HARSH INTERNAL TERROR. In Brazil a fascist terrorist organization has been mobilized, the so-called CCC, Comando de Caça aos Comunistas ('The Command for the Hunting of Communists'), a local version of the Ku Klux Klan.

THE PROGRESSIVE PRIESTS' MOVEMENT IS GAINING INCREASING STRENGTH and represents one of the most interesting features of the political situation on this continent . . . Brazilian prisons are packed full of priests, monks and nuns. They are persecuted and tortured . . .

IT IS WORTH NOTICING THE DISTINCT MOBILIZATION OF THE URBAN GUERRILLAS . . . The most active urban guerrilla movement now exists in Brazil, Guatemala and Uruguay.

UNTIL NOW IN WORLD POLITICS, LATIN AMERICA – WITH THE EXCEPTION OF CUBA – HAS PLAYED THE ROLE OF A SATELLITE OF THE USA . . . At present it has ceased to be a force of that kind, while at the same time taking on a new function as an independent political force.

[T]he focus of the fight being waged by the Third World against the forces of neocolonialism has at this point in time shifted from Africa and Asia to Latin America . . .[1]

Could a romantic who is racing about the world in pursuit of revolutions possibly have encountered a better time?

Kapuściński arrives in Latin America at a red-hot moment in the Cold War. Barely eight years earlier, Fidel Castro's revolution in Cuba broke free of dependence on the United States, creating an opportunity to overthrow the semi-feudal status quo in other countries in the region and prompting the hope of building a different kind of socialism – spontaneous, with the broad participation of the masses, without despotism or an omnipotent bureaucracy. Proletarians and peasants from other countries, often in alliance with segments of the regionally small middle class, start to rise up against local dictatorships or in opposition to governments that, while formally democratic, are run in the interests of a narrow élite. Villagers and workers from plantations demand agricultural reform and the dismantling of the *latifundia*, or large estates. The big-city world of labour calls for broad social legislation, examples of which it seeks not only in Cuba but also in the experiences of the recently overthrown Argentinean caudillo Juan Perón. Rebellious ideas from protesting Paris, agitated Berkeley and the burning ghettos of Chicago and Los Angeles reach the better-off middle classes. Even if they live relatively affluently, these people want to live more freely: to say what they want, write, publish and sing. The year 1968, which 'rocked the world', is just around the corner.

In Latin America, all these 'dangerous' aspirations have a particular context: they are spreading in a region of dramatic inequality, far greater than in the US and Europe – a region which Uncle Sam regards as his own backyard. Latin America has been treated as Washington's sphere of influence since the early nineteenth century. In the 1820s President James Monroe formulated a doctrine according to which the US assigned itself the right to intervene in any country in the Western hemisphere if American interests were threatened. Prominent Cold War–era politician Zbigniew Brzezinski once called this doctrine the equivalent of the Eastern European 'Brezhnev doctrine'. The latter assigned to the Soviet Union the right to engage in armed intervention ('fraternal aid') in any Warsaw Pact country if the local communist government – that is to say, the interests of Moscow – was in danger.

The victory of the revolution in Cuba, its romantic legend and infectious influence on emancipation movements in Latin America – leftist, communist or democratic, as well as those inspired by Catholic liberation theology – arouse concern in Washington, because it turns out that a few badly armed guerrilla units, with a handful of conspirators in the cities and support from peasants on the land, are capable of overthrowing dictatorships which are backed by the US and armed to the teeth. Thanks to the Cuban revolution's turn towards Moscow, followed by the missile crisis of 1962, which almost led to nuclear conflict between the US and the USSR, a small island in the Caribbean becomes the obsession of American politicians.

From now on, Washington will conduct a war against communism in Latin America. In practice, this involves supporting even the most bestial of tyrants as long as they are capable of stifling movements for social liberation, not just communist or pro-Soviet movements but also the softest movements for agricultural reform, social legislation, democratic elections and the dismantling of the post-colonial ownership structure. Under the influence of US policy and local uniformed warlords, a number of thoroughly moderate democrats in Argentina, Brazil, Guatemala and El Salvador become sworn revolutionaries, painted red.

Kapuściński arrives in Latin America (first stop: Santiago de Chile) a month after the death of Che Guevara, the missionary of socialism executed without trial in Bolivia, where he was trying to kindle the revolutionary flame. Students and rebellious workers pour onto the streets of the Latin American cities. In some – most violently in the Tlatelolco area of the Mexican capital – they are shot dead like animals in hunting season. In Peru it results in a semi-revolutionary experiment with social reforms introduced by a progressive military. In Bolivia a civilian–military alliance undertakes a similar attempt, with the support of the workers, the peasantry, the students and sections of the army. Whereas in Chile, the elections will shortly be won by democratic Marxist Salvador Allende, and hopes for revolutionary change take a peaceful route.

This is the time and place where History is happening.

A little while longer, and he might not have gone.

'What are you still doing here?' Roma Pańska, the *éminence grise* of the PAP, accosts him in a corridor at the agency's headquarters. It is November 1967.

'I'm getting ready to leave.'

'Really, Rysiek! Don't get ready, don't wait, don't delay, just get out of here at once or it'll be too late!'

'But . . .'

'Grab your bags and vamoose this instant!'

A couple of weeks earlier, Michał Hoffman asked Kapuściński if he wanted to go on another posting, to Latin America.

'Of course!'

The agency has a correspondent in Mexico named Edmund Osmańczyk, but the whole continent is boiling over, so it may be worth opening a second office in the south of the region. Kapuściński is to take a look around. Meanwhile, in Poland, the gathering wave of Moczar-ism does not pass the PAP by. Kapuściński has good connections, especially among patrons of the movement, but when shocks and purges are happening it is better to step aside and disappear. Anyway, who will get the chop? How will it end? Where will his protector pals land?

So he grabs his bags and disappears a few days later. Along the way, he sorts out a visa for Chile – the PRL is on good terms with Chile, where a socially orientated Christian Democrat party is in power, so he gets an entry permit at once – and *adios*!

Once again, as in India, Kapuściński is deaf and dumb. He makes a deal with his bosses in Warsaw: for three months he won't write anything, to give him time to learn Spanish.

In Santiago de Chile he meets Polish emigré Marian Rawicz.

'Marian, I'm in a hopeless situation, I'm sitting here in Santiago, I'm a foreign correspondent, but I can't even understand what they write in the papers, and in three months I've got to start sending in reports for my agency.'

'What can I do for you?'

'Please, please, I'll pay you properly, just devote a couple of hours a day to me for the next three months and teach me Spanish.'

They meet daily, while day and night Kapuściński devotes himself to words and grammar. He listens to the radio and starts to decipher the newspaper headlines. Having had French lessons in Dar es Salaam, Spanish isn't all Greek to him.

Two and a half months later, at the Chilean Institute for International Affairs, he gives a talk in Spanish on the political situation in Poland.

First blood: during an exchange of information with other journalists, he is given a leak about a potential coup d'état. In Chile the left-wing Christian Democrats are in power, President Eduardo Frei Montalva is conducting mild agricultural reform and introducing social legislation beneficial to the poor, but for the masses awakened by the changes and the general fever throughout the continent, it is not enough. It is becoming likely that the country's next leader will be a veteran of the left, Senate president Salvador Allende. The army in Chile upholds the legal order; here it is not just another political party, as is the case in many other countries in the region. Despite this, the right wing manages to convince a group of officers that the country is threatened by the Red plague. At the head of the conspiracy is General Roberto Viaux.

Kapuściński reports from Santiago:

Chilean public opinion is following the development of events with growing concern ... At the military garrisons the officers are holding stormy meetings, the course of which is not being made public. Yet people are saying that within the army two tendencies are clashing at the moment – one group thinks it necessary to carry out a full coup, overthrowing President Frei, dissolving parliament and suspending the constitution, whereas the other one is in favour of a partial coup, which means establishing a military government, but with President Frei staying in office.[2]

He warns that this report is destined *only* for the PAP's Special Bulletin, and cannot appear in the press: issuing this sort of speculative information, harmful to the good reputation of the country hosting the correspondent, could lose him his accreditation.

A few days later, he picks up the phone. Ambassador Dudziński is on the line.

'You've been thrown out.'

'What happened?'

'I don't know, but they called from the Chilean Ministry of Foreign Affairs: you're going to be deported.'

It is a repetition of what happened to Kapuściński in Kenya.

By mistake, the editor on duty at the PAP's Warsaw headquarters has tossed the restricted report into the normal service. On 10 May 1968, news about the threat of a coup d'état in Chile is published on the front page of *Trybuna Ludu*. Chile's embassy in Warsaw informs its government, and someone at the Chilean Ministry of Foreign Affairs decides to take away the accreditation of the reporter who issued the news.

Kapuściński is panic-stricken. There is political turmoil in Poland, he is *persona non grata* in Chile, and if he is deported, no country in the region will give him accreditation. For a correspondent, this is professional death.

'I went to see Allende, who was then president of the Chilean Senate,' he will recall many years later. 'The jovial Allende clapped me on the back and said, "Don't worry, we'll do something about it, we'll sort it out somehow."'

Kapuściński is summoned to the Chilean Ministry of Foreign Affairs.

'For things like this, we expel a correspondent within twenty-four hours,' a senior official tells him in a dry, formal tone. 'This time we're going to be more lenient.'

He gives Kapuściński to understand that someone important has intervened in the matter and that he is not going to be punitively expelled; however, he is to leave 'voluntarily'. Kapuściński suspects that it was Allende who arranged the ministry's generosity.

After leaving Chile, he goes to Rio de Janeiro, where he stays for several months. From there he writes to a close friend, 'I feel much freer here than within the much-vaunted Chilean democracy, which is a crappy regime, not a democracy – I simply hate Chile, but I'm in love with Brazil.'[3]

Before leaving Santiago for good, he reads in the bi-weekly *Punto Final* a sensational current publication: Che Guevara's Bolivian diary. For eleven months, until almost the final days before the defeat of his guerrilla unit and his execution, Guevara kept notes.

Kapuściński travels to Bolivia on the pretext of attending a conference for enterprises involved in tin mining. His real reason is different: to tour points along Che's guerrilla trail.

Nothing is known about the trip except the undetailed account he himself provides years later. The only event he mentions is being captured by the army and a drunken officer's attempt to execute him by firing squad. Che's successors, who will soon found a new unit, claim it is impossible for a correspondent from a communist country to have moved about freely in the areas where Guevara's unit was defeated. In 1968 this terrain was still militarized, and the presence of a white foreigner would have been noticed immediately. Journalists were treated as accomplices of the rebels, so a reporter from the Eastern bloc would have been regarded as a spy. Perhaps he only made it to Santa Cruz, the capital of the province, but never set off into this terrain?

Guevara fascinates Kapuściński: a romantic warrior fighting for a just world who died for his ideals. Shortly after the diary is published, Kapuściński leaves for Lima, where he shuts himself in a hotel and spends a month translating the final text written by the most famous martyr of the socialist revolution. He sends the translation to Warsaw; it ends up in the PAP's Special Bulletin, but there are problems publishing it for a wider audience.

The comrades in the Kremlin do not regard Guevara as a romantic hero: he was outside their control and did not act on orders from Moscow – as Moscow was aware. He brought about revolutions wherever he wanted, not where or how the Soviet comrades expected. Towards the end of his life, he lambasted the Soviet Union for its exploitation – as with other empires – of the small socialist countries subordinate to it and for handing the ideals of socialism over to bureaucracy. Che's death in Bolivia suited everyone: the politicians in Washington, Moscow and even Havana, where he was turned into a legend – the myth of the sacred socialist revolution.

The Bolivian Diary appears in Polish bookshops thanks to Frelek's intervention with Zenon Kliszko, who does, however, set a condition: the text must be provided with an introduction.

In the introduction, Kapuściński performs an intellectual balancing act. On the one hand, he writes with admiration about Che, his idealism and the idea of armed revolution in Latin America. However, Moscow opposes this idea, and, in accordance with its instructions, so do the Latin American communist parties. This is a time of contention between the Soviet Union and Cuba. The Soviet comrades do not want to inflame conflict with America; it is the era of 'peaceful co-existence' between the two superpowers, and Latin America is the United States' sphere of influence. Havana, on the contrary, is fuelling and encouraging armed uprisings on the model of the Cuban revolution. Guevara meant to incite an uprising of this kind in Bolivia, but he was defeated and killed.

How can Kapuściński write warmly about Che while also keeping to the 'Moscow line' opposing armed revolutions? He finds a way: he praises Guevara as an idealist ('The diary is one of the most beautiful documents of our era, written by a soldier of the revolution'); and at the same time criticizes Fidel Castro for condemning the Bolivian Communist Party, which in accordance with instructions from Moscow did not provide support for Che's guerrillas ('Fidel Castro's attacks on the Bolivian CP are simply unjust').[4]

'Rysiek was ashamed of that introduction later on,' says Józef Klasa, who has his own passion for Latin American affairs and was ambassador to Mexico in the 1970s.

For most of his time in Latin America, Kapuściński will feel torn between sympathies for the Latin American revolutionaries with guns in their hands and a sense of loyalty to the pro-Moscow decision-makers in Warsaw. This dilemma – and initially, his lack of a sense of direction or a feeling for the subtlety of local arguments – is noticeable in some of his reports.

The one that results in his having to leave Chile is written in accordance with the 'Moscow line': it praises the moderate Chilean Communist Party, obedient to directives from the Kremlin, whereas it accuses the more radical Socialist Party of 'a blind policy of opposition for opposition's sake'.[5] In turn, his fascination for Guevara is an expression of sympathy for the 'Christs with rifles on their shoulders' who are not loved by Moscow, the warrior-idealists who, with gun in hand, contrary to the dictates of their Soviet comrades, are fighting for a fairer world, more favourable to the people, especially to the poor.

22

Legends 3: Che, Lumumba, Allende

Kapuściński's fascination for Che Guevara gives rise to a legend according to which he conducted an interview with the revolutionary, knew him, and even remained on friendly terms with him.

The legend came into being because of a blurb on the cover of the British edition of *The Soccer War*. 'He befriended Che Guevara in Bolivia, Salvador Allende in Chile and Patrice Lumumba in Congo'.

Of these three people, Kapuściński – probably – met only Salvador Allende. All that is known of their meeting is what Kapuściński himself said in an interview towards the end of his life. It may be true that Allende protected him from the punishment of being thrown out of Chile. He never published a written text about meeting Allende, and he had never mentioned either this or any other conversation with him before the interview late in his life.

In his sketch 'Guevara and Allende', in the collection *Christ with A Rifle on His Shoulder*, Kapuściński writes not a single word about ever having met either of them in person. There is no ghost of a suggestion that they ever had a conversation, something that journalists are always in a hurry to tell us in the very first words of their reports. But there is a photograph, probably taken during a banquet, at which Kapuściński is sitting next to Hortensia Bussi, Allende's wife.

I ask Wojciech Jagielski, a journalist who specializes in the topic of Africa and is highly acclaimed among Polish reporters, if Kapuściński could possibly have met Lumumba.

'If you met Hugo Chávez or Evo Morales and you had a conversation with them, wouldn't you show off about it in a feature or a report? A reporter who meets anyone of that rank instantly grabs at least a sentence and issues the news that the guy told this or that to him, his paper, his agency. It's the ABC of our profession. In Kapuściński's work there is no evidence of any "meeting with Lumumba." '

The journalistic method that Kapuściński uses in his account of Lumumba (a feature in *Polityka* dated 1961, later included in *The Soccer War*) does not suggest that they ever met or spoke. In any case, Kapuściński

reached Congo in February 1961, when Lumumba had been dead for a
month.

Did he ever meet anyone else of 'that rank'? He was at the Hotel New
Africa in Dar es Salaam, where the rebels used to conspire – men who
would later be the leaders of African countries liberating themselves from
colonial power, such as Robert Mugabe, Sam Nujoma, Kenneth Kaunda
and others. But at that time they were not yet in the spotlight. During the
civil war in Angola, when Kapuściński met António Agostinho Neto,
leader of the MPLA socialist faction, he wrote about it directly in his reports
and then in the book *Another Day of Life*.

So what is the source of the revelations about his friendships with Che
Guevara, Allende and Lumumba?

One time when we were talking about Pinochet's coup d'état, Kapuściński
said to me: 'Oh yes, I was *there* then. It all started with the murder of General
Schneider.' Indeed, Kapuściński was in Chile in late 1967 and the beginning
of 1968, and then made return trips, including during the 1970 election of
Allende as president and Fidel Castro's 1971 visit to Chile, but he was not on
the spot at the time of the Pinochet putsch. 'I was *there* then' just meant that
he was travelling to Chile during those stormy years. However, at the time
of our conversation I was sure the maestro had been a witness to the coup
d'état (the PAP already had another correspondent, Zdzisław Marzec, in
Latin America by then, and it was he who reported on the Chilean drama).

Kapuściński used words to similar effect on another occasion when one
of us brought up the massacre that took place in Mexico City's Plaza de las
Tres Culturas – Tlatelolco Square – in 1968. Again Kapuściński said something like 'Oh yes, I was there then'. And yes, he was – a month later. The
massacre happened on 2 October, and at that time Kapuściński was in Rio
de Janeiro; he arrived in Mexico City in mid-November, as I now discover
while working on this book. The sombre atmosphere barely a month after
the crime undoubtedly made an impression on him – more than three
hundred demonstrators and random passers-by were killed, and two thousand wounded. He was a witness to that turbulent era, but he was not in
Tlatelolco Square, nor in the city at all, on the day of the massacre.

I think Kapuściński created the legend of his 'friendship' with Lumumba
and Che Guevara in a similar way. He may have told the British publisher
that he followed Guevara's trail in Bolivia, and the publisher understood
that he had followed it *with* Che. This myth-making relied on the way
suggestion can create certainty in the mind of a listener. Kapuściński himself
did not go into detail or tell the full story; if pinned to the wall, he could
back out, and it was impossible to accuse him of lying. Other people filled
in the story. We all did.

★   ★   ★

In the early 1990s Jon Lee Anderson, reporter and staff writer for the *New Yorker* and biographer of Che Guevara, did pin Kapuściński to the wall. 'I was in the very early stages of my research for the book about Che. I had read a great many accounts but had never come across a hint of friendship between Guevara and the Polish reporter,' says Anderson. 'Guevara didn't make friendships easily, and when I read on the cover of *The Soccer War* about his friendship with Kapuściński, I was excited. I thought it must have been some sort of secret friendship, but what a discovery!'

Kapuściński was giving a talk in London. Anderson cannot remember the date, but he does remember Kapuściński mentioning that he was working on his research for *Imperium*. Afterwards, Anderson arranged to speak with Kapuściński. He was very generous with his time; they had a drink and spoke for about forty minutes. After he had explained his own project, he mentioned his thrill upon reading that Kapuściński had known the late revolutionary. He asked Kapuściński: 'Tell me about Che.'

'Oh, that's a publisher's error,' replied Kapuściński.

'I felt instantly disappointed,' recalls Anderson. 'His reply struck me as sounding insincere. The disappointment was all the greater because I had always admired him as a reporter and writer – to me he was a legend, a "point of reference".' Anderson explains that nonetheless he kept his disappointment to himself, preferring to admire Kapuściński for the works he had produced, especially *The Emperor*, *Shah of Shahs*, and *Another Day of Life*. Then, and now, Anderson counts these as among his all-time favourite books.

A good many years later, in Liberia, Anderson was talking with a friend, and Kapuściński came up in the conversation. He told her about their London meeting of long ago, and about his disappointment. He remarked that he imagined the mistake had been corrected in Kapuściński's later publications. She got up and pulled a copy of the recently published *The Shadow of the Sun* from her bookshelf. There, still, was the claim about Kapuściński having 'befriended Che', and also Allende and Lumumba.

'Good publishers in the West almost always send writers the cover before printing, and ask them to write, or at least approve, the blurbs, and the same goes for the cover quotes,' says Anderson, who has published several books with prestigious publishers around the world. 'Even if it was different in Kapuściński's case, which I doubt, he could have corrected the mistake later, especially after I had raised it with him.'

The myth about Kapuściński's acquaintance with Guevara has been repeated. Long-standing director of the monthly *Le Monde Diplomatique* Ignacio Ramonet wrote that Kapuściński knew Che Guevara and conducted an interview with him. The legend was consolidated by journalists writing in-depth features about Kapuściński, for the British newspaper the *Independent* and the American magazine *Vanity Fair*, among others. Did

Kapuściński tell them about his friendship with Che during their interviews? Maybe he 'merely' didn't deny it?

Anderson came away with the impression that, despite his worldwide
fame and star status, Kapuściński still behaved like someone who lacked
self-confidence. During Kapuściński's public talk, Anderson noticed that he
kept emphasizing the fact that he had witnessed such and such a number of
revolutions, such and such a number of coups, and repeatedly mentioned
that while working on *Imperium* he had travelled sixty thousand kilometres
within the old Soviet Union.

'I remember thinking at the time, "My God, why does he keep on
repeating that?"' says Anderson. 'Sixty thousand kilometres is a lot, but why
mention it so often? It's as if he felt that the power of the statistics he cited
gave him greater title to expound on the matter. I thought to myself: "You
don't have to tell me that, you're Kapuściński!"'

Summary of a conversation:

'Why do people confabulate?' I ask Wiktor Osiatyński.

'To make themselves feel better than they really are. To show that to
others . . . To hide a weakness. For instance, a coward will invent courage,
and an aggressive person will make up his own tolerance. We usually lie
about things that cause us pain. I knew a man who used to tell colourful
stories about his father and his family, neither of which he ever had.

'In the case of a non-fiction writer such as Rysiek, the motive of making
what you are writing more attractive comes into it: to encourage people to
read, to draw attention to oneself.

'Confabulations usually occur when a person is not self-confident and
has to add something to himself or make up for something. It certainly
doesn't mean it is necessary, it's just the way he feels about himself. From
what you have established, does it appear that Rysiek confabulated the
whole time, or did the confabulations die out at some point in his life?'

'They die out, though there are some exceptions,' I answer.

'That would confirm my instinct. Once he became famous and highly
regarded, once he felt more confident and didn't have to prove anything to
himself or to anyone else, he stopped making things up.'

'He persisted in some of the confabulations,' I say. 'He did not deny
them.'

'That's understandable, because it's very hard to back out of a confabulation, especially for a reporter. If he had announced, "I confabulated!"
someone could have undermined everything he wrote.

'Additionally, when a person confabulates, a particular psychological
mechanism is set in motion: after a while he starts to believe in the things
he has invented, and he is absolutely convinced he is talking the truth.
Putting the facts straight demands an enormous effort, plus a good deal of

courage and self-knowledge.'

I pose a question: 'What could have motivated Rysiek when he suggested to me in a conversation that he was there during the massacre on Tlatelolco Square in 1968?'

Osiatyński answers: 'I think what was speaking out here was a strong need to identify with a great myth, a major historical event. He arrived in Mexico shortly after the massacre, felt the atmosphere of that event and identified with it.'

23

On the Trail of Che Guevara, *Continued*

After leaving Chile, he wanders without a posting. The idea of opening a second PAP bureau in Latin America seems less and less realistic: the agency hasn't enough money. So Kapuściński should take over the post in Mexico, but the PAP central office in Warsaw is having trouble with the correspondent there, Osmańczyk. He has no intention of leaving his job. ('He keeps thinking up new excuses – including a thousand incredible diseases – and he writes that he will leave when he wants to', the enraged Kapuściński writes to the Nowaks.)[1]

He has no idea what to do. Tired, resigned to continually having to take care of formalities such as visas and accreditation in each new country, and with no time for writing, for gaining knowledge, or for his own development, he wants to return to Poland. But at the agency they say, 'Be patient – you'll be going to Mexico soon.'

For the time being, he ends up in Rio de Janeiro. Newly appointed Ambassador Aleksander Krajewski has an ambition to create a dynamic post here, and offers to help the PAP. Kapuściński sighs with relief – but only temporarily.

His benefactor soon turns into a peculiar kind of persecutor. He fetches Kapuściński from the airport, takes him to the ambassador's residence, and refuses to hear of his guest moving out to live somewhere else. ('He wanted to keep an eye on me,' Kapuściński will recall. What for? We don't know.) He won't let the reporter use the telex machine. What sort of help is this, what sort of a favour?

Kapuściński declares a hunger strike. He goes to bed, covers his head with a sheet, and lies there without moving. He doesn't eat, drink, or get up. The housekeeper tries to break him, without success. Then the ambassador himself tries, but his efforts are in vain. With the sheet over his head, Kapuściński doesn't twitch. His stomach is rumbling, his bones ache from lying down, but he doesn't give in. It goes on like this for several days. The ambassador comes to the conclusion that his guest is a madman.

'If you must move out, the door is open.'

He rents a room with a kitchen in the Copacabana district, near the most famous beach in the world. He has a view of the ocean from his windows: it's the most beautiful place on earth! He falls in love with Rio, and he falls in love with Brazil. In a letter to Jerzy and Izabella Nowak he writes:

> This country is truly fascinating, and most importantly, the Brazilians are really great, fine people. They're extremely nice, and in that respect life here is fantastic. You can travel all over Brazil as if it were your own home. I've become very fond of Brazil and I'd like to come back here at any cost.[2]

These are the years of military dictatorship, but it's at its mild stage, and so Kapuściński writes in the same letter that 'the government is very liberal – despite what they write about it in the press'. A month after he leaves Rio, in December 1968, there will be an internal putsch within the army; the hawks will take power; the opposition will grab weapons, and urban guerrilla groups will be formed. From Mexico, Kapuściński will write about the rising influence of fascism in Brazil's political life.

Here, for the first time, he encounters a movement which becomes one of his fascinations: liberation theology. This is a trend within the Catholic Church that reviles anti-communist dictatorships and demands reform in a revolutionary Marxist spirit (which will soon displease the Holy See). In Brazil, liberation theology has advocates not just among rank-and-file priests and laymen but also the bishops.

Just as in Santiago de Chile, he hardly writes a thing. He leads a care-free life: the beach, the sea, sight-seeing. He belongs to the Foreign Correspondents' Club, thanks to which he receives invitations to dinners with government ministers. He learns Portuguese, though he can't stand it: 'an awful, ugly language. I have already mastered it tolerably well, and I can read quite fluently, but there's an irrational objection to this language at work inside me, so I keep ostentatiously speaking Spanish and refusing to talk Portuguese.'[3]

He avoids both alcohol and women, which in Brazil demands a good deal of will-power. He knows that as a correspondent from a communist country he could be watched or provoked, and in that way become easily compromised.

Towards the end of October he receives a telegram from Frelek (who returns briefly from his position as Kliszko's secretary to the PAP, as deputy head of the agency): there is finally a nomination for the job of correspondent in Mexico. The Mexican ministry of foreign affairs has already received a note from the PAP to say that Osmańczyk is ceasing to be the correspondent. There is relief and, once again, anxiety:

I am flying out of Rio next week and I'll be in Mexico City on 16 November . . . Now I've got an awfully hard time ahead of me with Osmańczyk, the most deplorable thing that could happen to me – you know how bad I am at things like that. What's more I'm going to lose another few months, damn it all, I simply haven't the strength, it's too much.[4]

Mexico City is a great source of fascination and an even greater source of frustration.

Here he has a flat with several rooms in the city centre at 57–503 Amazonas Street ('a palace', he writes of it). One room is a spacious study for him alone; this is comfort of a kind he has never had in Warsaw or anywhere else he has worked. Alicja and Zojka come to join him, so he won't be on his own. Socializing with the Polish embassy staff will also prevent him from suffering the torments of loneliness as he did in Kampala, Lagos, Lima and Rio. But he will be entirely alone with the great continent, which right now is a seething volcano.

Every day he reads piles of newspapers, listens to the radio, selects, copies, writes up and reports. In Brazil the guerrillas have kidnapped an ambassador, in the centre of Montevideo the corpse of a student has been found with the marks of torture, in Buenos Aires the Montoneros have shot an important general, some Soviet diplomats have been expelled from Mexico, Fidel says we won't give an inch, Venezuelan guerrilla leader Douglas Bravo says he's had enough of Fidel, in Chile Allende wins the elections, Nixon tightens his policy line . . . How can he master, explain and describe it all?

> [T]he longer stay here is a psychological burden for me, mainly because of my writing, which I cannot do here at all. The PAP has forced me onto the treadmill of daily information services, total idiocy that takes up all my time and energy and leaves nothing behind – no achievement or satisfaction. And I've got a few things to write up my sleeve: all locked away in files and dreams. The days and weeks go trickling through my fingers without a trace – dispatches typed out over and over, some ridiculous press conferences, the endless fiestas you can't avoid. On top of that an altitude of 2,500 metres, which I find tiring and very distracting. Enough, enough.[5]

Now sunshine, now rain, to quote a Latin American hit.

> My dears, I haven't written for ages, for what I would call psychological reasons, i.e., a very long-lasting feeling of total disaster on the Latin American front, a feeling that I'd never get anything done here and that I'd be wasting a couple of years. Luckily it seems this panic-stricken fear

of mine and my breakdown were not quite so entirely justified, because after returning from Poland I sat down at my typewriter and a week ago I finished a sixty-page text called *Latin America 1969*; today a PAP dispatch arrived from Zwiren [an agency editor] saying 'perfect, stunning, congratulations', etc. But what matters most is that I felt something unblocking inside me, my mind becoming clear, and my plans for the future starting to form, and in a nutshell, I was right on my way.[6]

And on a downer again:

Right now I'm sitting at home alone, the noise from the street is awful, it's sunny, but cold. Mexico City is tiring, oppressive, with ten million people, pollution, smog, two bank raids today, and yesterday – I read in the paper – a drunk was riding the bus, it reached the end of the route, so the driver tried to wake him up, the drunk was annoyed at having his sleep disturbed, so he pulled out a gun, killed the driver on the spot and went back to sleep. Then, wondering what on earth they wanted him for, he explained at the police station: *es que me molestaba, hombre* ['he disturbed me'].

And on that image I shall end. I promise to write again soon.[7]

Company from the embassy includes the ambassador, Ryszard Majchrzak, and his wife, Irena, and secretaries Eugeniusz Spyra and Henryk Sobieski (several decades later, his acquaintance with these two men will have consequences). They meet socially and as comrades at Party cell meetings at the embassy. Alicja Kapuścińska takes part in the meetings too. Kapuściński sometimes takes the minutes and is sometimes a speaker, delivering analytical reports – on Nixon's policy towards Latin America, for instance.

Irena Majchrzak, who later settled in Mexico and worked as an educator and anthropologist among Indian communities, remembers Kapuściński as a man living under 'tremendous inner tension': 'Never before or since have I ever met anyone so focused. There was something shamanic about him.'

They do not talk about politics at home or about the anti-Semitic witch-hunt, the echoes of which have not died down yet (Mrs Majchrzak is a Holocaust survivor). At that time everyone took cover, they were all on their guard, she says. They are in close contact, but in her view Kapuściński is self-contained: 'He conducted his own secret game with the world.'

What was that 'tremendous inner tension' like? Here is an example:

Armed conflict is just beginning between Honduras and El Salvador, a conflict which thanks to Kapuściński's reportage will go down in history as 'the soccer war'. A group from the embassy goes off to the ocean, to Acapulco, where the capital's middle class relaxes at weekends. The

Majchrzaks have rented a house and are waiting for the Kapuścińskis to arrive.

Meanwhile, since early that morning Kapuściński has been at home, listening to news on the radio about the developing conflict. Finally he says: 'I'm not going, I have work to do.'

Once the Majchrzaks have already started to give up hope of their friends' arrival, they appear. Both of them have come. Kapuściński is upset, tired by the long journey, and streaming with sweat. He keeps tapping his foot, and repeating: 'I'm going back in a moment. I have to return.'

'Where to?' asks Majchrzak.

'I'm going home, I have to go to Honduras.'

'Sit down, have a rest, jump in the pool. Let's have a drink.'

'No, no, no. I'm off.'

Finally he sits down, but only for a short while, of course. Majchrzak pours the whisky. An hour later, the bottle is empty. Kapuściński gets up.

'Now I really am off.'

'Where on earth to? You can't, you've been drinking!'

'I'm off, and that's final!'

At the Majchrzaks' stern request, Alicja almost forcibly pushes her staggering husband into the car and takes him to a nearby hotel. Let him sleep it off, he can go in the morning, they say. The ambassador and his wife breathe a sigh of relief.

A quarter of an hour later, Alicja turns up again.

'He's gone. I got out to unload the bags, he grabbed the steering wheel and was off.'

Alicja and the Majchrzaks spend the whole night awake, waiting for him to let them know he arrived safely. The next day, he calls to complain that Alicja let him go. When he stopped on the way for petrol, he fell out of the car. It's a miracle that he got there and is alive.

'The whole time, his duties to his family and friends were battling inside him with his professional duties and the most important thing – his passion.'

If he had chosen the sunshine and the ocean, the 'soccer war' would never have happened. If Alicja had held him back, maybe it wouldn't have either.

He loves these reporting trips, the short expeditions – whether to Honduras, Colombia or Chile. He always goes, the post's budget permitting. Even though it is difficult and sometimes dangerous work, the journeys are a breather from the daily routine, from the 'total idiocy that takes up all my time and energy and leaves nothing behind – no achievement or satisfaction'.

Dispatches from PAP special envoy R. Kapuściński:

TEGUCIGALPA: On Thursday morning, with the consent of the Honduran army's general staff, we went straight to the front of the war which has been going on for several days between El Salvador and Honduras. From Tegucigalpa to the town of Nacome . . .

Beyond that, we have to make our way forward under heavy artillery and mortar fire . . . It is a blazing hot tropical afternoon. At five we are on the front line among soldiers firing on enemy positions.

They are young lads, well armed. Around us there is evidence of prolonged, intensive fighting. This is a tough, fierce war, conducted in difficult, heavily wooded terrain. The fighting is happening almost face to face. There are a lot of human victims and significant material losses. Late at night we come back from the front.[8]

LIMA: I spent five days in the central and southern regions of the Peruvian Andes, where teams from the Ministry of Agriculture are conducting agricultural reform, confiscating landed estates. Depending on the circumstances, these *latifundia* are either being divided up among individual farmers, or transformed into production co-operatives created by the serfs and farm-hands from the relevant estate.

The Peruvian agricultural reform was initiated in June last year [1969] by a decree of General Velasco Alvarado's government and has already made enormous progress. This month the first, extremely important stage of the reform was completed: all the large sugar-cane plantations and the sugar factories and rum producers situated on their terrain, which are the property of foreign capital and the local oligarchy, have been transferred to the ownership of the work-force. These plantations, which are currently called 'agricultural production co-operatives', are managed by workers councils selected at meetings of the work-force.[9]

MEXICO CITY: The latest reports coming in from Miami indicate that reactionary Cuban emigrés are preparing an armed invasion of Cuba. This Sunday, Mexican television's Channel 8 broadcast a sensational report from Miami about preparations for this invasion . . . The viewers could see American landing crafts with groups of extremely well-armed men. A small unit of mercenaries was also shown, commanded by Vicente Méndez, who on 17 April this year [1970] made an attempt to land in Cuba to initiate guerrilla operations. Méndez's group was probably entirely wiped out by Cuban army units.[10]

SANTIAGO DE CHILE: [L]ast preparations are underway for a session of Congress which will meet on Saturday to complete the final vote for a president for the republic . . . no one has any doubt that the Congress will elect . . . the Popular Front representative, 62-year-old doctor Salvador Allende . . .

Throughout Chile there is an atmosphere of peace and civic discipline. The forces of reaction have failed to incite rebellion within the army, which remains loyal to the constitutional order. Nor has an attempt to terrorize society succeeded by organizing bomb attacks . . . In all, the extreme right wing has more and more evidently been pushed into defensive positions. Its history is gradually coming to an end.[11]

SANTIAGO DE CHILE: [T]he Chilean Congress has ratified the election of Salvador Allende as president . . . Joy at the triumph achieved has been overshadowed by the tragic fate of General Schneider, on whom the forces of reaction carried out an attack on Thursday, because as a loyal soldier he had prevented the oligarchies from provoking a military coup . . .

As I transmit this report, Santiago city centre is filled with crowds of people who have come in from all districts to celebrate their triumph. However, a big popular demonstration forecast to take place today has been called off at Allende's request because of the grave condition of General Schneider.[12]

Thirty years later, I question Kapuściński about the events described in these and other dispatches from Latin America, about how he sees the continent three decades afterwards and about his first observations. He replies that his Latin American experience is bracketed by two symbolic events: the death of Guevara in 1967 and the peaceful march of Subcomandante Marcos into Mexico City in 2001:

Thirty years ago – the slaughter of people who wanted to change the world for the better, who fought in the name of justice; now – the entrance into the Mexican capital of their heirs, who can fight by peaceful means and voice their demands in the city's main square, next to the presidential palace . . .

The death of Guevara, and then the entire protest movement of 1968, closed an era of incredibly violent and bloody confrontation between the forces of the opposition, which took the form of armed conflict, guerrilla movements with the participation of the peasantry, and the ruling élites, to a large extent dominated by the military. Because the 1960s in Latin America were a time of military dictatorships. In those days, some with hope, others with fear, people were expecting that two, three or four Cuban revolutions would recur, that there would be a domino effect and the whole region would become Castroist.[13]

The hope that this would happen was, at the time, also Kapuściński's hope.

24

Objects of Fascination:
The Latin American Icons

Allende and Guevara. They cannot be separated – they are both heroes of Kapuściński's love affair with revolution. He profiles them, paying tribute to the heroes of the common cause of socialism.

> Guevara drops his ministerial post, he leaves his desk and goes off to Bolivia, where he organizes a guerrilla unit. He dies commanding this unit. Allende is the opposite – he dies defending his desk, his presidential office, from which – as he always predicted – 'they'll only remove me in wooden pyjamas', i.e., in his coffin.
>
> So on the surface these are very different deaths, but in reality the only differences are the place, time and outer circumstances. Allende and Guevara give up their lives for the people's power. The former while defending it, and the latter while fighting for it . . .
>
> Can one say which of them was right? They were both right. They operated in different circumstances, but the aim of their activities was the same.[1]

The essay about Allende and Guevara is like a profession of faith by a revolutionary. Like any faith, this one, too, has its saints. What does he find so captivating? What makes these saints so impressive?

> Allende wants to preserve moral honesty.
>
> Guevara acts in the same way.
>
> Now and then Guevara's unit takes prisoners, ordinary ones and officers, who will be released at once . . . 'You're free,' they're told, 'we revolutionaries are morally honest people, we're not going to bully a defenceless enemy.'
>
> This principle of moral honesty is a characteristic of the Latin American left. It is the frequent cause of its defeats in politics and in battle. But we have to understand the situation. A young person in Latin America grows up

surrounded by a corrupt world. This is a world of policies formed in exchange for money and for the sake of money, a world of dissolute demagogy, a world of assassinations and police terror, the world of a prodigal, ruthless plutocracy, of a bourgeoisie greedy for everything, of cynical exploiters, vapid, depraved money-grubbers and girls who go from one man to another. The young revolutionary wants to reject this world, he wants to destroy it, but before he will be capable of doing that he wants to contrast it with another world, pure and honest; he wants to contrast it with himself.

The rebellion of the Latin American left always features this factor of moral purification, this sense of moral superiority, caring about maintaining a moral advantage over the enemy. I will lose, I will die, but no one will be able to say I broke the rules of the fight, that I betrayed them or let them down, or that my hands are dirty.[2]

Almost from the start of his work in Latin America, Kapuściński plans to write a big book about Guevara, but owing to the daily grind, his dream dissolves, recedes into the background and fizzles out.

He never does write a book about his hero of those years. There isn't enough time, what with the daily run-around, the treadmill, the constant trips abroad. In any case, another era sets in, and Guevara is not quite so sexy, not so cool anymore. To the very end, Kapuściński never loses his fondness for his old idol, and will never make a single remark to imply that he has changed his attitude or agrees with the anti-communist anti-legend about the ruthless revolutionary.

In the final years of his life, Kapuściński's nostalgia for Che's ideals manifests itself in enthusiasm for his continuator – in other circumstances, a different time and place – leader of the Indian rebellion in Chiapas, Subcomandante Marcos.

About Fidel Castro he writes next to nothing. While working as a correspondent in Latin America, he is not free to enter Cuba. A Cuban stamp in his passport will close the door to other countries in the region, excluding Mexico. Yet the Mexicans stamp 'arrived from Cuba' in his passport, which comes to the same thing.

He travels to the island only once, shortly after returning from his Mexican posting. He turns up at the Nowaks for Izabella's name day, and after a good few vodkas there is a fierce argument about Fidel and his revolution. Someone makes some nasty remarks about Castro, and Kapuściński is filled with revolutionary fury. He delivers a fiery defence of Cuban socialism and its leader, saying: 'What do you know about it all? Maybe they are making some mistakes, but those are their own mistakes! They are looking for their own, original way, but what are we doing? We've gone stagnant, we're not doing a thing, we've stopped bothering to look for anything!'

'I once had a fierce argument with Rysiek about Cuba,' recalls Izabella Nowak. 'His tendency to romanticize and his need for strong passions sometimes blinkered him.'

And from Jerzy Nowak: 'He wanted to believe it would be different in Cuba than in Russia after the Bolshevik revolution, different than in Eastern Europe, where socialism was brought in on Soviet bayonets. When in the early 1970s Fidel Castro visited Poland, he said to Edward Gierek, "We make mistakes, but they're our mistakes, not someone else's." That convinced Rysiek. It took him a few years to understand that his revolutionary idols in Cuba had moved away from revolutionary integrity. His fascination with Fidel Castro lasted until the end of the 1980s.'

Later on as well, however, Kapuściński dislikes the ahistorical condemnation and score-settling that becomes fashionable after the collapse of socialism. It is not his style, not his way of thinking. Only once does he speak critically – but without hate-filled embellishment – about the Cuban leader.

It is March 2001, at the Ibero-American University in Mexico City, during a conference running concurrently with workshops for reporters from Latin America.

Question from the audience: 'What do you think of Fidel Castro?'

Reply from Kapuściński: 'Castro is one of the world's few representatives and creators of authoritarian, dictatorial power. Someone who belongs to the past, as we are now living in an era of democratization on a global scale, though it is often just declarative democracy. Nonetheless, the democratic tendency is evident, and in the times ahead it is not dictators, not "single parties" that are going to do the ruling. That era is now coming to an end.'

'You didn't say the most important thing!'

When in the late 1990s I wrote a two-part feature on liberation theology for *Gazeta Wyborcza*, after the first part was published Kapuściński called with a friendly reprimand.

'You focus on disputes within the Church, but you don't say that liberation theology was an expression of emancipation for the Latino "lower-middle" level: teachers, petty tradesmen, small entrepreneurs, students, workers . . . Without them, liberation theology would have been nothing but a doctrinal dispute, which no one would have remembered, either then or now. Have you got time to add that in the second part?'

'Of course, Maestro.'

Liberation theology fascinates Kapuściński as a political movement, as yet another current of revolution.

Kapuściński's number-one hero from the sphere of liberation theology is Archbishop Hélder Câmara, 'the Brazilian Gandhi'. The archbishop's thoughts on the origins of violence in politics are spot on: 'Violence no. 1 – the mother of all violence – is social injustice.' Armed rebellion is just a reaction, violence no. 2, which people resort to in desperation. In preaching the principle of non-violence, Câmara does not approve the path of armed struggle taken by revolutionaries such as Che Guevara; however, rather than attacking the hordes of young Guevaras who take up arms, he attacks the source of the problem, the cause of their desperate choice.[3]

25

On the Trail of Che Guevara,
Continued Further

At the beginning of 1970, without moving from behind his desk in Mexico City, Kapuściński writes a piece of quasi-reportage, little remembered years later, about the kidnap and killing of the West German ambassador to Guatemala. This is a key text for understanding Kapuściński's world outlook, which was shaped by the years he spent in Africa as the continent was casting off colonial hegemony, and perhaps even more by the years he spent in Latin America while it was seething with revolutionary fervour. The story first appears in the PAP Special Bulletin, followed by an abridged version in the press, and is then published as a slim volume entitled *Why Karl von Spreti Died*.

The text stirs controversy, though there is no solid criticism of Kapuściński in Poland. The exception is an essay written by a friend of his, Wiktor Osiatyński, who puts forward a thesis as polemical as the story about the ambassador's murder: Kapuściński has justified political crime.

Is this what he has done?

During those years, in some Latin American countries, foreign diplomats are being kidnapped by left-wing guerrillas fighting against anti-communist civilian and military dictatorships. The kidnappings are designed to draw the world's attention to the persecution of the political opposition. In Brazil, Argentina, Uruguay, Nicaragua, and also in Guatemala as described by Kapuściński, the murders and 'disappearances' of oppositionists number in the thousands.

Abducting diplomats serves, above all, to publicize political crimes. The guerrillas choose diplomats as their target, because, as they see it, the world never hears about the kidnap or killing of a local expert at pulling out finger-nails or applying electric currents to the genitals. Whereas international opinion finds out the very same day about the kidnappings of representatives of governments that co-operate with dictatorships. All the information services and other mass media issue the news. As an additional motive, the guerrillas exchange the abducted diplomats for their comrades-in-arms who have been imprisoned by the regime. For those who are being tortured and are destined to 'disappear', this is usually their last chance at salvation.

One of the people kidnapped in these circumstances is the West German ambassador to Guatemala, Karl von Spreti.

In the early 1950s the social reformer Jacobo Árbenz comes to power in Guatemala. He is not a communist or an ally of Moscow; the communists are barely a part of his hinterland, and not fundamental. Árbenz's policies are aimed at emancipation of the poorest groups; he conducts agricultural reform, with a degree of compensation for the dispossessed American concern United Fruit Company. In response to these reforms, under the slogan of 'war against communism', Washington organizes a coup d'état which is really about protecting the interests of the American firm. The military coup initiates a series of bloody dictatorships and repressive measures, whose victims number some two hundred thousand people, murdered or 'disappeared'.

During the Cold War years, the US promotes the doctrine of 'internal war', which it implants in most countries in the region. It decrees that 'war against communism' is being waged not just on the global stage – between democracy and Red totalitarianism, between America and the USSR – but also on the internal front. The enemy never sleeps. So the military in Guatemala, Brazil, Argentina and other countries in the region cannot sit quietly in their barracks – there's a war going on, and in the name of combating the Red plague, democracy must be suspended. According to this doctrine, all sorts of methods can be applied in the fight against the adherents of Moscow and Havana. At the notorious School of the Americas in Panama, later transferred to the US state of Georgia, American specialists train Latin American officers to fight guerrilla groups. Among the topics covered by lectures and seminars at this school is how to inflict refined forms of torture. The Latino military become experts in the art of cruelty.

The brutal tortures which they apply turn carefree young dreamers into sworn warriors, ready to pull the trigger in extreme situations such as the one described by Kapuściński in his short book about Guatemala. The rebels believe they must shake the conscience of international opinion, force the Western powers to cease co-operating with the tyrants, and stop the criminal generals. And quite often their armed actions achieve the intended aim. In a report dating to that time – after an operation to abduct a diplomat – Kapuściński discusses the following facts, presented in an article in the *Sunday Times*:

> Some political prisoners have been released and given the opportunity to inform the public about police brutality in the prisons and about military operations by 'death squads' on the streets. The Latin American

governments have been embarrassed and humiliated. The 'gringo' has been totally thrown off balance. The revolutionary movements have increased in number and have also gained moral strength as a result of their renown. The climate is being set for revolution – or at least for essential reforms – within societies that are already unstable in any case.[1]

When the Guatemalan guerrillas kidnap Ambassador Karl von Spreti, Kapuściński is sitting in his office in Mexico City, reading the local – and not just the local – press, and is infuriated by what he reads. 'Hordes of United States security service agents are pouring into the cities of Latin America, attempting to seize the kidnappers of diplomats,' reports one of the British newspapers. Instead of a wave of interest in the situation in Guatemala, instead of questions about why it has come to the kidnapping of diplomats, there is a wave of one-sided condemnation of the guerrillas.

Out of the chorus of condemnation, Kapuściński extracts voices in a different tone – the ones explaining what lies behind Guatemala's tragedy and also clarifying why the kidnapping of ambassadors has been on the cards for a long while in Latin America:

> The issue of kidnapping people and hijacking aeroplanes is the central theme of the press here. Some of the Latino governments declare themselves in favour of Argentina's initiative, which proposes refusing the right of asylum to political prisoners set free in exchange for the release of kidnapped diplomats. Dr Héctor Cuadra, a member of the Law Institute at a Mexican university who is a leading authority on international law, is now debating this position.
>
> In Dr Cuadra's opinion, the kidnappings and terrorism will only stop if: 'the Latino governments respect the right to freedom of expression', and 'the Latino governments agree to treat political prisoners legally. These people spend years in the prisons of Latin America without ever being tried, and with none of the guarantees provided by the constitution'.
>
> Cuadra stated that 'Latin America is the land of political persecution'.
>
> In discussing the case of the death of Karl von Spreti, Dr Cuadra said: 'It was not a murder. According to martial law this is a case of the capture and execution of a hostage, and we should remember that there is a civil war going on in Guatemala. The government has lost control over the country, and the underground army – Fuerzas Armadas Rebeldes – is conducting strictly military activities.'[2]

Years later, Kapuściński admits that he wrote his book about the killing of Karl von Spreti 'to counter the misleading of world opinion by us – the journalists'.

What was my motivation in writing about Guatemala, for instance? The main point was to defend those people, to defend the guerrillas, to defend their dignity, their rationale. We hear terrible things about these people, the most disgraceful stories, because the entire information system distributed all over the world is a system of the right. It never utters a single word about what the dictatorships there are like, what the regimes are like, or the reality that forces those militants to fight. It will only keep on endlessly repeating its condemnation of 'terrorists'. But take note that all national liberation movements, including the Polish resistance movement during the last war, were defined by the official propaganda as terrorism. So my first impulse at the time, when after the killing of Karl von Spreti in Guatemala that whole wave of defamation poured out in a country where several dozen genuinely innocent people are killed on a daily basis, was a reaction of inner protest and moral defence of these people . . .

I can call them freedom fighters or heroes. I cannot pretend that the primary and fundamental, institutionalized terror does not exist, against which they are rising up, going to fight and being killed. That is the whole truth, and if anyone wants to stick at half or a quarter of the truth, then he is surrendering to or serving falsehood and mendacity.[3]

This forgotten little book includes what to my mind is one of the most brilliant passages in Kapuściński's entire oeuvre (a shortened version appears in *The Soccer War*):

The people who write history devote too much attention to the 'noisy' moments and do too little research on the quiet times . . . Silence is a sign of unhappiness and often of crime . . . Silence is necessary to tyrants and invaders, who make sure their activity is accompanied by it . . . What silence emanates from countries packed full of prisons . . . Silence requires a vast police apparatus. It requires an army of informers. Silence demands that the enemies of silence should disappear suddenly and without trace . . . It would be interesting if someone were to investigate to what degree world systems of mass media work in the service of information, and to what degree they serve quiet and silence. Which is there more of: what is said, or what is not said? . . . If I put on the local radio station in Guatemala and just listen to songs, beer ads or the only news from the outside world, that some Siamese-twin boys have been born in India, I know this radio station works in the service of silence.[4]

Writing with empathy for the Guatemalan guerrillas, Kapuściński finds himself in a politically ambiguous position. Of course the story about the murder of the West German ambassador is above all a major indictment of imperialism, despite which it does not suit the political correctness of the socialist camp. At the time, Moscow is opposed to the creation of partisan armies in Latin America modelled on Castro's and Guevara's guerrillas from the days of the Cuban revolution. The guerrilla movements are independent of Moscow and they spoil its policy of 'peaceful co-existence' with Washington – because the Americans regard every rebellion in Latin America as Soviet sabotage within their sphere of influence. Meanwhile, Castro is inciting schisms within the communist parties: urging the dissidents to create armed units and fight with guns in their hands against the right-wing, pro-Yankee dictatorships on the continent. Castro declares that the true revolutionary is the one who conducts revolution. Meanwhile, most of the communist parties in the region tend to fight using peaceful methods; from Havana's point of view, these parties are being eaten away by the virus of reformism.

Why Karl von Spreti Died is a story in the spirit of revolutionary socialism from Havana, not the bureaucratic kind issuing from Moscow.

In any case, the political winds are changing: after rebelling against Moscow's strategy, Cuba finally renounces its relative independence and support for guerrilla groups in the region. After the Soviet intervention in Czechoslovakia – the crushing of the Prague Spring in August 1968 – and the lack of firm reaction to this intervention on the part of the United States, Fidel Castro's fears will not go away. He is worried that as Washington did not react firmly to the invasion of Prague by Warsaw Pact troops, by the laws of analogy the still-possible – as he thinks – American invasion of Cuba might not meet with decisive opposition from Moscow.

Castro decides to protect himself in case of a US invasion of Cuba: he swallows his pride and, contrary to the expectations of people on the left the world over, including many Latino communists and some Cuban ones, he supports the crushing of the Prague Spring. He sends out a clear signal to the Kremlin: let's end the argument about the revolutionary path taken in Latin America – Moscow is the only Rome of world communism, and there won't be any more questioning of its leadership. He publicly expresses the hope that if socialism were ever threatened in Cuba, the Soviet Union would help.

The practical confirmation of Castro's new policy is his visit to Chile in 1971: he befriends socialist Salvador Allende, who is introducing revolutionary changes peacefully and democratically. Castro shows the face of a realist: he is afraid that the Chilean right, supported by the United States, will overthrow Allende's government on any excuse at all. That is why, during his visit to Chile, he cools the ardour of the left-wing radicals who are demanding that Allende introduce socialism immediately without considering the will of a large part of society.

As Kapuściński reports from Chile:

> Fidel Castro's visit and the speeches he made here prove that breaking the Latin American left into two currents is today a closed chapter in the history of the continent . . . Several times now he has repeated that the path which in Cuba led to the triumph of the revolution [i.e., armed fighting] is not the one and only path to victory. For many Latino leftist groupings, fixated on Cuba as the only ideal, these declarations must sound shocking . . . Some people will shift to the communist left wing, and the small unreconciled groups will descend to anarchistic positions devoid of ideals and will lose political significance.[5]

Havana's change of political strategy also has practical consequences for the work of the correspondent from Poland. Kapuściński – who should, as it were 'ex officio', be writing about the world in accordance with the Moscow line – is more sympathetic towards Havana's 'dissident' policy. Now his dilemmas are at an end; he writes it almost straight out:

> This general evolution of Havana's with regard to the problems of revolution in Latin America has equally important, positive significance for the policies of countries in the socialist camp on this continent. During the disputes between Fidel Castro and the local communist parties, our situation was difficult: on the one hand we supported Cuba, but at the same time we also supported the communist parties. This was not in the least comfortable for us.[6]

No longer must Kapuściński be torn between sympathy for Castro and loyalty towards the pro-Moscow decision-makers in Warsaw.

In his polemic against his friend's book about the killing of Karl von Spreti, Wiktor Osiatyński wrote:

> Kapuściński has substantiated a crime. He has justified murder committed in the name of the struggle against exploitation, oppression and dictatorship . . .
>
> What Kapuściński has written is enough to make us understand why the guerrillas kidnapped and shot von Spreti. I do not think it is enough to justify them. For Kapuściński it is. For from his book it unambiguously emerges that responsibility for the ambassador's death lies with: Guatemalan fascism, which forced the guerrillas to take up this form of struggle as the only one they had left; American imperialism, which kept

this fascism alive; Nixon, who failed to persuade the Guatemalan authorities, though he could easily have done so; and finally to some degree
Brandt, who did not put enough pressure on Nixon. The guerrillas are
not responsible at all.

And yet it was the guerrillas who put the gun to von Spreti's temple
and pulled the trigger.

After reading Kapuściński, I understood why they did it. However, as
distinct from the author, I was not convinced they had to do it. And I
didn't like this book.[7]

Kapuściński never commented on his friend's essay. 'Fine,' he will say on
occasion. Nothing more.

'I think here he was guided by a personal code: not to argue with his
friends, not to escalate the differences, to forgive them their errors,' proposes
Jerzy Nowak.

Perhaps he does not want to debate with Osiatyński, because in parrying
his friend's arguments he would have to find some convincing reasons for
the taking of someone's life – and in public discussion, isn't that suicidal?
How can you dispute an issue like that when at the same time you are
opposed to any sort of killing? How can you do it in such a way that the
debate does not become a defence of terrorism and political murder?

Kapuściński avoids the word 'terrorism' – he knows a word like that
makes everyone into a hostage, a prisoner of language. How do the phrases
'defence of terrorism' and 'defence of political crime' sound, and in what
way does 'recognition of armed struggle as one of the acceptable paths'
sound different? That is why Kapuściński uses the word 'guerrillas', not
'terrorists', and the term 'armed struggle', not 'terrorism'.

He does not regard Karl von Spreti as an incidental passer-by but rather
as a political player in the Guatemalan tragedy; the representative of a
government that gains advantage from exploiting the banana republic and
co-operating with a criminal junta justifiably viewed as an internal occupying force by those who have been repressed. As Dr Cuadra, the lawyer
quoted by Kapuściński, says: 'According to martial law, this is a case of the
capture and execution of a hostage.'

However, Kapuściński is not trying to find good grounds for murder –
there is no such thing – but to take a short walk in the shoes of the kidnappers, to feel his way into their situation, the drama of the country, the
tragedy of the oppressed. And then to ask questions: Can we understand
the actions of the guerrillas? Can we understand the young people from
Guatemala, Brazil, Uruguay and El Salvador who reach for rifles and bombs
in their struggle against the external or internal invader?

His years spent in the Third World teach Kapuściński empathy, teach
him to view things from the desperadoes' perspective: those who are affected

by repression, poverty and lack of prospects believe that situations occur in which there are no options left but bombs, guns, and sometimes suicide. When they're soon going to kill you, when you have to save your friends from torture, when you cannot see light at the end of the tunnel, all that remains is armed struggle (let it even be terrorism and violence) as the act of ultimate despair. It is hard to extol or eulogize this sort of fighting, but we can and perhaps should understand it.

Kapuściński does not substantiate political crime; he explains its anatomy, helps the reader put himself in the psychological situation of the desperate, and does it with such empathy and skill – and at the same time so cold-bloodedly – that some may rightfully feel shocked at their own reaction: if after reading this I can understand kidnappers and terrorists, am I justifying political murder? Doesn't Kapuściński go too far?

Why Karl von Spreti Died is not just a story about Guatemala but also a parable of the Cold War, as well as of latter-day and, to some extent, contemporary relations between North and South. It did not fit in with the political correctness of the socialist era, nor does it fit the kind prevalent since its collapse – certainly not in Kapuściński's country.

During the Cold War era, a vast number of Kapuściński's compatriots who dislike the communist regime live in the belief that Evil is always and only on the side of the Reds. Militants who refer to the ideals of emancipa-tion and the kingdom of justice, or who simply sympathize with commu-nism, bear – in the opinion of these people – the stigma of the forces of enslavement. By contrast, in the Cold War division, the forces of Western democracy – even if they throw bombs at civilians or run 'universities of torture' – represent Good.

Kapuściński shows without ambiguity that in the Third World countries the 'free' West shares responsibility for the enslavement of societies; it is an obstacle to aspirations towards liberation. In those countries, the commu-nists and left-wing radicals usually belong to the forces battling tyranny and bondage. Sometimes they are the only political force with which an honest person can identify without shame.

Based on his experiences working as a reporter in the Third World, Kapuściński soon draws the conclusion that viewing the world through the spectacles of the Cold War division into East and West, communism and capitalism, obscures rather than clarifies the picture. He finds the North–South perspective more important and more accurate – the division into the affluent world and the world of poverty and exclusion, and all the consequences of that division.

Thus, after the collapse of the socialist utopia he will not be infected by enthusiasm for capitalism, for modern ideas about 'spreading democracy' among 'savages', or for America-the-empire – practices and goals for which so many people in his country sigh with a love that is barely reciprocated. Nor is he attracted by the revision of twentieth-century history in the spirit of anti-communism. After reporting from Third World countries in the Cold War era, he has seen too much.

He has also understood that our 'better' world is deeply involved in the appearance, at the start of the twenty-first century, of 'Mohammed with a rifle', which he spoke about in interviews in the final years of his life. He was horrified by the 'war party' in Washington and the ease with which a superpower is able to trigger an imperial incident. He was also disturbed by al-Qaeda, which he regarded not so much as an organization but as 'an attitude, a mentality', as 'an attempt to send all outsiders to hell'.

He did not live long enough to write more on this great topic of contemporary times. What are the differences between 'Christ with a rifle' in the 1960s and 1970s and today's 'Mohammed with a rifle'? Where should we look for the criteria demarcating the line between a justified, but by no means good, armed struggle and the blind cruelty of terrorism, which is certainly not the weapon of the weak alone?

He did not leave a universal key, but his interviews and statements help us to think about the modern world and to pose questions about how to judge today's conflicts. The story of the kidnap and murder of Karl von Spreti is number one on this list. And although it does not contain any simple analogies, it exposes the mechanism of 'misleading public opinion', as well as political self-deception and illusions: supposedly, a battle is being fought against evil, whether it is called 'communism' or 'terrorism', but the illnesses, plagues and misfortunes against which the fight is ostensibly conducted become even more wide-spread because of its methods.

For now I'm getting on with the packing, rather feebly, but I am doing it, so I hope to send off my boxes on time, and then part with the land of the Aztecs. Altogether I will have had four and a half years in Latin America, which – roughly speaking – is enough for me.

I'm already wondering what I'm going to do in Poland. I know, and then I don't know. My ideal would be to do nothing and just devote myself to writing. That's my provisional plan, which might fall apart on contact with reality. I might stay at the PAP, but take unpaid leave in order to write, and then we'll see . . .

Aha, so what should I bring you? Ala wrote to say a dress shirt and various things of that kind, but perhaps there's something else? Maybe you could send me a list of your *pedidos* [requests]? In any case, I'll try to lug what I got via Ala to Warsaw.

So my dears, see you soon, very soon! I'm already eager to cross the Atlantic, to get to Europe, to Europe, there's no life outside Europe (we'll see what I say in a few months from now!), but maybe I'll say the same thing – *quién sabe* [who knows]? At any rate, I'm coming to a big turn, a dizzying bend in the road, enough excitement to make my blood curdle. Write, write, all I want to do now is write. Dammit, if only they'd leave me in peace, if only they didn't want anything of me, so I could hide, bury, lock myself away.[8]

26

Zojka's Escapes

Kapuściński's wife and daughter accompany him on his more than three-year stint in Mexico. Alicja works a little, and Zojka goes to high school. After a year and a half, Zojka wants to go back to Poland; she is seventeen and has enough determination to stand up to her parents. Especially her father, with whom she argues about everything.

From an interview with Alicja Kapuścińska:

Why did your daughter want to go home?
    I don't know. She had learned Spanish, and announced that she would rather be in Poland. That was her wish.
    Is she like him?
    No, like his mother.[1]

Alicja goes back to Warsaw with Zojka, thinking it is for ever, as she cannot leave her daughter on her own. A friend, Zofia Sztetyłło, offers to let Zojka live with her. 'Do you want to stay at Auntie Zofia's?' Alicja asks her daughter.

She was happy, she took her school graduation exams and got a place to do Hispanic studies. I came back a year later, and Rysiek six months after, as he still had to close down the post.[2]

Zojka's 'escape' from Mexico marks the start of a difficult relationship between father and daughter, as well as between daughter and both parents. The prelude to these complications comes a few years earlier, when Alicja travels to Africa to join her sick husband, leaving ten-year-old Zojka behind with her grandparents, against her wishes. Her mother explains that she is not going on holiday, but going to see her father, who is seriously ill.

Nevertheless, the regret and injury remain.

More than once I heard worried comments such as, 'She still feels like an abandoned child inside. No arguments are of any use here, it has to do with some mixed-up emotions.' The regrets and injuries manifest themselves for the first time when she is a rebellious teenager. She wants to go back to Poland from Mexico, and she does. No force could stop her.

During her student years, Zojka falls in love with a boy from Paraguay. Her parents refuse to hear of their daughter leaving for some unknown place; they have just begun to know Latin America in the era of social upheavals, revolts, coups d'état and terrible poverty.

Thanks to his connections within the Party, Kapuściński is in a position to arrange a grant in Poland for his daughter's boyfriend. And he does so – except that the 'son-in-law' does not turn up, shows no sign of life, and disappears without trace. Soon it turns out that the impoverished Paraguayan simply did not have the money for a ticket, and first had to earn enough for it. Neither the 'parents-in-law' nor the 'fiancée' had thought of that.

He turns up in Warsaw a few months too late – Zojka is now in love with a Canadian of Polish origin, who has come to Poland to get to know his father's country. That summer they hitch-hike their way to Sweden to work for a while, and then go to France on holiday.

When the new academic year begins, Alicja becomes worried because her daughter is not yet back from her holiday. Meanwhile Zojka is giving evasive answers. Finally she calls: Send my birth certificate, I'm getting married.

On Christmas Eve she gets married in Grenoble. Now she is called Zofia Grzybowska. Was Alicja at the wedding? 'Of course not. She told me about the wedding, but she didn't invite me.'[3] It is a sort of repetition of family history: Kapuściński's mother was not at her son and Alicja's wedding either.

> Rysiek was in Angola at the time. When he got home he was very angry. Any kind of family connections with foreign countries were very badly regarded, and could actually disqualify a journalist from going abroad as a correspondent.[4]

This was the second of his close relatives – his sister, Barbara, was the first – to choose life in the West. Kapuściński yells in rage that he is renouncing Zojka. Nowak smooths his ruffled feathers; calm down, he tells the father, it's her life, her right, her choice. Besides, she doesn't have to give up Polish citizenship; she'll get a consular passport.

Zojka leaves for Canada with her husband, 'escaping' for a second time.

Her marriage to the Canadian does not last long. Nevertheless, Zojka decides to remain in Vancouver. At one of the universities there she completes the degree in Hispanic studies that she began in Warsaw. Soon she meets another man, an American, and has a son with him, whose name is Brendan. Her relationship with her parents improves, and they exchange warm letters: it's great that you've stopped smoking, Dad; is there anything you need, daughter? Zojka is helped by her father's sister, who by a lucky coincidence lives in the same city. Little Brendan gets on very well with Barbara's sons, who treat him like a baby brother.

Zojka signs up for a typing course, enabling her to get temporary work in offices and libraries. But smouldering inside her are artistic aspirations. She is thinking about painting and also tries to write.

When in the 1980s Kapuściński becomes a world-famous writer and starts to receive more serious fees for his work, the parents' help for their daughter becomes more generous. Paradoxically, the tension returns to their mutual relations.

In 1984, when father and daughter meet in Palo Alto, California, there is an altercation typical of their relationship. For several hours, Zojka leaves the friends' house where they are staying. When she returns, her father makes a scene: why didn't she say where she was going and when she would be back? Zojka replies in a similar tone – he never bothered with her when she was little; now she is grown-up and independent; she has her own child and doesn't need to report to her father.

'He brought his daughter money, he was very proud of it,' remember the friends. 'Meanwhile, with her entire behaviour, she was communicating to him: "Don't think you can buy me for a few thousand."'

At the turn of the 1980s and 1990s, mutual relations take a turn for the worse. The number of grudges grows. Father explains to daughter that he is willing to help her, but he is not in a position to maintain her. He has earned a lot from several books published abroad, but it is not a bottomless pit.

Thanks to her parents' 'subsidies', Zojka rents an artist's studio in downtown Vancouver. During a visit to Canada her father comes to see the studio and gets the impression that renting a place in this location is an extravagance that neither he, and certainly not his daughter, can afford.

He calmly explains: Practising an art demands patience and humility, because in the modern day and age artistic creativity is the kingdom of excess, bursting with talent and products. To fulfil your artistic plans, first you have to earn some money; few people in today's world – only a handful of those most outstanding and acclaimed – can afford to live on their artistic creativity alone. The rest, in other words the majority, have to work within non-artistic professions and carry out their creative ambitions in their spare time, after work.

He is shocked by what's happening with his daughter: to tell the truth, he doesn't know much – only as much as he can see for himself and as she herself will tell him. He does find out that she gave up her job at the university library a few years earlier, and that she was planning to study psychology, followed by 'therapy through painting'. In Vancouver he is worried by the state of the apartment. Eleven-year-old Brendan spends days on end at home alone, in semi-darkness; he goes to school when he wants, and when he doesn't feel like it, he doesn't go. In Zojka's absence, his grandson tells him that he lives mainly on tins of baked beans in tomato sauce.

At the beginning of 1992, Zojka escapes for a third time: she writes her parents a short letter in which she announces that she is severing all relations with them. She tells them she is moving but doesn't give them the new address or telephone number. Only her bank account number remains unchanged.

Her parents cannot understand their daughter's behaviour. They are shattered. Kapuściński suffers torment, reproaching himself for not having been at home for years on end and for not having paid Zojka enough attention during the times he was there. But the milk was spilt long ago – what can be done about it now? He has been trying for years, helping as much as he can, sending money, sometimes against his better judgement. He blames himself for putting up with her immaturity for too long; he should have put his foot down ages ago. Both he and Alicja are in agony from their sense of helplessness. For months on end, they have no news of their daughter or grandson. (Zojka also severs contact with her father's sister, who has no idea why.)

'He suffered because Zojka cut him off from his only grandson,' a close friend tells me. 'One time when Brendan was in Poland, Rysiek tried to get close to him, to tell him something about himself, about the family and Poland. But he couldn't get his wishes across. The boy behaved just as if he had never left Canada: he tuned in to English-language channels on the TV and wasn't interested in anything but that. Maybe he was still too small . . . And then all contact with him was broken off.'

Months later, when Zojka finally gets in touch, the family psychodrama starts all over again. Her father demands that she get a job, and that if she can't find one, she should prove she has been trying by producing certificates from the employment agency. He is disappointed that the only topic their daughter ever brings up in their conversations and letters is money.

Some time later, Zojka presents him with the idea of an expensive journey around America, touring the famous art galleries. It is obvious who is supposed to finance this trip. Not for the first or last time, her father explains that in order to put extravagant plans into action, first you have to earn the money; he reminds his daughter that she is forty-five now and should take account of the financial resources and possibilities – her own as well as her parents'.

Now Zojka changes her name: henceforth she will be called René Maisner. She is a photographer and visual artist; she makes photographic and painted collages, and doesn't want anyone to think she owes any interest in her work to her famous father. 'Escape' number four . . . five?

When from time to time she comes to Poland, her father usually disappears from home. After one of these visits, Kapuściński has had enough, and doesn't want to see his daughter in the house ever again. For a while Alicja feels the same way, but later tries to soothe his anger. Zojka will cross the threshold of her parents' house many more times.

After her father's death, René Maisner, daughter of the famous writer Ryszard Kapuściński, travels around Europe. In Italy she and her mother accept prizes and meet his readers. In Pińsk in Belarus they unveil a memorial plaque on the house where Kapuściński spent his childhood. René Maisner goes on her own to Spain, where an exhibition of his photographs from Africa is on tour. In Granada she takes part in a conference about immigrants and cultural integration; she also receives the Harambee Award, which in Swahili means 'everyone pulling together'. At the University of Navarra in Pamplona she meets with students and professors, and answers questions about her father.

She gives the press several interviews – about her father.[5]

He was a man who showed his emotions but couldn't talk about them. He was a patient listener and was interested in what a person he met somewhere at the end of the world had to say, but he himself kept quiet. He treated me in a similar way. On coming home he would spend two days finding out what my life was like. Then he'd be absorbed by his work: meetings, conversations, writing . . . He was willing to pay the price for it, because in parting with the country for some time, he was also parting with his family.

My childhood memories are that encounters with him were usually unexpected. When he turned up, I was happy he'd be with us again. But on the other hand I wasn't capable of showing regret because of the separation. He simply spent too long in the other hemisphere. Dad understood that, and tried to make up for the lost time. When I was only a few years old, he used to bring me dolls. Ten years later he used to give me souvenirs and clothes made by folk artists from Mexico or Peru. Those were the days of flower children, and things like that were fashionable. Anyway, I still wear similar things today.

In October 2006 I brought him a 2007 diary, with drawings and words of wisdom by the Buddhist monk Thich Nhat Hanh. My father liked beautiful diaries and used to write down his notes, appointments and thoughts in them. 'I'm very grateful to you,' he said. He looked at it sadly, picked it up and kept it for a long time on the bedside table within sight and reach. Only later did I realize he was aware how ill he was.

Before the funeral I met a lot of people who loved Dad. They knew things about him which I had no idea about. That was painful. In those days my grief caused by Dad's passing was mixed with regret for the time we never spent together. I realized there were only a few shared moments. Too few.

In the autumn of 2008 René Maisner, photographic artist, has an exhibition at Warsaw's Kordegarda Gallery entitled *Elements*; her collages refer to the forces of nature: earth, fire, wind and water. *Gazeta Wyborcza* journalist Lidia Ostałowska interviews her. Maisner answers questions about her father reluctantly, sometimes irritably. She defends herself against the reporter's attempt to seek the source of her inspiration in her father's work.

Once the interview has ended, she declares that the questions about her father cannot appear in the text, nor can it say in her biographical note that she is the daughter of Ryszard Kapuściński. Ostałowska gives in, and decides not to have the text of the conversation edited for publication. The interview never appears.

27

A Committed Reporter,
a Black-and-White World

General Farrusco, commander of the city garrison, comes to fetch me from the shabby Fatima boarding house in the centre of Luanda. I wanted to stay at the Hotel Tivoli, where Kapuściński lived in 1975 during the evacuation of the Portuguese, when the wooden packing-crate city sailed away from here, then during the siege of Luanda, and finally when Angolan independence was declared, by coincidence on 11 November 1975, the same date as Poland's National Independence Day. But the Tivoli is fully booked two months ahead. In any case, it is no longer the same building – the façade and the decor have changed, and nowadays it is a four-star, not so modest little hotel, decent by local standards, from the late colonial era. You can no longer see the port or the bay from the windows, as they are now obscured by taller buildings.

Nor is Doña Cartagina here anymore – the white-haired old woman who cleaned at the Tivoli. Without her, so he wrote, it is hard to imagine Luanda, Angola, or any part of that war.

The civil war in Angola ended six years earlier, in 2002, but all over the city traces of it are visible. Some buildings have not been renovated for years, and part of the city is a construction site, as a result of which there are ghastly traffic jams. There are few hotels, and you need to make reservations months in advance, because few people come to a country where a civil war went on for thirty years. Now businessmen come here – involved in oil and diamonds – and it is they who take up most of the hotel rooms.

Farrusco, a tough fellow of small stature, speaks, or rather shouts, occasionally in crude language – now at the driver, now at other subordinates. He is emotionally on edge. 'Tell me how my friend Ricardo died. Was he ill for long? You speak just as he did. Meaning how? In Brazilian. Do you have photos? Give them here, quick!'

In the colonial era Farrusco was in the Portuguese commandos. The son of a peasant from southern Portugal, he stayed in Angola after completing his service and worked as a car mechanic. When the uprising against the

Portuguese broke out, one day he went to the headquarters of the MPLA – People's Movement for the Liberation of Angola, the Marxist liberation movement – and offered his assistance. 'I'll show you how it's done, how you should fight.'

Kapuściński met him on the southern front of the Angolan war and described him in a series of reports, then in the book *Another Day of Life*. He left his readers with his comrade from the trenches seriously wounded: when Kapuściński departed Angola, he did not know if Farrusco had survived.

Meanwhile, the wounded Farrusco had ended up in captivity. Told he should change sides to join the MPLA's Angolan opponents, he was offered treatment at a luxury clinic in South Africa. He refused. He ended up in prison, from where – as soon as he recovered – he organized an escape and then put together a guerrilla force in the south of the country, loyal to the MPLA's Marxist government in Luanda. Many years later his political enemies from UNITA, the National Union for the Total Independence of Angola, would murder his son – simply because he was his son.

Now, in his office at the city garrison, General Farrusco is looking at photographs taken by his friend from the front – the Polish reporter.

'Ricardo describes someone called Carlotta in his book. I've never met her.'

'That's her,' I say, pointing at one of the photographs.

'Is that really her? I did know that girl, but I never knew what her name was. She was with us in Benguela!'

'What was Ricardo like, as you remember him?'

'He was with us during the fighting in the south. We didn't treat him like an ordinary journalist.'

'But like whom?'

'Like one of us.'

'Because he was from a socialist country? Because he thought the same way you did?'

'He thought, but he did it the way that was necessary – he did some shooting.'

For a moment I'm unsure whether Farrusco has made something up. Kapuściński's political sympathies during this and other wars, conflicts, liberation revolutions in Africa and Latin America were always clear as day, and left no room for doubt. However, to sympathize and to shoot are two different things.

But in interviews with Kapuściński dating from the 1970s, I have no trouble finding confessions that dispel my uncertainty as to the General's memory:

Were you ever in a situation where you had to grab a gun?

Yes, in Angola for example. If you are at the front, you are often in a situation where you have to join in with the fighting.[1]

Did you ever shoot?

Yes. But those were exceptions to the rule. It's always better to go to the front with nothing, because if they catch you, you can defend yourself with the fact that you're unarmed, play the role of the guy who got mixed up in it accidentally, smile stupidly and show your honest intentions. Better not to have even a knife.

So why did you ever depart from that rule?

A journalist who specializes in being a war correspondent sometimes goes into action with a unit and then he feels involved with them. Even doubly so. He supports their cause and sympathizes with them, for one thing. Secondly, when the situation becomes dangerous, risky, he wants to give his lot support, not to be a burden that they have to take care of or look after. Under fire nothing else matters. No one is concerned about rescuing a reporter just so he can tell the world about this fight. He has to take responsibility for himself, shoot to avoid being shot. It's a fight for survival . . .

You can't be understanding towards someone who's got you in their sights. You cannot agree that he's in the least bit right. You want to live, so shoot.[2]

Many of Kapuściński's statements testify that it is not just about 'responsibility for himself' and survival. Looking at it purely theoretically, would he have fired at the MPLA's enemies in Angola? Would he have fired at the Latin American guerrillas if he had somehow got tangled up on the side of their enemies, in other words the military and the security service, and then told the story?

Everything he ever said on this subject implies he would not. A committed reporter, such as he considered himself to be, is on one particular side of the conflict, and sometimes gets involved to such a degree that he fires, along with the heroes of his reportage, at their (common?) enemy, not just because he wants to survive – not for that reason above all.

In any case, is it possible to be an objective war correspondent, commentator on revolution, or observer of great social upheavals? Kapuściński's life, his views and his writing provide an unambiguous answer to that question.

'Every time he came back from a new reporting trip, I never knew who I was talking to. A Bolivian guerrilla? An Ethiopian revolutionary? A Shi'ite fundamentalist?'

So says Hanna Krall, first lady of Polish reportage.

'Rysiek identified with the people he wrote about,' she says, 'with their experiences, sufferings and causes; he became one of them. Once he came back as a "Muslim" – he stopped drinking wine and eating pork. But when he started to write, the separation of the author from the world he was describing took place. I work the other way around,' she adds. 'I make my observations coldly, with detachment, and only walk in my heroes' shoes while I'm writing.'

On returning from Angola, Kapuściński identifies with the MPLA fighters and the Cuban soldiers supporting them, whom Fidel Castro sent to their rescue. Among the reporters for the weekly *Kultura*, where he works in the 1970s, legends circulate: that he fought in a Cuban uniform, that he showed someone his Cuban document – with a false Spanish name and a totally genuine photograph. How much truth is there in these, and how much myth?

He returns from Iran, where he has witnessed the fall of the Shah and the Islamic revolution, excited about the cause of the Shi'ite revolutionaries and their leader, Ayatollah Khomeini. Ewa Staśko, then editorial secretary at *Kultura*, gets into an argument with him (the story is told by her husband, Janusz Rolicki).

'You'll see what that dreadful old man will get up to,' Staśko warns Kapuściński provocatively. 'The French should have dealt with him.' Khomeini had spent time in exile in France.

'What do you mean?! You have no idea what the Savak [the political police of the Shah of Iran] used to do!'

The temperature of the quarrel rises so rapidly that the weekly's editor-in-chief, Dominik Horodyński, has to intervene.

Colombian journalist and professor of journalism Javier Dario Restrepo, whom I meet in Bogotá (where he holds the newly founded Kapuściński Chair), first became aware of the Polish reporter in the late 1980s, when, after one of the foreign publications of his book about Angola, someone accused him of a lack of objectivity.

'Did you also recognize the cause of the opponents of the MPLA's Marxist government, the FNLA and UNITA fighters?' a critical journalist asks Kapuściński.

'No one ever gave me the opportunity. War reporting is doomed to a certain measure of subjectivity,' he replies.

In an interview published in the Mexican newspaper *La Jornada*, which Restrepo gives his students to read, Kapuściński refutes the charge of a lack of objectivity and sets out his point of view:

I do not believe in impartial journalism, I do not believe in formal objectivity. A journalist cannot be an indifferent witness, he should have the capacity for what in psychology is called empathy . . . So-called objective journalism is impossible in conflict situations. Attempts at objectivity in such situations lead to disinformation.[3]

Formal objectivity, a dominant issue in American journalism, especially the news variety, is also rejected by Michael Kaufman, former correspondent for the *New York Times*, who befriended Kapuściński during the war in Angola. More than once he took advantage of the Polish reporter's knowledge to present news from the 'Red side' of the conflict, to which a correspondent from the United States did not have good access. It was from Kapuściński that he found out about the Cuban instructors who had come to Angola, and whom he had not yet seen for himself. Thanks to his friend from Poland, he could report to his paper in New York: 'According to a well-informed source from the eastern bloc . . .'

'When I started work in the profession,' Kaufman tells me at his New York apartment, 'many of my fellow journalists believed that if a policeman beats up an African American who is fighting for civil rights, the objective truth lies somewhere in the middle between the man being beaten and the man beating him. From the very start, this seemed to me to be nonsense.'

Both Kapuściński and Kaufman are interested in the spirit of the times, the Zeitgeist, not in measuring objectivity with a ruler. Both are pleased that the colonial era is coming to an end in Angola. Is their pleasure 'objective'?

Kaufman remembers the moment when independence was declared: a crowd of people dancing joyfully in the streets, shouting and singing. He wonders what sort of question to ask one of these excited people – the sort of question that can get to the heart of the matter.

'What is your wish for your child?' he at last asks an unknown woman.

'That he will live.'

'But live how?'

'Just that he will live – that is enough.'

It takes Kaufman quite a while to understand the simplest message encapsulating the meaning of the event he is witnessing.

And how does this meaning, how does that situation, relate to impartiality? How does it relate to the rationale and experiences of those who had to leave Angola, the colonists from Portugal?

We both smile at these questions – the demands of formal objectivity, which Kapuściński rejected.

On his return from Angola, with years of work as a correspondent in Africa and Latin America behind him, Kapuściński expounds his credo in several in-depth interviews – the credo of committed, 'non-objective' journalism. His point of departure is the situation in the world he is describing:

What am I concerned about? Above all, about restoring dignity to the man from the Third World, disdained and humiliated for centuries, because contempt was an inseparable condition and accessory for conquest. Contempt was necessary in order for conquest to be effective. This man had to be humiliated in order to be subjugated. This stereotypical way of thinking and behaving towards the man from the Third World was then disseminated by all the propaganda and the philosophy that lit the way for conquest. So now for me it is wildly important to restore to that man his full dignity in our eyes, his full human value.[4]

Kapuściński finds the roots of this attitude in biography – both his own and that of the generation which built socialism with such dedication and enthusiasm after the Second World War:

'[H]igh temperature' situations have the greatest effect on me, ones that involve commitment and emotional stress, and this is also how I interpret the experience of my generation in the 1950s. We were not the generation of stabilization, and that was not what determined our perspective, rationale and actions. Instead we were the generation of an era of inquiry and commitment, also sacrifices. First and foremost, we were aware that what mattered most and was common to all went beyond the individual sphere of issues of concern to each of us. Later, on my travels to Latin America, Africa and the Near East, while living there, I was always looking for those attitudes and people.[5]

Kapuściński claims that he developed 'something that in psychological analysis is called a fixation: we come to a halt at some stage of our experiences and then keep on following the same path, in spite of changing conditions'. In an interview with Andrzej Kantowicz he admits:

Things like a nice home, affluence, and peace and quiet were never in my thoughts . . . I needed movement and change. What suits me is a front-line, conflict situation, I like to be with people who are fighting, I don't want to stop at observation, I want to take part. At the heart of it I am monothematic. I have managed to extend a theme for myself: from attitudes within conditions of conflict in Poland, I have moved on to similar attitudes in the outside world. So there is a continuation. I am drawn to people who are conducting a direct fight at the risk of their own life. Who are fighting for their ideals, to transform the world . . .
  You are from a generation that liked the world to be simplified to the dimensions of good and evil. It liked strong incentives.
  Yes. I am opposed to complication. That is, I can see it, and I respect it, but I simplify. For philosophical and professional reasons. For clarity of

vision and for dramatic effect. In my youth I came to like unambiguous situations and I have remained faithful to them. It's a sort of speciality of mine: ideological tension, a state in which people no longer hide their true intentions. My speciality is also derived from my psychological predispositions . . .

But somewhere a greater rationale lies hidden. You dropped us . . . for very poor people. You declared solidarity with poverty. So it's the ideal of liberation from poverty? Love for one's neighbour?

Love for one's neighbour is our deepest rationale. But not everyone wants to be our neighbour, or anyone's neighbour at all. There are evil people too. Pathologically evil. Wherever they are, the world is pathological, sick; in places like that despair is born, a struggle against violence, a struggle for social justice.[6]

Wojciech Giełżyński, a fellow correspondent in other Third World countries, has doubts about Kapuściński's black-and-white, simplifying declarations:

You told Kantowicz that you like strong incentives – either you live or don't live – and simplified situations. I don't entirely believe in this declaration. It's too striking. Too simple. I don't believe you don't like disentangling all sorts of complications.

I really am opposed to complications . . . And that reality, African or Latin American, the reality of those conflicts is simplified.[7]

In Kapuściński's long journalistic trajectory I find episodes where his work has the features of propaganda, or prompts suspicions about the independence of his judgement. In the clearest case, there are striking coincidences between the political correctness in force at various times in the PRL and the reporter's judgements.

When Emperor Haile Selassie is on good terms with the authorities in the PRL, Kapuściński uses superlatives to write about him in a report from a summit of the Organization of African Unity held in Addis Ababa in 1963.

Despite his seventy-five years, Haile Selassie is a man of inexhaustible energy, sharp wit and deep sensitivity . . . one of those remarkable old men who astound us with their vitality and clarity of thought. As a man he is immensely amiable, cheerful and charming . . . The Emperor is undoubtedly the most eminent political intellect in the country . . .[8]

Paradoxically, the PRL has exemplary relations with the feudal ruler of Ethiopia, though they are limited by reason of distance and relatively few common interests. The roots of the paradox lie in the foreign policy of pre-war Poland, which, after the invasion of Ethiopia by Mussolini's Italy in 1935, recognized the Italian occupation. After the end of the Second World War, when the Polish Committee of National Liberation is formed in Lublin and then the pro-Soviet government in Warsaw, Haile Selassie – in revenge for the Second Republic's painful gesture towards him – ignores the grievances of the Polish government in exile and recognizes the communist regime. The PRL authorities did not forget the monarch's attitude, and in the 1960s they treated their distant ally as an honoured guest – a feudal lord who came with the message 'Small nations unite against big ones.'

Along with the ritual welcomes and honeyed words, *Trybuna Ludu* writes about 'the emperor's active policy on African affairs' and his 'wide-ranging activity within the international forum on behalf of peace and detente'.[9] Chairman of the Council of State Edward Ochab beats his chest in front of the Ethiopian monarch for the sins of pre-war Poland: 'The then Polish government belonged – unfortunately – to those who joined in with the disgraceful decision to recognize the Italian fascist occupation as a fait accompli.[10]

His Imperial Majesty Haile Selassie the Great!

During the emperor's visit to Warsaw, some comical confusion occurs. Haile Selassie is staying the night at the palace in Wilanów, where his beloved lap-dog Lulu suddenly gets lost (the same dog described by Kapuściński in the first few sentences of his most famous book, *The Emperor*). Perhaps Lulu has caught the scent of food and wandered into the palace kitchen in the hope of a treat? The emperor notices the dog's disappearance and rouses his lieutenants, who alert the officers of the Government Protection Bureau. Together they scour the Wilanów residence – the dog is nowhere to be found. The emperor's adjutant threatens that if Lulu is not found, his master will leave Poland the next day. The interior ministry's Nadwiślańskie Military Units (the internal security forces) are summoned to search the park surrounding the palace, but there is no trace of the dog. As the rest of the emperor's official visit to Poland hangs by a thread, at dawn Lulu the lap-dog finally has the good grace to emerge from her hiding place; the tiny creature had hidden somewhere in the kitchen and was afraid to come out. Haile Selassie's visit continued according to the original plan.

In the 1970s, when the emperor is overthrown by a group of officers who wave red flags and enter into an alliance with Moscow, for the PRL propaganda Haile Selassie ceases to be a statesman, a fearless warrior against fascism. He now becomes a representative of 'reactionary forces', while his overthrow is 'an epoch-making turning point in the country's age-old history'. In these words, another chairman of the Council of State, Henryk Jabłoński, welcomes the destroyer of imperial power, Colonel Mengistu Haile Mariam, to Warsaw.[11]

At more or less the same time, Kapuściński writes a report from Addis Ababa on 'terrorist activity by forces of the right involving feudal elements'. The student youth protesting against the Mengistu regime – as Kapuściński reports – come from 'mostly feudal, bourgeois families, and thus from strata whose interests have been damaged by the Ethiopian revolution'.[12]

Not a trace is left of the deposed Haile Selassie's eminence, his 'sharp wit and deep sensitivity'. There is only feudalism and reaction. Is it because from having earlier been one of the few truly free African leaders, he has now become the embodiment of the continent's political backwardness? In his most famous book, published almost on the eve of Mengistu's visit to Warsaw, Kapuściński portrays the emperor as a despot, an almost illiterate ignoramus.

During the war in Angola Kapuściński ends up in at least two situations (not counting firing at the front) in which he departs from the role of reporter or commentator on events, and takes strictly political decisions.

> [I]n Angola I was the only journalist in the world to have certain information which I knew at that moment to be top secret . . . if made public it could have changed the course of historic events. As one of very few people, I knew from the start about the presence of the Cubans.[13]

This knowledge involves information on the Cuban instructors and, later, also on the arrival of the first Cuban unit on 5 November 1975 – before Angola had declared independence. If issued publicly at that point, the news about the presence of Fidel Castro's troops in Angola could have been regarded as proof of outside intervention and could have given the green light for analogous military intervention by Western countries. Sending Cuban troops to Angola is Castro's own idea. The Kremlin is not keen to get involved in the African war, but Havana's military involvement presents Moscow with a fait accompli and entangles it for good in the Angolan conflict.

> I should have reported this [news] to Warsaw, of course not for publication at that moment, but on the other hand I know that this information could have been intercepted on the way. So then there's a problem of choice: whether to risk it, or not? The international effects, if the news had been stolen from me, could have been dangerous. So then I'm facing an important political choice, and I have to decide for myself, but on the other hand I find it exciting – after all, I'm a reporter, I've got a hit here, a bomb, you wait your whole life for an opportunity like this. Sometimes people ask me about censorship. I am my own censor, because I could spill the news about some vital matter, I have to decide whether to report

something for publication, report it under embargo, or not to deliver it at all, in view of the matter's importance and the chances of interception.[14]

In none of his reports from those days does Kapuściński mention the instructors from Cuba or the arrival of the first unit of Cuban troops; he speaks about it only a year later, in an interview. Would he have kept the information to himself if it had been a matter of intervention by, let us say, American troops in a country with whose revolutionary government he sympathized? This is truly a rhetorical question. He writes without restraint about mercenaries from Egypt, Portugal and South Africa fighting on the FNLA and UNITA side. On the help provided to the MPLA by Cuba and the socialist countries, he enigmatically drops just a hint: 'the MPLA's people's army is not alone'.[15] Nothing more.

It is the head of the PAP, his informal boss Janusz Roszkowski, whom Kapuściński tells about the second situation involving his departure from the role of reporter (at the time he is working for the weekly *Kultura*, but the PAP is paying for his foreign trips, including the one to Angola). The commanders of the Angolan MPLA cannot communicate with the Cubans and the then small number of Soviet advisers – there is a language barrier. Kapuściński is the only person in the vicinity – and also a sympathizer with the common cause – who knows all three languages: Portuguese, which the Angolans speak, Spanish, which the Cubans speak, and Russian, which the Soviet comrades speak. He takes part in the commanders' staff meetings as an interpreter. He hears everything and knows everything. How much of the information he gains there does he never report?

In his book about the Angolan war, there is an extract which hints at undercover sources of information (radio monitoring?). Kapuściński reports on a meeting held at the enemy camp, during which a strategy for the capture of Luanda is discussed. Perhaps the favour he did for the Angolan revolution did not go to waste?

I also found evidence of involvement in a far lower-calibre situation that was ambiguous for Kapuściński – an interview he conducted with the secretary general of the Chilean Communist Party, Luis Corvalán (he held this conversation along with Gomułka's former secretary, Walery Namiotkiewicz). Kapuściński addresses the leader of the Chilean communists in keeping with the rules of communist ritual and language, as a propagandist and activist, not as an incisive journalist:

> We are glad you were willing to devote a little time to us, and that outside your official talks with the leadership of our Party, despite such a short stay in Warsaw, you have met with us to answer our questions. We believe

that publishing your statements will be very positive and will meet with
great interest from our Party activists.[16]

However, on many occasions Kapuściński finds himself in diametrically
opposite situations, grappling with propagandistic and incompetent inter-
pretations of events in the Third World that have been published in the
press. This happens when President Ahmed Ben Bella is deposed in Algeria,
and his place is taken by Houari Boumediene. A correspondent for the
Italian newspaper *l'Unità*, the organ of the Communist Party, writes at the
time that the coup d'état is right-wing in nature, Ben Bella is a hero and
Boumediene is a fascist. Her text is reprinted in the Polish press and becomes
the official version of events in Algeria.

Meanwhile Kapuściński describes the Algerian revolution differently: he
writes that both politicians, Ben Bella and Boumediene, are leftists, but of
a different style. It is not about a change of political orientation – 'Algeria
will remain a left-wing country' – and the putsch is the result of the
complexities of local politics.

> So I had phone calls from Warsaw, making a dreadful fuss – what did I
> think I was writing? Boumediene is a fascist! The Italians probably know
> better, they're nearer, they shouted through the receiver. Then I got so
> upset that I wanted to go home immediately. But a few days later it was
> explained to me that it wasn't I who had blundered, but that Italian jour-
> nalist, who had a personal thing about Ben Bella. I can quite understand
> her – he was a very interesting man.[17]

Another time, in the PAP's Special Bulletin, Kapuściński argues with the
propaganda descriptions in the Polish press concerning a coup d'état in
Ecuador:

> On 22 June 1970 the president of Ecuador, Velasco Ibarra, declared
> himself the dictator . . . A few days later I learned from our newspapers
> that it was a reactionary revolution ('Reactionary coup d'état in Ecuador').
>
> Reactionary? Why? If the revolution was reactionary, it means that
> before then things were progressive. But is that true? I started to wonder
> about this coup d'état and about the criteria for evaluating political revo-
> lutions in the Third World. There have been and will be many of these
> revolutions, and so the issue is important.
>
> Let's say General Marota has deposed General Artum. Was this revolu-
> tion progressive or reactionary? It depends. It may have been progressive.
> It may have been reactionary. But it is very often the case that this sort of
> revolution is simply politically indifferent, that in the political sense noth-
> ing results from it: one general has replaced another general, that's all. In

the course of the past thirty years, there have been twenty-seven revolutions in Ecuador, but politically the country has not budged an inch – either to the left or the right. A revolution can be just an ordinary, mechanical turn of the carousel, without any ideological repercussions. In the most recent history of the Third World we can see dozens of such incidents. A general in place of a civilian, a thin man in place of a fat one, X instead of Y, but the essential thing – the regime's political line – remains unchanged.[18]

This argument superbly demonstrates Kapuściński's competence, his concern for accurate analyses, and also his struggle for a way of thinking that is independent from the political correctness of the socialist era.

Will he change his ideological opinions when the edifice of the PRL starts to totter, or later on, after the collapse of real socialism? Will his penchant for presenting conflicts in black and white remain a permanent element in his thinking and writing? And what about his outlook on the standards of the profession? What about his view that journalistic objectivity is in certain situations impossible, or even smacks of falsehood?

Till the end of his life he uses words such as 'imperialism' and 'reaction' – but in private conversations, never in authorized interviews or his own texts. In the new era, especially in the first few years after the fall of real socialism, he changes his written language, moderates his ideological expressiveness and goes with the flow, with the spirit of the new times, even though he cannot bear the anti-communist correctness which prevails after 1989, either the right-wing or the liberal version.

In this change in his own language, one might see his evolution as a writer or one might see opportunism. Or is it perhaps so-called practical wisdom, advising him not to close the doors to communicating with readers and listeners from another era who have different experiences and a different sensitivity? Because what Kapuściński says about the world – especially the Third World, known after the end of the Cold War as the South – is more or less the same as before; he remains faithful to his own values, his personal, committed outlook, without grating on the ear of his audience from another time, from another world.

But I am running ahead, jumping two eras . . .

Kapuściński returns from Latin America, which is fired up with revolutionary fever, travels to Angola, which is plunged in civil war, and then to revolutionary Ethiopia. Meanwhile, Poland reaches the next stage in the history of real socialism: let us call it 'consumer socialism'. It's like two different planets. Over there is a life-or-death struggle for a new order, for justice and solemn ideals; here is a struggle for a television set, a washing machine and a Fiat 126.

What will come of this clash, this contrast, this discord?

28

Christ with a Rifle in a Czech Comedy
at the Emperor's Court

His Majesty liked to visit the provinces, to give the plain people access to
him, to learn of their troubles and console them with promises, to praise
the humble and the hardworking and scold the lazy and the
disobedient.[1]

Now there is meant to be a 'second Poland', a different socialism. Enough
parsimony, enough struggling to make ends meet. The 'frugal mum' (the
old leader Gomułka) goes out to grass, and the 'generous dad' takes the
helm – new First Secretary Edward Gierek. He introduces a new style of
governance; he shows he is a benign master, a solid administrator and a
bountiful guardian. He travels about the country, trying to prove that the
authorities have not lost touch with the masses; quite the opposite – he
comes down the hill and seeks proximity with the people.

This new turn in the history of the PRL is designed to atone for several
dozen fatalities. When workers on the coast came out onto the city streets
with their demands for pay rises, the previous Party leader sent out the
army and the militia against them. As a result of the public shock, there is a
reshuffle of the élite at the top.

Kapuściński does not watch the Polish drama from close up, because at
the time he is in Mexico. When he comes home from his posting, he finds
a totally different atmosphere in Poland.

There is not a trace remaining of Gomułka's plebeian socialism. At the
beginning of the new decade it is far easier than in previous years to get
basic goods: food, clothing, household equipment. Life for the Poles
becomes more bearable, and Gierek's slogan in the first years of his government – 'May Poland grow in strength and may people live more affluently'
– is not far from the daily experience of the decided majority. The miners
are thrilled, because they are getting fabulous salaries and bonuses; the
farmers complain less, because Gierek does away with compulsory annual
supplies of agricultural products to the state at fixed prices.

The Gierek era is also a time when the PRL opens up to the West. It is easier to get a passport, and if someone goes off on a journey to the other side of the Iron Curtain he can officially buy a hundred dollars (earlier this was possible only on the black market, and was a hundred times more expensive). Previously condemned or ridiculed Western popular culture gains 'civic rights' – American films and serials on television are virtually one of the trademarks of the decade. Home-grown entertainment of a fairly good standard also appears; a boom in popular songs begins, and a couple of excellent cabarets open. Poland is having a good time drinking and dancing.

> His Highness showed particular vivacity and keenness. He received processions of planners, economists, and financial specialists, talking, asking questions, encouraging, and praising.[2]

As the new leader, Gierek has ambitious plans. On the advice of Party experts he considers some sort of semi–market reform but quickly drops these complicated ideas. Why bother? Poland can live on the reserves saved up by the previous first secretary, and shortly afterwards a miracle occurs – Western credits start to pour in.

The capitalist countries of the West are experiencing a boom, there is cheap money looking for an outlet, and socialist Poland willingly accepts loans of any size. There is no need to rationalize anything: abracadabra, and goods which previously you could only dream about appear in the shops. Salaries go up, and the hope returns that finally the affluent life everyone has been waiting for is just around the corner.

> If you use foreign capital to build the factories, you don't need to reform. So there you are – His Majesty didn't allow reform, yet the factories were going up, they were built. That means development.[3]

Prefabricated concrete construction takes off; people still have to wait for flats, but they are relatively cheap. Young couples get special credits, they buy fridges, washing machines, television sets and furniture – all on hire purchase, and if someone's really lucky he'll also get hold of a coupon for a car (still a deficit item).

> One was planning, another was building, and so, in a word, development had started.[4]

After a year of hard work there are cheap holidays and, for those who can manage it, even trips abroad – to Bulgaria, Romania or the Crimea. Youth organizations which in the years when the foundations of socialism were being built stood for ideological zeal, altruism and personal sacrifice are now concerned with 'fixing': first to arrange the supply of some deficit, hard-to-acquire goods for their activists, then some foreign travel.

Something like a socialist middle class emerges – a broad group consisting of most Poles, geared to consumerism. One of the leading dissidents of the era admits years later that this was the only period when he really did fear society and felt marginalized. Because almost all Poland approves of Gierek's socialism at the beginning of the decade, very few people are bothered by the lack of elections, the rule of a single party, or the limited freedom of speech. To live and not to die! Long live socialism and Comrade Gierek! Bravo, bravo, bravo!

> [H]e even liked progress – his most honourably benevolent desire for action manifested itself in the unconcealed desire to have a satiated and happy people cry for years after, with full approval, 'Hey! Did he ever develop us!'[5]

Kapuściński comes back from a world where socialism means a heroic struggle, the sacrifice of one's personal peace and quiet. Latin America is a revolutionary volcano: *Cuba sí, yanquis no*; the idol of the young is the recently assassinated Che Guevara; Salvador Allende is conducting a peaceful socialist revolution in Chile, which the Americans, the local oligarchs and the middle class want to overthrow.

Over there: For their belief in socialism, the young idealists are ending up in prison, being tortured, or dying in the jungle, and are often completely misunderstood by those whose rights they are demanding. Over here: For their belief in socialism, the young wheeler-dealers are the first to get a flat, a car and a trip to Sochi. There: great ideas, the clank of rifles; here: fairly OK cash, idle gawping at the TV, having a ball. There: rebellion, nonconformism, adrenaline; here: fake smiles, making the right faces for the authorities. If that is socialism, is this socialism too? Where can a man go, where can he find a place, how can he fit into life on this other planet?

Now he is a star on a national scale. During the past few years, while he has been away, several of his books have come out, strengthening the position of the talented reporter and expert on Africa and Latin America. Despite the limitations imposed by the system, it is much easier to write significant texts about the Third World; censorship is not as sensitive to an 'incorrect' tone in these as it is in articles and books on national topics or the West.

Kapuściński temporarily remains jobless. He has had enough of the PAP by now; he knows the agency treadmill will never allow him to write books – and that has become his main dream, plan number one. He has several unwritten volumes in his notes, files and head, but until now he has not had the time to sit down quietly, take stock and get on with it. He considers writing a separate short book about his then idol Che Guevara, and another one on Latin America, a sort of summary of the four and a half years he has spent in the region.

But first he must get a foothold somewhere, obtain a permanent salary and find something to live on. He looks around at the press in Poland and wonders which place would be best. He doesn't want to go where it will be hard to get permission and money for trips abroad. The choice should fall on a journal that has good connections with the decision-makers, his pals upstairs – because should problems arise, they will help solve them.

Kapuściński the romantic idealist has, at the same time, a good instinct for personal connections; he knows how to navigate the corridors of the Party court and how to secure for himself the right to realize his professional aspirations and dreams.

> Whoever wanted to climb the steps of the Palace had first of all to master the negative knowledge: what was forbidden to him and his subalterns, what was not to be said or written, what should not be done, what should not be overlooked or neglected.[6]

He seeks the advice of his chief patron, Ryszard Frelek, who has been promoted to a high post at the summit of power – he is now head of the Central Committee's foreign department. Frelek suggests he take a look around, wait a bit, and a good place is sure to be found.

For about a year – also on Frelek's advice – Kapuściński takes a job at the monthly *Kontynenty* (Continents), for which his patron writes a column on international affairs. This is the only magazine where he accepts an editorial post, to the extent of becoming deputy editor-in-chief. He also tries teaching – postgraduate lectures in journalism studies at Warsaw University.

'Outside the classroom there's this thin, tanned guy in a dark, tight-fitting roll-neck top and bell-bottom jeans,' recalls Ewa Junczyk-Ziomecka. 'Suddenly he starts to clap, like a school teacher chivvying his pupils "into class, into class, the bell has gone!" He looked so fit, I thought he was the physical education teacher. But it was *him*.'

The first lecture is on Latin America and Che Guevara: it is a disappointment. The great Kapuściński is not a very good speaker. The students are expecting the famous reporter who has come back from far away to tell them about his adventures. Instead he goes into the intricacies of Latin American politics and talks about figures of whom the young people have never heard. For this audience, the outside world is Yugoslavia, and of course France and Britain. But Mexico, Chile, Bolivia? They know absolutely nothing about the world Kapuściński is describing.

The lectures last for a term. Despite the chasm of experiences between Kapuściński and his small group of students, friendships which last many years are formed. Not long from now some of the female students will be his colleagues at the same newspaper office.

At more or less this point, Frelek signals to his friend that the right place has been found. The editor-in-chief of the weekly *Kultura* ('Culture') Janusz Wilhelmi, is leaving under a cloud. The new chief will be a friend of Frelek's called Dominik Horodyński; he'll be glad to have Kapuściński on his team.

Like most of the opinion-forming periodicals in the PRL, the weekly *Kultura* has its own convoluted political history. When it was founded in 1963, one of its tasks was to stifle revisionist tendencies among the intelligentsia. Its pages feature aggressive articles, and it conducts some brutal score-settling within the intellectual environment. Literary types boycott *Kultura*, and no one of merit wants to write for it.

In 1968, *Kultura* dodges its way through the student protests and the anti-Semitic witch-hunting. It does not resist the nationalist wave, but on the other hand does not support the nationalist-communists as strongly as certain other journals do. 'We came through 1968 as not entirely rotten bastards,' recalls one of the paper's editors.

As the new editor-in-chief of *Kultura*, Dominik Horodyński has to fill in the chasm between *Kultura* and the world of culture which his predecessor had dug. He has social connections among people in the arts. He's suave and likes to party. His views are liberal, and for some people his mere arrival changes the face of the magazine – his presence is a sign that *Kultura* will not be the organ of the Party stormtroopers.

A considerable number of young people now begin work at the weekly – ambitious reporters and commentators who are not easy to control.

'Kapuściński's arrival', recalls Maciej Wierzyński, deputy editor of the weekly, 'was like the ultimate validation that *Kultura* was a magazine you didn't have to be ashamed of. Why did Rysiek choose *Kultura*? That's what his patrons advised him to do, I think – here it would be easier for him to put his own plans into practice than, for example, at *Polityka*, which had worse connections at the heights of power in those days.'

The *Kultura* journalists, those young people who had just started out on their professional path, remember without any shame the magazine they created. They are convinced that *Kultura*, and no other periodical, had the best team of reporters in those days – reporters who describe the reality of the PRL in the lyrical style of Czech comedy, in other words with a combination of sensitivity to the absurd, plenty of satirical humour, a touch of melancholy, and a glorification of ordinary life.

Little of the atmosphere of previous decades is in evidence during the 1970s in the PRL, neither the heroic mood for believers in socialism nor the sense of dread for the few rebels. There are no great battles of ideas; there is just life from one day to the next, and the hope of making money. The staggeringly boring Party ceremonies broadcast on television are empty rituals; hardly anyone believes in the ideology, including those who preach it.

Kultura's reporters are superb at catching the satirical side of this reality. They are rarely able to write in a direct manner, so they discover the charms of ambiguity, allusion and metaphor.

Rather than an article stigmatizing the squandering of labour and resources, a feature is written on the long journey travelled by manufactured goods from the time they are produced to the moment when they end up on display in the shops. The article illustrates how everything must be stamped and 'accounted for' at every stage, using tons of paper and employing an army of people in the process. 'Paper reality' is the title of this report. Another report is about Brzeska Street in Warsaw's Praga district, where 'the wife might be on the street corner and a husband a drunk, but the children have to be normal'.[7]

The desperately dull, grotesque sessions of the 'Committee for the Evaluation of Toys and the Verification of Packaging' are an allegory (as well as a parody) of the endless Party confabs which lead to nothing.

A report on illusionists sends a subtle message on the decade of illusory affluence, which ends in the bankruptcy of Edward Gierek's Poland.

Dominik Horodyński is happy to share reminiscences of those days. He is eighty-five and quite unwell, engaged in a prolonged attempt at recovery from a broken leg (he will die a few months after our conversation).

'Do you know that some of the editors-in-chief informed on each other?' says Horodyński when I ask about relations between *Kultura* and the Party authorities.

'How did they inform? To whom?'

'To the censors, or to the Central Committee's Press Department.'

'What for?'

'For example, to divert attention from what they themselves were doing. They'd say to some comrade: "Look here, what are they getting up to at that Horodyński's paper?" '

'And then what happened?'

'Once a lot of denunciations, complaints and quibbles had accumulated, they summoned you to the Central Committee press office and imposed a punishment.'

'What sort of punishment?'

'They might sack you, or they might just tell you off, give you a warning.'

'But you had patrons within the government, didn't you?'

'If there was trouble, I called Staś Trepczyński, or Frelek, and they made whatever arrangements were necessary.'

'So you could say to a censor or a press secretary that if anything happened . . .'

'No, no. It didn't do to be either too wilful or too servile. If they reprimanded you at the Press Department, it wasn't wise to suggest you had support somewhere higher up – oh no! That could have done harm.'

'Can you remember the worst situation of that kind?'

'There were no big dramas. Don't forget that for people of my generation, the point of departure was the war – why should I get upset about the comments of some Central Committee secretary?' He laughs as he says this.

> [M]y bows were of a functional and efficacious character . . . they served a purpose of state, which is to say a superior purpose, whereas the court was full of nobles bowing whenever the occasion presented itself. And it was no superior purpose that made their necks so flexible, but only their desire to flatter, their servility and their hope for gifts and promotions.[8]

Maciej Wierzyński, Horodyński's deputy, tells me that his boss gave the staff a lot of free rein. Whenever charges were made by the censor's office or the Central Committee Press Department, he used to shift the problem onto his deputy, saying that his young colleagues were up to no good and that he knew nothing about it. So usually it was Wierzyński who had to argue with the censor and the Press Department.

Every time there is an irreverent report in the paper, there will be a call from the Central Committee to say: 'In your paper, comrades, the first page is at odds with the last!'

> [P]eople learned . . . another language, mastered it, and became so fluent in it that we simple and uneducated folk suddenly became a bilingual nation . . . Each of the two languages had a different vocabulary, a different set of meanings, even a different grammar, and yet everyone overcame these difficulties in time and learned to express himself in the proper language.[9]

If an article ends up at Mysia Street (the censor's headquarters) and is deleted there, there is usually no saving it, and it lands in the editor's wastebin. Quite often, however, allies are sought at the Central Committee Press Department. Sometimes the censor is afraid to let an article through that poses a risk to his own position, but the comrades higher up, his superiors, may be in a better mood right now, or may know what the flavour of the moment is, or where the boundaries are drawn, and the article manages to get rescued.

Zdzisław Marzec, deputy head of the Press Department, says that *Kultura* did not inspire sympathy within the Central Committee.

'I didn't like Horodyński and I never hid the fact at all.'
'Why?'
'Too much of a sharp operator.'
'What sorts of charges were laid against *Kultura*?'
'Mainly dodging.'
'Meaning?'
'Critical allusions, various bits of mockery, in short, an ambiguous attitude to the reality of the times.'

One tongue served for external speech, the other for internal. The first was sweet and the second bitter, the first polished and the second coarse, one allowed to come to the surface and the other kept out of sight.[10]

Wiktor Osiatyński recalls that each year they held a draw at the editorial office to decide who would write the text for the next anniversary of the October Revolution. And then everyone helped think of a way to pay off this collective easement so that the Party was happy and the author did not lose face.

Kapuściński finds himself in a schizophrenic situation. Thanks to his reliable contacts within the Central Committee, and to being regarded as a 'good comrade', he feels safe; he feels that no arrogant bureaucrat or boss can touch him. He is praised at the Press Department: an internal note states that his reports from Latin America are a model for other reporters.

He arranges his foreign trips on his own, without the mediation of *Kultura*'s senior staff. They are financed by the PAP, with which he continues to co-operate, or by the state publishing enterprise RSW 'Prasa', because *Kultura*, like all other periodicals, has no funding of its own for international reporters. His plans always have the support of the head of the Foreign Department, Ryszard Frelek. Everyone is happy: the PAP because it has up-to-date dispatches from the Third World, *Kultura* because it has the latest reports, the Party because it is receiving analyses of the political situation in the Third World from the best reporter in the country, and Kapuściński himself, because these trips are essential to his being able to keep track of events in the countries that fascinate him, and he also collects accounts, observations and impressions for his upcoming books. ('He was our star, our pearl,' says Janusz Roszkowski, head of the agency in the Gierek era and for a few years afterwards. 'Rysiek himself suggested the topics, and money was always found for him.')

At the same time, the reality with which Kapuściński collides in the Poland of the 1970s is like something from an entirely different planet. The horizon for most Poles, including many of his friends and acquaintances, stops at making money; People's Poland is about having fun and getting

Friends and fine art lovers from Staszic High School: (from left) Janek Mazur, Andrzej Czcibor-Piotrowski, Ryszard Kapuściński, Krzysiek Dębowski (squatting). Reproduced by kind permission of Andrzej Czcibor-Piotrowski.

PAP correspondent at Nairobi
airport, 1964.
Reproduced by kind permission
of Jerzy and Izabella Nowak.

On the beach in Dar es Salaam,
shortly after arriving at the PAP
posting in Tanganyika, 1962.
Reproduced by kind permission
of Jerzy and Izabella Nowak.

Somewhere in East
Africa, 1964.
Reproduced by kind
permission of Jerzy and
Izabella Nowak.

From a hospital in Kampala, while suffering from cerebral malaria, Kapuściński sent letters to Jerzy and Izabella Nowak in Dar es Salaam, October 1962. Reproduced by kind permission of Jerzy and Izabella Nowak.

In Dar es Salaam, 1962. Reproduced by kind permission of Jerzy and Izabella Nowak.

On holiday in Paris: Alicja and Ryszard Kapuściński with friend and *Polityka* journalist Agnieszka Wróblewska (right), September 1964. Reproduced by kind permission of Andrzej Krzysztof Wróblewski.

With Lech Wałęsa after signing of Gdańsk Agreement, 1 September 1980.
Reproduced by kind permission of Andrzej Krzysztof Wróblewski.

With wife Alicja (left) and Izabella Nowak, 1980s. Reproduced by kind permission
of Jerzy and Izabella Nowak.

With Jerzy Nowak, closest friend for forty-six years, New York, 1984. Reproduced by kind permission of Jerzy and Izabella Nowak.

Honorary degree ceremony at Jagiellonian University, Kraków, 2004.

With Gabriel García Márquez, who invited Kapuściński to conduct workshops for reporters from Latin America, Mexico City, 2001.

With participants in a workshop organized by the Ibero-American Foundation for New Journalism, Buenos Aires, 2002.

Kapuściński's loft kingdom, almost one year after his death, December 2007.

drunk. Even those who do not believe in socialism are pleased about it: things are better than before. Meanwhile, as a reporter from the Third World, he is in a state of ideological tension, in a black-and-white world. Being occupied with the revolutions and civil wars of the poor South is neither a job suited to making a fortune nor a painful practical duty – it is a passion (he adored that word), an intellectual, often strongly personal commitment. For Kapuściński, socialism and revolution are not a farce at a state farm or a satire at a committee; they involve sticking your neck out, risking your life for a cause, an ideal, a better world. His horizon, his perspective and emotions are often shaped by extreme experiences.

> Whenever I return to Latin America, it's a bit like going back to a ceme- tery. A lot of the people I knew, with whom I spent time, are no longer alive. And when I return to Africa, it's also rather like going back to my own personal cemetery . . . It may be that as a result I have a rather twisted view of the world – because I'm constantly moving within that reality, within those situations.
>
> Let's take Africa. Ben Barka [a Moroccan dissident], murdered in terri- ble circumstances. I had a friend called Pinto, who was shot the day after we had a conversation, as he was driving out of his yard . . . The story I described in my report entitled *Christ with a Rifle on His Shoulder* is symbolic in a way: those seventy-seven people, boys, who went out and who all died, one after the other. It was a known fact from start to finish that they would all die. And they knew it too. Because over there it's obvious when you set out that you'll never come back again. But never- theless, off they go, in the belief that they have to, that there is no alterna- tive. Saying to themselves: up to some point we have to keep dying in order to triumph later on.[11]

The series of reports which Kapuściński publishes on the pages of *Kultura* in instalments are about exactly this type of person, fighting for the cause of a society's liberation – and these reports form his next three books. *Another Day of Life* is about the end of the colonial era in Angola and the local revo- lutionaries from the MPLA. *Christ with a Rifle on His Shoulder* is about Palestinians fighting for the right to their own state, Bolivian guerrillas trying to incite a revolution, the kidnappers of the West German ambassa- dor to Guatemala (an abridged version of *Why Karl von Spreti Died*), people from the Mozambican liberation movement FRELIMO, and icons of the era Che Guevara and Salvador Allende. *The Soccer War* is a synthesis of the experiences of the decolonization era in Africa and revolutionary attempts in Latin America (here Kapuściński reproduces a number of reports from several previous volumes in slightly altered versions); among other things, it includes portraits of the heroes of independent Africa – Kwame Nkrumah,

Patrice Lumumba and Ahmed Ben Bella, and an account of the coup d'état in Nigeria. The report that gives the book its title is about the war between Honduras and Salvador.

As one reviewer wrote about this last book:

> In none of Kapuściński's previous books has the world been perceived as a coherent whole. Only *The Soccer War* makes us see that the view of the street in Guatemala during the kidnapping of Karl von Spreti, the view of depopulated Kinshasa, or of Luanda shut into boxes, and the view of a sunny alleyway in Tbilisi all have something in common. And there is so much of this common factor that from among the exotic cities and countries a sort of hometown comes peeping out at us, a familiar street, the face of a friend or a well-known person . . . We know that the world has this coherence and indivisibility thanks to the people who populate, destroy and build it.[12]

At *Kultura*, Kapuściński meets a new generation of journalists, for whom stories about idealistic freedom fighters sound like fairy-tales told by someone from another planet and do not mesh with any of their experiences. What's more, those fighters of 'his' are Red: why get upset about the fate of idiots, or at best naive people who want to make for themselves the sort of world we already know about, and of which we've had enough?

For the twenty-somethings at journalism school and *Kultura*, socialism is rather absurd, nothing but empty rituals and boredom. They dream of a comfortable life and the outside world: the West is where it's at! Someone is going on a scholarship to the States, someone else is off on holiday to Western Europe. In the West these young people get a large dose of new impressions, experiences and ideas.

> These people would return home full of devious ideas, disloyal views, damaging plans, and unreasonable and disorderly projects. They would look at the Empire, put their heads in their hands and cry, 'Good God, how can anything like this exist?'[13]

Yet Kapuściński comes back from that outside world and speaks of the West as having enslaved the poor countries of the Third World, and of the curse of 'American imperialism'. For the young people, the stories told by their colleague and master often sound like sheer cant, while for Kapuściński 'American imperialism' is not a platitude but an accurate description, something he has touched, sniffed and seen.

On his return from the civil war in Angola, there is a meeting at the newspaper office at which one of his colleagues, Tomasz Łubieński, asks provocatively: 'What do you find so thrilling about Angola? Who are those Angolan communists in league with the Cubans fighting against?'

'What do mean, who? American imperialism!'

For Łubieński, the answer smacks of propaganda. He and certain other journalists have a problem with Kapuściński: they like and respect their famous colleague, but at the same time they cannot understand his stubborn belief in socialism, or at least the Third World variety.

'You don't like America, but why do you carp at the French, too?' Łubieński, a sworn Francophile, asks on one occasion.

'You know the French from Paris – cultured, educated people', responds Kapuściński, 'but I know the ones from the colonies. They are barbarians! If you get in their way or frustrate their business interests, they'll kill you.'

Whenever he comes back from a trip, he drops in on Ewa and Mariusz Ziomecki, who live in Warsaw's Wola district. He brings whisky and Marlboros. Ewa Zadrzyńska, Ewa Szymańska and Maciej Wierzyński come along too. The young people sit on the carpet because the Ziomeckis have hardly any furniture, and gaze intently at their friend and mentor. Kapuściński tells stories until dawn: what he has seen and what he has lived through in the past few months on his travels – in the Near East, in Angola, in Ethiopia . . .

He narrates his future books aloud; he wants to hear them himself and test them out. When he talks about an overturned vehicle carrying a cargo of oranges, his friends can smell the scent of those oranges. When something is unclear, they ask questions – but rarely. This is not a dialogue; this is the master talking.

'He explained to us', recalls Ewa Junczyk-Ziomecka, 'that we might complain about the Soviet Union, but in Third World countries it is the Soviet Union that was helping oppressed societies push their way through to independence. This explanation allowed us to believe that Rysiek was on the right side.'

'You admired him as a master,' I comment. 'You adored him as a friend, but at the same time there was a gulf between you – his ideals were not the same as yours, his idols were not the same as yours . . . How did you cope with this disparity?'

'We often said among ourselves: "We should ask Rysiek if he has really let himself be taken in by all that. Because off he goes to Africa and Latin America, then comes back and tries to infect us with his belief in that sort of socialism, liberation movements and so on . . . Is he conning us, by any chance?" '

'And did you ask him?'

'No, unfortunately. He said for years that he was going to write a book about Poland, about himself. I was counting on his providing the answers to many questions. I think there are lots of his secrets that we will never know – maybe for the better.'

Mariusz Ziomecki, who starts working at *Kultura* while still an economics student, seeks a mentor and a father-figure in Kapuściński. He rarely sees him at the newspaper office, because Kapuściński drops in there once a week at most, and doesn't even have his own desk. If he does come, he shuts himself in the office with the editor-in-chief, so even then it's as if he isn't there.

They meet outside work. When Kapuściński starts having problems with his circulation (at the time he is still an ardent smoker) and with his spine, Ziomecki drags him on long walks. They try to play tennis, but without success; Ziomecki is not a good enough player to encourage his older colleague to practise regularly.

In this period the novice journalist looks up to the master. Ziomecki and a couple of other young reporters from *Kultura* are proud to call themselves Kapuściński's pupils, although Kapuściński does not read their articles or comment on them. He talks in general terms: you have to keep learning all the time, even once you achieve success; a successful person who rests on his laurels and does not continue to develop will soon fizzle out. So you know two or three languages? That's too few – you need to know six or seven! And you need to read serious, ambitious books, not give up, always keep advancing.

Fairly soon the master falls into the pupil's disfavour. ('After a period of intense fascination comes a stage in which the "son" distances himself from the "father",' says Ziomecki, smiling.) Kapuściński belongs to the Party, but Ziomecki is not even in a dilemma over joining; Kapuściński glorifies the Red revolutions in the Third World, but Ziomecki does not trust the master's accounts.

'Why is Africa so socialist–realist in your reports? Why are the freedom fighters saints, and the other lot bandits? The world isn't like that.'

'The Third World is like that!'

'He wouldn't enter into debate, he just dug in his heels,' recalls Ziomecki. 'Even when times changed and points of view changed with them, he stubbornly stuck to his line.'

During one of their conversations, Kapuściński takes offence at the lack of ideological zeal among the Poles he has met in the course of the Angolan civil war. They are trade representatives, selling the Angolans Polish lorries which work well in mountainous terrain.

'They don't give a damn about the war! Among the Cubans or the Russians you can see ideological commitment, but for our lot all that counts is a bit of trade and some booze!'

Frequently they discuss the master's membership in the Party and the young people's reluctance to join its ranks. On this issue they understand each other better.

'It's all right if you don't join the Party,' Kapuściński tells the young people. 'But that doesn't mean it would be a good thing if we oldies left it. There'd be a huge fuss; it would be regarded as a political demonstration, and we'd harm the paper.'

Ziomecki proposes an explanation: that in the countries of the Third World, his 'father' is seeking the land of his youth, the climate of commitment and ideological enthusiasm of the 1950s. The older man believes – and he works to convince the young people of this – that the Third World is purer, and the split between good and evil there more clear-cut. 'I'd like to believe that explains Rysiek's paradox,' says Ziomecki.

The idealistic Kapuściński is brilliant at moving about within the labyrinths of Gierek's non-idealistic court. Nowadays he drops in more often than in the past at his patron's new home on the first floor of the 'White House', as the Central Committee headquarters is known – often enough that several establishment comrades remember the situation as, 'He spent the whole time sitting in Frelek's office.'

He gets a commission from Frelek to writes analyses for the Foreign Department of current conditions in Third World countries. He observes the workings of government at close quarters, not just in a general sense but also their anatomy, behind the scenes, from the inside. He sees how people change as they acquire new positions and more power.

> [A] change in speech is another post-assignment symptom. Multiple monosyllables, grunts, clearings of the throat, meaningful pauses and changes of intonation, misty words, and a general air of having known everything better and for a longer time.[14]

He starts to understand how much in the world of power depends not on knowledge or individual effort, ideas or even ideological zeal, but on completely different attributes and circumstances.

> His Majesty never made appointments on the basis of a person's talent, but always and exclusively on the basis of loyalty.[15]

> [O]ne was more important if one had the Emperor's ear more often. More often, and for longer. For that ear the lobbies fought their fiercest battles; the ear was the highest prize in the game. It was enough, though it was not easy, to get close to the all-powerful ear and whisper. Whisper, that's all.[16]

He also sees at close quarters the rivalries of various coteries in the Party.

I would say that slowly, gradually, three factions appear in the Palace. The first, the Jailers, are a fierce and inflexible coterie who demand the restoration of order and insist on arresting the malcontent, putting them behind bars . . . A second faction coalesces, the Talkers, a coterie of liberals: weak people, and philosophizers, who think that one should invite the rebels to sit down at a table and talk . . . Finally, the third faction is made up of Floaters, who, I would say, are the most numerous group in the Palace. They don't think at all, but hope that like corks in water they will float on the waves of circumstance.[17]

Teresa Torańska remembers that when she made an appointment to interview a high-ranking Party dignitary without first confirming it with her supervising editors, Horodyński gave her a very hard time. She went to see Kapuściński, thinking she would find an ally in him.

'But instead,' she recalls, 'Rysiek said I had behaved disloyally. And he started explaining to me as if I were a child: "Listen, you have to understand that the editors have a particular political arrangement. If the interview appears, someone at the Central Committee will think our weekly supports that comrade – but is that a good thing for us right now? If in turn the interview doesn't appear, then the comrade in question will think we are against him." I didn't understand this complex structure or these abstract arrangements; I simply wanted to get an interesting interview.'

For Kapuściński, the Party's internal arrangements are not abstract. He has one gang of friends at *Kultura*, and a completely different one with his Party comrades at the Central Committee and the Ministry of Foreign Affairs. They also meet at each other's houses and out on the town. They have fun, chat and drink together. Kapuściński knows at first hand what is going on at the Central Committee, which coterie, trend or mood is on top, and who is being censured at any given moment.

Besides Frelek and Trepczyński, his gang includes colleagues he has met at embassies, consulates and commercial offices. United by their Latin American experiences and passions, these colleagues include Henryk Sobieski, a secretary from the embassy in Mexico; Janusz Balewski, a commercial adviser from Costa Rica; Józef Klasa, the former ambassador to Havana (not often present because he lives in Kraków); and Stanisław Jarząbek, attaché and secretary from the embassy in Cuba.

'In this company the departures and arrivals of friends to and from foreign postings provided a frequent occasion for a party,' says Jarząbek. 'Kapuściński was always there. He liked having diplomat friends, and sometimes stayed with one of us during his journeys.'

'We quite often ended up at Rysiek's flat in Wola at three in the morning in a fine old state,' recalls Balewski.

'I remember those tunnels between the stacks of books in the tiny room where his works were produced,' says Klasa.

Jarząbek again: 'We were fascinated by him – I was, for sure! At some party or other I delivered a paean in honour of Rysiek. He wasn't there at the time, and a female friend who knew him well whispered to me: "Be more realistic in your appraisals – take a closer look at Rysiek!" At the time I refused to accept that comment, which seemed to me malicious; I was enchanted by Kapuściński.'

Kapuściński has his friends from the diplomatic posts to thank for his first foreign publication beyond the socialist camp. Thanks to their personal connections with Mexico's deputy minister of culture Javier Wimer, Klasa and Balewski bring about the Mexican publication of *Another Day of Life*.

'It was Kapuściński's first book to come out in the West,' says Balewski proudly. 'And it was a great success.'

Many years later, however, his old comrades will bear a grudge against their former chum for turning his back on them in the new times, after the fall of socialism.

Owing to his firm contacts with people in power, Kapuściński observes at close hand how people are put out to pasture at the Party court. One of his friends, Józef Klasa, gets into bad repute with the Party leader. At the time, Klasa is secretary of the PZPR District Committee in Kraków. At first, thanks to Gierek, he is promoted, but then co-operation between the central ruler and the provincial governor does not turn out for the best.

For example, Klasa does not like the weekly *Życie Literackie* (Literary Life), which is published in Kraków; he thinks it and its editor-in-chief are compromising Polish culture. He takes underhand action to have the editor-in-chief removed from his job. Gierek, on the contrary, likes the weekly's top editor and defends him against Klasa's designs. It seems idiotic, but the Party leader is displeased by the provincial governor's wilful behaviour. After a couple of clashes, Klasa is sent off to the diplomatic post in Mexico – the job of ambassador being a way of sidelining a high-ranking bureaucrat.

> His Gracious Majesty wanted to reserve control of promotions to himself, and for that reason he looked with a malignant eye on any dignitary who tried to promote someone on the side. Such arbitrariness – immediately punished – threatened to upset the balance that His Distinguished Majesty had established; a bothersome disproportion would creep in and His Highness would have to worry about restoring the balance, instead of occupying himself with more important affairs.[18]

Is it from Klasa that Kapuściński hears what the former Party secretary in Kraków now tells me a few decades later: that Gierek is lazy, never reads a thing and has no desire to do so?

His Venerable Majesty was no reader. For him, neither the written nor the printed word existed; everything had to be relayed by word of mouth.[19]

'I think Rysiek started gathering criticism of our regime somewhere around 1976,' recalls Klasa. That year, 1976, is a time of workers' protests against increases in food prices. During the second half of the 1970s, the idyll of the first few years of Gierek's government changes into the daily torment of standing in queues for all sorts of essential goods. The wait for a flat is longer and longer, for washing machines and refrigerators you have to 'go hunting', and more and more errands and items that are crucial to a reasonably comfortable life have to be 'fixed'. The government introduces ration cards for sugar. The promises of consumer socialism begin to drift away. Once there is a lack of goods for ordinary people, the privileges start to be apparent, and the blatant unfairness of the system becomes markedly offensive.

At the tail-end of the 1970s, Kapuściński can tangibly feel what is happening to Comrade Gierek's 'other Poland'. He has always lived modestly – at the time in three small rooms in the Warsaw district of Wola – but in case of need, he does have ways to 'fix' almost everything. In those days he drives a Soviet Lada, and when the tyres wear out, he tries to buy new ones, but it's a problem – he cannot get them anywhere. He tries to 'fix' the matter at the level of the Central Committee. He turns for help to Frelek, who makes the necessary call. To collect the tyres, Kapuściński has to drive to a depot at Warsaw's Okęcie airport. When he gets there, someone shows him into a warehouse and opens a bolted door. He sees a gigantic space that is completely empty, except for one lone tyre sitting in the middle of the enormous hangar.

'This is the maximum you can get fixed through the Central Committee nowadays,' he tells a friend afterwards, 'one single tyre!'

It was a small dog, a Japanese breed. His name was Lulu. He was allowed to sleep in the Emperor's great bed. During various ceremonies, he would run away from the Emperor's lap and pee on dignitaries' shoes.[20]

Before writing about Lulu the lap-dog, he spends weeks lying on the floor in his flat in Wola, tearing his hair out.

'I can't, I can't go on writing the same old thing! Enough!'

He doesn't eat, he doesn't sleep. 'Let them throw me out,' he thinks. He disconnects the phone, and so his colleagues from the office send telegrams asking when the reports from Ethiopia will be ready. (This is how he tells the story in future interviews.)

Finally he presents the first instalment, just a few pages. He has an uncertain look on his face and, as ever, that apologetic smile. What will they say?

This is his first article in a completely new style, an unfamiliar genre.

'After just a few sentences,' recalls Wierzyński, 'I realized that here in my hands I had a brilliant piece of work. Is it reportage? More like a literary tale, a fable, or a treatise on power. We started making Rysiek bring us an instalment each week.'

The series appears under the title *A Bit of Ethiopia*, but everyone can sense that it is not about faraway Africa. Ethiopia and the court of the Emperor Haile Selassie are a disguise, a metaphor. Kapuściński's series is the universal story of the distortions of any sort of power, about the people at any court – including the comrades from the Central Committee, Gierek and the absurdities of Polish reality.

'Didn't the censors complain?' I ask Wierzyński.

'They felt stupid, because censoring an allusive story about Ethiopia would have been an acknowledgement of weakness. Sometimes in a mildly reproachful tone they would say: "Do you have to keep going on about these emperors, comrades?"'

His colleagues are amused by Kapuściński's story. They pick up the jokes, metaphors and ironical comments – about the unconcealed ambitions of the 'generous father' of the nation for the 'satiated and happy people [to] cry for years after, with full approval, "Hey! Did he ever develop us!"'; about the two languages for social communication which have 'a different vocabulary, a different set of meanings, even a different grammar', and yet 'everyone overcame these difficulties in time and learned to express himself in the proper language'; and about the fact that if you obtain foreign credits, no reform is necessary.

His colleagues even read about themselves in the series about Ethiopia: just like the young people in Haile Selassie's empire, they come back from journeys abroad 'full of devious ideas, [and] disloyal views', look around themselves and clutch their heads, saying: 'Good God, how can anything like this exist?'

Some people wonder which other Polish absurdities should be suggested to Kapuściński for ridicule. An opportunity arises when Gierek launches an ostentatious but preposterous plan to regulate the River Vistula, in order to distract people from the regime's troubles and the country's real problems. Kapuściński agrees to manufacture a bit of fun.

In the Palace, dejection, discouragement, fearful waiting for whatever might happen tomorrow – when suddenly His Majesty summons his counsellors, reprimands them for neglecting development, and after giving them a scolding announces that we are going to construct dams on the Nile. But how can we erect dams, the confused advisers grumble, when the provinces are starving, the nation is restless, the Talkers are whispering about straightening out the Empire . . .?[21]

Together, the instalments from the series called 'A Bit of Ethiopia' will form *The Emperor*, the book which in a few years' time will make Kapuściński world famous. Some of his friends, as well as experts on his work, will hail the book as 'a treatise on power', and its author as a brilliant expert on the issues of power as such, rather than necessarily an authority on Africa. This opinion of *The Emperor* becomes widespread – a somewhat defensive reaction when, after foreign editions of the 'treatise on power' appear, accusations are made about the accuracy of the facts of Ethiopian history cited in it.

Józef Tejchma, a member of the Politburo and minister of culture, does not remember if Gierek ever voiced his thoughts about *The Emperor*. He does not even know if he ever read the book, because, on the whole, Gierek read very little.

He does remember that when a rumour went round about allusions in Kapuściński's text, members of the Central Committee, too, began to read his series on Ethiopia as a metaphor for the workings of power and the Party court. Tejchma's diary entry for 16 March 1978 reads, 'It's about Ethiopia, but just as much about today's Poland,' and he notes, 'The nearer the end, the more outrageously people were tearing off a piece for themselves and lining their own pockets with total abandon . . . Palace life, though feverishly busy . . . was essentially full of silence, waiting and postponement.'[22]

'Criticism of Gierek's governments was growing,' adds Zdzisław Marzec. 'And along came *The Emperor*, which satisfied a public need to criticize the authorities. I don't know if that was Kapuściński's intention. It's a fact that he never dissociated himself from the allusive interpretation of his book. But neither the book nor the extracts from it published earlier in *Kultura* prompted any opposition among the censors or at the Central Committee Press Department.'

Politburo member Andrzej Werblan remembers that, at the time, the interpretation of *The Emperor* as a work of political allusiveness was being disseminated by Party hard-liners, who wanted to compromise in Gierek's eyes the 'liberals' who allowed such journalistic pranks. Yet Gierek chose to ignore these intrigues.

'Did you read *The Emperor* as a book about Gierek and his court?'

'I remember how Zenon Kliszko [who had had no government post since the fall of Gomułka] said to me: "Look here, Kapuściński has been writing about you lot!" I think he was writing about Haile Selassie, not Gierek. But he did capture the essential, recurrent features and mechanisms of any authoritarian power, including Gierek's regime. These mechanisms are more relevant here than the stage directions of one country or another. The book didn't have to be allusive; Polish reality saw its own reflection in it.'

'What didn't Kapuściński like about Gierek?'

'At first he was a fan, but then he started being annoyed by a certain court fashion on the one hand and by the lack of ideology, the technocracy, on the other. He was more keen on Gomułka's homespun style.'

Soon *The Emperor* is staged at Warsaw's Powszechny Theatre by well-known director Zygmunt Hübner. Tejchma goes to the premiere and clutches his temples.

'I remember sitting in the audience', he tells me, 'and hearing things from the stage like "It's a wonder it hasn't fallen apart!" People were laughing and applauding. At first I was laughing too. But after a while the thought occurred to me, "What am I laughing at? At myself, perhaps?" And I felt angry, at Kapuściński, whom many people at the Central Committee regarded as a friend, and even more at Hübner, for going much too far: he had sharpened the original text and highlighted all the allusions to the Polish situation.'

> [I]t occurred to no one that such a journalist, who had earlier praised, would dare to criticize later. But such is obviously the dastardly nature of people without dignity or faith.[23]

I no longer remember from whom I heard the following comment, which 'neutralizes' the astonishment at the fact that someone so idealistic and loyal to the Party as Kapuściński had suddenly run wild: 'Many of the ideologists of the generation which built socialism in the 1950s had been disappointed and were in the front ranks of the 1956 revolt. Then they were disappointed all over again when Gomułka backed away from reforming socialism. These people gained a positive obsession from their experiences, a sensitivity to the distortions of authoritarian power.'

Kapuściński, who in the revolutions and uprisings of the Third World seeks an ideal, moral purity, hope, and a new life – as well as his own youth – also sees there how authoritarian power can distort the loftiest ideals, transforming noble idealists into soulless bureaucrats, power addicts, and often cruel monsters. This experience makes him even more sensitive to the deformations of a regime when deprived of control.

> The last year! Yes, but who then could have foreseen that 1974 would be our last year? Well, yes, one did feel a sort of vagueness, a melancholy chaotic ineptness, a certain negativity, something heavy in the air, nervousness and tension, flabbiness, now dawning, now growing dark, but how did we go so quickly straight into the abyss?[24]

The biggest social rebellion in the history of the PRL is just around the corner. On which side of the barricades will the romantic revolutionary, who nevertheless has numerous connections with the people of the collapsing court, find a place for himself?

29

On Love and Other Demons

A woman is anticipation. Hence the highest embodiment of this attitude is Penelope.
Ryszard Kapuściński, *Lapidarium III*[1]

'Did you ever cry into your pillow?' Teresa Torańska asks Alicja Kapuścińska.
'No.'
'Never?'
'I don't think so. You're asking me for too many details. A person has to adapt to the situation. Life went on, and that's all. He had his work, I had mine.'[2]

Alicja is a highly regarded paediatrician. For thirty-five years she has worked at the Medical Academy hospital on Działdowska Street, from her first internship until her retirement. There are two kinds of employment there, academic and hospital. The academic jobs bring a higher salary, a shorter working day and a longer holiday, but also the obligation to become a specialist and to pass exams for academic degrees. Alicja has the 'worse' form of employment, a hospital job. Yet she also gives student classes; even without the compulsion imposed by an academic job, she takes first and second speciality degrees.

One time Alicja's boss, director Kajetan Kaliciński, says to her: 'Surely you don't live on what I pay you here?'

She replies: 'I have a husband, and he gets a salary.'

'So you just come to the hospital to practise your hobby.'

'You could put it like that.'

'And what's more we pay you.'

They had a laugh about it, and that was that. After all, Alicja's salary did not depend on the director. She says she was ashamed to admit how much she earned, even to her own father.

Years later she does a doctorate on celiac disease – gluten intolerance – in children. Her work is awarded a distinction. Wearing a gown and a mortarboard, she collects her degree at the Wielki Theatre. Ryszard sits in the second row, proudly watching her. She feels satisfied, thinking: You see, I'm no worse than the others.

The others:

> [H]e came into the Czytelnik café and all the girls gazed at him.
>
> And he favoured them with a smile. They must have been in love with him. I know they were. But what was I to do? I thought: let them be.
>
> *Didn't your heart ache?*
>
> Oh dear, sometimes it did, but it stopped whenever I saw that I did in fact matter to him.[3]

Women are attracted to him. He doesn't have to set out to conquer – instead, the lands to be conquered come sailing up of their own accord, offering an invitation to the conquistador. He can take his pick. He stands quietly to one side at the banquet, reception, or presentation; the social hub is somewhere else entirely, but his magnetism keeps working nonetheless.

What is it about him? It really is magnetism – the look in his eyes, his voice, his subtle manner – a very masculine subtlety, the incredible stories and the aura that surrounds a traveller who has toured dangerous countries, seen wars and revolutions. It is sex appeal. That smile.

Ryszard Frelek recalled how he used to charm the girls with stories about his hometown, Pińsk.

> He used to stir their sympathy, because he had a theory that that was the most important thing to do. 'There was great poverty in Polesie. When the first frosts came, Dad used to put me in a little sheepskin coat, tied it round with a strap or a piece of wire and only unwrapped me when it got warm again. And if anyone was sick he was rubbed with turpentine, laid on top of the stove and kept there until he was better.' I used to kick Ryszard's ankles under the table. What wire? What turpentine? Józef Kapuściński was a teacher![4]

One time he bewitched the secretary of one of the Party dignitaries, and she fell madly in love with him. To get his friend out of trouble, her boss relocated her to the diplomatic post in Havana.

One-night wonders do occur, but only occasionally. It's always about love – of one kind or another. He needs it. He needs admiration, he needs intimacy. He is the romantic lover, who races to the station at six in the morning, carrying a bouquet of roses, to meet the lady stepping off the train.

'But you have a wife.'

'Don't worry. She has someone.'

'That was the excuse he devised for himself,' a close female friend of his tells me, 'to soothe some of the women's pangs of conscience.'

Each one is the centre of the universe, a queen – as long as she wants nothing from the king and makes no demands.

As everyone knows, even the most enduring kingdoms are not eternal. Let us admit it: these are short-lived. A three-month rule usually applies: that is sufficient time for the initial enchantment to wear off; there's no need to drag things out. In any case, a longer time is impossible – there's writing to be done, a need to concentrate, continual trips abroad, and a wife. But it was wonderful, truly marvellous, like something out of a fairy-tale.

> Lady, be for me a fairy-tale moment
> a fairy-tale we make up for ourselves
> we don't need the sun or the moon
> the only light will be shining in your eyes
>
> We don't need bushes or trees
> instead of forests there will be your hair
> instead of rivers there will be your arms
> instead of waves there will be cradling
>
> And from this world that surrounds us
> let us take nothing but drops of dew
> so when the fairy-tale dream is over
> you may see your reflection in them[5]

(One of his male friends finds this 'dreadful, macho poem' offensive: 'He gets her to fall in love with him, breaks her heart, and then she's supposed to dream about him "when the fairy-tale dream is over". What appalling chauvinism!')

There is no need to go back and reignite something that has fizzled out. However, a few years down the line, if and when one of the former queens falls ill or has an accident and he finds out about it, he will leave his reigning consort in the middle of the street and rush to the hospital ward with a bouquet of flowers. She will feel that she still matters, that she has a place in his heart for ever, and that she is still queen, because he has not forgotten her.

The queen could be a secretary, a shop assistant, a student, an intellectual, a poet, a reporter, a translator, an editor, a copy-editor, a censor, an underground activist . . . Love knows no barriers or limits, it is above class and profession, above complexion (dark or fair), size (tall or short, thin or plump), experience (young or not so young), and civil status (single, married, or divorced).

'A man who is unsure of himself – and Rysiek was that type – seeks acceptance and confirmation of his own value in various fields, including relationships with the opposite sex,' explains one of his male friends.

'There is a simpler explanation: he had a large appetite for life, and that's all,' comments another.

He likes boasting of the number of his conquests.

'He kept count?' says one of his female friends in confusion and disbelief.

'Rysiek loved all mankind,' says the most genuine queen of all, bursting into laughter, 'but he loved the female half of humanily more.'

Hardly any women appear in his reports and books. Kapuściński the man may love the female half of humanity more, but Kapuściński the reporter rarely notices it. The exception is Carlotta, in *Another Day of Life*, the book about the civil war in Angola. Or *is* she the exception?

> Carlotta came with an automatic on her shoulder. Even though she was wearing a commando uniform that was too big for her, you could tell she was attractive. We all started paying court to her immediately . . . Our girl was a mulatto with an elusive charm and, as it seemed to us then, great beauty. Later, when I developed the pictures of her, the only pictures of Carlotta that remained, I saw that she wasn't so beautiful. Yet nobody said as much out loud, so as not to destroy our myth, our image of Carlotta . . . When [we] saw her in front of staff headquarters, she seemed beautiful. Why? Because that was the kind of mood we were in, because we needed it, because we wanted it that way. We always create the beauty of women, and that day we created Carlotta's beauty.[6]

And then Carlotta gets killed.

We will never find out what she thought or liked, or what her nature was. She appears only as an object of male admiration; we know what she looked like and, as the only girl in the group, what impact she had on the men. Not much more.

On one occasion, Adam Leszczyński, a reporter on Africa who is two generations younger, asks Kapuściński: 'Why is it that in writing about Africa you never write about sexuality? Africa is, above all, sexuality.'

'It's a matter of generation. For people of my generation, sexuality is a sphere you don't talk about in public.'

But in fact Kapuściński is interested in African sexuality. Cathy Watson and William Pike, at whose home in Kampala he stayed in the late 1980s, tell how he endlessly questioned their driver, Fred, about the sex life of the Africans. He was interested in polygamy.

However, in his book about Africa, *The Shadow of the Sun*, there are only two sentences about sexuality, far removed from the anthropological questions he put to Fred. He is at a crowded, noisy night club in Dar es Salaam that belongs to a Polish immigrant. 'Customers are drawn here by the charms of the chocolate-coloured Miriam, a beautiful stripper from the distant Seychelles. As a show-stopper, she has a special way of peeling and eating a banana.'[7]

In *Travels with Herodotus*, Kapuściński unintentionally reveals how he perceives the female half of humanity:

[T]he sales-ladies did not sit, but stood, looking at the entrance doors. It was strange that they stood in silence, rather than sitting and talking to one another. Women, after all, have so many subjects in common. Troubles with their husbands, problems with the children. What to wear, one's health, whether something burned on the stove yesterday.[8]

'Didn't I tell you he didn't make friends with women?' says Izabella Nowak, smiling, when I show her this quote from *Travels*. 'Now you know why.'

He was capable of being verbally brutal: when there is a crisis or conflict, when he says good-bye, or when a candidate for the throne is hesitating: 'Or maybe not? That's the brutality of someone who cares. Not a macho man, not a cold bastard.' (So they tell me.)

One of his male friends says, 'To many women, he was an attractive kind of bastard.'

Sometimes, as infatuated as a teenager, he gets restless: 'That's it, I'm finally getting divorced, that's enough.'

'If he really had wanted to get divorced, I'd have been the first to knock the idea out of his head!' says the true queen. 'Alicja was his mainstay.' His friends tell me that when Rysiek's car breaks down in Africa, he knows how to fix it himself, but when his car comes to a halt in the middle of a junction in Warsaw, he doesn't call the repair service; instead he calls Alicja to deal with it.

'Kuba, help!'

Kapuściński's pet name for his wife, Kuba, is invented after his return from Afghanistan at the very end of 1956. The sentry guarding him at the airport in Kabul, where he ended up without a visa, was pleased to learn that Kapuściński was not British. British – kaput; Russian – friend, he said. '*O, Urusi besyar khubas!*' ('Oh, Russians, very good!') Kapuściński plays with the sound of the words, repeating and reciting them. *Khubas* (good) is transformed into 'kubas', and 'kubas' metamorphoses into 'kuba', but with a capital letter.

'Kuba, help!'

But he keeps Kuba hidden from the world. The eternal bachelor.

'Why didn't you come to dinner at our place, Ala?' asks a friend.

'Because Rysiek never takes me anywhere.'

'He had a wife?' asks Elena Poniatowska, surprised. She is a Mexican writer whom I visit at her flat in Mexico City. 'He once mentioned a daughter.'

Daniel Passent: 'I had been acquainted with him for many years before I heard that he had a wife.'

A colleague from the weekly *Kultura* who regards himself as a friend: 'I saw Mrs Kapuścińska for the first time in January 2007, just before his death. She came to Warsaw University to collect the Franciszek Ryszka Prize on his behalf.'

Some friends of the Kapuściński family think that 'without Ala, Rysiek would have been lost'. When he became world famous and started receiving fees from various sources, Alicja studied the tax and copyright regulations. Whenever he went off on his travels, she found flight connections for him. She had dozens of other skills as a secretary, assistant and accountant; she helped create the administrative and logistic background to his career.

But throughout his life Rysiek kept her in the shadows. Only when he passed away did Alicja find herself in the spotlight; only then did she come into contact with a world she had not known in her husband's lifetime and begin to participate in his success.

He is about forty; she is half his age. He comes back from a long journey and goes to a party at someone's home. It is an international crowd. He tells stories and is intriguing. She already belongs to him, but he doesn't know that yet.

'What was it about him that attracted you?'

'Everything.'

'But most of all?'

'The most interesting part of a man's body.'

'Which for you is – ?'

'The brain.'

After partying all night comes an early morning farewell: 'So when will we see each other again?'

Then she, too, is crowned queen; he doesn't yet know it won't be for just three months. The enchantment, the infatuation, the mad passion last two years. They meet at the flats of friends who leave them the keys; in later years they meet at a studio flat in the Warsaw district of Służewiec, once she has her own place. 'There was nothing routine about him, nothing conventional, he was "creative", romantic – never any "get lost!" ' Affection, a sense of intimacy.

> Ever since you
> everything changes colour
> has an extra shade –
> of you
> ever since you
> the sounds change –
> they are imbued with your voice . . .[9]

'You know, once we're living together . . .', she says to him one day.

'He gave me such a look that I instantly realized I could either have what I had, or nothing. "Nothing" didn't enter into it. I chose what he gave me.'

Later, she herself would not have wanted a life together either. So she says. He needed a wife who would wait on him, be the head of administration, the accountant and purser. This is not for her. She is independent and ambitious; she has plans. She is an intellectual. She is attractive – in conversation, too. She's persistent and uses plain language. They construe the world in a similar way; nowadays she still says, 'I'm a Red. Is that unappealing?'

She will have many relationships, usually successful. Men were drawn to her just as women were drawn to him.

After a couple of months of passion, he announces it's the end. He has to write, concentrate; enough of this madness. Two days later he calls. She gives the caretaker five zloty to open the gate after eleven at night.

Then he breaks it off again, and again. The first few break-ups cause her pain. After the next few, she knows that in a couple of days the phone will ring anyway.

In one of his letters to her, he writes in the words of a poet: 'Now, when you know I love you, you will never do me any harm.' She knew he would not do her any harm either.

He writes that if he ever hurt her, he would hurt himself, because he would deprive himself of the right to what he holds dearest – the right to their love.

He does not think of marriage – yet even so, she is in charge of the situation. Only she knows when he is going abroad and when he is coming back. She takes him to the airport by taxi and comes to fetch him again. He goes to the Middle East only for a while, although officially the work trip lasts longer. When he is due to go to Angola, he admits to her that he is afraid of not coming back alive.

At roughly this point, after two years, she tells him it's the end. She has fallen in love with another man. There is no time for tears or farewells. He goes off to the war, while she starts a new life.

He comes back from the war alive, and it starts all over again. Now the odds have evened out: both of them are in relationships, so they will hide out together. For thirty-three years.

When she is far away, he writes letters saying he is in the middle of the desert – meaning a place where she is absent.

'Didn't you want to shine in his light?'

'Quite the contrary – I jealously guarded our privacy and intimacy, and nothing has changed, even though he is no longer alive. That's why my name will not appear in your book. I was with him for him alone, not because he was famous. In any case, when we met he was well-known only in Poland – it was at least fifteen years before he gained world fame.'

Sometimes he urges her to come out to a restaurant, a party or a premiere. Once she gave in. They go into a pub. They hear whispers: 'Oh, that's Kapuściński . . .'

'Finish your food,' she says to him. 'Let's get out of here.'

Later when he wanted to take her somewhere for dinner or to a party, she would say, 'I'll make you a sandwich . . .' They stay home and enjoy each other's company, and no one knows about it.

'He was the one who was indiscreet. If he hadn't shot off his mouth, you'd never have found out.'

There is nothing possessive about their love. They tell each other about their other relationships: 'Are you OK with him, are you OK with her? Great, I'm happy, I want you to be pleased.'

At one point she hooks up with a much younger boyfriend. He calls, and so she suggests that he come by.

'Surely you've gone too far this time,' he says to her.

'Was he jealous?' I ask.

'Jealous – no. But he felt uncomfortable about having to compete with a "handsome twenty-year-old". He himself felt like an "ugly forty-year-old."'

Another time she tells him, 'I think I'm getting divorced.'

'You've gone mad, I forbid you to! He's a friend of mine!'

When Kapuściński, approaching sixty, no longer has any desire to tell stories about his conquests, she thinks he must be hiding something. He disarms her by admitting, 'You know, in a writer's life there comes a moment when his most precious lovers are his own books.' (To a friend's regular question 'How are the girls?' he more and more often replies: 'I don't feel like it anymore, I'm tired, I haven't the time.')

He talks to her about Alicja. He is upset by his wife's wretched frame of mind and talks about her with concern. He is worried. He knows he is not innocent.

'Were you jealous of Alicja?'

'Never. I am eternally grateful to her for her tacit consent to our – Rysiek's and my – right to love. It is noble and admirable.'

She decides to love and respect everything that he loves and needs.

'Alicja was more important to him than might emerge from this whole story.'

She shows me a note he wrote in hospital just before he died: 'Kuba spends several hours a day with me. How grateful I am to her for that!' She says, 'At moments like that, you write the truth.'

I comment: 'So many years and you never lived together?'

She replies: 'Never for more than a few days.'

'You didn't become like brother and sister, mother and son, or father and daughter, as many old married couples do?'

'Never.'

The passion smouldered on to the end.

And the constant separations? These were just another test. They always knew that, as he wrote in one of his letters, only a few centuries would go by and their time would come. Their moment. It was lovely to think of every intimate moment.

He goes home to Alicja. He always goes home. First to the flat on the corner of Nowolipki Street and Marchlewski Avenue, next to the one on Pustola Street, and then to the one on Prokuratorska Street.

'So what if he was away from home more often than not? I don't even remember that anymore. Or maybe I don't want to. Physical presence isn't the most important thing. The most important things were the keys. "Oh dear, the keys! The keys!" he would cry out before leaving. He used to take the flat keys and pack them in his case. "I must be sure I have somewhere to come back to," he would say. He knew he had a home he could always come back to, whatever might have happened.'[10]

30

The Final Revolution, the Final Coup

> Whenever I came back from abroad, I always asked what was going on here. The stories I heard were increasingly permeated with a sense of hopelessness, a sense of being bogged down in the mud, a feeling that the quagmire was swallowing us up. The second symptom was the gradually intensifying impression that something was bound to happen. There was a conviction that this nation – stifled, crushed, deprived of a voice, deprived of the opportunity for self-fulfilment – would explode.[1]

In the summer of 1980 it finally does explode. The standard of living continues to worsen, and people have to queue for hours for all sorts of essential items. One day you might manage to hunt down some sugar, another time you may find some meat and cooked sausage. As their laughter turns into rage, people talk about how one day you can buy shaving cream but there aren't any razors, and when you can get razors, there isn't any shaving cream. Working conditions at many plants are deteriorating – there is no money to buy the necessary protective clothing, and people are often reminded of the miserly days of Gomułka. More and more Poles are escaping into alcohol – drinking is becoming a national epidemic.

Only on television, radio and in the newspapers does the image of the country stay the same. The propaganda of success praises the miraculous achievements of the past decade: we have built so many houses, we have made so many cars, consumption has grown. Meanwhile, in the summer of 1980 the PRL is close to bankruptcy, and the party that has gone on for several years on someone else's money is ending with an acute hangover and the fall of Gierek's court.

'The economic crisis was thus a necessary, but by no means a sufficient, cause of the revolution,' writes British historian of the Polish revolution Timothy Garton Ash.

> The decisive causes are to be found more in the realm of consciousness than of being. By 1980 this unique society, at once sick and

self-confident, frustrated but united, faced a weak and divided power elite which no longer had the means to win voluntary popular support yet had not the will to command obedience by physical coercion. Although the individual components are novel – the alignment of the Church [following the election of a Polish cardinal as Pope and his spectacular visit to the country a year earlier], the agitation of workers against a 'Worker's State' – the basic shift of political self-confidence and will from the rulers to a section of the ruled is familiar from the pre-history of earlier revolutions.[2]

Kapuściński writes: 'There was a conviction that the Party leadership had long ago put too much strain on society's psychological resistance, and as society is not organized, it reacts in a chaotic manner.'[3]

The centre of social shock is the Lenin Shipyard in Gdańsk, where a strike erupts. To begin with, the strikers simply try to win pay rises, bonuses, and the reinstatement of those who have been sacked for inciting rebellion. But as the days go by, the strikers demonstrate increasing obstinacy and determination, and observers – as well as the participants themselves – start to fear that the Party will crush the protest with the help of the militia and the army, as they did ten years earlier in the same place. Some do not rule out armed intervention by the Soviet Union, as in Czechoslovakia in 1968. The power of Moscow, real socialism, and the division of the world into East and West still seem inviolable, permanent and eternal.

These were visions of bloody slaughter, bloody revenge . . . These were catastrophic, apocalyptic visions. These visions emerged from the fact that the authorities had managed to bring about a considerable fragmentation of society, and that with the help of propaganda, all the pseudo-values advertised in the mass media, it had managed to create mistrust between people, an internal quarrel, and also disintegration in terms of social class or group.[4]

Having witnessed twenty or so revolutions, uprisings and coups d'état in the Third World, Kapuściński will soon see a spark flaring into a revolutionary flame in his own country.

Warsaw. I came to watch. The impression was huge. After years of stagnation, inactivity, intimidation and apathy, suddenly in the course of an hour I saw a different society. A public transport strike always has a visual impact. The trams and buses standing along Jerozolimskie and Marszałkowska Avenues formed a cross. It was a summer afternoon. People quite calmly started setting off to walk to remote districts, all the way to Służew or Bielany. Without any protest. It felt as if a sort of national community were starting to take shape. Society's resolution, its determination was visible. It was all the more striking that it was happening in Warsaw, a city where society is extremely disintegrated.[5]

On which side will the romantic revolutionary, the left-wing believer, find his place when the sharp end of rebellion is pointing at the regime that avows socialist ideals? Will he side with the mutinous people ('anti-social elements', as the government propaganda calls them) or with the Party, to which he has belonged for almost thirty years, alongside his pals from the Central Committee, who have always helped him whenever necessary?

The opposition movement in the PRL has been organizing itself for several years now. The Workers' Defence Committee (KOR) comes into being – a group of intellectuals who provide help to workers fired for taking part in protests against increases in the price of food. There is a 'flying university' in operation, as well as illegal trade unions, and independent political and cultural periodicals are getting published, by-passing the censors. This underground world has internal divisions into left and right. Some participants are formulating a programme to fight for complete independence from Moscow; others have a realistic view of the chances and will settle for greater freedom, adherence to human rights, and relative autonomy for Poland within the Soviet bloc. Some are closer to the Catholic Church, others further away. It is a makeshift version of the actual divisions that crop up everywhere in democratic politics.

This is a totally different sort of resistance to dictatorship than the revolutionary opposition movements that Kapuściński knows from the Third World. This Polish version is based on trying to act openly, within the framework of the existing law; it cites the authorities' international obligations to observe human rights. It rejects armed fighting, violence, and individual terror. But the authoritarian regime in 1970s Poland is also different from Third World tyrannies: its opponents do not disappear, they are not assassinated. Underground activists are usually arrested for forty-eight hours and then released, and the institutions of repression do not apply torture. The press is subject to censorship, but the Party allows a limited level of criticism (through allusions and metaphors), and the world of culture enjoys considerable freedom.

Kapuściński keeps his distance from the opposition; he is still a loyal Party member. When in 1976 workers in the city of Radom and in Warsaw's Ursus district demonstrate against food price rises and the opposition KOR is organized immediately afterwards, he publishes a series of reports from Angola in which he declares himself to be wholeheartedly on the side of the Marxist MPLA. While more dissident groups are formed and the underground publishing movement develops, Kapuściński monitors the

Red revolution in Ethiopia with sympathy. As the Poles get excited about
'our Pope', he reports on John Paul II's first foreign trip to Mexico, where
conflict arises with supporters of liberation theology. The Pope sees this
theology as 'infected' by Marxism; Kapuściński is one of its supporters. (In
Mexico City he stays with Józef Klasa, then ambassador. 'How Rysiek
loved that systematically atheist country!' recalls Klasa. 'What exactly did he
like about it? The fact that the Church had been put in its place.')

Before the Polish rebellion erupts, Kapuściński goes to Iran twice, where
he witnesses the fall of Mohammad Reza Shah Pahlavi, and the Islamic
revolution of Ayatollah Khomeini. Shocked by the cruelties of the Shah's
secret police, he identifies with his opponents. When the Polish people start
to grow weary of the crisis, fuses have been lit, and public eruption is just
around the corner, he writes a series of reports for *Kultura* on the Iranian
revolution. In many extracts – consciously or involuntarily – he touches on
the Polish situation. Read years later, they sound like prophecies.

> Here is a well-fed and well-entertained crowd that stops obeying. It
> begins to demand something more than entertainment. It wants free-
> dom, it demands justice. The despot is stunned. He doesn't know how to
> see a man in all his fullness and glory. In the end such a man threatens
> dictatorship, he is its enemy. So it gathers its strength to destroy him.[6]

Or:

> All books about all revolutions begin with a chapter that describes the
> decay of tottering authority or the misery and sufferings of the people.
> They should begin with a psychological chapter, one that shows how a
> harassed, terrified man suddenly breaks his terror, stops being afraid. This
> unusual process, sometimes accomplished in an instant like a shock or a
> lustration, demands illuminating. Man gets rid of fear and feels free.
> Without that there would be no revolution.[7]

How people who are exhausted by everyday life, anaesthetized and
worried about tomorrow, overcome their fear is something he is shortly to
witness at close quarters at the Lenin Shipyard in Gdańsk.

> After passing through the gate, you went to the health and safety build-
> ing, where the accreditation office was located. There were two girls
> sitting there, friendly but already very tired and dazed. They could either
> issue accreditation or refuse it. They either issued it for one day, or
> permanently. I got the permanent kind.[8]

Between the start of the strike and the appearance of journalists at the shipyard, the workers' demands undergo a radical change. The issue is no longer a pay rise, the reinstatement of fired workers, and an end to the repression of the rebels. Now the strikers demand recognition for trade unions that are independent of the Party and the employer; the right to strike; freedom of speech and the press; and a programme to bring the country out of the crisis into which Gierek's team has driven it. No one has made demands like these in the Soviet bloc for a very long time.

Kapuściński finds himself in a group of journalists who have turned up at the shipyard a few days after the beginning of the strike. No one yet knows how it will all end: will the authorities come to terms with the strikers, or will they send out the militia and the army for 'street negotiations'? Perhaps they will summon the help of their Soviet comrades? Kapuściński is aware that something important is happening – but does he already know which side he's on?

Journalists who belong to the Party have not come to the shipyard entirely of their own accord. The Party knows, the Party concurs – it's better to learn from their own people what's happening behind the shipyard gate. On the way to Gdańsk, one of them stops for the night at the district committee in Elbląg. Next day, still in Elbląg, he observes the striking workers, who shout at him, 'Hey, you fucking spies, what have you come here from Warsaw for?'

The Party's central office sends Wiesław Ilczuk, deputy director of the Press Department, to the district committee in Gdańsk. He is to keep an eye on the journalists and to relay whatever is necessary to the Central Committee. Some journalists who are Party members come along to report; Ilczuk or the local comrades give them permission to enter the shipyard. In the evenings they organize meetings at which the reporters describe the strikers' mood and what they heard behind the gate. Some of them try to convince their Party bosses that it is not a counter-revolution that is taking place, but a genuine workers' revolt.

'When Kapuściński went to the shipyard,' recalls one of his *Kultura* colleagues, 'he was not a member of the opposition or a dissenter, but the authorities' blue-eyed boy, a trusted comrade of the comrades on the Central Committee.'

In any case, first he turns up in Szczecin, at the local shipyard where there is also a strike. He goes at the request of Kazimierz Barcikowski, Central Committee secretary, who is going to conduct negotiations with the local Inter-Enterprise Strike Committee. They have known each other since student days. Barcikowski is right-hand man to Stanisław Kania, the person responsible within the Central Committee for security, and deputy first secretary. Barcikowski is regarded as a Party 'liberal'. He asks Kapuściński to get some insight into developments at the shipyard and the mood of the strikers, and then report to him. He wants information and an analysis from sources other than the Party and the militia.

'Rysiek made no secret of the fact that he had come to the shipyard in Szczecin at Barcikowski's request,' says a journalist colleague who spent a lot of time with him during the strike.

'How did you hear about it?'

'He told me himself.'

After Szczecin, Kapuściński goes to Gdańsk. Does he go because he realizes that this is the true heart of the revolution? Or, as with his trip to Szczecin, does someone prompt him to go?

The striking shipyard workers are mistrustful of journalists from the official media. More than one is refused accreditation on the shipyard premises.

The strikers felt that the press told lies and was an unreliable lackey of the regime. It was hard to explain to them what genuine broadcasting or information processing is like. Journalists were identified with the model of propaganda then in force, and it remained that way until each of them gained trust as an individual.[9]

The workers often took an indulgent attitude to us, as if we weren't to be taken seriously. One of my colleagues said he was a journalist. They talked for a very long time. Then they started having a go at something he said, and one of the shipyard workers rounded off the conflict by saying, 'All right then, let him be. Let him run along to his pal Gierek.'[10]

Thanks to the help of Wojciech Adamiecki, a commentator who sympathizes with the KOR, some people get an entry pass to the shipyard and, in addition, to the conference room for strike leaders and the government delegation. Kapuściński knows him from his early years as a journalist at *Sztandar Młodych*, during the heroic era of building socialism and then the revolt against the 'errors and distortions' of the Stalinist era. Now he can see that Adamiecki is not only siding with the workers' protest but is openly supporting the anti-government opposition.

Among the strikers and those camping outside the shipyard gate, Kapuściński notices people who – as he will relate years later – have brought his books with them to fill the long hours of idleness. It is hard to imagine a moment of greater satisfaction for a writer. He proudly signs copies of *The Polish Bush, Christ with a Rifle on His Shoulder, The Soccer War, The Emperor*. Moreover, he says, this 'immediately facilitated my entry into this environment'.[11]

Soon Kapuściński finds he has a much more useful entry pass at his disposal: knowledge of foreign languages. Foreign correspondents are now arriving at the shipyard, and the strikers need someone to explain their reasons and demands to the world's journalists.

'As soon as the strike committee announced that it was looking for people who knew languages,' says one of his journalist colleagues, 'Rysiek immediately came forward. They soon realized that someone like him was absolutely essential.'

One day, two Trotskyites from Spain turn up among the foreign observers. Kapuściński willingly agrees to be their translator, and takes them to see people from the strike committee.

'We want to become acquainted with your revolution,' says one of the Spanish visitors.

'You gentlemen are mistaken,' replies the worker from the strike committee. 'We're not having a revolution here. We're just sorting out our affairs. Sorry, but please leave the shipyard premises immediately, with no right to return.'

At the shipyard Kapuściński, whose knowledge of many Third World countries is excellent, comes to the realization that he has only a foggy idea of his own country.

> For many years I had had no contact with the working community, mainly because I wasn't in the country. For me, August was a great discovery . . . The way the system operated in the 1970s meant that the workers simply did not figure in the public forum. I am afraid many of my fellow journalists who covered national issues did not actually know the workers either . . . It was because of our society's disintegration. People were living in social environments that were completely isolated, cut off from each other.[12]

Most of the journalists from outside the Tri-City stay at the Hotel Monopol, not far from the main railway station in Gdańsk. Here they meet at breakfast, but no long conversations are held until late at night, at the end of each new day of the strike. They meet in the largest room, set up for several people, where their colleagues from the Polish Film Chronicle are staying, or else they gather in the flats of local journalists. They consider possible future scenarios, give each other hope, and allay one another's concerns.

'Our speculations and predictions usually failed to materialize,' recalls Ewa Junczyk-Ziomecka. 'We were almost always wrong, including Rysiek.'

Someone will later mention that he was struck by Kapuściński's calm and his belief in the rightness of what was happening there.

Someone else has never forgotten having heard him say that after witnessing so many wars, coups and revolutions, he finally has a sense of the significance of what is happening in Poland.

His colleagues know that, of their entire company, Kapuściński is the best informed on the reshuffles and manoeuvres taking place in Warsaw. They pump him for news – especially the people from the local press. They question him about the bigwigs who are leaving their posts and about the new ones being appointed in their stead. Who is who? What does this or that change mean? Please tell us, what is going on in Szczecin?

However, Kapuściński is not very talkative. He's cautious. 'He definitely wasn't the leader of the group of journalists at the shipyard,' says a colleague.

> The events that were happening, and our conversations about them, were a huge personal experience. We realized that matters were being resolved that would have an impact on our personal fate as reporters, and on what and how we were going to write.[13]

Official propaganda plays down the significance of the strikes on the Baltic coast. It reports on 'work stoppages' at some enterprises, but it keeps quiet about the scale of the protests and the demands of the rebel workforces. In addition, telephone communication between the coast and the rest of the country is cut off.

The journalists gathered at the shipyard decide to protest.

> We, Polish journalists, present on the Gdańsk coast during the strike, declare that much of the information published to date, and above all the way it has been interpreted, has not corresponded to the real nature of what is happening here. This state of affairs is conducive to disinformation.[14]

Now the real dilemmas begin. To sign, or not to sign?

Junczyk-Ziomecka: 'We stood under a small tree and signed our names below this declaration. Lots of us were scared. Finally one journalist couldn't stop himself − he seized the piece of paper with his own signature on it and started eating it. We rushed at him, crying: "Give it back!" We had to write out the text again.'

Thirty-six journalists signed the declaration, including Ryszard Kapuściński, Party member for almost three decades.

> For many journalists, signing that document was an enormous, life-changing decision. We wondered if there would be repression. I remember that one of my colleagues who had signed it came up to me the next day and said: 'So Ryszard, what do you think? I signed, but what's going to happen now?' He was terribly upset. We all felt we had made the right decision, but that it was a risky one. Nowadays it seems quite absurd, but at the time . . . on 25 August . . . In the end, we were protesting against the entire propaganda line with regard to what was happening on the Baltic coast.[15]

The workers don't really understand the journalists' dilemmas: they are already living in a slightly altered reality. When the declaration is read out to the shipyard workers, it gets some faint applause, but even the mildest 'no' gets applause at the time. One witness later recalls that the workers treated the journalists' political demonstration as 'the return of the prodigal sons', a vote by those who 'woke up rather late in the day, but a good thing too.'

On one of those days, Tomasz Łubieński runs into Kapuściński outside the shipyard, in the street. Agitated, Kapuściński whispers in his ear: 'I have information that there are Soviet tanks standing outside Elbląg in full readiness for combat.'

Giełżyński, too, remembers Kapuściński's panicked warnings: ' "They're on the point of invading," he kept repeating.'

'I think history had frightened him, and he frightened himself with it as well,' says Łubieński. 'On the other hand, his knowledge of it from his studies, and even more from his own life, gave him some detachment: he knew that one time it's like this, and another time it's different.'

Fear of intervention by the army or the militia, or of an invasion by Soviet troops, is the main theme of daily conversations. In later years Kapuściński says, 'Those portraits [of the Pope and the Virgin Mary that hung on the shipyard gate] acted as a protective shield. The workers said: "No Polish soldier will shoot at the Pope, no tank will drive through an altar." '[16] But everyone agrees that the Russians would have no such scruples.

'Kapuściński went his own way; he'd suddenly disappear somewhere and just as suddenly reappear,' says Lech Stefański, who wrote for *Polityka*. 'For a long time he didn't believe in a positive ending for the strike or in any optimistic "what next?" scenario.'

'I kept catching sight of him off to one side, by a fence or a tree, or sitting on a low wall talking to someone,' remembers Junczyk-Ziomecka. 'He didn't make any notes, but then he wrote the best article about the strike in the entire Polish press.'

> In a strike you don't do anything in particular. You sit around, listen, stand in a group of people, chat, sit again, smoke a cigarette and wait, and wait . . . Most of us who were there were not working. It was more about sharing a common fate for all those hours . . . Those were days of non-stop emotion.[17]

And also more than one personal transformation. One day Janusz Głowacki, a colleague from the editorial office who has a reputation as a playboy, turns up at the shipyard. Someone jokes that he just wants to take a snap of himself with the strike in the background, and then he'll be off.

'Well, so what's up, guys? Apparently you're on strike,' he blurts out, accosting Kapuściński and two other journalists standing there together. Hours later, he returns from the conference room, clutching his head and repeating: 'The Winter Palace! Revolution!'

For Kapuściński, as for most of the journalists, being present at the shipyard has more of a civic than a professional character. They write nothing themselves during this period, and they know no account of it will be published in the papers. What matters is that they are with the strikers, and that their minds and attitudes are undergoing transformation.

Kapuściński cannot avoid a sense of déjà vu from the Third World, for example, when he sees the alcohol ban ordered by the strike leaders, the discipline of the strikers, the communal prayers and the way the mass is sticking to these resolutions – the mass, which can only be controlled by itself.

> [F]or me it is an absolutely natural thing that in any organized revolt featuring a mass that has authority, this mass acts in a very ethical way . . . In the Iranian revolution, when there were demonstrations, not just of a hundred or ten thousand people, but two million, those two-million-strong demonstrations walked through the city, and when they came to a hospital, silence fell quite spontaneously, to avoid disturbing the patients. Alongside these demonstrations, groups of people formed spontaneously who walked along with plastic bags, picking up all the litter and refuse, in order to leave the city clean. Teheran usually looks like a giant rubbish heap, but after the demonstrations it looked like a city that had finally been cleaned.[18]

Two weeks after the strike, he writes:

> No one drank, made a scene or woke up with a thundering hangover. The crime level fell to zero, all mutual aggression came to an end, and people became friendly, helpful and open to one another. Total strangers suddenly felt as if they needed each other.[19]

(One of his colleagues describes the workers on duty at the shipyard gate as 'the guardians of the revolution' – yet another association with the revolution in Iran, which Kapuściński had recently written about in *Kultura*.)

One day Kapuściński observes the visit of five women from the local crafts co-operative. The women want to join the strike, but not because they want a pay rise; they're demanding that their chairman be sacked, because he is a lout, and all their efforts to teach him some manners have failed.

Kapuściński realizes that wages and economic issues are not at the heart of the Polish rebellion. The realization reconfirms his belief, formed by years spent in the Third World, that the main motor of most protest movements, uprisings and revolutions is not the fight for bread, but wounded dignity. A moment comes when people refuse to put up with any more humiliation. This will be the main idea for the essay he plans to write when all this is over. On this occasion he drops the usual method of reportage: one worker said this, another one said that. He thinks that sort of article will blur the crucial point of the events he is describing.

> It had to be a hard-hitting article, like a punch. An article that would move and shock. I wrote it with great passion, with a strong desire to reveal something incredibly important, something historic. The point was to show a different person, a different Pole, a different reality. To show that we are taking history into our own hands, and from this moment on everything is going to be different.[20]

Two weeks after the victorious strike, the fall of Gierek's court and the agreement of the PRL authorities to set up the Solidarity trade union – the first workers' organization independent of the Party in the entire Soviet bloc – Kapuściński publishes his punch-like article, 'Notes from the Coast', in *Kultura*:

> [T]he August strike was both a dramatic struggle and a sort of holiday. A struggle for rights, and Shoulders Back Day, Heads Held High Day . . .
> I do not know if we are all aware that whatever else happens, from 1980 onwards we are living in a different Poland . . .
> Anyone who tries to reduce the Coastal movement to issues to do with wages and living standards has not understood a thing. Because the chief motive for these events was human dignity . . .
> [T]here was no element of revenge, no desire for a payback, not a single attempt to fight out personal issues at any level . . . On those August days many words suddenly came to life, took on significance and shine: the word 'honour', the word 'dignity', the word 'equality'.
> A new Polish lesson began. The subject of the lesson is democracy. It's a tough, arduous lesson, under a stern, watchful eye that won't allow any cribbing. That's why there will be F grades as well. But the bell has already rung and we are all sitting at our desks.[21]

Before the article is published, it lands on the desk of Jerzy Waszczuk, the Central Committee secretary responsible for cultural affairs and the mass media.
'I talked to Kapuściński in person,' recalls Waszczuk. 'He was bewitched by Wałęsa, by the workers and the strike. He believed that the same sort of

thing had happened at the shipyard as he had been observing for years in the Third World, and that Wałęsa was someone like Che Guevara, but in a different reality, and that Poland was a link in the chain of worldwide revolutionary processes. I asked him to tone down his article.'

'Do you remember what specifically?' I inquire.

'I urged him to curb his enthusiasm for the rebellious workers and write something positive about the Party; to say that it had rejected the use of force, and had reached a compromise with the strikers. A compromise is always to the credit of both sides.'

'And did Kapuściński acquiesce?'

'Not at all. He refused to make any changes, not a single comma.'

'He was able to say no to a Central Committee secretary? Did he have such a strong position within the Party?'

'It was a time of crisis, of relaxed rules. The mechanisms of government were not operating normally. In a different situation it would have been impossible – I would have been more resolute, and Kapuściński would have been much more submissive.'

At a Central Committee meeting with the editors-in-chief of the newspapers and periodicals, one of them, a person known as a hard-liner, attacks Kapuściński: 'Such a great journalist and he so stupidly gave in to Solidarity!'

Still at the shipyard, right after the strike, a friend from the days of the '56 revolt, Andrzej Krzysztof Wróblewski, takes a picture of Kapuściński with the workers' leader, Lech Wałęsa. 'Rysiek was thrilled with Wałęsa, on his knees,' he says. 'He fell in love with him like a teenager with his first girlfriend.'

He continues: 'I fell in love with the revolution only once, in 1956. But Rysiek fell in love for the second time at the shipyard, maybe the third or fourth, who knows? He had seen more revolutions than anyone else. And he was in too much of a rush, galloping ahead, being uncritical. As if after all his experiences he had forgotten that you should never give credit to any revolution. He was behaving like a guy with no legs who leaps up to dance and can't see how funny he looks.'

'He always was the enthusiastic type,' says Andrzej Werblan, a friend from the Party side of the barricade. 'When he believed in socialism, he was genuine in his faith, sincerely dedicated to the Party. When he grew disenchanted, he was just as sincerely fascinated by the workers' rebellion. He was susceptible to the pressure of reality: when he took something to heart, he changed his views.'

But changing them in 1980 was not as simple as it may have initially appeared.

Our entire editorial team at *Kultura* joined Solidarity. I was extremely excited and involved at the time.[22]

But he himself does not join Solidarity – that is what his *Kultura* colleagues, who did sign up for the new union movement, remember years later. Nor did the people in charge of the weekly join it either.

As divisions appear among the journalists, Kapuściński maintains good relations with people who are making a variety of political choices. At *Kultura* there are no major clashes anyway, as almost the entire team sympathizes with Solidarity. Things are different at *Polityka*, where the journalists have divided into supporters of Solidarity, its open enemies, and those who are critical or sceptical; in addition, editor-in-chief Mieczysław Rakowski has just been made deputy prime minister.

Immediately after the end of the strike at the shipyard, Kapuściński sets off on a tour of Poland, once again at the request of his comrades on the Central Committee.

'Just as he was asked to go to the striking shipyard in Szczecin, he was probably asked to do it by the same man, Barcikowski, though today I could not swear his name came up in conversation,' says a colleague from *Kultura*. 'Rysiek certainly said his Central Committee friends had asked him. They wanted him to provide an analysis of the situation within the country, as seen by a reporter who was an expert on revolutions and mass social movements.'

His comrades from the 'White House' still regard him as their man.

Kapuściński visits striking enterprises, spends days and nights with various committees, and observes the incipient social movement and the 'self-limiting revolution'. He discovers a different Poland.

On the tenth anniversary of the massacre of workers on the Baltic coast outside the Gdynia shipyard gate during their 1970 demonstrations against price rises, Kapuściński takes part in a mass commemorating the tragedy. With him is Teresa Torańska; after the mass they go together to a large room within the shipyard where they listen to witnesses recalling the events of 1970. These people come out on stage and for the first time ever speak publicly about their experiences of those days. Kapuściński records their accounts on a small Sony cassette-player.

A doctor describes how the wounded were brought to the hospital; everything was supervised on the spot by the security service. He remembers a lad who was in danger of having his leg amputated, and how he was taken by helicopter to another hospital. 'I don't even know if he survived,' he says, and at that moment a voice is heard from the crowd: 'It was me, I'm alive!'

A mother describes her son's funeral, held – on security service orders – in secret at night.

'Rysiek soaked it all up,' says Torańska. 'He was discovering a Poland he didn't know.'

Some Solidarity activists and supporters think complete victory over the system is just around the corner. In one conversation at the newspaper office, someone compares the Party to a small dog trying to stop a speeding train: in other words, Solidarity.

At that juncture, after one of the biggest crises in relations between the Party and Solidarity, Kapuściński and Torańska are on their way back by car from Bydgoszcz to Warsaw. Kapuściński explains that the entire Polish upheaval is not just about Solidarity. 'There's a fight going on for Poland's independence,' he declares.

'It was six in the morning, we were sitting in my Fiat 126 parked outside his house, and he said it almost in a whisper, as if revealing the biggest secret, as if he had discovered America,' says Torańska, smiling.

'Why was that?'

'Because up until that moment he had believed in the system, and in his friends at the Central Committee. He was always saying, "Barcikowski said such-and-such" or "when I saw Barcikowski". A good few months after the Solidarity uprising, he still regarded himself as a Party man. He could see that some amendments and reforms were needed, but he thought the system should be maintained. On the way from Bydgoszcz to Warsaw, during that conversation outside his house I noticed for the first time that he was going through a metamorphosis.'

> I have started writing a book about our Polish affairs, our contemporary ones, but also with reminiscences going back to the 1950s. The working title is *The Demand*. I want to show the evolution of my generation, the generation that has been through a whole series of crises. The most recent one, in August, found some people on this side, and others on the opposite side. I pose questions about the mechanisms that have led to this parting of the ways, to these transformations. I am not concerned about the fate of individuals, but about trying to show what has occurred inside us, the circumstances that have influenced and are still influencing the way attitudes are shaped.
>
> I will devote the spring and summer to writing this book. I aim and hope to have the first instalment published in *Kultura*.[23]

He will not write the promised book, or even a single feature about Poland during the 'carnival', the name given to the sixteen months between the strikes of August 1980 and December 1981, when General Jaruzelski introduces martial law, ending the era of hope for the reform of socialism.

In interviews he gives at the time, as if avoiding direct statements on the new movement, he escapes into general reflections, which do not place him unambiguously on the rebel side. He talks about the maturity of the Poles, the need for renewal, and the significance of the ongoing events. The name 'Solidarity' is occasionally mentioned, but not often.

Maciej Wierzyński, who in those days is working in television, makes several attempts to invite Kapuściński to the studio to tell the viewers about his travels around Poland in rebellion. 'I always got the same answer – no. As if he didn't want to talk about Solidarity. After a short period of enthusiasm, he had a presentiment that it would all end badly. Maybe that was why he refused?'

During the 'carnival', Kapuściński is more involved with renewal of the Party than with Solidarity. He regards with sympathy the internal unrest: of the activists who are on strike along with the work-forces. They think the Party has lost public support but is not yet beaten. It still has a chance, it just has to democratize, to meet the expectations of the working world halfway.

Kapuściński travels to Toruń, where he meets initiators of the movement for Party renewal.

It starts at Towimor, a plant that makes ship fittings, and at Toruń University. At Party committee meetings at both institutions, the activists choose their executive bodies at the grass-roots level, without the agreement of the city committee. The newly elected executives establish mutual co-operation, also without agreement from above.

The movement for renewal within the Party acquires the attractive name *poziomki* (meaning 'wild strawberries', but also literally 'horizontals') – because horizontal structures within the organization had reached agreement without the blessing of the higher echelons, although the Party structure is vertical. In turn, people from the Party apparatus who are not keen on these changes christen the new movement the 'Toruń plague'.

Kapuściński understands that establishing new structures within a neo-Stalinist type of party is an almost revolutionary act. The system of providing information and making decisions within this kind of organization has been run the same way since time immemorial, with the involvement of a higher authority. Meanwhile, the two committees in Toruń have broken this cycle and introduced an uncontrolled element, a virus from outside the system.

> [T]he movement for grass-roots renewal within the Party began as a consequence of the August wave of strikes, when the Party members taking part in the strike came to the conclusion that they must find a way out of the crisis the Party was in by democratizing it . . . [T]he boldness of the demands, the firmness of the postulates put forward by the so-called Party grass roots in many cases goes incomparably further than the demands formulated within the postulates of Solidarity.[24]

The *poziomki* activists wear two badges in their lapels or on their sweaters or shirts: one for Solidarity, and one for the PZPR (Polish United Workers'

Party). They do not want to dissolve the Party, they want to strengthen it and come out to meet supporters of the new social movement halfway.

Kapuściński often discusses Party renewal with Andrzej Werblan (his closest Party friend, Ryszard Frelek, is out of the country at the time, having been appointed Poland's ambassador to the UN). In this period Werblan loses his job on the Central Committee but remains a member of the Sejm (the lower house of the Polish parliament), representing Toruń. After some initial tensions with the *poziomki*, Werblan moves closer to the movement for internal Party renewal.

'At the time Kapuściński was afraid the Party would disintegrate,' says Werblan. He sympathizes with the *poziomki*, seeing in this movement hope for rebuilding the Party's credibility and influences within society. Kapuściński's reasoning relates to the experiences of Hungary in 1956 and Czechoslovakia in 1968. In those countries it came to armed intervention by the Soviet Union, not because movements that defied or disobeyed Moscow had been formed, but because the local communist parties had fallen apart and had become incapable of controlling a social upheaval. (The Kremlin was annoyed by Nicolae Ceauşescu, leader of Romania's Communist Party, for instance, but he guaranteed peace and order, and so they never resolved to oust him.)

'At the time,' says Werblan, 'our concern was to make the Party into a force worthy of public trust, which in case of violent conflict with Solidarity would be capable of controlling it and preventing the collapse of state structures. If they did collapse, Soviet intervention would be 100 percent certain.'

One of the reporters' colleagues, Wojciech Giełżyński, doubts whether the calculations Kapuściński made at the time were correct. 'It was the *poziomki* who were splitting the Party from the inside, weakening it,' he contends, 'and they could have brought Soviet intervention down on us by doing that. In the eyes of the Kremlin, it was the *poziomki*, and not Solidarity, who were leading the Party towards disintegration.'

Another colleague observes: 'It was always possible to describe Solidarity as a counter-revolution. But on the other hand, what Moscow feared was that the Party itself would be at the head of the changes. A similar scenario in Czechoslovakia in 1968 had ended in armed intervention.'

The *poziomki* insist on an urgent Party congress. The top brass are holding off. Finally there is a congress in the summer of 1981: the *poziomki* lose ground, and the Party closes ranks against Solidarity. (Does it also avert the threat of 'fraternal aid' from Moscow?)

Kapuściński's wish, to some extent, comes true – the Party does not disintegrate. However, it does not become stronger by rebuilding credibility or by coming out to meet the Solidarity movement halfway, but by increasing discipline and entrenching itself in positions that for this revolutionary era are conservative.

Following the congress, the enthusiast changes into a pessimist.

From conversations he had with Kapuściński at the time, Werblan remembers that he was enchanted by Solidarity and by the integrity of the movement, and also that he was afraid of the anarchic factor and of excessive aspirations that were impossible to satisfy at that time. 'He thought of himself as someone who connects both sides. He had good contacts with people in both camps.'

And so in the 'carnival' months Kapuściński sits astride the barricade. On the one hand, he supports the *poziomki* and reform within the Party, but on the other, along with intellectuals who are close to Solidarity, he signs an appeal for consideration addressed to the radicals on both sides. The indirectly stated context of the appeal is the threat of intervention by Soviet troops.

Kapuściński is not just an experienced reporter, but also someone from the Borderlands – he is aware that the Polish situation cannot be viewed in isolation from geopolitics. Poland is part of the Soviet camp; at this point in time, ideas of independence, of limiting the power of the Party, and of a Polish withdrawal from the Warsaw Pact, for which the impatient Solidarity people keep clamouring, are pipe dreams. Images from his childhood come back to him: the Soviet soldiers on the bridge into Pińsk aiming their rifles at him; his sister's screams, his mother's cries, fear and despair; the NKVD men coming to the house for his father. 'Whenever he talked about the Soviet Union, he lowered his voice,' recalls a friend from the *Kultura* team.

On numerous journeys across Poland, he listens in during negotiations between members of the work-forces, people from Solidarity, enterprise directors and Party activists. Afterwards he will say that the dramatic development of events was influenced by the low level of conflict at the local, enterprise level, a lack of serious political reflection, some radical phraseology and arguments being reduced to interpersonal games. However, once Solidarity has been broken up by the Party, and thousands of its activists have been imprisoned, he comes to the belief that it was not one or the other group that was to blame, not the leaders of one or the other side: the obstacle to democratic changes was the political system, by its very nature incapable of assimilating them. A Greek tragedy on the River Vistula.

Just before martial law is declared he talks to Frelek, who has just returned from New York. They meet at the Ambasador café on Ujazdowskie Avenue in Warsaw. Kapuściński tells his friend he is off to Gdańsk, where the Solidarity leaders are holding a conference – for the last time, as it will turn out.

'He was jittery,' Frelek recalls years later. 'I had just come back from the States, and the Americans had been showing me maps marked with the deployment of troops on the borders.'

Frelek shares this news with his friend.

On 13 December, when the phones throughout the country are no longer working, Frelek uses his connections to make sure nothing has happened to Kapuściński and to find out if he has come home safely from the Baltic coast.

He has. A patrol checked his I.D. on the journey back to Warsaw – that was all.

The streets are full of snow, soldiers and armoured cars. The day after the introduction of martial law, Kapuściński goes to the *Kultura* office on Wiejska Street. Like all periodicals, the weekly has been suspended. Janusz Rolicki and three other colleagues also turn up at the office. They are all members of the PZPR's Basic Party Organization at the weekly.

According to Rolicki, it is he who suggests disbanding the office's Party organization. Everyone agrees. They pass their membership cards to the secretary of the organization, who is to take them to the district committee. Instead he takes them to the editor-in-chief, Horodyński.

Horodyński thinks his Party-member colleagues' decision is rash.

'It will be a nail in the coffin of *Kultura*,' he says when he finds out about it. His intuition proves correct: disbanding the Party organization at *Kultura* means that the journal will never be issued again, unlike most of the other suspended periodicals . . .

'Leaving the Party must have been a difficult, a pretty dramatic decision for Rysiek,' says Wiktor Osiatyński, his friend from *Kultura* who was not a Party member. For his entire adult life, Kapuściński had belonged to the Party. He believed in socialism, he believed the Party was his place, and the Party regarded him as its man. By making this decision, he drew a line through much of his own past, burned a lot of bridges, and broke many of the connections which until then had allowed him to travel abroad and function within the reality of the PRL.

That same afternoon, Kapuściński goes to see a friend from the Polish Journalists Association. Her three-year-old daughter greets him by saying: 'If you've got any books at home, you'd better get them out and hide them quickly, because when they come they'll take them from you.'

And then she adds: 'I know all that because we've got lots of books too, and we've already got them all out.'

He goes to see Frelek. They talk for hours and hours.

One day he drops in at the PAP office, where he worked for many years. People are having friendly conversations, trying to cheer each other up. Everyone is worried about what will happen next. Peace and quiet, or the opposite — strikes, demonstrations and street fighting? Ryszard Piekarowicz, a long-term PAP correspondent based in Asia, notes in his diary on the evening of 17 December:

> Kapusta ['cabbage', a nickname] says the situation is not good and will get worse. It will come to passive resistance, people will not go on strike but they won't work properly, they'll just pretend to be working. There are years of sterile dictatorship ahead of us, from which nothing good will come.
>
> Jaruzelski has made an error by not accepting power clearly in the name of the army to save the state, in the name of the nation, as a mediator between Solidarity and the Party. He could have said that he was intervening because Solidarity and the Party were not capable of reaching agreement and were starting to get into a fight. So it was necessary to avoid civil war.
>
> The young people are only thinking about how to leave Poland. No one believes things can change for the better.
>
> In Hungary in 1956 a large part of the opposition, the most active part, escaped abroad, which immediately weakened resistance. Hardly anyone has run away from Poland.[25]

A few days later he adds the following postscript:

> Is martial law meant to prevent Soviet intervention, or is it just a prelude to it? Kapusta reckons intervention is inevitable.[26]

In a conversation with Mariusz Ziomecki several days after this, Kapuściński once again predicts imminent intervention.

'He painted the blackest possible scenarios, he was scaremonger number one. He said blood would flow and there would be terrible carnage. And when it came to it, they would crack down on us journalists first of all. Then I realized that his familiarity with the dynamics of coups d'état in the Third World had not equipped him with wisdom appropriate to our, Polish situation.'

The martial law regime does come down on the disobedient journalists: anyone who wants to continue practising the profession must appear before a so-called vetting board. The board consists of Party functionaries who decide whom they will allow to carry on in the profession and whom they will not. Refusing to submit to vetting is regarded as an act of disloyalty towards the state, slamming the door on practising the profession within the official mass media.

Kapuściński makes a decision: 'I am not going to any vetting.'

Like most of the journalists who do not appear before the board (or are rejected by it), he is summoned to the headquarters of the publishing enterprise RSW 'Prasa', which publishes almost all the country's newspapers and magazines. In the PRL the main employer is the state, and it is RSW 'Prasa' that now gives the disobedient journalists notice in the name of the state and, shortly afterwards, offers them jobs in other branches and professions, usually at the Social Insurance Institution (ZUS).

Teresa Torańska appears at RSW 'Prasa' just after Kapuściński. When he comes out of the room, she asks, 'What did they offer you?'

'Senior inspector at the ZUS.'

'I burst out laughing. Meanwhile Rysiek ran off without saying a word. The absurdity of it amused me, but he was hurt, perhaps at the fact that they had dared to offer him, Kapuściński, something like that. He had no sense of the ludicrousness of the situation, or any sense of humour with regard to himself.'

Naturally, Kapuściński does not accept the job at the ZUS.

Since his death, Kapuściński has sometimes been presented as a victim of repression by the government of General Jaruzelski. In response to one of these suggestions, then government spokesman Jerzy Urban wrote in a letter to a *Gazeta Wyborcza* journalist:

> I declare that at the beginning of 1982, after making the relevant efforts and arrangements, I invited Kapuściński to come and see me at the government spokesman's office, and I officially made him the following offer: let him choose himself any periodical, suspended at the time or not, but financed by RSW 'Prasa', and he would go as its correspondent to any Third World country he wished. I explained that I was suggesting a periodical, and not a newspaper or the PAP, so that he would have no ongoing obligations. Kapuściński said on the spot that he wasn't interested in the offer, without giving any reasons, and I took this on board without discussion. The political motives for his refusal went without saying at the time. However, it was Rysiek's decision. So even if it is true that some government unit tried to vet him, met with a refusal, and offered him a job at the ZUS, it is not the whole truth about how Kapuściński was treated by the authorities of the time.[27]

The authorities have a problem with Kapuściński: how are they to treat a man who has been a loyal Party member for thirty years, an old friend, who has just performed a political *volte-face*? In addition, he has close friends from the same branch who are now members of Jaruzelski's government. The general's speeches are written by Wiesław Górnicki, a former PAP correspondent in New York, the Middle East and the Far East, whose talent as a reporter is sometimes compared to Kapuściński's. The deputy prime minister is Mieczysław Rakowski, his former boss from his days at *Polityka*.

The government spokesman Jerzy Urban is another former colleague, also from *Polityka*.

Kapuściński's books continue to be published in the 1980s without any obstruction on the part of the authorities. A few months after the introduction of martial law, *Shah of Shahs* appears – his book about the Islamic revolution in Iran, which is often regarded as one of his two greatest works, alongside *The Emperor*. Three further editions of *The Emperor* come out, and *Shah of Shahs* – usually read as an allegorical, universal tale about the workings of revolution – is reissued twice in that era.

Kapuściński does not entirely break off all contact with his old comrades, not immediately. He no longer wants to be associated with the Party, and distances himself from the authorities, but sometimes arranges to meet his old pals for dinner or a drink.

When Stanisław Jarząbek, the ambassador in Havana, comes to Warsaw, he meets up with Kapuściński at a pub in central Warsaw. Kapuściński complains that everything's getting worse, there's no work, there's nowhere to publish.

'Maybe you could come to Cuba?' suggests Jarząbek. 'I can provide you with everything you'll want. You could teach at the university, you'd also get something out of it for your writing. I've already had a chat with Rakowski, and no one from the government is going to cause you any obstruction.'

'But how much will the Cubans pay me?' asks Kapuściński.

Jarząbek is dismayed.

'I realized he didn't give a hoot about my help, but he didn't want to say so openly. The question about money was meant to make me stop pressing the invitation.'

'How did your conversation with Rakowski go?' I ask Jarząbek.

'I told him I wanted to help Kapuściński, and to invite him to Cuba. I also asked if he would receive Kapuściński to talk about it. Rakowski replied that he was always willing, and that Kapuściński knew the way to him, and didn't need any intermediaries.'

Kapuściński never showed up at Rakowski's office.

Unlike many of the journalists who have split with the Party, Kapuściński does not denounce the government and his former comrades. However, as he does move closer to the opposition at this point, Urban aims a dig at him of his own accord. After BBC TV broadcasts a documentary about the Polish reporter, Urban mentions at one of his press conferences a scene in which Kapuściński asks the film crew to switch off the camera just as they are driving past one of the Ministry of Internal Affairs buildings. The government spokesman comments sarcastically,

This suggests to the British that filming Kapuściński is prohibited by the police and lends the British film-makers' work a heroic dimension. That is childishness. Kapuściński is not a military facility or a state secret. He can be filmed in any place and in any manner. Making Poland into a dangerous place is misleading for the British viewers.[28]

Kapuściński now only very occasionally meets up with his old friends from the Party, such as Frelek and Trepczyński. In a letter to Jerzy Nowak he writes from Philadelphia that he's rushing to the train station because he's going to New York 'to hand this letter to Staszek Trepczyński'. However, the fact that he is moving away from his former comrades, who have supported his career for years, is beginning to be obvious to them. And painful. In his personal diary, Frelek notes that the man with whom he has spent thirty years in a close friendship, and whom he has supported and protected for all this time, has turned his back on him.

Meanwhile, Kapuściński finds himself unmoored:

> I didn't know what to do. The rhythm of my life has always been like this: I went abroad, came back, wrote a book about it or a series of reports and went abroad again. This rhythm was interrupted by martial law. What am I to do here? I wondered.[29]

The journalists connected with Solidarity, like those who have recently broken away from the official media, try to find places for themselves. Some change profession, others leave the country, for good or just for a time, and others get involved in organizing the underground press.

Kapuściński comes to meetings of the unofficial Polish Journalists Association. They talk, debate, discuss. Some decide to publish in newsletters that are being issued illegally, outside the control of the censors, while others keep their distance from underground activity for fear of being put in prison.

'Rysiek was simply there with us.'

A woman who took part in meetings of the underground association emphasizes this fact.

'No one expected him to run about with leaflets and appeals. As long as he was in the country, he came to our meetings, and that in itself had significance for us.'

Yet one of his colleagues, Maciej Iłowiecki, remembers that Kapuściński was cautious, perhaps overly so. He did sign some of the Polish Journalists Association's declarations, but if he thought the wording too strongly anti-regime, he declined.

'He was afraid they wouldn't let him go abroad, and he couldn't live without those trips. I even had a private grudge about it, but nowadays I understand him much better.'

During martial law, many people from many environments who earlier kept their distance from the Church now find a refuge at parishes run by priests who are Solidarity sympathizers. Kapuściński, who has had no contact with the Church as an institution since his high school days, comes to the parish of Saint Stanisław Kostka in the Warsaw district of Żoliborz. Once a month the Solidarity chaplain Father Jerzy Popiełuszko holds masses here 'for the Homeland', which bring together thousands of people and become demonstrations of support for the Solidarity underground and of opposition to martial law. In the autumn of 1984, Father Popiełuszko is kidnapped and murdered by agents of the security service.

> I took an active part in the underground talks organized by Solidarity. I attended a great number of meetings. At them we talked about the situation in Poland and the international situation. At the time there was a universal loss of confidence in the official press. Many of my colleagues had left the country, and many had been interned, so there was a huge need for this sort of illegal, secret talk. They were mainly held at presbyteries and in churches. Sometimes in private houses too, but that was rare, because it was dangerous. There was still intense surveillance going on. These meetings meant a great deal to people – not just in terms of information, but also integration. What mattered was that we were together. Two Polands had started to exist: the official, ruling one, and the underground, samizdat one.[30]

Several times, friends and colleagues who have crossed the next Rubicon and are now editing and publishing underground newspapers, try to persuade Kapuściński to work with them.

He never agreed to write an article for the weekly *Tygodnik Mazowsze*, the biggest underground publication. Anna Bikont, who co-edited it, met with him several times to record his thoughts on the international situation. An article written in this way about the situation in Afghanistan did appear in the weekly, signed with the initials N.D.

Ernest Skalski, a colleague from *Kultura* who edited one of the underground journals after martial law, remembers that Kapuściński avoided co-operation with his paper by citing an agreement he had apparently made with his American publisher: 'I have sold them the rights to everything I'm going to write. They'd be upset with me if I published something elsewhere.'

> Dear Jurek,
>   This evening I got your letter and the *New York Review of Books*, for which many thanks . . .

So I'll repeat my basic thesis for the present day (I stress the word
'present', because the situation is still far from stabilizing): there is a sense
that at this point the threat of intervention has shrunk to the minimum,
and the threat of civil war has seriously diminished too. In short, all the
solutions involving force have receded into the background, and what's
becoming more realistic is a scenario involving a lengthy, exhausting
crisis, in which no blood will be shed, but we will all get worn to a nervous frazzle.[31]

In this letter, written a few months after the introduction of martial
law, Kapuściński informs his closest friend, who is on a diplomatic posting in New York, about the mood in Poland and how events might
develop.

In short, I'm asking you and Izunia to stay calm about how the situation
in Poland will develop, and to your question about what's going to
happen, I will give you exactly the same answer as I give every day here
at meetings with my readers: NOTHING'S GOING TO HAPPEN.
There will be lots of scrambling and lots of trouble – that's all. It is simply
a feature of the Polish process that it has no lasting, substantial internal
solutions. Something has to happen outside Poland for this process to be
able to make a real move forwards.

These days, Kapuściński has a lot of spare time – he is not working
anywhere, nor for the time being is he going abroad. He is now fifty, and
problems with his circulation and his spine are also taking their toll. External
circumstances force him to devise a new form of literary expression besides
reportage. In a letter to Nowak in November 1982, he writes:

Right now I'm sitting over a new book, conceived as the first part of a
series of my thoughts about the world and modern times. In keeping
with the theme, the book will consist of notes, quotes, sentences, opinions and mini-essays – in short, it will include some philosophical experiments, set in various years and various places around the globe: a structure of intersecting verticals and horizontals. Well, first I have to write it,
and then we'll see what comes of it.
    The book's title, *Lapidarium*, explains its character and the technique
used to write it (a lapidarium is a museum for stone remnants, pieces of
ancient sculptures the whole of which can no longer be reconstructed –
in short, it's a sort of artistic rubble heap, something that has fallen apart
and can't be put back together again) . . . here my not just axiological, but
also eschatological ambitions are coming to the fore, but only this sort of
writing has value for me these days.

That's what's keeping me occupied now, in spite of all that is happening around me, but if I gave in to the prevailing mood, I'd never do another thing, but I do want to write several more books . . .

My dear friends, the main thing is to bear up, carry on and try to be oneself. Here we are filled with great optimism, because regardless of the immediate difficulties and all sorts of nastiness, we are on the right track, moving along with good people and having good thoughts. Really – chin up! Step back, switch off, cocoon yourself! . . . Yours, Rysiek.[32]

Kapuściński has a reason for his sudden burst of optimism right in the middle of the depressing atmosphere of the battle between Poland and Jaruzelski. A major lifetime opportunity has just appeared. *The Emperor* is to be published in the United States.

[A]s I wrote before, *The Emperor* is about to come out in N.Y. with a serious publisher called Harcourt Brace Jovanovich. My translator is flying to N.Y. soon – I hope you won't mind if he gets in touch with you. The publisher has already approached me for world rights to my work. They advertise themselves as owning the rights to Günter Grass, Max Frisch and Georges Simenon, and they want to include me in this pantheon too. In short, it's starting to look interesting. I'm counting on the support of Mr Nagorski [Andrew Nagorski, *Newsweek* correspondent in Eastern Europe], among others, who has been so kind to me, as well as Susan Sontag and others.[33]

It is the writer–reporter's second birth – this time on the world literary scene. Fame, international prestige and finally some decent money are only a step away.

31

Worth More Than a Thousand
Grizzled Journofantasists

Helen is over eighty ... she was once friends with Thomas Mann and Hannah Arendt, and she emigrated to the States with them in the 1930s ... Helen – profound, intensive culture, the fine art of expressing thought – the now dying milieu of European intellectuals from the first half of the century, who regarded conversation as an art; behind the simplest remark they uttered a brilliant upbringing, eager, ardent youth, years of study and communing with the world of thought and spirit could be felt.[1]

Helen Wolff from the New York publishing company Harcourt Brace Jovanovich is delighted by *The Emperor*. Thanks to her, from one day to the next the Polish reporter, whom no one in America has heard of before, is now familiar to America's leading intellectuals, writers and reviewers. She has an affection for authors from the 'Old Continent' and a talent for spotting them. Her husband, Kurt Wolff, published the works of Franz Kafka in Germany before the war. Once in America, they jointly published a series of literary works by European writers, including Günter Grass, Boris Pasternak, Max Frisch and Italo Calvino.

An extract from *The Emperor* lands on Wolff's desk just before her retirement (Kapuściński claims it was her very last day at the publishing house). She decides to respond to William Brand, the translator, who sent her the manuscript.

Brand found out about Kapuściński's book from his Polish wife, Katarzyna Mroczkowska. In the spring of 1979 Mroczkowska was travelling from Poland back to the United States, where she was a doctoral student at the University of Rochester. One of her friends handed her a book, saying, This is for your journey, this is what everyone is reading in Warsaw nowadays. It was a copy of *The Emperor*.

At first the Polish doctoral student is pleased she has finally found a Polish book worth recommending to her colleagues, American scholars of literature. In time another thought starts to take shape: maybe *The Emperor* should be translated? A year later, she writes a letter to Czytelnik, Kapuściński's Polish publisher, in which she proposes the idea of translating the work, in collaboration with her husband, who is a native speaker and English scholar. However, she warns, the work would be a bit of an experiment, as they have never translated a book before. Kapuściński sends an enthusiastic reply.

They meet in person a year later, in the late spring of 1981 in Kraków, when the translation of *The Emperor* is essentially ready. 'With that beard, you look like a mujahidin,' is the first thing Brand remembers Kapuściński saying.

The translators are having a few problems with the archaic language in *The Emperor*, the stylization; the adjectives are especially tricky. Kapuściński solves the problem this way: 'Do whatever you want, just have fun with it.'

The translation is not the hardest nut to crack, though. How are they going to find a publisher in America for a book by a reporter from a middle-sized country in the Soviet camp who is completely unknown on that side of the pond? At the time, translations from foreign languages constitute barely 1 percent of all the books published in the US. How and whom can they convince that a slim volume about the emperor of Ethiopia, written by a Polish journalist, should be included in this exclusive club?

On returning to the United States, Brand sends samples of the translation to about a dozen publishing houses, both well known and less well known. Some politely refuse, others do not reply. Only Helen Wolff from Harcourt Brace Jovanovich says yes.

How did Brand come up with the idea of sending *The Emperor* to her in particular?

> Needing some distraction, I happened to pick up a copy of the *New Yorker* that was lying nearby and started leafing through the ads: for fur coats, champagne and diamonds. Suddenly a rare sight grabbed my attention – a page entirely covered in text. It was an article about Helen Wolff, widow of Kafka's pre-war publisher, Kurt Wolff. This refugee from Nazi Germany was a cult figure in New York. Translations of the greatest European writers were the foundation stone of her career . . . I rushed off to find a guide to the publishing market, in search of her address. Early on Monday morning, just before leaving for the airport, I sent the manuscript with a letter addressed to Helen Wolff at Harcourt Brace Jovanovich.[2]

A few weeks later, a telegram from Helen Wolff arrived at the Brands' flat in Kraków, announcing that she would call in a few days – 'she had a warm voice and got straight to the point'.

The American edition of *The Emperor* was essentially agreed.

*   *   *

Kapuściński appoints Brand his proxy. On the final day of November 1981, Brand travels to New York, where in Kapuściński's name he signs a contract with Harcourt Brace Jovanovich. Meanwhile, in Poland martial law erupts, the country is cut off from the rest of the world, and Brand is stuck in America for longer than planned.

In the weeks while he awaits the opportunity to return to Krakow, there occurs the most absurd event in the entire international career of Kapuściński's book. As Brand recalls:

> One day a lawyer called from Harcourt Brace. It was obvious he didn't want to talk about writing style.
>
> He said there were some legal declarations and authentications that he needed.
>
> I told him that Mr Kapuściński would not be able to sign any sort of declaration or authentication until the situation in Poland cleared up.
>
> 'It's not necessarily about something Mr Kapuściński has to sign,' he said. He needed declarations and authentications from the Ethiopian citizens described in the book. He wanted to get signed documents, certified by a notary, including their true names and addresses, in which they would guarantee the authenticity of their statements and would release the publisher from ultimate legal responsibility.
>
> Those people are palace officials, I replied, in hiding from the revolutionary Marxist regime. They talked to the author confidentially, on condition of full anonymity. Merely attempting to get in touch with them could put them in lethal danger.[3]

After some thought and without consulting Kapuściński – in the early days of martial law there are no phone connections with Poland – Brand tells the publisher's lawyer that Kapuściński and he, as his representative, will take responsibility for any complaints or legal claims the Ethiopians might make. The obstacles to publishing Kapuściński's first book in America are eventually removed.

The Emperor appears at the beginning of 1983. On the cover of the first edition, an endorsement by the famous futurologist Alvin Toffler, at the time a favourite of the mass media, encourages people to buy and read the book: '*The Emperor* is the nightmare that men of power dream when they are most alone. It is a bone-chilling, brilliant tale, as precise in its cut-glass literary style as in its political insights'.

'We printed five thousand copies,' says Drenka Willen, the book's editor and the successor to Helen Wolff, in a phone conversation. She, too, is an émigré from Europe (from Yugoslavia). 'We decided to wait and see how the reviewers and critics would react.'

The response exceeded the expectations of the publisher, the author, and everyone else. As Peter Prescott writes in *Newsweek*:

[This book's] mordant humor rises from its interior, like gases from a swamp. The effect is rather as if Kafka had written 'The Castle' from inside the keep . . . An allegory of totalitarian governments today? Almost certainly. Haile Selassie is a stand-in for Stalin, for Big Brother, the ruler who brings his country to a condition of near perfect stasis. It's a fascinating performance, seductively written and translated as if there were no language barrier.[4]

A review by John Updike makes a significant contribution to the book's success, thanks not only to this author's popularity but also to where it is published: in the prestigious political and cultural weekly the *New Yorker*. Toffler also did a lot to popularize *The Emperor* in America, by talking about the book to potential reviewers, media people and intellectuals.

After Updike's *New Yorker* review, other voices full of admiration appear, both in the American and the British press. The reviewers see Kapuściński as an Eastern European proponent of so-called New Journalism, creative non-fiction writing, or, as some call this type of literature, 'faction'. This trend, combining the aims of traditional reportage with the writing techniques used in fiction, was popularized in the 1960s and 1970s by Truman Capote, Norman Mailer, Hunter S. Thompson and Tom Wolfe.

In the British paper the *Sunday Times*, Salman Rushdie names *The Emperor* his book of the year for 1983. 'Kapuściński's writing,' says Rushdie, justifying his choice, 'always wonderfully concrete and observant, conjures marvels of meaning out of minutiae. And his book transcends reportage, becoming a nightmare of power depicted as a refusal of history that reads as if Italo Calvino had rewritten Machiavelli.'[5] Soon after this, Rushdie and Kapuściński meet in person; Rushdie will become one of the most faithful promoters of his Polish friend's writing.

'Thanks to the critics' rapturous response, we sold all five thousand copies,' says Drenka Willen. 'We decided to print five thousand more. Unfortunately, we only sold some of those extra copies.'

'In America great literature does not have large print-runs,' adds Brand.

Is that the only reason? I remember a conversation with Mark Danner, the eminent reporter and essayist, who knew Kapuściński and who teaches journalism at the University of California, Berkeley. Danner has worked for and published in America's top journals, including the *New York Times*, the *New Yorker* and the *New York Review of Books*, and has several acclaimed books to his name, including one about the involvement of the CIA in dirty wars in Central America and another about the Iraq war and the use of torture at Abu Ghraib.

I asked him if he analyses Kapuściński's texts with his students. 'Yes,' he replied, 'we read *The Emperor*, *Shah of Shahs* and *The Soccer War*, but it sometimes takes students a while to appreciate their brilliance – what is distinctive about them.' Why? 'I expect,' says Danner, 'that it is partly owed to Americans' specific understanding – or lack of understanding – of power and what it is. Americans believe that, in general, power – even if they happen not to like one or another particular government – serves the good of people. That is their "default position": that power is about solving problems, about attaining progress and promoting development. That is the aim of exercising it. Meanwhile Ryszard's work – I'm thinking here of *The Emperor* in particular, though it is true of *Shah of Shahs*, *The Soccer War* and his other books as well – exposes that myth; it shows that the main point of power is power itself – attaining it, keeping it, holding it, nothing more.'

Alongside generalities about the fate of ambitious literature in the US, this is certainly another valid explanation, rooted in American experience. Is this why Kapuściński's popularity in America is not a mass phenomenon, but is limited to the intellectual élite, known writers and academic circles? Is that why he isn't a guiding star for American journalists?

Kapuściński's position in the United States and Britain is consolidated by his next book, *Shah of Shahs*, about Iran's Islamic revolution. It is received with even greater praise than *The Emperor*.

However, *Shah of Shahs* as presented to the Americans and the British is not exactly the book known by Polish readers. The American edition, and after it the British, which prompted such great enthusiasm among reviewers, displays a riddle that we can probably never solve with complete certainty. Thanks to a hint from a close friend of Kapuściński's, once I have almost finished writing this biographical account I discover that all references to a CIA plot and US involvement in deposing the democratic government of Mohammad Mosaddegh and supporting Mohammad Reza Pahlavi, who was loyal to America, have disappeared from the US edition. How is this possible? Who censured Kapuściński and in what circumstances?

A total of about fifteen pages of the original text have disappeared from the American edition. Readers in the United States did not find in their copies of *Shah of Shahs* the following extract, among others:

As the American reporters David Wise and Thomas B. Ross write in their book *The Invisible Government*: 'There is no doubt at all that the CIA organized and directed the 1953 coup that overthrew Premier Mohammed Mosaddegh and kept Shah Mohammed Reza Pahlavi on his throne. But few Americans know that the coup that toppled the government of Iran was led by a CIA agent who was the grandson of President Theodore Roosevelt. Kermit "Kim" Roosevelt ... is still known as "Mr Iran" around the CIA for his spectacular operation in Teheran more than a decade ago. One legend that grew up inside the CIA had it that Roosevelt . . . led the revolt against the weeping Mosaddegh with a gun at the head of an Iranian tank commander as the column rolled into Teheran. A CIA man familiar with the Iran story characterized this as "a bit romantic" but said: "Kim did run the operation from a basement in Teheran – not from our embassy." He added admiringly: "It was a real James Bond operation." '

Of course the United States has never officially admitted to the role played by the CIA. Dulles himself [head of the agency] said relatively the most on the topic when he appeared on a CBS television programme after leaving the CIA in 1962. When asked if it was true that 'the CIA people spent literally millions of dollars hiring people to riot in the streets and do other things to get rid of Mosaddegh', Dulles replied: 'Well, I can say that the statement that we spent many dollars doing that is utterly false'.[6]

I start my attempt to explain the riddle by putting some questions to Agata Orzeszek, Kapuściński's translator into Spanish.

'Did the entire text of *Shah of Shahs* appear in other languages?'

'It certainly did in Spanish.'

'Did you ever talk to Rysiek about why the American translation was cut?'

'I asked at once. He replied that those were his own corrections. It was obvious he didn't want to talk about it.'

'Those are very specific corrections – everything about the role of the US in deposing Mosaddegh and supporting the vile dictator has gone. We know what a critical opinion Rysiek had of America's support for dictatorships in the Third World.'

'That was why I pointed it out to him, in no uncertain terms. He replied that he had shortened the text at the request of the American publisher. "And you agreed?" I asked. "I wanted the book to be published." He clearly had no desire to go deeper into the subject.'

I check which version appeared in several other languages. The French and German editions are mutilated the same way as the English-language edition – the French translator translated the book from English; the German did translate from Polish, but a publisher's note tells us that it was done on the basis of the American edition published by Harcourt Brace Jovanovich. The Spanish, Norwegian and Hungarian editions, all translated from Polish, are the same as the original version.

I call William Brand. I try to establish whether he translated the entire text of *Shah of Shahs* or whether he was given different guidelines by Kapuściński, such as a shortened text. He cannot remember. Nor can he remember any conversation with Kapuściński about changes to the original text. He is surprised by everything I tell him. He does recall that only once did he receive a typescript from Kapuściński – it was a much later book, *Lapidarium*. He suggests I contact Drenka Willen, the book's US editor.

During our phone conversation, Willen, too, expresses surprise that the American edition of *Shah of Shahs* was cut. She asks me to point out the places where the cuts were made, which I do. For the purposes of our conversation, I translate several sentences into English off the cuff, and once again I explain that most of the 'vanished' text refers to the role of the United States in deposing Mosaddegh and keeping the Shah in power. When I say: 'Kapuściński admitted to someone that he made the cuts at the request of the publisher,' Willen replies that it is impossible. There is no censorship in this country, she tells me.

I suggest a hypothesis: 'Perhaps – like some people living under real socialism – Kapuściński transposed to America the rules of the game one plays with the censor in Poland? And, thinking this way, he removed the extracts in question himself, just in case?'

'But he had been to America before,' says Willen [in 1983, for the publi-cation of *The Emperor*]. 'He must have known things in this country are different.'

There is a note of concern and surprise in Drenka Willen's voice. Once again she assures me that the text of *Shah of Shahs* appeared in America in the shape in which Kapuściński delivered it. It's not unusual to do a little editing of the text, of course, but not a cut of several, let alone more than a dozen, pages.

Do I have other hypotheses? Yes. I believe the editor's explanation that neither she nor anyone at Harcourt Brace Jovanovich demanded that Kapuściński delete the passages in the book that were critical of American policy. In the 1980s publications appeared about the crimes of the CIA, about the involvement of administrations in Washington in overthrowing democratic governments in the Third World, and about their support for tyrants such as Shah Reza Pahlavi in Iran, Pinochet in Chile, Somoza in Nicaragua and Suharto in Indonesia, or for the racist apartheid system in South Africa. Why should anyone demand that Kapuściński remove passages containing information that was available in other books?

And so I think Kapuściński was censored by Kapuściński himself. But why?

It is not impossible that he followed this line of reasoning: Even if there is no censorship in the US, why run the risk of making revealing statements about the country's policies? Writers who had been critical of American policies, such as Gabriel García Márquez or Carlos Fuentes, had had trouble getting into the US during the Cold War, had been blacklisted and refused visas for years. Kapuściński knew their histories, but he very much wanted to travel to the United States once his books had started to appear and the world had begun to appreciate him. That is the first hypothesis.

Another one goes like this: After the success of *The Emperor* Kapuściński started receiving invitations to give talks and attend conferences. He was given a grant to spend several months in the US. Criticizing the American government did not necessarily close the door to further invitations and grants, which are usually awarded independent of a country's political authorities. But the man who had spent his life in the world of dictatorship and censorship and had no illusions about the workings of power, including democratically elected power, took action 'just in case'.

Third hypothesis: He may have decided that America, which in the 1980s was giving moral, and not just moral, support to the Poles' aspirations to freedom as they rebelled against real socialism, did not deserve harsh criticism on the part of a Polish reporter – even if this criticism concerned decisions made by US governments from the distant past. Not now, not at this moment. And note that in the 1980s Kapuściński's attitude was undergoing an evolution – from faith to lack of faith in real socialism – and it is not impossible that at this moment the political neophyte triumphed over the critical reporter and writer.

Finally, Kapuściński may have calculated that in an era of ideological offensive by the right – this was during the presidency of Ronald Reagan – criticism of America in a book by a correspondent working, nonetheless, for a communist press agency, would be an easy target for a polemical attack, and it would not be hard to undermine the author's credibility if anyone chose to do so. This in turn could have harmed the reception of *Shah of Shahs* and could have affected the fate of further titles. Such attacks, though only marginal in their scope, did in fact occur. As Kapuściński's translator recalls, Iran 'was at the centre of US interests – the Shah was an important ally, and the hostages at the embassy in Teheran were Americans. [Young fundamentalists occupied the US embassy for more than a year, provoking a major crisis in relations between the two countries.] Soon one of the freed hostages started talking – among other things – about too much indulgence towards the Iranians and, even worse, about factual inaccuracies in Kapuściński's account.'[7]

When I summarize my hypotheses to one of Kapuściński's close friends, he says: 'Your theories are noble. Unfortunately, I have a less sympathetic one.'

Rather than betray it now, I will return to it later, as my account approaches the moment when an episode from the past comes back to haunt Kapuściński, during the final years of his life.

Within a few short years, Kapuściński comes to be regarded as the author of classic works of literary reportage. More books come out – first in

English, then in more than a dozen other languages. After the two major books come *Another Day of Life*, *The Soccer War*, and, at the start of the 1990s, *Imperium*. Reviewers call him 'the legendary correspondent', his adventures are compared to those of Indiana Jones and James Bond, and his work is compared with the writings of Joseph Conrad, Graham Greene, George Orwell, Ernest Hemingway and V.S. Naipaul.

His loyal reader and disinterested promoter Salman Rushdie writes in the *Guardian*:

> In his books on Haile Selassie and the Shah, and now in *Another Day of Life*, his descriptions – no, his responses – do what only art can manage; that is, they fire our own imagination. One Kapuściński is worth a thousand grizzled journofantasists; and through his astonishing blend of reportage and artistry we get as close to what he calls the incommunicable image of war as we're ever likely to by reading.[8]

One of the critics declares Kapuściński to be 'the king of journalists' because he has – as he writes – all the right attributes: Shakespeare's insight into the heart, the narrative flow of Dickens, the existential distance of Camus, and the simplicity of Orwell and Hemingway. (Beautifully said!) A reviewer in the *Wall Street Journal* praises him this way: 'In fact, Mr Kapuściński, in English translation, is a more beguiling, intelligent, witty writer than just about anyone I can think of writing in English to start with.'[9]

By the end of the 1980s *The Emperor* has come out in Italian, German, French, Spanish, Dutch, Danish, Swedish, Norwegian, Japanese, Russian, Persian, Hebrew and Hungarian. It is also made into a stage play, and the most famous production, directed by Jonathan Miller at the Royal Court Theatre in London, is described by the critics as 'faultless'. The stage show is accompanied by another performance – on the street outside the theatre, where some Rastafarians hold a demonstration, because they regard Haile Selassie as a god and reject the absurd conviction that he is dead – God can never die. 'Death to Kapuściński,' they shout, 'death, death to Miller, death!'

When the Soviet empire collapses, people in the West – and later, beyond the West – find out from one of Kapuściński's most famous books, *Imperium*, how the colossus disintegrates and what sort of inheritance its collapse leaves to the world. They are given the opportunity to compare the mechanisms and nature of their own countries' colonialism and imperialism with Soviet colonialism and imperialism. As one reviewer notes in the *New York Review of Books*:

> What is striking about Kapuściński is his ability to capture the historically telling image we would not otherwise see. In the Ukraine, he glimpses

through a train window an abandoned part of the vast Soviet arsenal: a row of new artillery pieces sunk deep into the mud, only the gun barrels and shields protruding.[10]

On my travels in Kapuściński's footsteps to several African countries, I met William Pike, a journalist who lives in two capitals, Kampala and Nairobi. He told me how he and Kapuściński once went together to the north of Uganda, where negotiations were underway between the government and the rebels. Like most of the journalists present, Pike listened to the official talks; meanwhile, Kapuściński disappeared somewhere. His British colleague tracked him down only after the negotiations were over; Kapuściński was talking to some ordinary soldiers, who were treating him to a cup of tea in a hastily cobbled-together shack. They were sorry their commanders were not giving them any pay and that, as a result, they were forced to rob the local villages instead of protecting them from the guerrillas. Pike contends that by talking to the private soldiers, Kapuściński gained a better understanding of the character of that war, its sources and the real problems facing the Ugandans than he did.

Is it in showing great events and great history from the worm's, rather than the bird's, eye view that Kapuściński's magic lies, the secret of his popularity? Unquestionably this is one of its major sources.

There are countries where he is simply a known author, countries where he is admired and legendary, and lastly countries where his readers worship him with the sort of adoration enjoyed by rock stars and religious gurus.

The Spanish and Latin Americans were affected by a serious form of 'Kapumania' (the Latino reporters for whom in the last few years of his life he ran workshops gave him the nickname 'Kapu'). According to a journalist working for Mexican television who was torn to shreds during a debate by some students because of her channel's political manipulations, 'For every charge they laid they had a footnote, a quote or an aphorism from the books and lectures of Kapuściński on the profession of journalist and the role of the media. They crucified me with Kapuściński.'

In Spain his career was crowned with the Prince of Asturias Award (known as 'the Nobel of the Ibero-American world'), which he received in 2003 jointly with Father Gustavo Gutiérrez and Brazilian president Lula. In Latin America he was lauded for his co-operation with Gabriel García Márquez's foundation.

While many Spaniards and Latinos treat him with respect or even adoration, the Italians are absolutely crazy about him. According to Wiktor Osiatyński, who has taught students on several continents, 'In Asia they always asked me about Polish soccer players – how are Lato and Boniek doing? In Latin America they always asked about the Polish pope. In Italy they asked if I had read anything by Kapuściński lately. For many Italians,

Kapuściński is their first association with Poland. Rysiek's fame in that country is not limited to universities, intellectuals and journalists, but is universal, on a mass scale.'

What demand does his writing meet? What is the source of such great popularity within certain linguistic and cultural environments?

I put this question to my various interviewees around the world, but apart from William Pike's telling anecdote, the most interesting answers come from Kapuściński's Polish friends and also his Polish critics, though Kapuściński had hardly any of those.

As Adam Daniel Rotfeld says: 'He had an unusual talent for interpreting reality through the senses – he was able to write about smells, and to perceive the texture of things. He was a sensual rather than an intellectual writer, and most people take in the world via the senses first and foremost. He had a perfect feel for the fates of ordinary people, he understood their world and was then able to describe it accurately, to tell their stories. Readers on other continents recognized themselves in these accounts.

'He was also,' Rotfeld continues, 'a writer of a new genre, who recognized the mentality of modern man perfectly. His writing breaks through the borders of genres – it includes elements of reportage, philosophical thoughts, and fiction. And it is comprehensible to a wide range of readers.'

It is true that when you read Kapuściński's books you get a bit of everything: a thriller or adventure story, information about major world events, some rather lyrical reverie and general philosophical reflections on life. All in one – and beautifully written.

According to Wiktor Osiatyński, 'He provided people with a poetical, literary and altogether fairly straightforward description of the world and its complexities through human experience and people's real lives, not theoretical considerations.'

Translator and writer Antoni Libera, who clearly does not rate Kapuściński's writing highly ('those poeticized descriptions meet the demands of the tourist who has a limited experience of travel, who admires the sunset, the exotic climate and so on'), makes an interesting suggestion. When asked why Kapuściński is so popular in the West, Libera replies:

> Because he satisfies the need for Western European and American culture to take itself to task – to perform the highly popular, though extremely hypocritical, task of doing penance. Western culture never stops beating itself on the chest for the sins of the past and the prosperity in which it lives, which turns into a ritual of self-negation typical of any civilization on the wane. By dumping blame on the West for the rest of the world's poverty, Kapuściński slots into this way of thinking perfectly.[11]

Unlike Libera, Kapuściński touched, felt and had inside knowledge of 'the rest of the world's poverty' caused by the West. He also understood that robbing this 'rest', within which most of humanity lives, did not end with the colonial era, but continues to this day in other forms. What the uninformed viewer of the television news regards as bloody tribal fighting in Africa is usually yet another war over raw materials, incited and covertly run by Western corporations, more and more rarely – and not so openly as was once the case – by the governments of Western countries. If it is the sensitivity of people in the West to the injustices committed in their name and described by Kapuściński that is the source of his popularity, then perhaps Europe, the West, the world is not dead yet. Perhaps there is still hope.

Worldwide popularity, books translated into many languages, invitations from far and wide to give lectures and attend seminars and conferences change Kapuściński's life on several levels. Towards the end of the 1980s he and Alicja move from their cramped flat in a block in Wola to a two-family house in central Warsaw. At their new home they have three main rooms, and Kapuściński has the loft to himself – his own kingdom, where he spends most of his time when he is in the country.

With the advent of international fame he gets to know the prosperous countries. All his professional life he has been travelling to Africa, Latin America and less often Asia, and has seen the world from the perspective of the South. Now he has the opportunity to take a look at the world from the perspective of the North. It is a totally different experience. He travels to America, Britain, France, Italy, Spain, Sweden and Germany, not as a reporter but as a famous writer, who is driven in a fine car from the airport to the hotel, from the hotel to the meeting with readers, from the meeting with readers to the television interview, from the television interview to the radio interview, from the radio interview to dinner at an excellent restaurant, and then back to the hotel. Next day it is the same thing again.

As Wiktor Osiatyński recalls, 'He put a lot of work and effort into his new "life of a famous writer". In the course of just six months he polished up his English so that he could comfortably give interviews and take part in conferences and meetings with readers without needing an interpreter. It is rare for a man past fifty to achieve such great progress in his knowledge of a foreign language. He had his teeth done – that might sound amusing to some people, but for a public figure, especially in the West, it is no small thing. He changed his reporter's working outfit for a jacket, and sometimes he even put on a tie.

'He reckoned that if the world wanted to talk to him, he should make a bow in its direction and prepare himself for the encounter. He realized that unless he did so, he would not achieve success, and that fame and an international career have a price and some occasionally tiresome stage directions, such as conducting regular correspondence. That is highly time consuming; it can be boring and can distract from the writing of books, but you have to do it if you want to keep up important contacts and receive invitations – if you want to join in the world of famous literary figures. And although Ryszard's wife took most of this work upon herself, Rysiek earned his success abroad not merely through his books but also through this daily toil, which "servicing" his work demanded.'

Sometimes he feels cut off from the reality of the average person in those countries. Only when he travels for longer, for several weeks or months, as a visiting professor – now to New York, now Philadelphia, now Oxford – does he have the chance to take a closer look at the countries which in his eyes were the invaders and persecutors of the Third World, the world where he has spent most of his professional life. For more than two decades, he has closely observed hungry people fighting for survival from one day to the next; sometimes he has shared their fate. Now it confuses him when, dining at his new literary friend Susan Sontag's home, she offers him a steak the size of a large platter. 'What an orgy, what glamour!' he confides in someone later on, slightly shocked.

His first observations in America also involve food:

From morning to night, in cafés, bars, clubs and restaurants, they eat. The subjects of conversation are: where shall we eat, what shall we eat, what did we choose from the menu, what did they serve, what was it like. All this at length. They end with the conclusion: we eat too much. Some of them decide to go running. Others read magazines about slimming. Their concern about their figures and fitness is most endearing.[12]

Despite some initial reserve, he starts to enjoy the dynamics and energy of the North, especially when he compares it with the drabness of Poland during martial law and the years that followed. In a letter to the Nowaks, who have just returned from a several-year posting to New York, he writes (from Philadelphia):

I have a lot of classes here, and even more offers, various meetings, readings, literary events and so on. Only here, when you leave Poland and live – as I am doing for the first time – within American society, do you feel what a crazy difference there is in the dynamics of life; in Poland there's vegetation and waiting for the end, here there is a pace, everything is planned years ahead, there's incredible urgency and productivity.[13]

Kapuściński consciously notices that, despite the view of many of his compatriots, Poland is not the centre of the universe or even of the Reagan

Cold War era, as some people with a hostile attitude to the regime like to delude themselves. After his first trip to the United States, in 1983, he notes:

> Their [the Americans'] attitude to Poland (and to other countries too): friendly indifference.
> 'Oh, yeah?'
> 'Really?'
> 'Far out!'
> 'Well, well.'[14]

Only here, in the world of affluence, meeting the most famous writers on earth and the most lauded intellectuals as an equal, as a colleague, and as a partner in conversation, does Kapuściński realize how far he has come from Pińsk, via Warsaw, New Delhi, Accra, Dar es Salaam, Lagos, Rio de Janeiro, Mexico City, Luanda and Addis Ababa to New York, London, Paris and Berlin. 'At the age of twelve,' he notes in New York, 'James Joyce was writing remarkable letters; at the same age I was running after cows in the fields and had never yet read a single book.'

In respectable company he feels bewildered and lost. After a reception held during a PEN writers conference in New York he gives vent to these feelings:

> Inside it is crowded and stuffy, with a deafening hubbub of voices animated by alcohol. They are serving white wine, nothing but white wine, and there are cases full of this wine everywhere. In the crowd the flushed faces of Mailer, Vonnegut and Gaddis flash past me, and somewhere overhead hovers the sombre face of Danilo Kiš (I didn't know he was terminally ill at the time), the smile-free face of Günter Grass, and the intense face of Doctorow, as if trying to hear someone's whisper. Suddenly I trip (or rather I am pushed) onto a small, cowering figure sitting against the wall. It is an old man, who holds out his hands in a gesture of self-defence. I stop and grab him so he won't crash to the floor. It is Claude Simon, the great French writer and Nobel Prize winner.[15]

'As the years went by he became a member of the intelligentsia, an intellectual even, but he came from a poor background, from the provinces, from ignorance, and was not brought up among books or the cult of knowledge – am I right?' queries Michael Kaufman, the former *New York Times* correspondent who befriended Kapuściński in Angola. 'He got nothing from life thanks to his parents' social position as simple teachers. He had to make a superhuman effort and do some incredible work on himself to get to the top, to reach the position he achieved at the end of his life.'

Some of the people who heard him give lectures or speak at conferences remember that he would get terribly disconcerted. He did not speak well, and sometimes even stammered. Was this really the great Kapuściński?

His old friends, the journalists Agnieszka and Andrzej Krzysztof Wróblewski, whom he visits in America in the 1980s, notice with some incredulity his struggle with everyday matters.

'That lion of the desert, who had half the world wrapped around his little finger, was suddenly behaving like the biggest feather-brain in the world,' says Wróblewski. 'I couldn't believe what I was seeing.'

Travelling a few stops on the subway is a problem for him. He tells his friends how 'I get pushed into that awful tunnel' and then 'dragged out of it'. His chats with journalists lack spirit. 'Nice to meet you,' he says, and then basically there is nothing to talk about. At a dinner after one of his literary events, people gossip that it was boring. They are disappointed.

I ask Ewa Junczyk-Ziomecka, who organized a lecture for Kapuściński at the University of Michigan, Ann Arbor, how he fared with the university audience. It was just after the American publication of *Imperium*, and he was speaking about the book and – the hottest topic of those years – the collapse of the Soviet Union. Crowds of people came, including professors and students.

'How did he do as a lecturer?'

'He was all right, but no great shakes. He went down worse than I had expected.'

'Wasn't he a good speaker?'

'No.'

'What was the reason for his lack of confidence, his timidity before an audience, in spite of his fame and his lofty position in the pantheon of journalists and writers?'

'I think there was still a poor boy from Polesie lurking inside him. And when he found himself in front of a large audience at a major university, he felt more like that boy than like a great writer who has come to great big America to talk about the collapse of an even bigger empire.'

Now and then in America, for the first time in his life, Kapuściński comes up against another attitude to him and his work besides adoration.

'He sounded devastated when he called,' says Wróblewski. 'Someone had written something critical about him, and he took it as a disrespectful slight. He was terribly upset. He got angry: "What a little shit!" and "How could he?"'

Maciej Wierzyński, his former boss and colleague from *Kultura*, who was living in Chicago at the time, has a similar memory of his reaction to criticism: 'There was a meeting with Chicago's Polish community. Someone in the audience criticized Rysiek for his left-wing views and long-term association with the communist regime. He was distressed by it; he became confused and shrank back. We got pretty drunk afterwards. I think what surprised him the most was that he could prompt emotions other than awe and delight. And no wonder – in Poland for all those years he had grown accustomed to nothing but tributes and admiration. Criticism must have been all the more painful for him.'

Soon he will have to take it on board. In what sensitive spot will the critics strike? Will he pick up the gauntlet they throw down?

32

Lapidarium 4: Why Did Kapuściński Have No Critics in Poland?

The question arises in conversation with the reporter Małgorzata Szejnert, who since the fall of real socialism has schooled numerous young reporters at *Gazeta Wyborcza*.

Kapuściński had no critics because he neutralized the critics himself. He knew almost all the influential reviewers in person, and they all liked him. He was one of those rare cases of a highly successful journalist who does not arouse envy among his fellows. The others were his fans and wished him well. So did the decision-makers on the Central Committee, who thought of him as their representative. He disarmed potential critics by his friendliness, his personal charm, and his timid smile. He was capable of offering help – not just the professional kind but also ordinary human assistance. Many people boasted of knowing Kapuściński, and after a single conversation with him plenty of them thought of him as an old friend. How could one write anything critical about a man like that?

It was a conscious strategy on his part. It was his way of protecting himself from critics and criticism. He was protecting his work, which cost him his health, as he frequently risked his life to do it. While a reporter in Third World countries he was a pauper, with never enough money to live decently there. He lived wherever and ate whatever, and his work cost him a huge amount of time and effort. He read a lot and studied a lot. Then he had an extremely difficult time putting it all together into an account, a report, or the latest book – and he wrote slowly. For him, writing was a grind.

And if, after all that, some smart alec who knew little, had experienced little and had barely even flicked through his book was going to take this monstrous effort to task . . . What if an unfavourable review had an adverse affect on making more trips abroad, which he could not live without? He also knew he was thin-skinned and easily hurt or offended.

And so he devised a self-defence strategy: to defuse the bomb before it went off.

No one touched his writing with a single critical word for years on end, decades. He lived inside a glass bubble. Isolated contentious voices began to appear in Poland only at the end of his life.

He reacted to all critical comments with fits of rage, distress, or grief bordering on depression. Izabella and Jerzy Nowak recall that even gentle critical suggestions – coming from his closest friends – provoked his fury. He was capable of ripping up a page of his own work before their very eyes out of anger.

Tomasz Łubieński remembers meeting him once outside the Palace of Culture and Science in Warsaw. He began by congratulating Kapuściński on his latest award. Kapuściński, though, was looking sad and downcast, like a beaten dog. It turned out that a couple of days earlier at a conference in Gdańsk a well-known critic named Tomasz Burek – a one-time Marxist who in the 1990s had assumed a new incarnation as an anti-communist and right-winger – had made some unfavourable remarks about his work.

'It struck me', says Łubieński, 'that he didn't say, for instance, "That Burek was spouting nonsense – to hell with him!" He was really distressed; he was fretting because someone had said something critical about him. But he had such a strong position in the country and worldwide that he could have totally ignored that sort of criticism, said nothing, taken no notice.'

He had a similar reaction to an impudent, lying attack – alleging that he had worked at the PZPR's Central Committee press office – in one of the weeklies by a columnist and ideologist with a professorial title, mocking Kapuściński's rather obvious thesis that colonialism bears responsibility for the backwardness of the Third World.

'I told him to ignore such clumsy taunts, but he got upset anyway,' says Jerzy Nowak.

Wiesława Bolimowska, his former colleague at the PAP, who in the 1990s became the editor of a university periodical called *Afryka*, informed Kapuściński that she planned to publish an essay by an expert on the life of Haile Selassie which was critical of *The Emperor*. She wanted him to comment on the charges laid against his book. He never replied to the invitation. (Another Africa scholar from Warsaw University says the expert's text was offered to various newspapers and weeklies, all of which politely turned it down.)

He reacted with a mixture of irritation and sadness to a critical article by Ernest Skalski in *Gazeta Wyborcza*. Skalski took issue with Kapuściński's view that the murkier aspects of globalization provided the context for the 9/11 attacks in America. Skalski's piece was elegant, and rather mild in tone, devoid of personal taunts. Yet Kapuściński was furious, as if he had been brutally attacked. He bad-mouthed his colleague and clearly sought support. 'What does Ernest think he's doing? What sort of nonsense is this?'

He was also pained that *Gazeta Wyborcza*, which after 1989 he regarded as 'his' place, had published something critical of his thoughts about the world.

He was probably even more upset by the criticisms of Henryk Bereza, chairman of the jury for the NIKE Literary Award, concerning *Travels with Herodotus*, his final book. It had been shortlisted for best book of 2005, and unofficially people were saying that the final round was between Kapuściński's *Travels* and Andrzej Stasiuk's *On the Road to Babadag*. Stasiuk's book won, and Kapuściński's was awarded the Reader's Prize. After the award, Bereza was asked in an interview why Kapuściński had not won the NIKE. He replied that he did not regard *Travels with Herodotus* as a great enough book to deserve Poland's most prestigious literary prize. With unconcealed bitterness, Kapuściński later told Wiktor Osiatyński: 'As long as Bereza is chairman of the jury, I haven't a hope of winning the NIKE'. He took it as a major defeat.

In the final year of his life, he was sick at heart because of some sharp criticism by Maria Janion in her book *Niesamowita Słowiańszczyzna* (Remarkable Slavism), all the more so since he regarded Janion as the very best scholar of Polish literature. Approvingly quoting Western and Russian critics of *The Shadow of the Sun* and *Imperium*, Janion accuses Kapuściński of harbouring prejudices towards Russia and the Russians, of having a patronizing attitude, of ascribing certain political pathologies exclusively to Poland's eastern neighbours and failing to perceive exactly the same ones in the countries of Western Europe (e.g., the sanctification of monarchs). In Janion's view, Kapuściński's thinking – regardless of his empathy for 'the Other', the weaker, colonized man – was not free of the influences of 'orientalism', an idealized vision of the East permeated by myths, stereotypes and prejudices.

In something of an effort to excuse himself for his fear of criticism, Kapuściński included some general remarks on this topic in *Lapidarium II*, in which he does not betray that he is writing about himself as well:

> The generations brought up under totalitarian systems have a particular attitude to criticism. Within a democracy, criticism is a form of opinion, a view, an attempt to influence the attitudes of others, to shape reality. In a totalitarian country criticism conceals a dagger, a noose, or a bullet, and can be a death sentence. Therefore people who know the practices of this system instinctively react to criticism with fear, they run away from it in horror, feeling as if they have been caught in a trap with no way out.[1]

During the PRL era, when such fears might have been warranted, Kapuściński had no critics. Some half-hearted polemics began to appear once democracy had taken over, but not until a couple of years before his death.

Finding silly, malevolent attacks just as upsetting as attempts at discussion made by serious people, he never responded to critical commentaries. He consciously adopted the strategy of keeping silent. He did not like (or did not want?) to confront or argue. He was oversensitive, and he knew it. He wanted to be loved and admired. He liked to be listened to; he didn't want to sing one part among many – especially as he felt more competent regarding his chosen subject matter than any potential polemicist in Poland (perhaps with the exception of the Russian theme). He also thought – no doubt correctly, from the viewpoint of his strategy for his life and his writing – that to react would simply prolong the life of the criticism and create an aura of controversy around him and his work, rather than the aura of greatness and admiration on which he depended.

Małgorzata Szejnert says to me: 'I am afraid the lack of criticism in Poland that accompanied him throughout his life will be mirrored, by the law of the pendulum, in excessive, unjust criticism. Nothing in nature can disappear.'

Not for the first time I catch myself fearing that, without meaning to write an exposé, I am discovering facts about the master's life which I would rather not know at all, and that I am creating a platform for massively negative opinions of him.

'And you're going to put it all down?' asks a reporter colleague, when I tell her about some of my discoveries.

'Do I have an alternative?'

After all, a portrait of Kapuściński in which frailties and flaws are visible is more genuine than a beatified icon. Quite simply, it is realistic. In any case, isn't this version of Kapuściński more interesting than the one that is flattered to death? More instructive than the falsified one? More human than the one raised on a pedestal, covered with laurels and showered in mindless rapture?

I am reminded of a conversation I once had with Clayborne Carson, a professor of history who published the letters of Martin Luther King and in whom the great leader's widow, Coretta Scott King, placed her trust. Carson, to whom King's widow had passed all her husband's papers, discovered that King had committed plagiarism in his doctoral thesis, and he made that fact known in the press. The widow was not pleased, and her relationship with the historian cooled. In time she understood that an honest scholar could not have done otherwise.

I asked Carson if he had been shattered by the unpleasant discovery. He replied:

I never regarded King as a god, but as an ordinary man (albeit one with some special qualities that made it possible for him to play a unique role in the African-American freedom struggle.) As a historian what fascinates me most is how people leading ordinary lives are able to rise above themselves and do extraordinary things. Such a man was Martin Luther King. I admire Gandhi – I think that if any man was close to sainthood, it was he. However, I wouldn't like to be Gandhi's wife, because as a historian I know that Gandhi the husband was a far more than difficult person.

It isn't good to admire people for being perfect, because if they turn out to have faults or stains on their résumé – and they always have – our faith is bound to collapse in ruins. Better to admire our idols for the extraordinary things they do, *despite* being completely ordinary people.[2]

How fitting the words of this American historian seem for my account of Kapuściński.

33

The Reporter Amends Reality, Or, Critics of All Nations, Unite!

On a small display table at Barbara Goshu's art gallery in Addis Ababa is a photograph of Emperor Haile Selassie. It was taken in 1971. That was a big day in the lives of Barbara and her husband, the well-known Ethiopian painter Worku Goshu, because His Royal Highness officially opened their new gallery.

Barbara has lived in Ethiopia for more than forty years. She and her husband met as students at the Academy of Fine Arts in Kraków; after graduating, the pair decided to live in Worku's hometown, Addis Ababa. Both of them produce religious art, and the gallery is filled with icons. Barbara's great passion is to preserve the dying primitivist tradition of Ethiopian folk art, and her stylized pictures are imbued with this spirit.

'I can tell you,' she says, 'Kapuściński was a charming man. Enchanting, warm and friendly. As soon as he arrived in Addis he always dropped in on us; he liked to chat, to listen and have something to eat with us. I never looked into his soul, but we all loved him. But . . . you know what . . . that *Emperor* . . . it's like a tale from *The Thousand and One Nights*.' She smiles broadly. 'Some of it sticks to reality, but less rather than more.

'What is untrue? You'd better ask what's true, it'll be easier to say. It's all fairy-tales, nonsense, fantasy. He writes that Haile Selassie never read any books, but he had such a brilliant mind! Extraordinary intelligence! Apart from that, it is impossible that Kapuściński visited Ethiopians at their homes and that they told him all those stories there. I'll tell you why not: the Mengistu regime was on the rampage. You cannot imagine what was going on here; there was a police curfew, and people from the emperor's court were being virtually hunted down. No one would have taken the risk of inviting someone to their home at night, let alone a white man, who would draw attention. A journalist? It's quite impossible. You should also know that the Ethiopians don't invite people to their homes. At home you eat and sleep, there is no place where you might receive a guest. Here the prevalent culture involves going out to a bar.

'Who did Kapuściński talk to? I'll tell you: he met them at dinners at the embassy. Someone whispered something to him on the side, and then he ... well, you know. He added colour. He fantasized. He split one account into several. Apparently one of the emperor's people once took him to the palace, on the quiet, to have a look around. That's what he said, I don't know if it was like that.'

One Polish diplomat, who asks not to have his name revealed, says that Kapuściński's interlocutors were indeed people from the court – alcoholics whom he took out for a drink. He treated them, and they told him things. Barbara Goshu reckons that, too, is doubtful: the army were everywhere, so were the political police, and no Ethiopian, certainly no one from the deposed emperor's court, would have dared go into a bar with a white man, a reporter – that would have attracted attention. No, no, it's not possible.

A critic of *The Emperor* once pointed out that even after the fall of Mengistu, Kapuściński did not reveal the identities of his informers, despite the fact that they were no longer under any threat and that, at the time, people from the imperial court were giving evidence as witnesses at the trials of those behind the Red Terror.

'Did I ever talk to Kapuściński after *The Emperor* was published? Of course,' says Goshu. 'I told him at once that it was dishonest, and that he had presented an unfair picture of the wonderful man Haile Selassie actually was. How did he react? Like this: he made a face like this' – she makes the surprised face of a small boy who has done something naughty – 'then he quickly changed the subject. Never before or later did he ever say what he thought about the emperor or about Mengistu. He used to ask questions, draw out confidences, steer things onto a topic that interested him, and then listen.'

These spontaneous comments from Barbara Goshu, whose fascination for the emperor makes it hard to regard her comments dispassionately, tally with the criticism of the leading expert on Haile Selassie's life, the late professor Harold G. Marcus. Marcus taught at Michigan State University in East Lansing, and also at Addis Ababa University during the emperor's reign. He published the first volume of his monumental biography of Haile Selassie but did not manage to complete the second. Apparently, an unfinished, working version is slated for publication. In a scholarly article on books about Africa, he writes:

> Kapuściński had written a flawed book because he had uncritically believed his informants, several of whom told tall tales about the short monarch. A few examples will suffice to clarify this point.
>
> One, Mr Richard as he is called by several raconteurs, reported that the emperor had a little dog that was permitted to urinate on the shoes of

courtiers and that there was a servant whose sole duty was to wipe the offending shoes dry. True, the emperor enjoyed small dogs, but he never would have permitted any animal to humiliate his courtiers.

Second, Kapuściński recounts that the emperor's sole teacher was a French Jesuit, who never was able to inculcate reading into his young charge. In fact, the young Haile Sellassie had several teachers, among them two Capucins but nary a Jesuit. His Ethiopian Capucin, Father Samuel, introduced his student to the classics of Ethiopian and Western philosophical literature and instilled in him a profound respect for reading and learning.

Third, Haile Selassie was, by all reports, a sedulous reader in Amharic, French and, later, in English. He not only perused books but also reports, newspapers, and magazines. Furthermore, he wrote instructions and orders, giving the lie to Kapuściński's absurd statement: 'Though he ruled for half a century, not even those closest to him knew what his signature looked like.'[1]

Professor Marcus makes additional charges, but does not deny that Kapuściński's book has certain merits:

> *The Emperor,* therefore, is flawed but often insightful; it should be read with care and Kapuściński's facts ought to be carefully checked against the historical record.[2]

Addis Ababa, November 2008. A panel discussion at the university on *The Emperor* provides an unexpected counterpoint to the stern criticism levelled at Kapuściński.

I ask my fellow panellist, professor of literature Abiye Daniel, what he thinks about the charges laid against Kapuściński by experts on Ethiopia and on Haile Selassie's life – that he repeats rumours from the street and distorts the image of the country and its inhabitants, and that the dog Lulu could not have peed on the courtiers' shoes because in Ethiopian culture that would have been – as they put it – 'humiliation beyond all humiliation'.

'We never knew anything about Haile Selassie except rumours,' replies the professor. 'Kapuściński painted a portrait of the emperor that we didn't want to know at all. Many of us Ethiopians had a mythical image in our minds: of the good master who hands out money to the poor from his car. Kapuściński shatters this image, and a very good thing too. That is the great virtue of his book.'

A voice from the audience, a man of thirty-something, declares: 'This book is offensive. People of my parents' generation, who lived in the days of the emperor, feel disgusted, hurt and disappointed by what this journalist has written.'

The professor replies calmly. 'Some people are annoyed that a foreigner has presented us in this light and that he had no right to do so. But why shouldn't he have? This book has a wonderfully ironical and sarcastic spirit; there are excellent passages about the faces of the courtiers pushing forwards into the emperor's range of vision, about the omnipresent ears eavesdropping. The dog Lulu couldn't have pissed on the courtiers' shoes? The knowledge we have on the subject of dogs suggests that dogs do piss on things. Why should anyone insist that Lulu the dog could not have pissed on someone's shoes?'

Abbas Milani shakes his head. He says: small mistakes, big mistakes, inaccuracies, the certainty with which he writes but to which he had no right – in other words, not enough knowledge. Professor Milani read *Shah of Shahs* years ago and retained a fairly good impression from his first reading, but before our conversation he read the book again.

'Undoubtedly your friend knows how to listen,' says Milani, 'and captures the atmosphere of the place and the moment superbly. Unfortunately he hasn't the energy to do more reading, more research, more checking. Reading this book a second time, I was amazed how many mistakes he could have avoided if he had only done a little more reading.'

Milani is the director of Iranian Studies at Stanford University in California. For ten years he has been working on a biography of Reza Pahlavi, Shah of Iran and hero of one of Kapuściński's two most famous books.

'You can open *Shah of Shahs* at any page,' he says, 'point to a passage, and I will tell you what is wrong or inaccurate.'

I give it a try. I open the book at random and read out: 'Roosevelt asks Churchill what has become of the ruler of this country, Shah Reza . . .'[3] 'Stop!' Milani interrupts. 'But we know Roosevelt didn't ask Churchill about the Shah,' he says, 'because he was better informed about the internal situation in Iran. Kapuściński suggests that the US president was ignorant on this matter – nothing could be further from the truth.'

Another passage at random, from the last part of the book: 'The Shah was resolute about retaining his throne, and to this end he explored every possibility.'[4] 'That's a fascinating point,' says Milani animatedly, and reads a few lines aloud himself. 'If we can say anything about the Shah with absolute certainty, it is this, that he was not a resolute person. While working on his biography I came across eight crisis points in the period from 1941 to 1979, when he was ready to abdicate and leave the country. And at a certain moment he even did leave . . .

'I am annoyed', he says, 'by the certainty with which the author writes about some events. Not even historians have that sort of certainty, even they argue about many facts. An example? The photograph of the Shah's father. He describes it splendidly, the style of the book is admirable, the problem is that no one knows if the man immortalized in the photograph really is the Shah's father; there are even some who claim no one knows who his real father was. Does that mean a journalist has to acquire complete, detailed knowledge of his subject, like a scholar of the period, a historian? No. But he should write with greater care, be aware of what is certain, and what prompts doubts.

'This lack of care,' continues Milani, 'also betrays the sort of person Kapuściński was talking to: he had left-wing and centre-left friends, who told him their version of events. He employs the exaggeration typical of his interlocutors. Somewhere he writes about the thousands of people murdered by the Shah, but actually during his reign about fourteen hundred prisoners were executed. He writes about hundreds of thousands of political prisoners – when I was in prison there were 4,500 of us.

'If your friend had "sold" this book as "faction" – a literary account of the revolution based on real events – one could have applauded him. The trouble is, he is selling it as journalism. The "model reader" of this story, to use Umberto Eco's term, is someone who likes reading but who hasn't the faintest idea about Iran. This is not a book that will still be read – like Montesquieu's book about Persia, or de Tocqueville on America – in a hundred or two hundred years' time. I would recommend it at most to someone who wants to find out something not so much about the Shah, the revolution, or the culture of my country, as to get a sense of the atmosphere of events. That Kapuściński really did manage to reflect well.'

Warsaw University historian Marcin Kula does not hide his irritation when I summarize the charges brought against Kapuściński by these experts on Ethiopia and Iran.

'I can't bear that sort of review,' he says. 'They are typical of a certain category of historian: the narrow specialists. Within the social sciences, the cult of specialization has proliferated, which reduces to absurdity, disenables, the creative circulation of ideas. Whenever I write something on a topic that does not strictly belong to my field of specialization, I instantly come in for criticism or silence on the part of the specialists. A particular category within this group – and I say this on the basis of many years of observation – are the Orientalists, mainly the philologists who specialize in rare languages. They are convinced they are the only ones who know anything about "their" countries and cultures. Anyone else who touches "their" subject is committing a crime.'

And yet reading *The Emperor*, Kula goes on to say, as a monograph on the era of Haile Selassie, or *Shah of Shahs* as a textbook on the modern history of Iran, makes no sense. Kapuściński creates literary and intellectual constructs, and seeks models of power and recurring situations to help him portray the universal rules of human behaviour and the mechanisms of power and revolution. The Bible is full of historical mistakes and inaccuracies too, and what is the result? Focusing on uncovering them might be interesting for amateurs, but intellectually it is fruitless.

Two reporters and feature writers connected in the past with the *New Yorker* and now both professors, at New York University and UC Berkeley respectively, react the same way as Kula; they are Lawrence Weschler and Mark Danner.

Weschler: 'The rhapsodic quality in Ryszard's book-writing is conspicuous; it is pitched at a different register than his daily reportage, it is couched in a telling-stories-in-recollection-at-a-distance sort of cadence, a quality the intelligent reader picks up on at once (and again one that is not to be confused with standard day to day journalism, which he was also capable of doing). *As such*, and as conspicuously allegorical writing, Ryszard's writing in, say, *The Emperor* and *Shah of Shahs* transcends the usual fiction versus non-fiction dichotomies and calls out to be shelved under the category Literature.'

Danner: 'I've never thought the question of factual accuracy was the central one when it comes to Ryszard's work, especially books like *The Emperor* and *Shah of Shahs*. Obviously, specialists on Ethiopia or Iran have a different view. But *The Emperor* is not supposed to be a history of a particular time – at least, not primarily. It is a piece of literature, of literary reporting, an account that comes as much from the traditions of Machiavelli's *The Prince* and Stendhal's *The Charterhouse of Parma* as from the practices of daily reporting. In this light, is the question of whether or not Lulu the Emperor's dog really did pee on the courtiers' shoes really so crucial?'

I am surprised: both speakers are evidently free of the obsession of American journalism with checking every detail. At some newspaper offices in America, the fact-checking procedure is a real nightmare for the reporters. Are they saying this because they do not regard Kapuściński's books as journalism, but as literature? Great literature?

Years ago, Danner wrote an essay in which he grapples with the obsession: fiction vs. non-fiction. I summarize: there is no such thing as the purely factual, just as there is no such thing as pure fiction. Fiction draws on life by the handful, and non-fiction makes use of artistic means of expression. The authors of both genres use the same literary techniques. At the centre of the story there is always an intrigue, a character, a symbol around which the story gets going and continues to develop.

But how does the story as told relate to the 'truth' about reality? Isn't that at the heart of the controversy? Of course. And can one answer with the question, What 'truth' are we talking about? Nora Ephron describes the Washington élite in a roman à clef called *Heartburn*; it is a book that belongs on the fiction shelf, yet it is easy to identify the settings and the time described in it, and who is who in real life. In Kapuściński's *The Emperor* this sort of identification is impossible, but this is a book in the 'true stories' category, non-fiction. Which of them is to a greater degree a work of pure art, which is the more fictional, and which do we ascribe to the category of non-fiction? There is no simple answer.

In fiction, poetry, and drama, we have no choice but to trust the author; he or she alone knows the whole story from start to finish, and the protagonists' motivations; there is no room for alternative scenarios or different endings. In non-fiction – whether historical, journalistic or biographical – there are always some questions that remain unanswered: What were our hero's motives? What was he thinking? Could history have turned out differently? There is always something else we have not discovered or cannot grasp in full.

Kapuściński had his own theory about crossing the borders between fiction and non-fiction. He expounded it in the simplest way in the course of an argument with his close friends.

'When we were still living in Africa,' says Izabella Nowak, 'he gave us an article of his to read about the riots in Dar es Salaam. Africans had beaten up whites, and my husband had been at the site of the incident, so we knew exactly where and how it had occurred. I pointed out to Rysiek that he had got some details wrong, because the fight had taken place on a different street, in different circumstances. He shouted at me, "You don't understand a thing! I'm not writing so the details add up – the point is the essence of the matter!"'

Jerzy Nowak explains what he meant by 'the essence of the matter' by adducing an example from real life (because Kapuściński did not ignore accuracy solely in his reporting). One day he introduced Kapuściński to another of his friends, Adam Daniel Rotfeld, and his now late wife Barbara. The Rotfelds, who loved to eat well, invited Kapuściński to dinner. Afterwards Kapuściński gave the following report: 'You can't imagine it – I'm sitting at table, and they keep bringing things in, first some legs of pork, then hams, then half an ox, then turkeys, then some stuffed ducks'. As Nowak says, 'Of course that wasn't strictly true, and half the details needed correcting, but Rysiek's account conveyed the essence of the Rotfelds' hospitality.'

Some years ago, Kapuściński held a discussion with another reporter, Wojciech Giełżyński, on the extent to which a journalist is free to subject reality to some 'reworking':

RK: I am incapable of making anything up. If I could, I would write novels.

WG: I'm not thinking of fiction. I'm excluding fiction. I'm thinking of some fact, some typical event which really did take place, but – as bad luck would have it – on another day or in another place . . . Do you admit that it's possible to distort the sequence of facts slightly, for instance to adjust the chronology in order to achieve a better cognitive or artistic effect?

RK: Yes, you can do that: you can rebuild reality, but taking authentic elements from that reality. That sometimes helps to convey a deeper meaning. It all depends how it is done, and whether it sits within the particular realities, within the climate, or whether it is artificial, invented, deceptive. You can sense that at once. The reader can sense it. Every made-up ornament, embellishment or added horror sounds false. But there is no sense in exaggerating the factual precision either . . . In the end it doesn't matter if this guy was killed by three or five bullets. What matters is to convey the essence of the incident.[5]

Kapuściński, who on principle did not respond to criticism or attacks, had a problem with them nonetheless. Therefore, in his *Lapidarium* books – his loose collections of notes about the world – he often returned to his thoughts on the topic of reportage, the literary techniques used in journalism, and the direction in which the contemporary media were heading. These were his indirect answers to the critics.

Reportage as a genre is going through an evolution from journalism to literature.[6]

Or:

A collage, a symbiosis: nowadays reportage often makes use of techniques that are typical of novels or short stories, and so-called 'fine literature' is happy to borrow from the achievements of reportage. But it has been like that in the past too. In the care they took to gather material, novelists were no different from reporters . . .

One of those who contributed to this 'muddying of genres' was Bruce Chatwin. Chatwin, who died in 1989, is the biggest name in contemporary British reportage . . . Susan[nah] Clapp, the publisher of his book [*In Patagonia*], writes about the difficulties of giving a precise definition to this sort of literature: ' . . . Chatwin rejected the formerly traditional demand of reportage to be true to the facts and used techniques which are employed by novelists. The result was reportage which reads like a story . . . It is reportage, but at the same time it is a historical essay, and also, on top of that, a novel. It was a new kind of writing, which made non-fiction into a broader, richer genre'.[7]

Wasn't Kapuściński using these loose reflections and quotes to sketch a self-portrait? Wasn't he driven by a similar intention when he mentioned the names of the American precursors of so-called New Journalism?

In a mini-lecture on the history of the press and the reporter's profession, Kapuściński tries definitively to disarm the controversies surrounding truth and fiction, as well as objectivity and subjectivity, in his journalism/ writing:

> Misunderstandings about reportage also arise from the differences between the Anglo-Saxon press and the continental European press.
>
> Anglo-Saxon journalism comes from a liberal tradition, from the conviction that the press is a public institution and that it expresses the interests and opinions of all citizens equally, and therefore it must be independent, impartial and objective . . .
>
> The roots of the continental European press are different. The press here comes from political movements: it was a tool for the Party struggle. And so by contrast to the Anglo-Saxon press it was characterized by partiality, commitment, the fighting spirit, and a party bias. Here information and commentary were not separated . . .
>
> Knowing about these two models of the press, it is easier to answer the question of whether reportage is a journalistic or a literary genre. In the Anglo-Saxon world it is decidedly literary. Within the model of the Anglo-Saxon press there is no room for such a personal product as reportage, the strength of which lies in the author's presence at the site of events, his physical presence, but also his emotional one, his impressions and thoughts. And so there, reportage is printed in literary periodicals and published by book publishers. No one is in any doubt that books by V. S. Naipaul, James Fenton or Colin Thubron are 'fine literature'.
>
> In the countries of continental Europe it varies. Here for some time there used to be, and in places there still is, journalistic reportage. It fulfilled a particularly important role in countries where there was censorship, because it was a form that gave greater freedom for independent, critical expression. In Europe there was also literary reportage, practised mainly by writers. Those who wrote this sort of reportage were usually not professional journalists.[8]

And so there is no single kind of journalism, no single tradition. In the reporter's profession there is no universal method for conveying the truth about events, there is no one-and-only justified means of expression.

But is this the only conclusion to be drawn? Doesn't Kapuściński's argument create theoretical permission to be nonchalant, and to ignore what we are used to calling the hard facts?

'I'd prefer there to be as few inaccuracies or factual errors as possible,' says Marcin Kula, defending Kapuściński from the 'detail-monger' critics. To the question of inaccuracies resulting from inattention or ignorance, there is no good answer. The 'continental European' tradition of committed reportage absolves one from subjectivity, but does not absolve one from making mistakes. Not every 'reworking of reality' can be explained by the 'higher truth' or the 'synthetic truth'.

During my journey in Kapuściński's footsteps, and also in the course of reading, I come across several tricky examples.

Santa Cruz, Bolivia. In the waiting room at PreVida, a small private clinic, I am waiting for Dr Osvaldo Peredo, known to his friends as Chato. On the wall there are portraits of the doctor's two brothers, Coco and Inti, both of whom fought in Che Guevara's unit.

After both his brothers had been killed, Chato set up his own guerrilla unit. At Teoponte, despite the fact that he made an alliance with the miners, he lost the battle. Salvador Allende's plane removed him from the city, which was under siege by the army, and took him to Chile. He came back and organized attacks against activists on the fascist right. He hid behind a variety of names, until finally he realized that the days of guerrilla warfare were over. He was arrested not for conspiracy, but for possessing fake documents.

Nowadays he works as a doctor and still keeps in close contact with politics, just as his entire family always has.

Kapuściński described the Peredo family, including Chato, his dead brothers and his father, in his reportage *Christ with a Rifle on His Shoulder*. I show Chato the Spanish translation, which came out many years ago in Mexico. He reads:

> The Peredo family could be the subject of an entire story. In Cochabamba, Bolivia's second largest city after La Paz, our commander's [Chato's] father Rómulo Peredo used to publish a scandalous newspaper entitled *El Imparcial*. He wrote the whole thing himself. He drank like a fish as he did it. The following item appeared in the newspaper: 'The parish priest at Pocon raped a sixteen-year-old girl!' The next day the priest came to Cochabamba shocked and offended.[9]

'Hmm.' Chato vocalizes, probably in disapproval, and reads on.

> 'I, Mr Peredo? A sixteen-year-old?' Peredo made a concerned face and wanted to help the priest somehow. 'It's a tricky matter,' he said. 'The only thing that can be done is to issue a disclaimer, but that will cost you a hundred pesos.' Which was a lot of money. The priest paid, and next

day *El Imparcial* printed: 'Yesterday we published the news that the parish priest at Pocon had raped a sixteen-year-old girl. We apologize for the mistake. The story was about the parish priest at Colón.' The day after that, the priest from Colón came along, and so on.[10]

Now Chato is shaking his head.

However, not everyone was willing to pay for a correction – lots of people came to make a fuss and beat up the editor. In this situation Rómulo Peredo appointed the famous Bolivian boxer, Ernesto Aldunate, as a manager of the newspaper. Aldunate biffed anyone who came to interfere. After a while the interference stopped.[11]

'Where did you get this? It's pure fantasy!'

'Is there something incorrect?'

'This is fiction – it may be colourfully written, but it's entirely untrue. Well, almost entirely.'

Chato takes a fat Bolivian encyclopaedia down from the shelf, looks up 'Rómulo Peredo' and reads aloud that his father was a publisher, editor-in-chief of a serious newspaper, a top-flight politician, and in the 1940s a senator, patriot and democrat who was forced to flee to Chile to escape the repressions of a series of dictatorships. The description in the encyclopaedia implies that Rómulo Peredo was *somebody* – a serious person, not a scandal-monger, scoundrel and con man.

'That . . . how could he . . . what a bastard! A man devoid of morality!'

'Do you remember when you met?'

'I never laid eyes on him. Someone spun him a yarn, because I admit there is a bit of truth in this, but he has picked up some rumours as well, and invented the rest.'

I ask him to read on. Now and then he points out further inaccuracies in the details – this brother worked as this, not that; another fought for two years, not one; he was killed in a gun battle, not in his sleep, et cetera.

Further on, Kapuściński quotes an account, transcribed from a tape recording, by Guillermo Veliz, a guerrilla from Chato's unit. It's the same thing again, he says, Guillermo couldn't have said that, not in that way. Facts mixed with fiction. What sort of a guy is this? What sort of a guy is this? Chato keeps repeating.

I can overlook the inaccuracies. Anyone who writes knows that even the most meticulous author makes errors. In the end, what significance can it have for the 'essence' of the account if Inti continued to fight for one more year after the death of Guevara, or two? However, the scale of the oversights is worrying – there are too many, and they occur too often. And the portrait of the father of the Peredo family is even more distressing.

If, as it would appear from the encyclopaedia (a son's reaction is not necessarily the best barometer), Rómulo Peredo was a respected figure in Bolivian public life, why did Kapuściński present him in such a distorted mirror? I do not know, and I will never find out; I can only hypothesize. Perhaps somebody hostile to Peredo the editor or Peredo the senator, who may have been wronged by him, told Kapuściński his or someone else's story. Kapuściński liked to quote even the most improbable rumours, because, as he contended, they form part of the social landscape, they tell us about people's consciousness at a given time and place, and so they are 'social fact'. But instead of writing that 'rumour on the streets of Cochabamba has it that Rómulo Peredo . . .', or 'at the La Cueva bar I heard a story that Rómulo Peredo . . .', Kapuściński has passed along a second-hand story (which happens to be highly comical) as the truth about a man who has a first name, a surname, a biography and a reputation.

Or maybe he described the man accurately? Maybe he checked the gossip? I doubt it. If Kapuściński had taken care with the details, then in presenting a sketch of the elder Peredo he would have said he was a politician (his chief occupation) and a senator, and that he spent time in exile because of political persecution. He clearly did not refer to any sources, and so I tend towards the hypothesis that he 'bought' an amusing story, which played its role in his reportage and suited the image of 'exotic' Bolivia. He may have thought, Who would ever check the details of a story about someone called Peredo, especially in a text written and published in Polish?

In Kampala I come across a different sort of anecdote in which Kapuściński is carried away by fantasy. Here I talk to husband-and-wife journalists William Pike and Cathy Watson, who have been living in Africa for several decades. They tell me about the joint trips they made with Kapuściński to guerrilla camps in their home country of Uganda and in neighbouring Rwanda.

Cathy points out that in Rwanda, Kapuściński was not interested in the sort of information that news reporters always ask about: who, where, when, with whom, against whom, why and what for? He asked the guerrillas for their personal stories, the reasons they were fighting, their aims, and their dreams for the future. He wanted to understand what it means to be a fighter, and why people choose such a fate. The rest, in other words the so-called hard facts, were just stage directions for him, of secondary importance.

William is the unnamed co-star of the chapter entitled 'The Ambush' in Kapuściński's African summing-up, *The Shadow of the Sun*. He says the book's account of an incident in northern Uganda, when they fell into an ambush set by the guerrillas for the government troops, corresponds more or less to the actual course of events. He smiles at the exaggerated details – Kapuściński refers to a 'narrow, laterite road, full of holes and ruts'[12] – and shows me some photographs of that very road. It is smooth and wide. It doesn't matter, says William, it's just poetic licence.

His only confusion arises from a passage in the chapter about Idi Amin:

> Suddenly, a band of children came up the street that led up from the lake, calling 'Samaki! Samaki!' (fish in Swahili). People gathered, joyful at the prospect that there would be something to eat. The fishermen threw their catch onto a table, and when the onlookers saw it, they grew still and silent. The fish was fat, enormous. These waters never used to yield such monstrously proportioned, overfed specimens. Everyone knew that for a long time now Amin's henchmen had been dumping the bodies of their victims into the lake, and that crocodiles and meat-eating fish must have been feasting on them. The crowd remained quiet. Then, a military vehicle happened by.[13]

'That was a well-known story in Uganda,' says William. 'In the 1950s, when the British were still there, someone came up with the idea of forcing the development of the fishing industry. An experiment was conducted that turned out to have awful results – the Nile perch was introduced into Lake Victoria. The fishermen had superb catches, but the perch, which is a predator, killed off other species of smaller fish, causing an environmental imbalance. Moreover, because of the availability of so much food, the perch grew to an incredible size. The suggestion that they fed on the corpses of Idi Amin's victims fits in with the blood-chilling stories about the horrors of his dictatorship perfectly, but it is pure fantasy. The Nile perch just fed on smaller fish.'

John Ryle, who in 2001 in the *Times Literary Supplement* published the best-known criticism of Kapuściński's African writing, includes a whole list of his gaffes, inaccuracies and mistakes. That the Sudanese Dinka and Nuer tribes live not just on milk, as Kapuściński suggests, but also eat grain, fish and meat. That Sudan was not a British colony, but was jointly governed by the British and the Egyptians. That the Bari do not come from Uganda but Sudan. Et cetera.

As for Kapuściński's claim to have visited the only bookshop in Ethiopia in the 1990s – at Addis Ababa University, and devoid of books to boot – Ryle laughs at this 'observation' and doubts that can have been the case in Addis in the early 1990s. My sources say Ryle is right, not Kapuściński.

Once again, I could shrug off the tiny inaccuracies that do not make *The Shadow of the Sun* any less fascinating. But moving away from the details, Ryle lays another charge, of fundamental importance in evaluating Kapuściński's writing on Africa. And not just Africa.

[I]n a typical episode of *The Shadow of the Sun*, he travels to a distant, dangerous location, falls ill and confronts death. And he is witness to dreadful events, from which he emerges with a deeper understanding of the further reaches of human nature . . .

The baroque note in Kapuściński's prose confirms the movement away from fact towards the realm of fantasy and symbol. The African universe, for him, is a place of absolutes and extremes, extremes of poverty, of climate, of violence and danger . . .

In this mode of writing – the tropical baroque style – nothing can be ordinary or familiar. Everything is stretched and exaggerated, the opposite of home . . .

The direction of his own blurrings and inventions and exaggerations becomes clearer in the light of this inadvertent self-criticism. Africa is a continent without bookshops, he avers. Its rulers are illiterate. Its inhabitants are prisoners of their environment, or of their bloodline. They are afraid of the dark. They live on nothing but milk. (Who knows? They may well have heads beneath their shoulders too . . .) Europeans, it is clear, can never really understand such people . . .

[T]he single historical experience that the inhabitants of this hugely various continent do have in common with each other [is] the experience of colonization (or military occupation) . . . Despite Kapuściński's vigorously anti-colonialist stance, his writing about Africa is a variety of latter-day literary colonialism, a kind of gonzo orientalism, a highly selective imposition of form, conducted in the name of humane concern, that sacrifices truth and accuracy, and homogenises and misrepresents Africans even as it aspires to speak for them . . .

In the last chapter of *The Shadow of the Sun* there is a culminating generalization that embodies his ambiguous attitude to factual reportage, and corresponding attraction to the realm of poetry and fiction. 'The kind of history known in Europe as scholarly and objective,' Kapuściński writes, 'can never arise here because the African past has no documents or records, and each generation, listening to the version being transmitted to it, changed it and continues to change it . . .'

'As a result,' he continues, 'history, free of the weight of archives, of the constraints of dates and data, achieves here its purest, crystalline form — that of myth.'

This characterization of the role of collective memory in African societies is, to say the least, under-informed. On the one hand it is now well-established that oral history can be chronologically accurate and that traditional genealogies can be precise. On the other, Kapuściński's account ignores more than a century of scholarly research and the existence of hundreds of universities and libraries in African countries, not all of which are empty or malfunctioning, and some of which burgeon with the work of African scholars.

What this account of African history does reveal is a telling indication of Kapuściński's own narrative aspirations. Here in the domain of myth, in a realm untouched by literacy, where the subject never answers back, a reporter is freed from the constraint of dates and data, the tedium of checking and cross-checking, the tyranny of documents and records. Here facts are no longer sacred; we are at play in the bush of ghosts, free to opine and to generalise about 'Africa' and 'the African' – and invent – without criticism from scholars, or indigenes, or self-appointed guardians of facticity . . .

From this place, deep in an imaginary Africa, the writer may return with any tale he pleases.[14]

About flesh-eating fish. About Addis Ababa having no bookshops. About a gang of dogs on the run in Luanda. From Latin America, by right of analogy, about a publisher who cons a series of priests into paying for newspaper disclaimers. About the man's son, a guerrilla, who was shot in his sleep, although he was wide awake when he was killed . . .

Do such tales really convey the 'deeper meaning' of what was happening in Africa, or get to the 'essence of the matter' in Latin America? Do they decipher the universal mechanisms of human attitudes and behaviour?

As Ryle aptly points out:

The force of his writing depends to a considerable extent on an air of certainty, on the voice of experience, the authority of someone who, we are told in *Shah of Shahs*, has survived twenty-seven coups and revolutions, who has driven through burning road-blocks and stayed behind in besieged cities, the only foreign correspondent who remained when the rest of the press-pack left.

On the other hand, perhaps the comments of Catalan theoretician of journalism and literature Lluís Albert Chillón provide a good counterpoint to Ryle's accusations?

Kapuściński practises a kind of literary journalism that is impossible to categorize – as different from New Journalism as it is from the new European journalisms, which combines into a formerly unknown symbiosis the information-gathering techniques that belong to investigative journalism, the art of observation that is typical of reportage, and a quest for a kind of poetic truth, which through a narrative mode that is closer to myths, legends and folk tales than to realistic novels, transcends the boundaries inherent in simple documentary truth.[15]

But if, from the viewpoint of the rigours of journalism, Kapuściński's writing gives rise to so many doubts about the accuracy of the events he describes, then . . . For the first time, I start to wonder whether it matters if we put his books on the 'journalism' shelf or the 'fiction' shelf.

During one of our conversations, his school friend Andrzej Czcibor-Piotrowski says: '*The Emperor*? It's the best Polish novel of the twentieth century!'

Criticism of the accuracy in Kapuściński's writing does not undermine – as I understand it – either the literary excellence of his books or his perspicacity in decoding the mechanisms of power, revolution, human attitudes and behaviour. Instead it poses the question of whether some of his works can stand as a model or reference point for journalists and journalism, if even for its least rigorous form, literary reportage. Also a more fundamental question: How much licence does a reporter have? Because in journalism, increasing the 'capacity', 'enriching' literary reportage, 'adjusting reality', crossing the borders between genres and entering the terrain of fiction have a high price, an unfortunate flip side – they weaken credibility.

In the margins of the argument about reporters' accuracy, about embroidering and inventing, it is impossible not to ask questions about the 'truths' conveyed via 'rigorous' journalism. How reliable are the big information agencies and television networks that are connected with economic and – indirectly – political power? Don't 'rigorous' journalists and commentators sometimes modify the details or omit the essential circumstances of events, when publishing them would strike a blow at the interests of the powerful media owners, advertisers and sponsors? In the final years of his life, Kapuściński often bemoaned the fact that the mass media go in for manipulation; they oversimplify, they 'have ceased to be the opposition to the system', 'they have settled down with power, they no longer protest or challenge the principles'.[16] This is not a justification for the inaccuracies of literary reportage – it is simply another aspect of the debate about journalistic credibility.

Kapuściński is not the only eminent reporter to have been criticized for a lack of precision, mistakes or downright invention. Another is the Colombian Nobel Prize winner Gabriel García Márquez, who wrote literary reportage, especially in his youth. The standard example of García Márquez's confabulation is a piece called 'Caracas sin agua' (Caracas Without Water); in it he invents a German scholar named Samuel Burkart, who, because of the lack of water in the city, shaved himself using peach juice. García Marquez was accused of a lack of credibility in this and other feature articles.

One school of thought concerning literary reportage proposes that a journalist has the right – for the good of the text, to convey 'a higher truth' – to create, let us say, a fictional character out of several real ones. Some journalists did this in the PRL era, in order not to expose the people featured in their reports. It is also done by Wojciech Jagielski, for example, in his book *The Night Wanderers*, about child soldiers in Uganda.[17] But Jagielski gives a clear warning in the introduction that these are fictional characters; in an interview he calls his book a story, not reportage, because, as he puts it, 'in reportage, to protect the heroes I can change their names, but not create characters'. He is absolutely fair to the reader. I also like the fact that he says:

> You cannot allow yourself too many liberties in journalism. You may say: 'I'll only go a short way off the path of journalism, just this once'. But it doesn't matter how many times you do it, or how far you go. What matters is that you went off the path.[18]

The trouble with Kapuściński is that some of his works can stand as indisputable models for journalists, and some – often the greatest in literary terms – not necessarily. The latter are more like books from the fiction shelf, and the highest one at that; perhaps they should not be presented to the public as works of reportage, even if a major part of the material was gathered through reporting methods and the author makes use of reportorial narrative tools as well. This sort of fiction is 'the truth of lies', to use Mario Vargas Llosa's term, but perhaps it is not journalism.

I daresay Kapuściński would not have been offended if some of his books were placed among works of fiction. Where is the proof? Here you are:

> In 1981 the *Washington Post* published a feature by a young journalist called Janet Cook, entitled 'Jimmy's World', about a black eight-year-old drug addict. Cook won the Pulitzer Prize for it, but just as she was about to be awarded it, the report turned out to have been a hoax, and the prize was withdrawn.
>
> I like what Márquez said on this occasion: 'You didn't give it to her for journalism? You should have given it to her for literature!'[19]

Most of all, he wanted to be a writer. For years he dreamed of being accepted among the élite of writers. Journalism was something inferior and utilitarian, below his aspirations. At best it was a route into literature.

Before he achieved the heights of fame, Kapuściński once said sadly and rather enviously to a friend who was a writer and translator: 'You are a poet in the Polish Writers Union, but I'm just a journalist'.

Most certainly not 'just'.

34

Legends 4: Kapuściński and Kapuściński

Now I understand better the intuition I have felt since starting to write this account: Ryszard Kapuściński – the hero of Ryszard Kapuściński's books – is also a fictional character.

Yes, of course, he has a great deal in common with the prototype. The literary Kapuściński is an invaluable ally in understanding the real Kapuściński. He reveals, so clearly that it couldn't be clearer, what the real Kapuściński would, for example, have liked to forget, erase, hide and burn. The sort of person he would have liked to be, if only now and then, and the way in which he would have liked to be perceived and remembered. The sort of Kapuściński we are to love, the sort we are to admire.

The literary Kapuściński (the one from *Travels with Herodotus*), who starts his career as a journalist in the era of de-Stalinization, has the task of hiding the fact that the real Kapuściński was a journalist earlier, in the era of raging Stalinism.

The literary Kapuściński (the one from *The Soccer War*, and also from many interviews), who is going to be shot by the Belgians at Usumbura, suggests that we are to admire the real Kapuściński as a fearless, macho adventurer.

The non-literary (but 'invented', in fine literary style) Kapuściński who befriended Che Guevara, Lumumba and Allende, and even knew the cruel Amin, creates the legend of the real Kapuściński: isn't someone who was on such close terms with all those legends a legend himself?

Yes, the real Kapuściński – the theoretician of literary reportage – is right: by 'reworking reality', by 'rebuilding' it, one can obtain the 'higher truth' and understand the 'deeper meaning'. For instance, the meaning of the dreams and yearnings of the person writing.

The real Kapuściński did not like to confide, confront or look in the mirror. He had secrets, many secrets – as one of his close friends says – personal, political, and as a writer. The literary Kapuściński reveals only some of them to us, in fact not many, but he does help us – contrary to the wishes of the real Kapuściński – to get at least a brief look into the soul of the real one. Even so, we know that 'brief' is a lot: in non-fiction we never get to know the hero entirely, something always remains undiscovered, uncertain and incomprehensible.

I am comparing the real Kapuściński with the literary Kapuściński, and yet both of them are as genuine as could be. One is the mirror image of the other. They are one and the same person.

Because the Kapuściński who is immersed in fiction and invention, the literarily processed Kapuściński, who is also doubly on his guard, opens the door to the real one, to understanding who he really was and what he really thought.

35

Our Friend Rysiek

Jerzy Nowak, his closest friend for almost half a century, lists several of 'Rysiek's essential traits':

Above all, from when they first met, he has been characterized by strong independence of mind and self-reliance. He listens to others but does not yield readily to suggestions; he trusts his own senses, observations and evaluations. When his friends criticize details in one of his texts, he is capable of angrily tearing it up in their presence, though in the corrected version he rarely takes notice of critical comments.

He is a particular kind of pessimist – whatever evil might happen, it has to happen anyway, it has to do its thing.

He combines erudition and the approach of the intellectual reporter with a simplicity that gives some people the impression of his being a rather ignorant simpleton or an exceptionally modest man. He is neither of those. He has an inner sense of greatness, or rather a belief in the significance of what he writes.

He tends to be given to passions – personal as well as political ones.

He is sensitive to falsehood – he easily detects it in people and in the written word.

World fame does not change him one iota, at least not in relation to his closest friends.

He listens carefully, but even so he thinks and writes what he wants to.

He cannot cope with popularity. He is incapable of saying no – to meetings, interviews, invitations – although in time he will learn to. (Alicja will act as a barrier, and so will the answering machine, saying in his voice: 'This is telephone number XXXX, please leave a message after the beep. Thank you.')

In friendship he is guided by the principle that you forgive your friends more.

He often calls and asks what's new or how he can help. He gives you the feeling that he will not let you down in case of need: 'He once admitted to me that for him the measure of friendship was whether a person whom he regarded as a friend was someone with whom he could be in the trenches.'

The chief principle that guides him in life is, Never hurt anyone, even if that does harm to you yourself, even if you have to tell a lie to avoid wounding someone.

One time they do not see each other for five years – the Nowaks are in Buenos Aires, and he is in Mexico City. He cannot visit them because of the visa difficulties that Argentina imposes on correspondents from socialist countries. His letters survive – full of romantic, almost amatory terms. 'My darlings', 'my dearests' . . . There are numerous confessions of how painfully he is missing them, and lots of affection.

> People, you have no idea how much I've missed you! Five years, God in heaven, will you recognize this old man, whom you last saw when he was still a young pup? But now he's got a walking stick, and a bald patch, and dementia, and his eyes are misted over. Son of a gun![1]

Years earlier, in a letter from hospital in Kampala, where he was sick with malaria, Kapuściński drew a heart and wrote next to it: 'I'm sending you my heart'.

When the Nowaks are expecting their second child, he writes a separate note to Izabella:

> Dearest Izabella,
>   I'd like to send you a cheerful message to make you feel relaxed when you go to get the new Krzyś [the name of the Nowaks' first child], but you know I'm not good at jokes, so I'll just wish you no pain at all, my darling, and that's my only wish, because even without my wishes I know you're going to give birth to something just as wonderful as Krzyś, something we're all going to be proud of, from Tierra del Fuego to Mexico City. When I come to Buenos, I promise to spend a whole night awake rocking the creature that will be crying and weeing in its cradle.[2]

After the birth of the 'new Krzyś', who turns out to be Dorota, he writes, 'My joy and emotion, and – frankly – my sense of relief that it all went well are without bounds.'[3]

On Dorota's eighth birthday, Kapuściński writes a little poem called 'Some Ho-Hum Lines Written on Dorota's Birthday':

> In the sunshine birds are singing,
> In the sunshine frogs are springing.
> When the night is gone at dawn,
> The sun comes up to greet the morn.
> Then it shines much hotter,
> And says hello to Dorota.[4]

Dorota Nowak remembers that one day when she was only a few years old and her brother was in his teens, they had a competition to see who could do a headstand. When Kapuściński sees the Nowaks' son standing on his head against a wall, he immediately enters the contest: 'I can do that too, look at this.'

Without a warm-up, in the middle of the room instead of against the wall like Krzyś, Kapuściński tries to stand on his head. When he is nearly there, with his legs in the air, he suddenly loses his balance, and the home-grown athlete crashes to the floor. Krzyś and Dorota burst out laughing. For a while Kapuściński is bewildered and cannot catch his breath, but then he, too, starts laughing, and the moment of danger is over.

When grown-up Dorota takes up equestrian sports and requires money to buy a horse, without hesitation Kapuściński tells her: 'Just say how much you need.' Dorota is coy, and then he says in a slightly louder, paternal tone: 'You mustn't give up your passion! Your passion is the most important thing in life!' And then calmly adds, 'So how much do you need?'

Dorota borrows the money, and he says she doesn't have to pay it back. After Kapuściński's death, she repays the debt to Alicja.

They were neighbours on an estate consisting of four-storey blocks of flats in the working-class Warsaw district of Wola. Kazimierz Bosek is a friend from a totally different sphere to Nowak. Like Kapuściński, he is a journalist, but unlike him, Bosek is ill-disposed towards the PRL.

Right at the time when Kapuściński is a ZMP (Union of Polish Youth) activist at Warsaw University, Bosek – the son of a pre-war police chief – is thrown out of college as a 'class enemy' (he had withheld the information about his father in a form asking for personal details). He is conscripted into a penal army battalion and forced to work in the mines, which years down the line will affect his health.

In over forty years of friendship, the two men avoid conversations on political topics, as they have almost nothing in common on that front.

Their strategies for life are different. Kapuściński knows that nothing is achieved through conflict, so he always smoothes the sharp edges, gets on with his bosses and generally avoids confrontation. When he sees that someone is talking nonsense, he doesn't continue the conversation. 'Yes, yes, of course you're right' – that's the way he closes conversations which aren't going anywhere. Bosek, on the contrary, is the type who always knows better and has to show it; because of this, he often has trouble at the work-place.

They are alike in a different respect, though: both are emotional. They also share similar 'problems' with their daughters. In defiance of her father, Zojka emigrates to Canada, while Bosek's daughter from his first marriage, Agnieszka, goes away to France and gets married there against her father's will. They confide these fatherly experiences to each other, support each other and have instant mutual understanding on these matters.

His friend's flat provides Kapuściński with one of his hiding-places from the world. When Bosek and his second wife, Marzenna Baumann-Bosek, go away on holiday, they leave him the keys (to their new flat in the Sadyba district); in their absence, Kapuściński often spends several weeks there.

He consults Baumann-Bosek, who is also a journalist, about fashion and appearance – how to dress, where to buy clothes of tolerably good style in times when there are not many nice things in the shops. When he starts to go bald, she advises him not to do a comb-over to cover the bald patch because it looks pitiful. 'Just cut it short' is her recommendation.

'When Rysiek started having spinal problems, he couldn't sit down and spent whole days lying on a hard floor, and he became depressed. My husband used to come and cheer him up,' she says. 'In turn, when my husband and I both started to be seriously ill, Rysiek always took an interest in us, gave us psychological support and quite often financial help too.'

When Bosek starts to have exactly the same problems with his circulation (leg pains) as his friend is having, Kapuściński calls Marzenna and gives instructions.

'He mustn't eat fat and absolutely no alcohol.'

'Well, you know he doesn't drink.'

'Ah, no one ever knows that.'

'Rysiek was very fond of Bosek,' says a mutual friend of theirs, 'but he was quite forbearing towards him.'

In the new Poland after 1989, when Bosek campaigned for allowances and pensions for soldier-miners, Kapuściński regarded his friend's efforts without understanding, with indulgence, as a bit of craziness. On the other hand, he appreciated Bosek's passion for the Renaissance poet Jan Kochanowski. Bosek discovered the site of the poet's first burial and brought about the ceremonial interment of his remains in the city of Zwoleń. The patron of the ceremony was Cardinal Franciszek Macharski, and many figures from the world of culture attended.

Thanks to a journey they made together in the mid 1980s to Czarnolas, the village where Kochanowski lived – Kapuściński took his friend there, who had a broken collar-bone and could not drive – he wrote his first poem in thirty years. He included it in *Notebook*, a collection published quite soon after that. (Originally he dedicated these lines to the memory of Kochanowski.) An excerpt:

> Why
> did the world
> fly past me
> so quickly

it did not let itself be held
approached
addressed in the familiar[5]

Bosek, who is the same age as Kapuściński, dies six months before his famous friend. At that moment Kapuściński feels, not for the first time but very acutely, that his days are coming to an end too. He is already weak, with a bad hip and a failing heart.

Wojciech and Maria Giełżyński quickly fall silent, or rather finish their story about their friend before it has really started. He dropped in on them over the years, they ate, drank and felt as if they were having fascinating conversations. But about what? They cannot remember. What did he say, what did he like, what was he like? Now they realize they were the ones who did the talking. Rysiek kept quiet. They knew him, but they didn't know him.

This 'formula' recurs in many people's friendships with Kapuściński.

Many of his acquaintances call him their 'friend' because he let them believe they had made friends. In fact, they knew each other a little, and from time to time they had a nice conversation. Kapuściński created the impression of listening intently. Almost everyone came away from a conversation with him convinced the master thought of him or her as an exceptional person, the most important conversationalist in the world, a pal, a friend, a pupil.

The reporter Wojciech Jagielski tells with a smile how the most trite banalities became pearls of wisdom (in the speaker's imagination) whenever Kapuściński was listening to them:

'That's incredible, how did you find that out?'

'That's a great thing, my heartiest congratulations.'

'Wonderful, what you're telling me is truly wonderful!'

Jagielski says ironically that many people came away from a meeting with Kapuściński feeling six inches taller.

The fat came away feeling thin. The reticent and the boring came away feeling like the most wonderful raconteurs. The average came away feeling outstanding, and the scribblers like virtual Nobel Prize winners.

'Rysiek seduced women, he seduced men, he seduced old people and he seduced children,' says Mariusz Ziomecki, laughing.

Seduction was his strategy for life. He wanted to be loved, and he put a great deal of effort into making his wish come true: he was loved.

Most of his acquaintances – the good ones and the very good ones, the even better ones and the close friends – are convinced he never said a bad word about anyone. 'Just once in a rage he described a certain well-known writer as a "loathsome yid!" ' says a close friend who knew Kapuściński for more than thirty years. The writer in question had behaved despicably, as he saw it. My source stresses that it was the only time he ever heard Kapuściński use such crude words about another person.

A few of his close friends challenge this legend, saying that they often heard him make critical comments about other people. 'A hopeless hack' was how he sometimes dismissed writers whose talents he did not value, even if he liked them very much personally.

'Speak well about everyone' – that was yet another of Rysiek's masks, a strategy for conquest and seduction. Not often, and not with everyone, did he allow himself to be sincere.

Dorota Nowak remembers that Rysiek once praised the merits of a well-known writer in her presence. ' "Among the living Polish writers he is undoubtedly the greatest stylist," ' he said, as she recalls. A few days later, a friend of hers who is a book reviewer for one of the papers recounts a conversation he's had with Kapuściński. They got onto the subject of the 'greatest stylist', and Kapuściński turns out to have told her friend that the 'greatest stylist' is a very poor writer.

Did Rysiek tell each person something different?

Did he tell people what he thought they wanted to hear from him?

Ewa Junczyk-Ziomecka travelled with Kapuściński to Ann Arbor, where he was to give a lecture at the University of Michigan about the fall of the Soviet Union (*Imperium* had recently been published). Just before passport control they were accidentally parted: Junczyk-Ziomecka went through immigration first, and Kapuściński got stuck.

It turned out he did not have the invitation with him, nor did he know what hotel he would be staying at – he had put all the paperwork in his checked luggage. Meanwhile, Junczyk-Ziomecka, who had copies of it with her, had long since gone through passport control. The immigration official started asking Kapuściński all sorts of questions, the way they interrogate someone who seems to be trying to cheat their way into America and then stay there illegally. Kapuściński took one of his books in English out of his bag to prove he really was a writer who had come at the invitation of the university.

'When he finally appeared,' says Junczyk-Ziomecka, 'he started screaming at me so loudly that the airport security people ran up to ask if I needed help. I thought he might even have been capable of hitting me.'

She adds, after a pause, that this sort of behaviour testifies to a close friendship; he would never have let himself lose control of his emotions like that towards someone who wasn't a very good friend.

*   *   *

'He was friendly in a lovely way,' recalls Małgorzata Szejnert, who does not regard herself as a close friend of his but rather as a colleague, an acquaintance.

In the early 1980s, when the authorities had broken up the Solidarity movement, Szejnert wanted to emigrate to America. She was afraid the border guards would turn her back at the airport. Kapuściński offered his support: he would go to the airport with her and watch from a distance to see what happened.

'If they stop you, wave at me. They all know me there, so if anything's wrong I'll go and try to fix it so they let you through.'

Kapuściński waits several hours at the airport. In fact Szejnert does not need his intervention, but she greatly needs his support at such an anxious moment.

A female colleague who is a well-known reporter shares the following memory:

In the early 1990s, when *Imperium* had just been published, a group of reporters from *Gazeta Wyborcza* visited Kapuściński in his study at the house on Prokuratorska Street in Warsaw. It was meant to be an informal, frank conversation between the young reporters and the master. They asked Kapuściński a lot of tricky questions and made quite a lot of critical comments about his new book on the Soviet Union. Only one reporter kept praising him; her colleagues felt she was sucking up to him and, in their view, was talking nonsense.

After the meeting Kapuściński called one of the women reporters who had been at the meeting and with whom he was on friendly terms. He was unhappy with the conversation and complained about the trainee reporters. At one point he said, 'Only one clever girl there.'

'That made me think,' says the woman who was his friend. 'Despite his position as the master, despite his worldwide success, he had a shaky sense of his own value. He liked the cheap, mindless compliments, but the serious conversation had saddened and annoyed him.'

'He had many fine characteristics, and perhaps the finest of all was his unfeigned kindness towards people,' says Wiktor Osiatyński. 'His friends could count on him to listen, to go for a walk, and if he only could, he would help. He also treated the strangers who were introduced to him seriously and kindly.'

I try to confront him with a view I have heard more than once in conversations about Rysiek: he was good at pretending to be listening to others.

'Sometimes it went in one ear and out the other. He really did listen to those who had something interesting to say, especially on the professional front, though he did not usually share his own reflections with them. But I do also remember some profound and fascinating conversations: about how the character of the media and of power in the world is changing, and about the challenges of globalization.'

Other observations by a close friend: he was the type who panics ('What will happen, what will happen?'); he could be awkward in his relations with people, and he sublimated this deficiency in literature.

'Were we good friends? He used to say that of me. Did his friendship make itself felt? Yes indeed, and often. Whenever I was sick he came to visit me in Konstancin. Many times, out of pure altruism he looked for the best doctors for my complaints, for which I am eternally grateful to him and which I was unable to reciprocate. But he also refused various requests – he was capable of being tough towards his close friends.'

Osiatyński feels awkward talking about it, but I know that in fact he was one of the friends who experienced that 'toughness': he had helped to promote *The Emperor* in America and took the book to Alvin Toffler, but years later when he asked Kapuściński for a short note for the cover of his own book, Kapuściński claimed to be too busy.

There were lots of strangers whom he did not refuse. Kapuściński cared about creating a good image, so that no one would think the great writer was too big for his boots, but he did say no to his friend. The books whose covers carried a recommendation from him, or which he reviewed, were often ones he did not value; sometimes he showed his friends piles of them in his study, commenting with irritation, 'Look what they've brought me. Am I supposed to read that? Write about that?'

'But even so I adored him,' adds Osiatyński.

'One more thing: he had a dreadful, agonizing feeling that he had to write, and that if he didn't write, his life was worthless. The only state that justified not writing was illness. Maybe that was the source of his hypochondria? He was always complaining or dying of something, but then he'd pick up his suitcase and go abroad anyway.'

One of his final memories: less than a year before Kapuściński's death they go on a week-long trip together to Siena, where Osiatyński is teaching a short course. They stay in an old monastery that has been converted into a university conference centre. Every day Rysiek goes for a walk in the garden, where he enjoys looking at the flowers, trees and gardening tools. Every day they eat dinner with the academics. Rysiek eats very little and very slowly, so slowly that the dinner hour goes by, and the cooks, waiters and gardeners start laying the table next to theirs for their own dinner.

'Before then he had been engaged in our conversation, but at that point he stopped talking, and with childish delight he started watching those tired people, eating, chatting and laughing. He spoke in admiration of their straightforward manner, coupled with their attention to cleanliness and form. He sat there so intent that I had to drag him away from the table.

Moments like that made me realize that his curiosity about ordinary people was full of respect, devoid of any kind of superiority. Just then I discovered something extremely important about him as a man, and also about how he worked as a reporter. Without that curiosity and respect, there wouldn't have been a Kapuściński.'

36

Where to from Socialism?

Kapuściński lost a unique opportunity to talk about his dedication to the idea of communism. Although he travelled around the collapsing Soviet Union during the last two years of its existence and wrote a famous book about this journey, *Imperium*, he never said a word about his own connection with the idea of communism, which was fundamental to the creation of the empire.

This part of the story began in September 1939, just after the outbreak of war. Little Rysio and his mother and sister are on their way home to Pińsk after their summer holidays, but the Soviet soldiers prevent them from entering the city – they scream, threaten and point their rifles at the small family. Afterwards come hunger, fear, and deportations, and so the Kapuścińskis move from being under Soviet to being under German occupation. *Imperium* is not an 'objective', calmly written history book; it is 'a personal account of a journey', a reflective journal of the author's several 'encounters' with the empire. It is also an account which gives rise to numerous questions.

For example, Kapuściński devotes several dozen pages to his encounter in the late 1960s, but we are not told in what circumstances he went to the Soviet Union on that occasion. Yet these circumstances are not merely worth mentioning, but entirely necessary. He was in fact sent there by the PAP, on whose commission he was meant to write a propaganda piece for the fiftieth anniversary of the October Revolution – a series of reports on the USSR's Central Asian republics. (Slipping out of the trap, he managed to write a fascinating series of articles.)

Kapuściński personally escorts us about the *Imperium* and is present throughout. The exception are passages in which he speaks of the nightmares of the Stalinist terror and the Gulag, and when he deliberates on the nature of Soviet communism, the way it changed victims into executioners and vice versa, and the human costs of this seven-decade experiment. At those points *Imperium* turns into the cold account of a historian and analyst; the Kapuściński who encountered the empire several times vanishes. This account of the Soviet Union seems to be the product of a man who at the start of the Second World War was a victim of Stalin's aggression towards Poland (which he was), and several decades later is travelling about the collapsing superpower as . . . who exactly? A former victim returning to the country of his childhood? An impartial observer from another planet? A historian? Any reader unaware of the author's life story would be entitled to come away with a variety of such impressions.

My sense that the book could be thus interpreted is unintentionally confirmed by a journalist from Hong Kong, who asks me some questions about the master. It was she, a long-time fan of Kapuściński's, who recommended *Imperium* to a Chinese publisher.

'Until now, as a book by an anti-communist, *Imperium* has not been able to appear in China,' she tells me.

'An anti-communist? But for most of his adult life, Kapuściński was a member of the Communist Party.'

'Impossible!' she cries in amazement.

In the book, not once does Kapuściński mention that for nearly his entire adult life he subscribed to the idea that powered the building, and then the politics, of the empire, or that his own country was a sort of province of that empire. What choices did he make at the time? Why those and not others? To say nothing about this seems quite odd in the context of a personal and political reflection on his experiences of the history of the Soviet empire and of the most alluring idea of the twentieth century, which, once realized, ended in a nightmare or, in the most benign instances, failure.

In the spring of 1989, reading the news arriving from Moscow, I thought: It would be worth going there. (Others were pushing me in the same direction, since, whenever it comes to life, Russia starts to interest a lot of people.) It was a time when everyone felt a sense of curiosity about and anticipation of something extraordinary. It seemed then, at the end of the eighties, that the world was entering a period of great metamorphosis, of a transformation so profound and fundamental that it would not bypass anyone, no country or state, and so certainly not the last imperium on earth – the Soviet Union.

A climate conducive to democracy and freedom prevailed increasingly across the world. On every continent, dictatorships fell one after the other: Obote's in Uganda, Marcos's in the Philippines, Pinochet's in Chile. In Latin America, despotic military regimes lost power in favor of more moderate civilian ones, and in Africa the one-party systems that had been nearly ubiquitous (and as a rule grotesque and thoroughly corrupt) were disintegrating and exiting the political stage.

Against this new and promising global panorama the Stalinist–Brezhnevian system of the USSR looked more and more anachronistic, like a decaying and ineffectual relic. But it was an anachronism with a still-powerful and dangerous force. The crisis that the Imperium was undergoing was followed throughout the world with attention, but with anxious attention – everyone was aware that this was a power equipped with weapons of mass destruction that could blow up our planet. Yet the possibility of this gloomy and alarming scenario nevertheless did not mask the satisfaction and universal relief that communism was ending and that there was in this fact some sort of irreversible finality.

Germans say Zeitgeist, the spirit of the times. It is a fascinating moment, fraught with promise, when this spirit of the times, dozing pitifully and apathetically, like a huge wet bird on a branch, suddenly and without a clear reason (or at any rate without a reason allowing of an entirely rational explanation) unexpectedly takes off into bold and joyful flight. We can all hear the shush of this flight. It stirs our imagination and gives us energy: we begin to act.[1]

The spirit of the times takes Kapuściński to the Vorkuta mines and the old forced-labour camps at Magadan and Kolyma.

There were 160 camps – or, as they are also called, Arctic death camps – in Magadan and Kolyma. The convicts changed over the years, but at any given moment there were around half a million residents. Of these, one-third died in the camps, and the rest, after serving years of hard labor, left as physical cripples or with permanent psychic injuries. Whoever survived Magadan and Kolyma was never again the person he or she once was.

The camp was a sadistically and precisely thought-out structure, having as its goal the destruction of the individual in such a way that before death he would experience the greatest humiliations, sufferings, and torments. It was a barbed net of destruction from which a man, once having fallen into it, could not extricate himself.[2]

When did he find out about all this? Did the Kapuścińskis, who escaped from Pińsk in fear of being deported, ever return to the experience in their family conversations? Did the eighteen-year-old Rysiek set about building socialism with knowledge – if only displaced – of the Soviet system, believing that in Poland it would be different? Or did he only later find out about the atrocities of Soviet Stalinism? When?

I am not asking these questions with a view to 'squaring accounts' or 'hunting Reds', as was fashionable after the fall of real socialism. I have neither the right nor the desire to pillory anyone. I simply wish to understand my hero better, and perhaps to find out something universal: what are the mechanisms that make it possible to reconcile irreconcilable information about crimes with one's dreams of a better world? And I'd like to find that out from Kapuściński.

If he had not written *Imperium*, would I be asking these questions? Yes, but less adamantly. I would have recognized that behind the lack of public consideration of his own former involvement hide trauma, pain, a secret. But here, in *Imperium*, Kapuściński himself takes us on a tour of the Soviet Union, of the camps, of the history of the Stalinist purges, the specific facts of Soviet colonialism, which is different from the British or Spanish variety. He invites us to talk about this topic; more than that, he draws up a tally of the injustices and losses, but – in what is ultimately a personal account – he says not a word about himself or his own belief in the idea which engendered the Union of Soviet Socialist Republics. Absolutely nothing. With his talent for observing human attitudes and behaviour, with his unique capacity for empathy, he could have brought something new to our knowledge of the history of communism and of the twentieth century. Instead of which he offers interesting and not necessarily original thoughts, but they are sterile, bereft of personal perspective.

Perhaps only once – and even this is not certain – does he come close to confronting his own résumé, when he writes:

> One walks along the streets of Magadan through high-walled corridors dug out in the snow. They are narrow, and when another person is passing one must stop to let him by. Sometimes at such a moment I find myself standing face-to-face with some elderly man. Always, one question comes to my mind: And who were you? The executioner or the victim?
>
> And why am I moved to wonder? Why am I unable to look at this man in an ordinary way, without that perverse and intrusive curiosity? For if I could summon up my courage and ask him this question, and if he responded sincerely, I might hear the answer: 'You see, you have before you both the executioner and the victim'.
>
> This too was a characteristic of Stalinism – that in many instances it was impossible to distinguish these two roles. First someone, as an interrogating officer, would beat a prisoner, then he himself would be thrown into prison and beaten; after serving his sentence he would get out and take revenge, and so on. It was the world as a closed circle, from which there was only one exit – death. It was a nightmarish game in which everyone lost.[3]

When I think about Kapuściński's life and the times in which he made his political and personal choices, other questions arise. Even in the worst years, communism in Poland cannot by any measure be compared with communism inside the Soviet Union. With the exception of a few years of

Stalinism, which claimed thousands of murder victims, real socialism in the PRL was probably – may those who suffered harm forgive me – one of the mildest dictatorships of the second half of the twentieth century. Therefore, putting the question 'Were you the executioner or the victim?' to Kapuściński makes no sense. Others do, however: What did he know about all this? Had he heard of the camps or the frozen hell of the Gulag, as he picked up a pencil and sketched his poem in honour of Stalin? Did that poem ring in his ears as he filled the pages of *Imperium* with facts about the Soviet tyrant's crimes?

I am not demanding remorse or self-criticism – I just want to understand. I would like to hear the voice of a man with unique experience behind him: victim of the empire, then builder of a province obedient to imperial power, witness to the disintegration of Western colonialism in Asia and Africa, observer of countless revolutions, uprisings and coups, chronicler of human poverty and greatness, human dreams and cruelties on many geographical latitudes. But instead of his voice – that most exceptional voice – there is silence. A silence I find disappointing and grating – and which I am also trying to understand.

Wiktor Osiatyński thinks that the atmosphere in Poland after 1989 was not one in which one could talk unguardedly about one's own experiences with communism, including Party activities, ambiguous choices and compromises. Perhaps this is the key to Kapuściński's silence on the topic of his own involvement. How many former Party activists, especially people in the spotlight, politicians, journalists, artists and cultural figures, were subjected to a public lynching without any inquiry into individual blame or any effort to understand their life stories or the tangled history of one's own country? The so-called squaring of accounts was a tool in the fight for power, a whip to beat the enemy, picked up whenever it brought applause and votes. As he was thin-skinned, fearful of confrontation and sickened by polemic, Kapuściński hadn't the slightest chance of levelling with his past under such conditions, of talking about it without fear of being spat at and stamped on.

Now it occurs to me that *Imperium* was in fact a chance of this kind – the only one he ever had. Perhaps a personal account by the greatest living reporter about his belief in communism, his hopes and disappointments, built into a journey around the collapsing Soviet Union, would not have got him into any trouble at all. Perhaps an unforced account – because, at that point, those who were eager for decommunization and lustration (the public exposure of those who had collaborated with the secret police) had not yet waylaid Kapuściński – would have had the quality of an intellectual journey into the past, a search for the truth about himself and all the people who were captivated by a great idea. Even if he had been attacked, he would have had armies of defenders, both in Poland and abroad.

He evidently wanted to forget about the past, not discuss it or grapple with it. His literary and civic activity at the time martial law was introduced suggests he found his Red past a burden, and didn't know how to handle it, what attitude and strategies to adopt towards it. It is only now, having taken a three-year tour of Kapuściński's life, that I sense this. As I read *Imperium* now, for the first time I hear a false note. I would like to know what sort of thoughts and feelings prey on a man as he writes about crimes, when his own past work includes a poem written years ago in honour of the criminal. What does the sixty-year-old, wiser with age, think of the eighteen-year-old who is filled with excitement or the twenty-something who has seen a great deal but cannot yet have understood much? What would the older man have to say to the younger one?

One of his friends offers the following thought in the form of a question: 'Maybe he wouldn't have said anything? He knew a lot, a great deal about the world, and about other people, but he knew little about himself. He didn't know himself.'

The 1980s mark the start of Kapuściński's great international career, but also of troubles with his own past. He has already left the Party, he rejects his former comrades' offers ('Choose whatever posting you like in the Third World'), goes to masses for the motherland, and occasionally appears at underground SDP (Polish Journalists Association) meetings but does not become openly involved on the side of the illegal Solidarity union. Something stops him. His own résumé? Definitely. But there is another reason, too: he wants to go abroad, and openly declaring himself to be on the side of the underground opposition could, at least in the first half of the 1980s, complicate if not prevent trips abroad on grants, lecture tours, and, above all, events surrounding the foreign publication of his books.

In his personal notes for 1982 he writes, with some irritation:

A man of compromise, flexible. In Poland such people are not liked. They'll say he's ambiguous. Here a person has to be unambiguous. Either black or white. Either here or there. Either with us, or with them. Plainly, openly, without hesitation! Our vision is Manichaean, front-line. We get upset if anyone disturbs this high-contrast image. This arises from the lack of a liberal or democratic tradition with a wide range of shades. Instead we have a tradition of fighting, extreme situations, the ultimate gesture.[4]

Where has the activist gone, who 'openly and without hesitation' sided with the ZMP revolution, clamoured from the 'front line' for the changes of October '56, and in his reports from revolutions in the Third World declared himself – in 'Manichaean' style – to be 'opposed to complications', who liked 'unambiguous' situations and stayed faithful to them for so long?

Age does its work. Kapuściński is over fifty and has seen a lot. He knows too much to keep painting the world in black and white, on top of which he is having trouble with his old commitments – that is why he now sings the praises of compromise and flexibility, and feels the lack of 'a liberal or democratic tradition with a wide range of shades'. He records the state of his own 'political' spirit in a poem (after a thirty-year hiatus, he returns to poetry):

> Ah yes
>
> it took a long time
> before I learned to think about man
> as a human being
> before I discovered this way of thinking
> before I took this path
> in this salutary direction
> and speaking of man or contemplating him
> I stopped asking such questions as
> is he white or black
> an anarchist or monarchist
> fashionable or outmoded
> ours or theirs
> and I began to ask
> what in him is of human being . . .[5]

This is the confession not only of a mature man who is increasingly aware of the shadow line, not only of a successful writer acclaimed at home and abroad but also of a person at a political turning-point, for whom the questions of black or white, Party man or Solidarity member, oppositionist or defender of the status quo are awkward.

Only once does he try to level openly with the past, but it is a mere sketch for the argument which he will never develop, never wring out of himself. In *Lapidarium* he writes:

Those who lived through Stalinism, and those who find out about it from books and stories, cannot understand each other, because they are living on entirely different levels of information; it is not just about the fact that someone didn't know, but also that he preferred not to know or refused to know: to ask a jarring question disliked by the authorities was a suicidal act. A ZMP instructor had to report on meetings to the board, telling not just what sort of statements were made, but who asked what questions.[6]

This internal fight as he grapples with himself can also be seen in his social and political behaviour. He goes out for a drink with his old comrades, meets with government spokesman Jerzy Urban (though refusing his offers) and takes advantage of minor assistance from an old Party comrade, but admits in his personal notes:

> They point out to him that he has changed. But does that deserve condemnation? You have to start with the question, From whom has he changed to whom? They reproach him for having taken what was on offer in the past. They think badly of him for refusing to take any more. They have lost a partner – hence their fury. It's the typical morality of the criminal gang: bonded by complicity in abuse. The moment you cease to do evil, you are doomed to condemnation on the part of those whom you have exposed through your act of refusal. The longer you stay in the gang, the more you will feel doomed to the gang. One day you want to leave the gang. But at once the question will arise: Will the other side accept me as one of them? The force that makes us stay in the gang is not so much fear of the gangsters' revenge, as concern that we won't be accepted by the people outside the gang.[7]

The other side will, however, accept and applaud him; after all, its participants include many people with exactly the same political biography as he – former communists whom real socialism has disappointed, but just a little earlier.

And once again he sides with the revolution!

In May 1987 Kapuściński receives an invitation to a meeting with Lech Wałęsa, who has just mustered several dozen opposition activists and sympathetic cultural figures to meet at a church on Żytna Street in Warsaw. After the meeting Kapuściński notes:

> 31.5. Meeting with Wałęsa. Those he invited included Łapicki, Samsonowicz, Osmańczyk, Beksiak, Edelman, Strzelecki, Turowicz and Tischner. I hadn't seen Wałęsa for a long time. He has greatly matured. At one point I thought he reminds me of Witos.[8]

Eighteen months later, from the initial group invited by Wałęsa, the 135-member Citizens' Committee (KO) emerges, which, at the Round Table talks and without the firing of a single shot, negotiates with the PRL government to end real socialism. At the time Kapuściński, who is formally a member of the KO, will be touring the Soviet Union as it decays from the inside, observing the disintegration process as it happens within the empire, without which the Round Table in Poland, the end of the old system, and the fall of the socialist bloc would be impossible.

★   ★   ★

In the new Poland, following the change of system, he burns his bridges with the past.

In October 1989, there is a reception at the Hotel Marriott to mark the visit of King Juan Carlos of Spain. Kapuściński bumps into an old comrade from the Party diplomatic pack, Stanisław Jarząbek. A broad smile, a warm embrace, it's been ages! But soon Jarząbek sees Kapuściński go pale and stiffen, and from an old chum he changes into a cold stranger – and suddenly walks off.

'His first reaction was natural, friendly, but shortly thereafter he realized he had made a faux pas. He was there in the company of Bronisław Geremek and his colleagues from Solidarity; he must have been aware that I, a comrade from a different era, was a shady customer, and that in this new environment it wasn't right for him to admit to such intimacies. After that I watched him for the rest of the evening; he didn't step away from people on the new team, perhaps to avoid bumping into any of his old pals, a good many of whom were circulating at the party. That was the decisive moment when I changed my mind about Rysiek.'

Some time later a similar situation arises. Following a funeral mass for an old acquaintance, Henryk Sobieski, a colleague from the same old guard as Jarząbek comes up to Kapuściński. He tries to give him an effusive greeting, but comes up against a brick wall. 'What's up, Rysiek, times have changed and you don't want to know your old friends anymore?'

'Sobieski said it very loud, plainly to draw attention to himself,' says a witness to the event. People in the church began to look round, and Kapuściński hurried off in another direction.

The message behind both these situations is spelled out by a social clash that occurs in a totally different milieu. Shortly after the change of regime in Poland, Kapuściński is talking to his close friend and translator Agata Orzeszek and a friend of hers who is an avowed anti-communist. The friend puts Kapuściński in the firing line: 'All your life you were a Party man, but what about now? You've made yourself so pro-Solidarity, you've followed the herd, gone with the environment.'

'She's not very bright,' says Orzeszek later, once they are alone.

'You know, she's not so dumb at all. It's true I've gone with the environment. Who should I have gone with?'

What does 'gone with the environment' mean?

Like most leading figures in the world of journalism, Kapuściński greets the end of real socialism with relief and enthusiastically supports the new, democratic market order. First of all, he supports Lech Wałęsa's candidates in the partly democratic elections to the Sejm and the Senate held in 1989, when they rout the *ancien régime*. Then, for the most important issues of systemic transformation, he stands alongside the liberal intelligentsia: among other things, initially he approves of Leszek Balcerowicz's shock therapy, which transforms the planned economy into a neo-liberal version of a market economy (so his friends remember, because Kapuściński never made any public statements on this topic).

When former comrades from the fight against 'the commune' start to argue about power and the road to a better future, Kapuściński, like the majority of the liberal intelligentsia, supports the first non-communist prime minister, Tadeusz Mazowiecki, in his dispute with the recent Solidarity leader, Lech Wałęsa. During the 1990 presidential elections, which Mazowiecki loses, Kapuściński is a member of his election committee, as are many other stars of the cultural and academic world.

In the parliamentary elections of the 1990s he supports the Democratic Union and its continuation, the Freedom Union, both of which defend Leszek Balcerowicz's social and economic course and believe that to transform Poland into a democratic, capitalist country it is necessary to gain wide public consensus, tighten their belts and restrain social claims (he lends his name to honorary election committees, which involves no effort). Like most of the liberal intelligentsia, he expresses a dislike – only in conversations with friends, never writing anything about it – of squaring accounts with former communists, of witch-hunting or reproaching people for the past. He anxiously watches the expansion of the Church into the political sphere and its attempts at creating a confessional state.

In spring 1991, in a letter to Nowak, who is then Poland's ambassador to Austria, Kapuściński outlines the atmosphere in the new Poland following the early political shocks:

Dearest Jurek,

Just a few words to tell you I'm still alive and haven't forgotten you. I miss seeing and talking to you very much. The desertion from Poland of lively, curious minds still continues, unfortunately, and it's hard to find anyone here whom you can talk to in a down-to-earth and interesting way. By and large there's nothing sensational happening here. The situation is full of extremely bizarre contradictions, but then every revolution is typified by that sort of state of affairs.

The Khomeini-ization of the country is getting ever more intense. The mess and the political fragmentation are immense, and the brutalization of political life is huge and painful too. But there's more talking than real political or personal decision-making. In other words, far more slandering than actual beheading.

Yesterday evening, 3 May, I was at a reception at the Castle given by the President. It turned out much better than expected. I talked to Wałęsa for a while. He said he's very affected by it all, which makes it hard for him to maintain the calm and detachment appropriate to his function. In short, he shared his impressions of what it's like when you become president.

I talked longer to Balcerowicz, and he asked me chiefly about the situation in the USSR. The impression of the new team [of Jan Krzysztof Bielecki, who became prime minister after Wałęsa's presidential victory in December 1990]: they are still feeling rather unsure in the saddle, but they're doing their best to be likeable and to make a good impression.

I think the most important thing in the country is a slight improvement in the atmosphere. There are lots of new shops opening, you can buy everything, here and there you see some beneficial changes, there are all sorts of new initiatives (especially out of town), in short, you can see a few brighter points.[9]

As his home turf in the new Poland, Kapuściński chooses *Gazeta Wyborcza*, the biggest opinion-forming daily paper, established at the moment of transformation by people who came from the underground press, and run by legendary democratic oppositionist Adam Michnik. The paper's political line determines (or expresses) the position of a large proportion of the liberal intelligentsia in Poland's major public debates after communism.

Kapuściński drops in at the *Gazeta* office on Iwicka Street, later Czerska Street, not to work but to visit, for a bit of friendly gossip. He likes to know what's being discussed. He meets familiar people, gets to know the new generation of journalists, and creates a positive aura around himself. During his regular visits, once a month or sometimes every second month – as long as he's in the country – he usually looks in on the deputy editors: Helena Łuczywo and his old friends from the PRL press, Juliusz Rawicz and Ernest Skalski.

'Helena and I have established an iron principle: we don't talk about *Gazeta*,' he once told me, and shortly afterwards related some anecdotes demonstrating that the main topic of conversation was in fact *Gazeta*.

'So what do you talk about?'

'Everything; what's going on here and there, what's happening in Poland and abroad.'

(That is how I remember the exchange, to which I attached no significance; at the time it had never occurred to me that one day Rysiek would die and I would write his biography.)

After he was gone, I asked Helena Łuczywo herself what she and Rysiek talked about. She thought for awhile, and replied that she couldn't remember anything in particular. 'The news, current affairs.'

Kapuściński needed to feel a sense of belonging. He was usually independent-minded – perhaps with the exception of the first few years of democracy, when he 'went along with the environment' – but he understood that for success you need not just work and talent, but also a group that supports you, giving you strength, approval, and safety. He believed that a journalist, reporter or feature writer needs friendly surroundings where his work can flourish. And *Gazeta Wyborcza*, with which he felt far more connected than distanced regarding Polish affairs, proved to be just such a place for him. The differences between his and the newspaper's positions, which crop up to a minor extent in the late 1990s and in international affairs after the attacks of 11 September 2001 in New York and Washington, never lead to open conflict or a parting of the ways. Kapuściński remains on friendly terms with *Gazeta*, its chiefs and its many journalists to the end.

Just as in the previous era he first published each new book in instalments in the weekly *Kultura*, so in the new times he does exactly the same in *Gazeta*. This is the way *Imperium*, *The Shadow of the Sun*, *Travels with Herodotus* and volumes of *Lapidarium* get published. As he used to say, having the weekly discipline was the only way he could be mobilized to write systematically; it provided an obligation that permitted him to drop the perfectionism that was so fatal for creativity, that prevented him from accepting his incomplete knowledge of a topic and held him back from starting work on a book.

His writing, too, also shows evidence of going along with the environment. How much of his grappling with his own past involves adjusting his views to fit the new times? How much is the genuine evolution of those views? How much is plain disorientation – totally understandable at the time of a historical watershed?

In his notes from the early 1990s he writes:

> The tragedy of the former communists: that they remain in the orbit of the issue of communism. Obsessively, incurably. Their entire thinking, their activity is animated, powered, motivated first of all by the fight for communism, and after that the fight against communism.[10]

It is striking to see the former communists presented as 'they'. The comment that comes to mind is that Kapuściński is having trouble coming to terms with his own past – which is the attitude of many people who have had similar experiences.

Further on he writes:

> The environment also forces the former communist to keep harping on the issue of communism (why he joined, why he withdrew, et cetera). The environment puts pressure especially on those who are capable of saying or writing something. Meanwhile, these very people often have

little to say, because they have been living in good conditions and never came up against the crimes of the system. The fact is, the system was anonymous and relied on anonymous people, on a colourless, nameless army of bureaucrats, policemen, inspectors, guards and informers. The entire fiendishness of the system lay in its greyness, fogginess and mediocrity, in its shabbiness and torpor.[11]

This is hugely imprecise: the system also counted among the ranks of its faithful people from the world of culture, scholars and journalists; it had an attractive – up to a point – social programme, and a vision for the future that fired the imagination. Whence the suggestion that only victims of the system and people living in poor conditions within that system can have anything essential to say about communism?

During the 1990s, in his *Lapidaria*, Kapuściński sometimes happens to refer to the Marxists this, the Marxists that, 'against the expectations of the Marxists'. He points out Marx's incorrect prophecies, for example that the working class would eliminate capitalism, when we are actually witnessing how capitalism eliminates the working class. He says nothing about the role of Marxist thought in his own intellectual biography for several decades: he himself was a Marxist. As with the former communists, the Marxists become 'them'.

Perhaps it was because of a desire to erase the past (possibly out of fear that while hunting former Reds, someone will remember his past?) that he affirmed the view that 'nowadays there is no left or right, there are just people with an open, liberal, receptive mentality, turned towards the future, and people with a closed, sectarian, restricted mentality, turned towards the past'.[12] In so doing, Kapuściński repeats the thinking of intellectuals such as Leszek Kołakowski or the British sociologist and ideologue Anthony Giddens, who, in saying good-bye to the left, applauded the post–Cold War shift in politics towards the centre and heralded the utopia of the purported 'end of History'.

Nearly a decade later, Kapuściński says his farewells to this line of thought – alien to everything he has written his entire life, everything with which he has identified, and of which he has been in favour. Soon he will re-adopt his left-wing thinking and return to the person he was before 1989 – but in a new language, more palatable in the era of 'the end of History'.

Meanwhile the mainstream declares him 'Journalist of the Century'.

In 1999 the trade monthly *Press* invites fifty well-known Polish press, radio and television journalists to cast their votes. Each of them offers the names of three people in the media whose achievements set an example for future practitioners of the profession.

Kapuściński wins the vote, against such candidates as Jerzy Turowicz, Jerzy Giedroyc, Melchior Wańkowicz, Adam Michnik, Hanna Krall and Ksawery Pruszyński.

Ryszard Kapuściński is the grand master of reportage. His works have gained recognition not just for professional technique, but also for literary language and idiosyncratic turn of phrase.[13]

This is an era of laurels at home and abroad: statuettes, honorary doctorates, lectures . . . He is at the height of his fame. In Italy, Sweden, the Spanish-speaking world, and – though to a lesser degree – the Anglo-Saxon countries, he is treated like a top celebrity, the grand master of reportage, an eminent writer. As a master of the journalist's profession, Gabriel García Márquez invites him to the school of reportage that he has founded at Cartagena.

It seems Kapuściński has nothing more to achieve.

37

Lapidarium 5: Was Kapuściński a Thinker?

It is a reporter's dream to be recognized as a writer. It is a writer's dream to be recognized as a thinker.

The road to this dream is paved with Kapuściński's *Lapidaria* – his books of brief reflections, quotes from philosophers, fragments of reportage in miniature, loose notes, and, more rarely, broader analyses of things happening around the world. Each successive volume of the five *Lapidaria* is more sparing in form than its predecessors, evolving towards collections of 'golden thoughts'. The books are uneven.

Where did the *Lapidaria* come from?

This is Adam Daniel Rotfeld's hypothesis: 'He wanted his writing to be comprehensible to a wide audience, but at the same time he was ashamed that because of the simplicity with which he told his stories, the great would regard him as a nonentity. That was why he thought up the *Lapidaria* – full of quotations from clever books and comments on various themes; unfortunately, not always the best, sometimes annoying and pretentious. As if he wanted to show us: "I read a lot too, I'm an intellectual too". There was no need.'

'Why do you publish your *Lapidaria*, Rysiek?' Wiktor Osiatyński asks him one day.

'Because people want to read them.'

'Why don't you write a serious book about the things you touch on there?'

No reply. Just a smile.

'Nowadays', Osiatyński tells me, 'the *Lapidaria* seem better to me than they used to, because Rysiek is no longer here. It's fabulous that he left something like that behind!'

'Was he a thinker?'

'He wanted to be regarded as a thinker, and in a way he succeeded. He was an invited guest at universities, he went and gave lectures around the world. But in my view he wasn't a thinker.'

'Why not?'

'A thinker makes generalizations, creates syntheses and looks for similarities. Rysiek was the opposite – he looked for differences, his world was the world of detail, and he was brilliant at showing those details, the various colours of the world.'

'Did you ever learn anything from him that you have never read in any book by a contemporary thinker?'

'What he said about globalization was an intellectual discovery for me: that here we are watching globalization on CNN, but meanwhile vast stretches of the world are going through the opposite process – de-globalization, which means separating themselves from the rest. All over Africa in the immediately post-colonial era, you could communicate in English and French; nowadays in many of the cities on that continent, apart from the major metropolises, you have to know the local languages in order to communicate. That is one of the signs of de-globalization which he noticed, and which many Western thinkers have not.'

He could be original and innovative – for instance, in his investigation of the world-views that were the sources of colonialism, conquest and the crimes of the twentieth century:

> The ideology of the slave traders was based on the belief that the black man is not human, that mankind is divided into humans and subhumans, and that with the latter one can do as one will – preferably, exploit their labour and then dispose of them. In the notes and records maintained by these traders is laid out (although in a primitive form) the entire later ideology of racism and totalitarianism, with its core thesis that the Other is the enemy; worse – subhuman. The philosophy that inspired the construction of Kolyma and Auschwitz, one of obsessive contempt and hatred, vileness and brutality, was formulated and set down centuries earlier by the captains of the *Martha* and the *Progresso*, the *Mary Ann* and the *Rainbow*, as they sat in their cabins gazing out the portholes at groves of palm trees and sun-warmed beaches, waiting aboard their ships anchored off the islands of Sherbro, or Zanzibar, for the next batch of black slaves to be loaded.[1]

In the nineteenth century, contempt for the 'subhuman' was barely noticeable within Europe. Kapuściński's reflection expands our knowledge of 'the origins of totalitarianism' – to quote the title of a fundamental work by Hannah Arendt – as it appeared in the next century. It is as if he were asking, Are the cruelties that the Europeans inflicted on each other in the twentieth century all that surprising, given that they inflicted them on others earlier? Why did the Europeans notice them only when they were the ones affected, when it backfired on them, and not earlier? What does that tell us about European consciousness?

Kapuściński presented Western readers with many stories about their world as seen from the perspective of the South; he was not the first or the only one, but he did belong to a small company of popular, fairly widely read writers who adopted this non-Eurocentric viewpoint.

Here is another reflection on the history of the twentieth century from a point of view other than the usual Western one – concerning the map of the world:

> [I]n the middle of our century the Third World woke up. This was an extraordinary historical event. The twentieth century was unique, not just because of the experience of totalitarianism, but also because of the birth of the Third World. If we place a political map of the world in the first half of the century alongside a map dating from the second half, we see two completely different worlds. On the first map the world was arranged hierarchically. The earth was dominated by a few independent countries, and the rest of the world had the status of colonies, semi-colonies or dominions. Everything was part of a structure ruled by Western Europe and the US. Today we are looking at a completely different world. We can see almost two hundred independent states, and we have a map without colonies, semi-colonies or protectorates . . .
>
> The domination of the stronger over the weaker has assumed different, more subtle and complicated forms.
>
> . . . [T]he second half of our century is the era of major, final decolonization, the political promotion of hundreds of tribes, nationalities and nations, their entry onto the world stage, their gradual transformation from the objects into the subjects of history. This change and this promotion have opened the way for the civilization process, for mass migration from villages to cities, a movement that has taken on a global scale.[2]

And the issue of dignity? Kapuściński stubbornly maintained that revolutions do not necessarily erupt because people have no bread – not first and foremost – but because they can no longer put up with the humiliation, the contempt of their rulers, or the violation of their dignity. This is a factor that is not appreciated by the professional commentators, including historians, political scientists and political philosophers.

When does it result in revolution? When are people capable of taking action against tyranny? As soon as the fear breaks down, when one lone person in the crowd stops fearing the policeman and then others follow him, copy him and step into a new world – without fear: 'the man [in the crowd] has stopped being afraid . . . this is precisely the beginning of the revolution.'[3] In Poland, Iran, Chile, Mexico . . . everywhere.

What about his comments on the Third World and poverty?

My main topic is the life of the poor. That is how I understand the concept of the Third World. The Third World is not a geographical term (Asia, Africa, Latin America) or a racial one (the so-called coloured continents), but an existential one. It refers to the life of poverty that will be typified by stagnation, structural inertia, a tendency to regress, a constant threat of the ultimate collapse, and a general lack of alternatives. Poverty has many forms, lots of masks and shapes, lots of shreds and holes, rust and stumps, rags and patches.[4]

He cites the brilliant discovery which in the early 1980s did the most to change daily life in many parts of Africa – the plastic container!

A dozen years ago, this container revolutionized life in Africa. Water is the sine qua non of survival in the tropics. Because there is generally no plumbing here and water is scarce, one must carry it over long distances, sometimes ten or more kilometres. For centuries, heavy clay or stone vessels were used for this purpose . . . Then the plastic container appeared. A miracle! A revolution! First of all it is relatively inexpensive . . . it costs around two dollars. Most important, however, it is light. And it comes in various sizes, so even a small child can fetch several litres of water.

All the children carry water. You see entire flocks of youngsters, play- ing and teasing one another as they walk to a distant spring. What a relief this is for the exhausted African woman! What a transformation in her life! How much more time she now has for herself, for her household![5]

He had an unconventional view of the Cold War, which for half a century 'was regarded as the central, in fact the only conflict, which obscured all other conflicts and problems. All that counted was how many bombs one lot had, and how many the others had. Who had what influences and where.' This thinking, he believed, has been transferred into the contempo- rary scene, hence the surprise at the attacks of 9/11, hence ideas involving 'spreading democracy' by way of war, hence disregard for the dangers posed by global poverty – the biggest bomb threatening the planet.

Kapuściński often noticed things that escaped the attention of those who have the status of thinkers. He did not express his observations in the language of theory, but simply, in a way that was comprehensible to a mass audience, in exactly the same way his reportage was framed. As one of my sources says, 'He was innovative and original wherever he came into personal contact with another land, smelled another reality; wherever he toiled and sweated. The "library" Kapuściński was flat and derivative.'

But he did have 'library' ambitions, too. In the *Lapidaria* and in inter- views, he often argued with the most famous Western thinkers of the post– Cold War era.

Above all, the end of the Cold War is misunderstood. It is regarded as the end of conflicts and wars in general. The most prominent expression of this way of thinking was Francis Fukuyama's essay 'The End of History', published in 1989. Fukuyama's reasoning was as follows: history is over, because communism has collapsed, and for liberal democracy there is no political alternative. The system of liberal democracy functions best in the United States, ergo it will automatically be adopted by everyone, as it is the most rational system. Thus history as a certain drama, collision or rivalry has come to an end . . .

This position – that liberal democracy wins out as the only possible variant for the development of mankind – has brought in its wake two practical consequences: the rapid development of consumerism as a philosophy for life, and the radical transformation of the mass media into tools for entertainment . . . Our entire world has become a great big amusement centre. Entertainment has become the main content of culture. And as both consumption and entertainment demand peace and a pleasant atmosphere, the media have started to create this atmosphere for us, by shifting the world's real problems out of our sight: poverty, hunger, diseases and wars.

Thanks to this we have forgotten that we, the people of the West, are only a small part of mankind on our planet, and that our entertainment and amusement is accompanied by a deepening division in the world, growing inequalities. The world is starting to divide into a 20 percent minority of people who benefit and an 80 percent majority of people who are marginalized. It is not just about real poverty or hunger, but also a sense of being marginalized; an internal grudge, the bitterness and frustration of people who can see that in the race for ever more splendid consumer products there is no room for them.[6]

He never developed his polemics into the form of a longer essay or a book; he challenged both Fukuyama and another American political scientist, Samuel Huntington, with short commentaries in the *Lapidaria*, but nothing more.

After meeting Fukuyama in person in Warsaw, he made subtle fun of him:

20 November 2001.

A day with Francis Fukuyama. I was intrigued by his way of thinking, his view of the world.

Fukuyama is middle-aged, modest and polite. His manner, his conduct towards others is calm and courteous, not to say shy, whereas in debate he is a very tricky partner, or to be more precise, it is impossible to debate with him at all, because he doesn't allow an exchange of opinions to happen. He has a ready answer to each question, which he presents immediately, without hesitation, in a confident tone, brooking no opposition. In this thinking there is no room for doubt, no question marks or scepticism. If there's a problem, sooner or later it will be resolved. Poverty? It will be eliminated. Diseases? Drugs will be developed. Air pollution? Filters will be installed, etc., etc. Reality puts up no resistance, and if it does, it will be broken. In Fukuyama's world difficulties can of course appear, but they are all sure to be overcome. This is total, victorious optimism.

In this way of thinking there is nothing you can latch onto in order to get a conversation or a dialogue going. The surface of the debate is smooth, aerodynamic, easily conquering the forces of resistance.[7]

He also felt uncomfortable in the company of the American thinker because Fukuyama did not treat him as an equal partner. Their discussion was held at the Warsaw University library, but it was Fukuyama who did the talking, while Kapuściński – who came off as rather uninspired at public appearances and was not good at being himself in polemical debate – could not break through; only once or twice did he take the floor for a while. In comparison with Fukuyama's celebrity he looked pale, even though – to my mind – he had more interesting and innovative things to say than the American political scientist.

This scene also has a symbolic dimension: it illustrates Kapuściński's poor 'ideological frame of mind' after 1989, his disorientation during the dominance of neo-liberal ideology, when the problems of poverty were ignored, oversimplified answers were given to complex challenges, and the over-optimism of 'the end of History' prevailed.

In his short book *The Other* he set out his intellectual manifesto, his political and moral message. The modern world is a place where various cultures coexist, none of which is or will be dominant – in the way in which European culture dominated the world for many centuries. It remains for us to listen to each other carefully, to hold a dialogue; there are already more than six billion of us, and we are sitting on a powder keg.

Osiatyński thinks Kapuściński wrote a serious piece of nonsense in this book, namely that in relations between Europe and Others, the Enlightenment closed a period of 'wildness' and opened a new, modern era, in which a new language appeared, as did the conviction that the Other is equal to us, the Europeans.

'So where's all the nineteenth-century colonialism, the ideology of racism that Rysiek wrote so much about? Those atrocities were engendered by the post-Enlightenment era. I told him about it, and he promised to make corrections in the next edition of the book. He never managed to.'

Another absurdity that Osiatyński heard from his friend was that human rights cannot be the universal political philosophy of mankind because 'they place the individual above the community'. That's nonsense, says Osiatyński, an expert on the matter: human rights determine only what kind of coercion the community may not apply to the individual, which does not mean that the individual governs the group – that is a misunderstanding.

In one of the *Lapidaria* Kapuściński wrote: 'We understand human rights too institutionally. We usually accuse the state of breaking these rights – the government, the bureaucracy, the police. And yet another person, an entirely private individual can crush someone else's human rights.'[8] Once again there is a confusion: human rights are a discipline from the borders of law and political philosophy, defining mutual relations between the individual and the state, the individual and the community, not individual-to-individual relations.

'I think Rysiek believed in his own greatness and started to formulate general reflections without having solid foundations for them,' says Osiatyński. 'He read selectively, he was less interested in the processes, and he didn't always perceive the general laws. But he saw the details perfectly.'

'The experience of spending many years among distant Others has taught me that friendliness towards another human being is the only attitude that can touch a chord of humanity in him.'[9] In the final years of his life Kapuściński develops the concept of the reporter as an interpreter of cultures, a friendly observer and builder of bridges across cultural barriers. The first such interpreter was Herodotus, and he himself is the modern-day equivalent. In one interview he says:

> The value of my work as a reporter relies not only on the fact that I come into contact with another culture, but also that I have to tell someone else about this other reality. So I have to look for the key that opens other worlds. Without that, this profession is pointless. The reporter is a bit like a scout who infiltrates foreign customs and situations, and a bit like an interpreter who tries to transfer those observations into a language, concepts and images typical of his culture.[10]

The reporter as interpreter of cultures is doomed to defeat, however – as Kapuściński knows. The world is too rich, and it is hard to penetrate another culture and understand other kinds of behaviour, other customs and a different history. In *Travels with Herodotus* he describes being in Rome, where he put on a new shirt, a new suit and a trendy spotted tie, but even so everyone knew he was foreign. In Algeria, after the overthrow of Ahmed Ben Bella, he notices a crowd forming and runs to the site of the incident, but it turns out that people are just rubbernecking at a car smash in the street. The 'interpreter of cultures' is unable to recognize the simplest indicators in another culture; nevertheless, despite a string of failures, he goes on trying, even if he might again be unsuccessful. He is dealing with the impossible.

This impossible task, however, encapsulates an ethical and political programme for the world, of which the reporter–scout simply provides an example: listening to each other, coming out to meet the Other, global solidarity. Otherwise we will all kill each other.

In this area of his thinking he went radically against the trends prevalent in global politics after the Cold War.

38

Where to from Socialism? *Continued*

When does he realize that in erasing traces of the past and adapting to the mainstream of thinking after communism and the Cold War, he is not occupying his own skin?

Perhaps at the point in the late 1990s, when he notes:

> Several tenets of economic dogma are lying in ruins. The most important one is that the development of investment, trade and technology will increase the prosperity of the whole of society. The situation is different: nowadays the people getting rich are the ones who were already rich to start with. Mankind can be divided, on the scale of each country and of the entire planet, into two groups – winners and losers.[1]

Or certainly when he writes:

> More and more is being said about globalization, but it is understood not as the way cultures and societies come closer and get to know each other, but as a financial and economic operation, as the right of capital to act on all world markets, infused with the spirit not of closeness but domination . . .
>
> The particular harmfulness of neo-liberalism pervaded with egoism lies in the fact that it became the practice of wealthy states the moment when, as the result of a demographic explosion, vast crowds of poor people, numbering hundreds of millions, appeared on our planet, who without the support of the richer people cannot find themselves a fair place on earth.[2]

In 2001, when he observes the entry of Subcomandante Marcos's guerrillas into Mexico City – in the first rebellion against neo-liberalism – he again becomes the reporter he once was, with his heart on the left: always siding with the rebels against big capital and power, always in defence of the losers.

Now he calls himself an 'interpreter of cultures' – a formula that springs from an ideological stance, a world outlook, a left-wing attitude. If we live in a world where the winner takes all, imposes the rules of the game, and exploits those who are weaker, usually including people from cultures other than his own, and if the old left-wing language of criticism has lost its credibility, its penetrating force, we should seek a new language, replenish the old diagnoses and criticism, draw conclusions from our failures and formulate a message appropriate for the present day.

'Marx still has his uses,' he says one day, when I recount my observations from a journey to Brazil.

I had been travelling around the Brazilian interior, and in Mato Grosso I was told about the dead bodies that are cast up now and then on the banks of the Araguaia River. These are the corpses of peasants who have illegally occupied plots of land, often agricultural wasteland. Earlier they would have worked for owners of the *latifundia* for starvation wages. When they lost their jobs, they had nowhere to go. The only possibility that occurred to them was to trim off a piece of their former master's land and live off it. Hunger and despair having driven them to infringe the sacred law of ownership, the landowners' private police forces now hunt them down and throw their dead bodies into the river.

'A classic class conflict, straight out of Marx,' is Rysiek's diagnosis.

He understands perfectly why the 'fashion for Marx' is returning: because there are conflicts for which Marx's description is an exact fit. Even *The Economist* devotes an issue to the renascence of Marxian thought, even though it still firmly defends the neo-liberal form of the market. In the 'post-socialist' era, Kapuściński treats Marxism not as the skeleton key to open all doors, but rather as a set of observations about the world, or sometimes a method for analysing events and posing questions. Marxian thought, he contends, has kept its vitality and is useful in many situations: 'The whole of Marx has been too hastily thrown on the rubbish heap.'[3]

Once again there is the same detachment, the same reluctance to admit to an error: 'has been thrown', not 'we have thrown'.

In the late 1990s Kapuściński the commentator begins to speak and write entirely openly in the language of the left-wing critics of neo-liberalism and globalization. Essentially he never parted from left-wing thinking, but at the beginning of the 1990s he was unable to find a spiritual and intellectual space for himself; in the realm of neo-liberal ideology, where the market is elevated to a pedestal, ruthless competition is deified and the losers are ignored, he felt unmoored. This disorientation and this attempt to find a place for himself in the new reality are the impetus for commentaries and opinions in the first few *Lapidaria* that do not fit with anything he wrote either before or after. When, towards the end of the decade, criticism of capitalism and social (global as well now) inequalities returns to the scene, and new protest movements appear, Kapuściński revives, feels the wind in his sails and finds his homeland – except that this homeland is usually outside Poland. It is abroad, not in Poland, that he has an audience who really listen to him; his evaluations are respected and have penetrative force in Spain, Italy, Mexico and Argentina – if only this one from the *Lapidaria*'s penultimate volume:

> Globalization is not global, because it involves almost exclusively the North, where 81 percent of all foreign investments are made . . .
> The rapid, dynamic development of the world brings along two dangerous distortions:
> - firstly, this development generates inequalities (inside a country and on a planetary scale);
> - secondly, everywhere the strength and wealth of the centre are growing, while the outskirts are getting weaker and poorer.
> Everywhere, all of us are taking part in a game, the principle of which is that winner takes all (e.g., the boss earns as much as all the rest of the staff put together). In short, it is a new form of feudalism: at the top there is the master, the ruler, the sovereign, and lower down there is the entire feudal world subordinate to him – the vassals, servants and yokels.[4]

Left-wing protest movements, especially in Europe and both Americas, but also in some countries in Asia and Africa, have a good ear for these issues. The final volumes of Kapuściński's *Lapidaria* include catalogues of social scandals – hunger, poverty, exploitation, new inequalities – which harmonize with the themes taken up by the anti-globalization movement since the second half of the 1990s.

Nonetheless, towards the end of his life Kapuściński shies away from political affiliations. He sees himself as an unaligned, critical commentator on world affairs; being associated with a particular tendency or labelled as an anti-globalist – although on basic questions he said the same things as the anti-globalists – could have irritated him.

He does his best to preserve his independence.

In *The Shadow of the Sun* he records a spectrum of disappointments, though he presents them in the form of conversations with other people. One of his African commentators notes that religious and ethnic fanaticism is dangerous for decolonized Africa. Another says that Africa must wake up.

'Before he got down to writing *The Shadow of the Sun*,' says Jerzy Nowak, 'he went to Africa to check which elements of what we had formerly admired could still be defended. Afterwards he told me that one could come to the sacrilegious conclusion that it is worse than it was in the colonial era – though he does not blame the Africans for that, but rather the affluent North, which is in no hurry to help, although it could. Instead of help, the prosperous countries are only interested in exploiting Africa's raw materials, nothing more.'

The world of late Kapuściński is getting complicated. He remains an advocate of Africa, but admits it is questionable whether African cultures are capable of being self-critical, ergo of achieving progress and development. He still demands the affluent world's help for Africa, and shares the following thought:

> Europe's image of Africa? Hunger; skeletal children; dry, cracked earth; urban slums; massacres; AIDS; throngs of refugees without a roof over their heads, without clothing, without medicines, water, or bread.
> The world therefore rushes in with aid.
> Today, as in the past, Africa is regarded as an object, as the reflection of some alien star, as the stomping ground of colonizers, merchants, missionaries, ethnographers, large charitable organizations . . . Meantime, most importantly, it exists for itself alone, within itself, a timeless, sealed, separate continent.[5]

In his other favourite region, Latin America, he is delighted by the 'springtime of the peoples', the new left-wing wave which started at the end of the 1990s.

> We are witnesses to a great new awakening, the ethnic rebirth of the part of Latin American societies derived from their indigenous populations . . .
> The heart of the matter is a total change of atmosphere in almost all the countries I recently visited in the region; also a belief that a positive scenario of events is possible for this part of the world. Latin America has ceased to be a continent where global tensions are concentrated, and has begun to be a laboratory for some new social and cultural forms, the site of various experiments. The twenty-first century will be Latin America's century.[6]

Some people think that in old age he squared accounts – in *The Shadow of the Sun*, among other places – with the revolutions, rebellions and revolts that fascinated him in his youth. What does 'squared accounts' mean here? That he turned away from what he wrote earlier? Negated what he had seen and experienced? Revisited his former judgements? As expert on his work Andrzej Pawluczuk writes:

> I once asked Kapuściński if nowadays, twenty years on, he would have written those books of his the same way, identically: *The Soccer War* and

Christ with a Rifle on His Shoulder. Yes, identically, he replied without hesitation.[7]

To the end, he asserted it was 'evil' Moscow, not the 'good' West, that was helping Third World countries push through to independence; the West was a force enslaving the societies of the South. So what if the Soviets had made their own economic and geostrategic deals along the way? Should the Africans continue putting up with colonialism just to prevent that? To help the West in the Cold War? Rubbish. What was in it for them? Kapuściński regarded it as absurd to make retrospective judgements of the legitimacy of revolt, the independence struggle or revolution on the basis of later defeats.

Of course, Moscow did not support wars of liberation or revolutionary rebellions in every corner of the Third World during the Cold War. More than that − it opposed them when it was concerned about peace with Washington, or when some movement or revolt did not suit it ideologically and did not recognize Moscow as the revolutionary's Rome. At that point, Kapuściński's sympathies usually leaned towards the heretics − not necessarily for ideological reasons. It was more a matter of empathy, solidarity with the desperate or with idealists who despite all sorts of adversity pick up a gun and sacrifice their own peace, often their lives, to go and fight for a fairer world.

Kapuściński now returns to his own path, from which he deviated in the early 1990s. He breaks free of the political correctness of the new era, just as he broke free of it in the days of the PRL. At the same time, he stays in the mainstream as the biggest star of Polish journalism − exactly as in the previous era. But what he now writes and says about contemporary conflicts and challenges has a limited influence on the thinking of Poland's political and journalistic establishment. He is not the first or the last idol to be totally ignored.

Following the 9/11 attacks on the World Trade Center and the Pentagon, the rift in world-view between Kapuściński and the 'environment' of mainstream thinking (certainly the mainstream in Poland) becomes manifest.

A few days after the incident, he calls me to say, 'Come by, we must have a chat.'

I have never heard this tone in his voice before, full of irritation and impatience.

'It's awful what they're writing in the paper − it's all wrong, with no thought put into it. Stuff and nonsense!'

'Shall we do an interview?'

'Ask if they'd like that.'

I arrive with Aleksander Kaczorowski, who is then in charge of *Gazeta Świąteczna*, the weekend section in which *Gazeta Wyborcza*'s longer essays, features and interviews appear. Kapuściński sketches a panorama of globalization as the context for the 9/11 attacks:

> The phenomenon of globalization does not function on a single level, as is often said, but on two, or even three. The first of them is the official one, in other words the free flow of capital, access to free markets, communications, supra-national companies and corporations, mass culture, mass goods and mass consumption . . . But there is also a second form of globalization, in my view very powerful, negative and disintegrative. This is the globalization of the underground, criminal world of mafias, drugs, the mass weapons trade, money laundering, tax evasion and financial fraud . . .
>
> And there is a third level of globalization too, which covers various forms of public life: international extra-governmental organizations, movements and sects. It testifies to the fact that people no longer find answers to their needs in the old, traditional structures – such as the state, the nation, and the church – and so they go looking for something new. So while the beginning of the twentieth century was characterized by the existence of strong states and strong institutions, the beginning of the twenty-first is characterized by a weakening of the state and a great expansion of various kinds of small, extra-state, extra-governmental forms – both civil and religious. The context and structure in which man used to live is changing . . .
>
> This is an extremely vital circumstance for understanding events such as 9/11, because it shows that we may be dealing with forces over which no one has control, and which will be hard to control in the future.[8]

Not for the first time, he postulates the idea of global solidarity:

> This is not about short-term aid of the kind provided in the case of a flood, an earthquake, a famine or other disaster. What we need here is an overall conception of goodwill on the part of the developed world. Something like that has never yet come into being . . . If we do not help the poor, if we don't smooth out the inequalities in the world even to a minimal degree, we shall end up killing each other. I think we are going through a dramatic crisis in humanitarian thinking.[9]

Towards the end of the interview he strikes an oppositional tone, critical of the main current of thought on what happened in New York and Washington on 9/11:

> I cannot bear to hear any more statements about Islam or Arab culture, on which suddenly everyone seems to be a great expert. Or about plans

concerning whom to kill, on whom to be avenged, or whom to bombard. Of course the perpetrators of the attacks in America should be identified and punished. But the horizon of thinking about the present crisis should not be like this. If we are only going to think about military revenge, we will not get far. If after a military response we return to the blissful state we have been stuck in for the past decade, in a short while something else will give us a shock . . .

9/11 revealed how terribly fragile this world of ours is. Awareness of this fragility seems to me incredibly important – for further reflection on the world, and above all further action within it.[10]

A week later, the only time in the history of *Gazeta Wyborcza*, a polemic arguing with Kapuściński appears: although mild in tone, it firmly opposes the current of thought he represents. It is written by the paper's former deputy editor, Ernest Skalski.

Here are some extracts:

One can agree with Kapuściński or not, but his knowledge and the standard of his analyses oblige one to do some thinking . . .

'I think the most important thing at this moment is to establish and understand the context of this event', says Kapuściński. I am ready to agree that this is the most important thing, but here the eternal conflict appears between importance and urgency. Understanding demands consideration, and consideration takes time. The thinkers may come to various conclusions, and so it will be difficult to establish anything. Meanwhile we must start to take action, to avoid being surprised by yet another terrible attack while we're doing all this thinking . . .

Practice tells us that sharing out wealth is not a solution to poverty. In any case, organized terror is not generated in extreme poverty and stagnation, but where something has got moving, where new aspirations have appeared, and are outgrowing the potential to satisfy them. The Palestinians have a higher standard of living than the Yemenis. Nor is it worth deluding ourselves that all the world's difficult problems can be solved within the remit of the fight against terrorism . . .

[I]n the democratic countries all forms of aggression and violence have passed their expiry date and should no longer be tolerated. This also applies to the anti-globalists. Civilized debate on the topic of globalization is certainly needed. Acts of aggression are definitely not.[11]

Skalski's article is a good illustration of the *Gazeta* editors' line of thinking at the time. Kapuściński is annoyed and upset. He takes the piece as a sort of blow, from the least expected direction. Yet he does not respond.

The differences between his evaluations of the world situation and those of *Gazeta*'s editors become even clearer during the propaganda campaign designed to justify US aggression against Iraq. *Gazeta* openly sympathizes with the Bush administration's plans for war. In the words of editor-in-chief Adam Michnik, it recognizes the invasion and the military overthrow of Saddam Hussein's dictatorship as a necessary evil. The paper's commentators see a threat in the global spread of 'anti-Americanism', not in the imperial tendencies of Washington policies. They applaud the idea of 'spreading democracy' with the help of the American (and Polish) armed forces.

Kapuściński argues with this way of thinking in *Gazeta*, in an interview given on the eve of the American invasion of Iraq.

'[A]nti-Americanism'. This term prompts my doubts. America is very many things, it is a vast number of wonderful achievements that are the dream of millions, if not billions of people worldwide. America means fabulous science, an impressively disciplined society, technological achievements – nowadays all this is the motor of development for the entire planet . . .

Many people in the world are opposed not to America, but to the American 'war party'. They are opposed to America's imperial designs, which is understandable. People are opposed to any kind of domination; such is the nature of man – man is in favour of freedom, and against being controlled or having something imposed. Here lies the problem of 'anti-Americanism'. There is an attempt to define people's mood as anti-American, when it is actually an anti-imperial, anti-war mood . . .

[I]n America they talk about 'anti-Americanism' perhaps in order to create the belief within society that people in the world outside are hostile to their homeland . . .

I interpret all the talk about exporting Western democracy as an attempt to justify expansion operations. In colonialism, too, conquest was justified by the fact that it brought progress, higher civilization, and conversion to the true faith. And that does in fact happen, but at the price of great bloodshed and several centuries of occupation and domination. So it is not a new idea, and history knows many examples of bringing 'the barbarians' another, 'higher civilization'. These justifications accompanied the entire, more than five-hundred-year history of European colonialism. Yes, it's not a bad idea . . . but first you have to estimate how many millions of human beings it will cost. Who will take responsibility for that? How many generations will it last? How many hundreds of years?[12]

'He took a critical view of America's and Europe's actions conducted within the remit of the "war on terror"', recalls Jerzy Nowak. 'I defended the American intervention in Afghanistan, but Rysiek thought it would only lead to the country's further ruin. He did not support the war in Iraq. He was critical of the Israeli government, and spoke of Israel with regret, saying that it had started from an ideal, only to rely on force thereafter. Towards the end of his life there was a great deal of pessimism in Rysiek's thinking about the ongoing conflicts in the world.'

About national politics he keeps quiet, on principle. He has a growing conviction that Poland is a political and intellectual backwater, a tin-pot country. He doesn't want to know who dislikes whom, or who is plotting with whom against whom. He doesn't want to know, though while partaking in political gossip he asks questions about everything. Then he forgets. On his lips, names that are well-known from television sometimes sound as if a foreigner were saying them, someone who has only just heard them for the first time and is making sure he has remembered them properly.

As I now try to trace how his attitude to the post-communist order in Poland changed, all that remains are my own memories, and those of his other friends and acquaintances. Just crumbs of information, no statements or interviews on the topic.

Wiktor Osiatyński: 'He felt euphoria in the days of the Mazowiecki government, and then watched the scrimmage, the chaos, the invasion of boorish elements, and the weakening of quality of the political class with increasing anxiety. He was worried about the weakness of the left and disturbed by the growing inequalities.'

At some point Jerzy Nowak says that a comparison of Rysiek's views and sensitivities with those of Jacek Kuroń is justified.

Kuroń was a minister in two governments after 1989, and built capitalism in order, as he put it, to have something to share afterwards. Towards the end of his life he blamed himself for having built an unfair order, full of injustice and inequality. Kapuściński's thinking about the transformation in Poland had a similar pitch, a similar tone, though it was never verbalized into a coherent evaluation.

I remember a comment he made about Balcerowicz, in the final years of his life: 'doctrinaire.'

At the same time he could not bear populism, boorishness, or the mob's demand for rights in the name of those who had been wronged. As early as the 1980s, when no one had dreamed of a political movement such as (the nationalist party) Samoobrona (Self-Defence), he noted:

> Steer clear of the rabble, or you'll come to a bad end, because it will sink you and destroy you. Treat those people as carriers of plague, give them a wide berth. In the rabble there is a sort of will to conquer, a jealous desire to destroy everything. The rabble's aim is to disturb your peace,

make your work impossible, and make progress impossible for mankind. The rabble movement is always a backwards movement, it is a motionless movement.[13]

'Why did someone as left-wing as Rysiek dislike populism so much?'

'Because the populists spoiled his conception of the world.' So says Hanna Krall.

He took a warm view of the initiatives of the young left in Poland, though he had no profound thoughts about them. 'That quarterly, *Krytyka Polityczna*, is all right, don't you think?' he partly asked, partly assured himself.

He gave one of his essays, on 'encountering the Other' as the main challenge for the future, to the Polish edition of *Le Monde diplomatique*, a left-wing monthly to whose French edition he had subscribed for many years (it was always lying on his desk). In conversation he was always referring to comments and information he had found in its pages, and he and the journal's long-time editor-in-chief, Ignacio Ramonet, had a mutual regard.

But usually he went on about the right.

'Dreadful chaps!'

'It's turning into fascism!'

'You can't imagine what's going on here!' he fumed in the summer of 2006, when I returned to Poland after a year away. (For more than six months Lech Kaczyński had been president, and his brother Jarosław had just become prime minister.)

Above all it was about lustration, in other words exposing the co-operation by well-known figures in public life with the PRL's secret service. And also about squaring accounts in the broader sense – which involved branding people in politics and culture who had once belonged to the Party and believed in socialism.

'He went on and on, saying, "You'll see, now it's the end, the *Kaczory* [a popular nickname for the Kaczyński twins] are going to sort us out!" ' says one of his friends.

He shows anxiety, concern, and even fear whenever, with each successive political crisis and election, the issue of 'former agents' comes up again – always as a weapon in the fight for power, almost never with the aim of learning about the history of post-war Poland, the workings of the system or how to understand people's careers. His opposition to lustration links him strongly to the *Gazeta Wyborcza* environment.

In the early 1990s, at a party given by the ambassador of one of the Western countries, Kapuściński listens as a post-1989 Ministry of Foreign Affairs official lists – in the presence of everyone – the names of current Polish diplomats who in his opinion were Soviet agents. As the party comes to an end, the assembled company hear an altercation in the corridor. Rushing to intervene, they find Kapuściński holding the ministry official by the lapels of his jacket, pinning him to the wall and shouting, 'How dare you, you bastard!'

In the second half of the 1990s one of the right-wing journalists (earlier a press acquaintance in the PRL era) writes in a niche weekly that Kapuściński 'had very good knowledge of all the inside facts and complexities of Party in-fighting, rises and falls', and that 'even if he wasn't a staff intelligence agent', he 'was quite often used on an ad hoc basis for covert operations'.

Kapuściński laughs at his denouncer, but his laughter is not unrestrained – he is afraid.

'I could see the fear growing in him that eventually they'd drag out his connections with the intelligence service,' says Osiatyński.

'Did you ever talk about it?'

'Yes. He said, "I'm sure to have something in my documents." '

In the final months of his life, rumours reach him that in one of its features programmes the public television channel intends to reveal his connections with the PRL's intelligence service. He doesn't know exactly 'what they've got on him', but he is horrified, doubled up with anxiety.

He calls his friends and acquaintances at *Gazeta*.

'Do you know what they're planning?'

Two months before his death he goes to a book launch for Krzysztof Teodor Toeplitz, accused by public television a few days earlier of co-operation with the security service. Daniel Passent from *Polityka* was 'outed' at the same time.

'We took Rysiek's appearance as a gesture of solidarity,' say both Toeplitz and Passent.

'He called to say he'd come half an hour early for a chat,' says Passent. 'He was agitated. It felt as if the clouds were gathering over him, too, but none of us said it at the time. He came to show us he was with us, and that he didn't agree with this people-hunt that the right wing was conducting.'

In one of their last conversations, he tells Osiatyński that he doubts whether 'what we have in Poland can be called democracy yet'.

39

The File

The bomb explodes four months after his death. The weekly *Newsweek Polska* publishes documents from the archives of the PRL's special services concerning Kapuściński's collaboration with intelligence, which lasted several years. Within the framework of Polish political debate after 1989, co-operation with the communist state's secret services is generally regarded as something between treason, indecency and opportunism – whatever the material content of the co-operation.

The revelatory force of the sensational facts published in *Newsweek* is mitigated by an interview with Ernest Skalski, a friend of Kapuściński's, a journalist who had intermittent contact with the intelligence service in his own history. (Before leaving for Denmark on a scholarship in 1967, Skalski was approached by a Ministry of Foreign Affairs official and asked to take an interest, in the course of his stay, in some West German reporters whose statements 'could pose a threat to Poland'. Skalski did not co-operate with the Ministry of Foreign Affairs.) Skalski's basic thesis is that if Kapuściński had not agreed to co-operate with intelligence, he would not have gone abroad as a PAP correspondent, so books such as *The Emperor, Shah of Shahs, The Soccer War* and others would never have been written, and the great reporter and writer Ryszard Kapuściński would never have emerged. The price he paid for his consent was not high: he never harmed or injured anyone.

Newsweek found itself in the line of fire between supporters and opponents of lustration. The right-wing journalists did not hide their satisfaction: here lay yet another authority in ruins – left-wing or liberal, in short, 'not one of us'. The man had proved to be an opportunist, 'up to his neck in it'. Environments friendly with Kapuściński, above all *Gazeta Wyborcza*, objected to 'the dramatic distortion of the truth about a great writer', and 'casting a shadow on an honourable man' on the basis of 'unverified security service documents'. There were also declarations such as: 'We believe more in his books – in what he wrote and said to his readers and audiences, than in what he allegedly said surreptitiously to blackmailers from the secret police'.

Close friends and defenders also spoke up abroad. As British journalist Ian Traynor wrote in the *Guardian*:

> [Kapuściński] is the latest prominent Pole to be 'outed' in what critics call a rightwing witchhunt orchestrated by a paranoid government that sees 'reds under the beds' everywhere in Poland.[1]

Or Italian journalist Paolo Rumiz in *la Repubblica:*

> Polish lustration involves selective acts of vengeance, the aim of which is to attack free people who are credited with promoting the country's good name. Lustration threatens to besmirch everything and is a game for hyenas. Kapuściński was a victim of the pitiless machine which was set mainly against those who had been abroad. Nonentities from Warsaw society could not forgive him his success and accused him of writing nonsense.[2]

An ideological war serves neither to establish the truth nor to promote calm consideration or subtle judgements. The lustrators are uninterested in the complex truth about the past, free of cheap moralizing, and in their turn the defenders of those lustrated – like it or not – become hostages for the attackers, and, unable to see that they are doing so, enter into their ways of thinking. Thus it happened up to a point, I think, in the case of Kapuściński. I sympathize with the defenders of Rysiek's good name, and I wrote a good deal about the post-1989 witch-hunts, but neither of these facts exempts me from establishing – within the possibilities available – the truth about the hero of this account.

So, did Kapuściński co-operate with the intelligence service or not? If he did, what does it actually mean? What exactly did he do? Why? What did the PRL's intelligence service generally do in the parts of the world to which Kapuściński travelled as a PAP correspondent? How useful was his co-operation? How did he himself regard it? How, in general, should one judge the co-operation of journalists with the secret services?

I often sensed – and this I now know for certain – that fear of the surfacing of the file from the special services archive, and fear of being publicly pilloried as a consequence, weighed on him physically and mentally during the last dozen or so years of his life. I also think that at least once this fear exerted an influence on his writing (a hypothesis I shall explain later). And so I want to, and must, find out what Kapuściński was so terribly afraid of. Did he have reason to be afraid? Did he, as some people now think, conclude an unwritten pact with the devil: co-operation with the intelligence service in exchange for trips abroad? Or perhaps the situation was actually completely different?

I can understand the chief motive for his never speaking of his own co-operation – the atmosphere in Poland after 1989 was not one in which a person could, without fear of being chewed up, spat out and branded, openly admit, 'Yes, I co-operated. I did it because . . . I'm sorry that . . .' Or, on the other hand, 'I'm not sorry, because . . .'

It is time to tell this story in a manner that is free of moralizing blackmail, and free as well of the fear of it.

First of all, the file.[3] What does it contain?

A key item is a conclusion drawn up by an anonymous Ministry of Foreign Affairs functionary in 1972: 'he was used operationally for the identification and exposure of employees of intelligence HQs [in Latin America]. During his co-operation he showed much willingness, but did not hand over any vital materials of interest to the Security Service'.

Chronologically, the earliest items in Kapuściński's file are notes compiled in 1963 by officers in the Ministry of Foreign Affairs' Department I (intelligence). Kapuściński was then a PAP correspondent in East Africa, and probably had no idea the secret services were interested in him. The notes contain perfunctory information on which schools he attended and which organizations he belonged to; that his parents were teachers, his wife a doctor, and his sister a student. One of the notes contains information about Kapuściński's feud with the playwright Drozdowski, whom he had accused of plagiarism. 'The subject is under investigation by us as a potential candidate for co-operation', confirms a Department I officer in this note.

On the basis of the documents available at the Institute of National Remembrance, where the PRL's secret service archives are stored, it is not possible to establish when the intelligence service first got in touch with Kapuściński.

Chronologically, the next two notes written by a Ministry of Foreign Affairs officer date from the spring of 1965; after a short stop in Poland, Kapuściński is getting ready to leave for West Africa. At this time he transfers the PAP's African post from Nairobi to Lagos, the capital of Nigeria. Then a personal conversation with a Ministry of Foreign Affairs officer takes place. In his account of this meeting, the officer refers to Kapuściński by the cryptonym 'the Poet' and calls him an 'information contact'. He also summarizes his African travel plans (and writes in error that Kapuściński is going to East Africa).

In a note for the officer, Kapuściński describes the probable route of his next tour of Africa; he has not yet decided whether the PAP's new headquarters will be in Accra (Ghana) or Lagos (Nigeria). A document has survived in vestigial form that lists the intelligence service's expectations of Kapuściński: they are interested in information about the activities of

American institutions, companies and organizations. The Ministry of Foreign Affairs officer informs Kapuściński that in Africa someone will get in touch with him, using the password 'Greetings from Zygmunt'. He is to reply: 'Has he sold the car?'

Kapuściński receives instructions 'for information and execution', and signs them. However, there is no trace in the file of his co-operation with the intelligence service during his time in Africa, not a single piece of information, note or mention. It is not even known if anyone ever approached him with the password established in Warsaw.

The intelligence service remembers Kapuściński again before he leaves for his posting in Latin America. In late autumn 1967 he meets with Major Henryk Sobieski, who reports afterwards: ' "The Poet" is familiar to our apparatus from African terrain. Among all his personal acquaintances he enjoys complete trust and a very good reputation. He made a very positive impression on me too. He is close to us in class terms and has a strong ideological commitment. His attitude to working for us is very good.'

During the meeting, Sobieski tells Kapuściński that in Latin America the Polish intelligence services are interested in the activities of the United States' spy network. 'In view of his highly political position', Kapuściński's instructions from the Ministry of Foreign Affairs 'will not diverge from the aims of his work as a journalist'. The intelligence service expects Kapuściński to 'point them towards' journalists 'who have connections with the environment of counter-intelligence employees, or who from their official positions (they run the crime sections in their papers) have access to these institutions'. He will also 'gain information on some issues connected with the activities of Zionism, the Americans and the Federal Republic of Germany'. The remaining topics of the conversation described in the note are of a technical nature: how Kapuściński is to get in touch with the headquarters in Warsaw (via a cryptographer at the embassy in Santiago de Chile; in Mexico City, someone yet to be identified will get in touch with him) and also how to hide from counter-intelligence.

Two years later, the intelligence service extends its expectations to include 'identifying and reaching CIA and FBI cells deployed on Mexican territory or in other Latin American countries', 'gaining information on individuals connected with the activities of these institutions', 'gaining insight into environments and places frequented by CIA and FBI functionaries and identifying their contacts with citizens of local origin', and also 'hostile activity against the PRL', conducted 'above all by the intelligence agencies of the USA, Israel and the Federal Republic of Germany'.

During more than four years spent in Latin America, Kapuściński – as it appears from the archive material available at the Institute of National Remembrance – provides the intelligence service with only a few notes. He signs them with the pseudonym 'Vera Cruz'.

He tells them about the Centro de Estudios del Desarrollo (CENDES), an institute for development studies at the Central University of Venezuela in Caracas which, according to his findings, is 'a major centre of CIA penetration and reconnaissance within Venezuela'.

(Many years later, Sandra La Fuente, who attended Kapuściński's journalism workshops and whom I told about this note, will laugh and say that the maestro twisted everything: 'CENDES has always been the most progressive institute in all Venezuela,' she says. 'Some people from the intellectual hinterland of Hugo Chávez's governments come from there. It seems improbable that CENDES could have been a CIA cover'.)

Here are some extracts from a description of Pablo Morales, editor-in-chief of the Latin American edition of the monthly *Reader's Digest*, 'co-financed by the CIA':

> He has been living in Mexico City for several years. Spanish by origin, but a US citizen. As well as Spanish, he speaks English fluently with an American accent . . . age about 45–48. Tall – about 6 foot 3 inches. The manly type, very good-looking . . . Drinks often, but doesn't get drunk. Always spending time in the company of women (Americans). Polite and courteous. The idle type, sophisticated, always smartly dressed. As a rule he is reticent. Never takes up conversations on serious topics . . . He is polite towards socialist correspondents, but shows no desire to establish contacts. Gives the impression of being an apolitical person, who likes good food, women and alcohol.

On the activities of fascist organizations in Latin America inspired by the CIA:

> Inspired by the American special services, and particularly the CIA, terrorist organizations exist in Latin American countries whose activity is aimed against communist parties and any kind of progressive movement. The members of these organizations are usually representatives of the financial oligarchy and haute bourgeoisie who belong to the extreme right. Some of the members are also recruited from the lumpenproletariat. The organizations are financed by the CIA and extreme right groupings within the Latin American countries.

Kapuściński's texts on a conference of US ambassadors accredited in Latin American countries and on a Trotskyite movement in the region have not survived, and are known only from a note by one of the officers in charge of him, pseudonym 'Benito'. Kapuściński's account of the American ambassadors' conference was 'passed [by Polish intelligence] in March this year [1970] to Cuban comrades'.

A text on Cuba's aspirations to normalize relations with the Latin American countries is identical in form and language to reports he wrote for the PAP's Special Bulletin.

Kapuściński states among other things that guerrilla groups in the style of Che Guevara are dying out, and that Cuba 'is withdrawing its support for this sort of movement and activity'. Isolated in the Western hemisphere, the socialist country governed by Fidel Castro

> is expressing readiness to renew diplomatic and trade relations with each of the individual Latin American countries, but on the other hand it does not want this normalization to happen via the OPA [Organization of American States]. Fidel Castro calls the OPA 'the US Colonial Ministry', and believes that within the framework of this organization, which is dominated by the United States, Cuba would lose its existing independence.

From the documents at the Institute of National Remembrance, it emerges that the intelligence service wanted Kapuściński to obtain materials from a congress of science and technology held in Tel Aviv. To this end, during a holiday in Warsaw he was supposed to meet with the vice-chancellor of a Mexican technical college on his way back from Israel. No information is available to say whether this meeting took place. (The interpreter of this material, whom I will introduce later, claims it did not.)

The largest number of unfavourable comments about Kapuściński, furtively expressed after the publication of the *Newsweek* piece, were prompted by his note about Maria Sten. An employee of Warsaw University and a scholar of pre-Columbian cultures, she was sacked from her job on the wave of anti-Semitic purges of 1968 and emigrated to Mexico. Kapuściński, who, as he explains in the note, did not know her previously, gives this account of their meeting:

> Maria Sten had come straight from Poland. She presented a picture of what was happening there, calling it 'a nightmare'. During the conversation, Sten brought up the following issues:
>
> she said that 1968 was the most tragic year in the history of Poland, because 'the best people', in other words the Zionists, had been 'forced to leave the country',
>
> she expressed surprise that in the meantime, while she was on her way from Warsaw to Mexico City, there had been nothing in our press about 'the dismissal of Comrade Świtała and Comrade Szlachcic for installing a bugging device in the offices of Comrades from the Party leadership – Gomułka, Cyrankiewicz, Gierek and so on',

she was surprised that Comrade Kępa had remained First Secretary of the Executive Committee, because when she left 'there had already been a decision to remove him',

she 'could not understand' why Solecki and Kolczyński had remained, who were also 'going to be removed',

she expressed her concern that 'that whole gang hasn't been driven out', on which she was counting,

from her statements with regard to her future it emerged that she plans to remain in Mexico City and is looking for an apartment.

The note contains clichés typical of the official, anti-Semitic propaganda (Kapuściński calls Poles of Jewish origin who were forced to leave Poland at that time 'Zionists'). By passing this information about Maria Sten to the intelligence service, could he have done her harm? Probably not. Sten was not planning to return to Poland, and Kapuściński knew that. Despite this fact, does the note have the tone of a denunciation? Unfortunately, yes, it does.

Danuta Rycerz, a close friend of Maria Sten's, to whom I talk about my impressions, claims that Sten actually demanded of Kapuściński – with whom she was later on friendly terms for many years – that he relay her critical views to people at the top of the Party. I take this comment at face value, though I do not conceal my doubts: it sounds as if it were added after the fact, with the noble intention of defending her friend's good name.

Sten is the only person about whom Kapuściński wrote this sort of note, although in Mexico he came into contact with other Poles who were critical of the government in Warsaw. One of these people was Professor Jerzy Plebański, a physicist from Warsaw University who went to Mexico in the 1970s as part of an academic exchange. Józef Klasa, shortly to become ambassador to that country, says that the intelligence service tried to recruit Plebański, but he resisted. He was threatened with the consequences of his refusal, and perhaps that was why in the end he decided to stay in Mexico for the rest of his life. 'Rysiek,' recalls Klasa, 'used to meet with Plebański, and must have known his critical views about our government, but he never reported them to anyone. Rysiek was a decent man and would never have hurt a soul.'

Maybe he really did write, at her request, what Maria Sten thought about the Warsaw comrades?

There is one other note in Kapuściński's file which provoked some biting comments after being published in *Newsweek*. It concerns Alice B., an Englishwoman, an alleged intelligence service agent, 'playing the part of an ultra-leftist'. Kapuściński met her in Angola in 1975. According to the note, Alice B. was 'ugly' and 'had sexual relations with blacks'. However, it was not Kapuściński who drew up the profile of her, written in the language

of the secret-police subculture, but a Ministry of Foreign Affairs functionary quoting a conversation with him.

Three other statements have survived, signed with the pseudonym 'Vera
Cruz', in which Kapuściński declares his expenses 'in connection with
performing tasks': 350 Mexican pesos (about thirty dollars).

In 1972 the intelligence service archived Kapuściński's documents, which
means that the co-operation had been discontinued. According to materials
available at the Institute of National Remembrance, it was renewed only
once, during the liberation war in Angola. Whether and what sort of information Kapuściński provided to intelligence at that point is unknown; there
are no relevant documents.

The intelligence officers who 'minded' Kapuściński in Latin America were
two employees of the Polish embassy in Mexico. Privately they were his
friends: Eugeniusz Spyra, who used the pseudonym 'Grzegorz', and Henryk
Sobieski, aka 'Benito' – the man who presented Kapuściński with the intelligence service's expectations before he left for the post, and the same man
who many years later is offended when Kapuściński refuses to greet him
warmly at the funeral of a mutual friend.

Kapuściński once mentioned Spyra to me in hushed tones, as if revealing
a great secret: 'That Spyra was our intelligence service resident for the
whole of Latin America'.

They knew each other well, often spoke and visited each other's homes.

Both Kapuścińskis kept up social relations with Sobieski and his wife for
many years after leaving Mexico. When Sobieski became ambassador to
Venezuela towards the end of the 1970s, Kapuściński visited him in Caracas
(he had come to Venezuela to give a series of lectures). One of his former
comrades says that after 1989, when his old contacts began to be a burden
for Kapuściński, Alicja occasionally kept in touch with the Sobieskis.

Both Spyra and Sobieski refuse to talk to me in person about Kapuściński.
I manage to have a chat with Sobieski over the phone.

'I'll tell you one thing,' he says, 'the revelations in *Newsweek* are trivial. If
anyone thinks it was possible to tell Kapuściński to do something, they
know nothing about him. He was the one who could fix various things for
me, not I for him – it was he who had the contacts high up.[4] . . . No one
could touch Kapuściński, he was out of reach . . . People from Rakowiecka
Street [the Ministry of Foreign Affairs head office] could obstruct him but
not harm him. He was good friends with Frelek, and Waszczuk . . . Besides,
Kapuściński was no eager collaborator, as some people are writing nowadays, but an expert at ducking and diving!'

That would make sense. In a handwritten note for his superiors in
Warsaw, 'Benito' explains that although Kapuściński 'has a very good
approach to our service and his political attitude does not arouse the

slightest reservations', yet he is overwhelmed by an excess of duties as a correspondent and hasn't enough time to 'implement our operational tasks'. 'Benito' admits that, to date, he has gained little from 'operational conversations' with Kapuściński. The key passage about his 'expertise at ducking and diving' goes like this: 'Once he deals with finishing a book about Che Guevara (he is at the final stage), despite the afore-mentioned difficulties he will be able to set aside a little more time to perform the operational tasks assigned to him'.

Indeed, Kapuściński was planning to write a book about Che Guevara, but he never even started it. He must have told Sobieski that, on top of the daily PAP toil, he was also writing a book – which he was not actually writing – and that he didn't have time for anything else. Or perhaps the friends agreed that Sobieski would write this sort of thing to his superiors so they wouldn't keep bothering him? Because Kapuściński really was terribly busy with his own professional matters.

Examining the context is crucial to understanding the issue of 'Kapuściński and the PRL intelligence service'. Without the context, the file from the Institute of National Remembrance is 'a tale told by an idiot', a collection of residual bits of information from which little emerges and which are, in addition, easy to misinterpret. What was the significance of the few notes and analyses he provided to the intelligence officers? Why did he write so few of them in the course of more than four years? Because he was unimportant as a collaborator? Or inept? Because Latin America was unimportant?

I will call him the Interpreter, because he explains the contents of the file and also the circumstances and rules in force at the point of contact between the intelligence service and foreign correspondents. In the absence of such explanations, nothing about this matter would be clear or comprehensible. I cannot write who he is. I can perhaps write only that his knowledge of the 'Kapuściński case' coincides to a very broad extent with the knowledge of the officers in charge. I trust the Interpreter, which means I am sure he explains the heart of the matter reliably, though I must assume he keeps some information to himself.

'What was of interest to Polish intelligence in Latin America during the Cold War?'

'Let's start from a different point: which countries were within the sphere of interest of Polish intelligence in that era? What were the priorities? Without this hierarchy, something important will slip our notice.'

And so, our intelligence service was interested above all in the Western countries, first and foremost the United States and West Germany. That was where the main agents operated. The correspondents who went to postings there, as well as to other Western countries, were given tasks by the intelligence service and provided valuable, often very valuable information.

For journalists going to Third World countries, the situation was slightly different: they, too, were involved in co-operation, but it was done more for the sake of principle. In other words, each reporter who went abroad to a posting in Africa, Latin America or Asia was asked for information and to write reports, but their co-operation did not usually have great significance, nor was great weight attached to it.

'Why not?'

'Because the Third World as such was not important for our intelligence and only counted as a field of competition between America and the Soviet Union.'

'But something did interest Polish intelligence in Latin America or Africa, for instance.'

'Yes, the activities of the United States on that terrain, their agents, companies and organizations. In countries such as Mexico or Angola, to which Mr Kapuściński travelled as a correspondent, various intelligence services recruited collaborators. These collaborators were usually "dormant", used sporadically, if the moment came when information from them could be useful.'

'And did Kapuściński help to select and recruit these collaborators?'

'Your question sounds rather as if Mr Kapuściński were some important agent, or had special duties. But he was just small fry, very small fry. On top of that, he travelled to regions of the world which were not strategically important for the politics of Poland at the time, or even for the Soviet Union. If not for the fact that it could sound impolite, I would say that as an intelligence service collaborator he was virtually a nobody. That file is a collection of rubbish.'

'Rubbish? So why did the intelligence service need – for instance – a profile of the editor-in-chief of the Latin American edition of *Reader's Digest*?'

'The journal was known to have connections with the CIA, so a profile of the editor-in-chief was compiled just in case. Intelligence services collect information about anything that might come in useful, usually without any specific aim. Most of the information never gets used, but you have to have it, just in case . . . That's what this work is all about. The intelligence service usually gathers the same sort of information as the journalists, and does its best to have a fraction of a percent more of it than the press. Because one or another detail might prove useful, who knows when or in what circumstances. The profile of the *Reader's Digest* editor, moreover, like every other profile, has been compiled on the basis of several sources; what Mr Kapuściński provided was just one of the elements.'

'Was he an important figure? An important CIA agent?'

'As far as I know, he wasn't. Intelligence services collect information not just on "reliable" agents or candidates for agents. The information about the *Reader's Digest* editor was gathered just in case.'

'Couldn't a full-time intelligence employee have gathered it?'

'Of course he could, but it's always about having observations, information, comments from various sources. That is why Mr Kapuściński was asked for them – he knew the man.'

'Was Kapuściński's information that the CIA was financing right-wing terrorist organizations in Latin America who were murdering left-wing activists important to the intelligence service?'

'That was known about without Mr Kapuściński. His report was just further confirmation.'

'Maybe he had the right to believe that by providing such information he was exposing criminal activity by the enemy during the Cold War.'

'But you know what all those death squads were, La Mano Negra, Triple A and many others. They committed monstrous crimes. Mr Kapuściński had wide knowledge on the topic.'

'Why did the intelligence service order political analyses from Kapuściński, such as the ones about the "anti-communist turnaround" in Mexico's policies, or about Cuba's attempts to normalize its relations with other countries in the region?'

'Because Mr Kapuściński was an excellent observer who wrote superb political analyses and had a wider view than the average intelligence employees. The intelligence services aim for that sort of analysis.'

'And could the information he provided, about that editor for instance, have been dangerous for that person, as Kapuściński's lustrators suggested in the press?'

'You're joking . . .'

'One of Kapuściński's lustrators wrote: "The profiles of foreigners included in his reports could have been useful to Polish and Soviet intelligence. And the information that appears there stating that someone might be 'an agent of the [American] secret services' could prove lethally dangerous for that person" '.[5]

'That's nonsense – we're talking about the real world. But anyone who takes James Bond films seriously imagines that's what intelligence work is like.'

'Wrongly? Why do you think it's nonsense?'

'Because intelligence services are involved in gathering information, not killing the other side's agents.'

(In the memoirs of John Stockwell, CIA resident in Angola in the 1970s, I find a passage that provides a good response to the lustrator's accusations: 'In my twelve years of case officering [from 1966 to 1978] I never saw or heard of a situation in which the KGB attacked or obstructed a CIA operation'.[6] In other passages in the book, Stockwell describes friendly conversations and drinking sessions enjoyed by CIA and KGB agents in Angola. He explains the iron principle of the intelligence services: their work relies on gathering information, and on 'turning' the opponents' collaborators to get them to work for 'our' side, not killing them. Murder is a professional error, always a failure.)

'I heard a rumour that after returning from his travels to Third World countries, Kapuściński used to go to Moscow. This rumour includes the suggestion that the Soviet comrades made use of his services too, and therefore he was a very important agent . . .'

(Laughter.) 'Those are tales in the style of "how little Johnny imagines those days to have been" . . . Mr Kapuściński was even small fry for Polish intelligence. For Soviet intelligence he was non-existent, no one there knew about him or had ever heard of him . . .'

'Is it possible that he provided the intelligence service with more information, but it was destroyed or got lost?'

'No. If anything got lost, it was nothing essential. The file from the Institute of National Remembrance shows exactly what the importance of Mr Kapuściński's co-operation with intelligence was. Minimal, almost non-existent.'

During conversations with some of Kapuściński's acquaintances, the following refrains recur:

'He had to play some sort of game with those guys from intelligence.'

'He had no alternative, he had to agree.'

'If he hadn't co-operated, he wouldn't have gone abroad and there would never have been Kapuściński the writer' (this was one of the things Skalski said in his interview for *Newsweek*).

'Does it emerge from your findings that Ryszard wriggled out of co-operating? I hope it does.'

'Play a game', 'had to', 'wriggled out' . . . All the hypotheses sound removed from historical context and are uttered from the perspective of post-1989 Poland, from the viewpoint of opponents to real socialism. They're burdened by the mindset of anti-communist inquisitors and lustrators, even though they're spoken by people who are far from belonging to the right-wing camp; some are even former Party members. In these wishful suppositions lie the unspoken assumptions: that People's Poland was not Poland; that having contact with the intelligence service was just as morally reprehensible as giving information to the secret police who were spying on opponents of the dictatorship; and that Kapuściński was a decent person, so if he did co-operate with intelligence, it was not because he wanted to but 'had to', and if he 'had to', then he was 'playing' or 'wriggling out'.

'Don't you think the situation might have been quite different?' I suggest to one of my interviewees, who was very much hoping that Kapuściński had 'wriggled out' of co-operating. 'That Ryszard Kapuściński wasn't a warrior for the anti-communist underground, but a loyal Party member for almost thirty years? Not a careerist, but a true believer, who really did have faith in socialism for most of that time? People's Poland was his Poland, even if he became disenchanted with Gomułka after his departure from the ideals of October '56, or later on with Gierek. Kapuściński used to encourage his friends to join the ranks of the Party in order to make that reality better.'

My interviewee ponders these facts and admits, after a pause, that he has never thought about it like that before.

Meanwhile, to my mind, this is the only key to an explanation of Kapuściński's life story, how he behaved and the choices he made – none of the others fit, they just grate in the lock, turn it halfway and move no farther. Only when we look at his political life in this way does sporadic co-operation with the intelligence service cease to look like a sinister agreement or an immoral pact with the devil, selling his soul for trips abroad, promotion, or a career.

There was no devil, at least not for Kapuściński. The old system may have appeared diabolical in the eyes of the sworn anti-communists and declared oppositionists, or even those members of the Party who joined its ranks only for career purposes. Kapuściński was a communist, a socialist, a left-wing believer. With the passage of time he had less faith, but more pragmatic approval; he recognized that, despite its deficiencies, socialism is a fairer system than capitalism. In any case, what could any sensitive person think who was familiar – from having spent time in the countries of Africa, Asia and Latin America in the Cold War era – with capitalism's colonial, post-colonial, and imperialist versions? Kapuściński had the right to regard passing on information about sinister CIA operations and its agents to his *own* country's intelligence service and writing a few political analyses as a morally good deed (a patriotic one perhaps?), in all certainty not as something reprehensible.

If he did 'wriggle out', if he did behave like 'an expert at ducking and diving', it was more likely because he was overwhelmed by the weight of his duties as a correspondent. From Mexico City he was covering the whole of Latin America – every day he had to read dozens or hundreds of newspaper articles in a foreign language, listen to radio and television broadcasts, write numerous brief reports and notes, and meet with numerous people. He didn't have enough time for an extra-professional life.

Someone tells me that after returning from Latin America he complained to Frelek that the intelligence service was pestering him and that, through his connections, Frelek arranged for the gentlemen from Rakowiecka Street to leave him in peace. I doubt if the complaint sounded like anti-communist tale-telling, in which PRL intelligence played the role of a criminal institution. Kapuściński is more likely to have complained because he didn't have time, while Rakowiecka Street was being insistent, demanding analyses and reports and bothering him.

In fact, thanks to his connections at the heights of power, he might have been able to refuse the intelligence service earlier, but perhaps it didn't occur to him. From the meagre output in the file we can see that he did not commit himself to co-operation and certainly did not build his career on it.

Did he come to feel at certain moments that writing reports and analyses for the secret service even occasionally is not a proper occupation for a reporter? That it crosses a line which a journalist should not cross? Not because it is for the intelligence service of a communist state, but simply because it is for an intelligence service.

While reviewing the press clippings on 'Kapuściński's file', now and then I come across evidence that even some of the commentators who are well-disposed towards Kapuściński fall into the trap of anti-communist political correctness.

'Aren't we absolving him too easily?' ask the *Newsweek* chiefs Wojciech Maziarski and Aleksander Kaczorowski. 'If it came to light in the US that a famous reporter who had won the Pulitzer Prize had co-operated with the CIA, he'd be compromised in the eyes of the readers.'

This thesis prompts me to examine how co-operation between journalists and the CIA was treated in 'good' America during the Cold War – yet another mirror to reflect the issue of 'Kapuściński and PRL intelligence'. Possibly it will allow us to see the whole affair in another context, in different tones and proportions?

In the mid-1970s two committees of the US Congress – headed by Congressman Otis Pike and Senator Frank Church – conducted inquiries into CIA covert operations. In the course of these, it came to light that recruiting American journalists to co-operate with the CIA was standard practice for the agency. From the very start of the inquiries, the administration in Washington, led by President Gerald Ford and his secretary of state, Henry Kissinger, posed obstructions, and pressure both from former CIA chiefs and the then current chief, George H. W. Bush, stopped the members of congress and the senators from making further inquiries (restraining the latter with greater effect). The CIA chiefs argued that revealing such information would harm American foreign policy. However, some of the revelations, especially from Pike's committee, were leaked to the press, prompting journalists to investigate the collaboration of some individual reporters, as well as entire media institutions, in intelligence activity.

Of the publications that appeared on this topic, the best known at the time was an article entitled 'The CIA and the Media', published in *Rolling*

Stone magazine in October 1977. At the time its author, Carl Bernstein, was one of the two most famous reporters in America – to this day he remains one of the leading US journalists. Only three years earlier, his investigation into the Watergate affair for the *Washington Post*, jointly conducted with Bob Woodward, had led to the resignation of President Richard Nixon.

The following is a summary of 'The CIA and the Media':

As CIA documents clearly show, in the course of a quarter century, starting with the early 1950s, more than four hundred American journalists secretly worked for the CIA. Their relations with the intelligence service were of various types, from 'innocent' conversations or exchanges of insights to completely open co-operation, for example, the acceptance of commissions strictly focused on intelligence. The journalists shared the information they gathered with the CIA, and they were hired as liaison officers between headquarters and professional spies, for instance in communist countries. In the view of senior officials of the agency, they were among the CIA's most valuable 'tools' for gathering data. Freelancers, stringers, full-time journalists from the biggest media, Pulitzer Prize winners regarded as informal ambassadors for their country abroad, and also the chiefs of opinion-forming newspapers, radio and television channels – all co-operated with intelligence.

Among the directors of large media concerns whom the agency officials name as individual collaborators with the CIA are Arthur Hays Sulzberger, publisher of the *New York Times*, William Paley of the Columbia Broadcasting System (CBS), and James Copley of Copley News Service (CNS). The following companies co-operated with intelligence: the American Broadcasting Company (ABC), the National Broadcasting Company (NBC), Associated Press (AP), United Press International (UPI), Reuters, Hearst Newspapers, *Newsweek*, Mutual Broadcasting System (MBS) and many others. In the view of senior CIA officials, the agency's most useful connections were with the *New York Times*, CBS and Time Inc.

How did this institutional co-operation work in practice? Usually the CIA director himself or one of his deputies established a friendship or acquaintance with someone from the management of the newspaper or television channel. The newspaper took on a CIA employee as a journalist or gave him its accreditation. The newspaper or channel's offices abroad shared the information they gathered with the CIA agent. Sometimes the intelligence agents were employed at the office as administrative or technical staff.

The formal relations between the actual reporters and the CIA varied: some signed confidentiality agreements with the agency, some declared that they would never reveal their co-operation, and others functioned under contracts that resembled agreements for employment or temporary commissions. Many kept in looser touch, though they were often entrusted with the very same tasks as the reporters on contract.

What sort of tasks? The CIA used the journalists, above all, to recruit and run foreign agents, to obtain and analyse information, and also to produce disinformation, stirring up confusion and disseminating falsehoods among the political élite in the given country.

The agency's 'standard expectations' of journalists – according to the account of a senior CIA official – went more or less like this: 'We wanted to ask you a favour. You've just come back from Yugoslavia, right? What are the roads like over there? Did you see any sign of the presence of troops? Where exactly? Are there a lot of foreigners there? Just a moment, would you spell that name again . . .'

Briefing conversations before a journey were similar: what to watch out for, whom to meet, with whom to strike up an acquaintance. The CIA treated these journalists as its agents; they often regarded themselves as trustworthy friends who were doing the CIA a favour – usually for no financial gain but for patriotic reasons, for the good of the homeland.

The journalist Joseph Alsop, whom the CIA sent to the Philippines in 1953, just as any other employee would be sent abroad, later said openly, 'I am proud they asked me and proud to have done it. The notion that a newspaperman doesn't have a duty to his country is perfect balls.'

Co-operation between the media and the CIA during the Cold War had its ideology: the fight against 'world communism', the same ideology that justified co-operation between the intelligence service and many other institutions, corporations and companies. It was easy for the intelligence service to penetrate the world of journalism, since the borders between the political, economic and media establishments in America were never all that transparent. Whenever the CIA made use of the co-operation of jour-nalists or their back rooms – in other words, the offices abroad of newspa-pers, radio and television channels – it was almost always with the knowl-edge of the owner, the editor-in-chief or some other key management figure. This means that the most powerful mass media – a total of about twenty-five organizations, corporations and media agencies – carried out functions for the intelligence service.

Involving the media and their foreign correspondents in co-operation with intelligence on a grand scale was begun by Allen Dulles, who became director of the CIA in 1953. Hearing the reports of correspondents coming back from abroad, and obtaining notebooks from them full of contacts and observations, became standard practice for CIA officials from Dulles's time onwards.

Intelligence employees were not in the habit of revealing the names of those who co-operated with them. They argue that it would not be fair to judge the conduct of those journalists in isolation from the context of the times in which – as one senior CIA officer says bitterly – 'it wasn't considered a crime to serve your government'.

However, from time to time some names did surface, such as Jerry O'Leary of the *Washington Star*, or Hal Hendrix of the *Miami News*, who won the Pulitzer Prize. According to agency officials, Hendrix provided the CIA with 'extremely useful information' about Cuban exiles in Florida, and O'Leary about the situation in the Dominican Republic and Haiti. The CIA has in its archives extensive reports on the activities of both journalists, from which it emerges that they received no money for their services.

According to the officials, O'Leary regularly worked for the CIA, yet the journalist himself saw it differently. He claimed that it was not work or co-operation, but ordinary conversations, an exchange of observations. He admitted to being on friendly terms with CIA agents, but it was they – he avowed – who were more helpful to him than he was to them.

This divergence is a good illustration of the non-transparency and ambiguity of the situation in which journalists who maintain contact with the intelligence service find themselves: they might think they are just having conversations with agents and gaining information from them that is necessary for their own work, but meanwhile they are regarded by the intelligence officials, in this case the CIA, as 'our people' or, quite simply, agents.

Certain American journalists were given clearly defined tasks by the CIA and signed contracts; for them, it would be difficult to contend that they were 'just' having conversations (Bernstein provides several names).

The ambiguous, 'grey' nature of the situation regarding agreements with intelligence – in this case institutional agreements – is well illustrated by the case of Arthur Hays Sulzberger, publisher of the *New York Times*. In the years 1950 to 1966, his newspaper provided cover for ten CIA agents. The CIA owed the privilege of close relations with the most influential newspaper in the United States to Sulzberger's friendly relationship with Allen Dulles. It was a deal made by two powerful people and two powerful institutions: both benefited from the agreement, and so it would be difficult to speak of 'pressure' being exerted on a weaker party by a stronger. Sulzberger signed a secrecy agreement with the CIA, the content of which is the subject of controversy. According to some sources, he only agreed not to reveal classified material made available to him 'for information', not for publication; according to others, he swore never to reveal any of the newspaper's dealings with the agency. Sulzberger never hid from his editors and reporters the fact that the newspaper co-operated with the intelligence agency. However, information concerning which reporters or employees performed intelligence tasks in addition to doing their jobs for the newspaper, or who was a CIA employee for whom the paper provided cover, remained confidential.

In 1976, in the course of the inquiries by both committees of Congress, the then head of the CIA, George Bush Sr, promised publicly that the agency would not enter into any paid or contractual relationships with journalists employed within the American media. At the same time, he let it be understood that the intelligence service expected journalists to provide voluntary, unpaid co-operation.

One of the key messages of Bernstein's article is that the job of the intelligence service is to gather information and that it needn't be hampered by the ethics of the journalistic profession. That is the problem of journalists and their chiefs, the owners of the media. 'If even one American overseas carrying a press card is a paid informer for the CIA, then all Americans with those credentials are suspect,' says a former *Los Angeles Times* correspondent.

It would be hard to offer a more apt conclusion.

I ask five well-known American foreign reporters from the press and radio: Were they ever importuned by the CIA, were attempts ever made to recruit them or to talk them into an informal exchange of information? Each of my interviewees travelled to various conflict zones during the Cold War and subsequently: to Soviet bloc countries, including Poland, to Africa, Latin America, the Middle East, to Vietnam during the war and to Iraq following the American invasion in 2003. They all know the context of my question – that it relates to providing a broadened background to the case of Kapuściński and PRL intelligence, and showing how the intelligence services on both sides in the Cold War made use of journalists. Each of the five knows of Kapuściński's lustration.

Only one answers the question in the affirmative: yes, the CIA did try to involve him in co-operation. Another admits to a conversation with American military personnel and 'maybe intelligence too' in Iraq, although nothing was ever said directly, and no offers were made. Someone else replies that the CIA never tried to get information out of him, but later in our conversation admits to a friendship with the CIA resident in one of the countries where he worked as a correspondent.

The only one of my interlocutors who says openly that CIA personnel made him an offer has so many articles to his name exposing criminal operations by American intelligence that I think it pointless to ask him how he responded.

This reporter points out that foreign correspondents, especially in conflict zones, can never be certain whether they serve as a source of information for people from the intelligence community, or if they figure in CIA archives as 'operational contacts' or 'collaborators'. Because, he asks rhetorically, what is the natural place an American reporter heads to as soon as he arrives on site? The US embassy. If there isn't one in that particular country, he goes to the headquarters of an American corporation doing business there, and corporations are sure to have their share of intelligence agents. It is entirely natural for a journalist to go to a meeting at a corporation, because that's where he can find the support of his compatriots on foreign soil, and gain contacts and insights. Can he be certain, while exchanging comments with anyone who works at the embassy or for a big company, that he isn't providing information to the CIA? Never. He has every reason to assume that the embassy's political attaché he's talking to will repeat his views to whomever necessary. And if he speaks directly to the ambassador and tells him something he has seen, heard, or unearthed to which diplomats do not have easy access, is he exceeding the appropriate limits? At what point can it be said that he is already co-operating with intelligence, or not yet doing so? For he can be quite sure that the ambassador will repeat a reporter's revelations to CIA personnel.

'So what's your advice?'

'Caution. You should never say too much. But to tell the truth, there is no good advice.'

I ask if the CIA still makes use of journalists nowadays. Of course, he says, though since the days of the Pike and Church committees it is more cautious and does not involve them so openly in co-operation as before.

'How do you view the similarities and differences between the "Kapuściński case" and co-operation between American journalists and the CIA?'

My interlocutor draws a diagram on a piece of paper to illustrate the structure of the relationships between the political authorities and the media in the socialist countries and in America in the Cold War era. In the communist countries it is a vertical pyramid: authorities – medium (newspaper, press agency) – journalist. The press agency or weekly where Kapuściński worked was not independent; simply put, the authorities could issue orders to the chiefs of the press agency or newspaper. Considered hypothetically, if the journalist were to refuse to co-operate with intelligence, the country's political authorities could order his employer to punish or fire him. The system enables this option, regardless of whether and to what extent it is used.

The sketch showing the relationship between the authorities and the media in America has no vertical dependencies. The authorities can speak directly to the journalist as well as to his bosses. It can influence the owners and managers of the media, but it cannot order them to do anything.

'These differences between the systems are important in the political analysis, but in practice, when it came to a journalist or a media organization co-operating with intelligence, the nature of the information transmitted, the possible consequences and the ethical dimension were exactly the same.'

'Meaning?'

His response is similar to what is found in Bernstein's article: 'If one correspondent is co-operating with intelligence, then we are all suspect. Co-operation with intelligence is a bloody dangerous practice for our profession. Not just because of credibility, the moral aspect; there are lots of "grey" situations that elude unambiguous judgements. But it's also about our plain human safety. If suspicion falls on one person, no one can feel safe.'

Is this the main moral of the story about the reporter who is involved in collusion with the secret services? By co-operating with intelligence even occasionally, whether out of noble intentions or opportunism, Kapuściński wasn't committing the sin of selling his soul to the 'Red devil', as the anti-communist inquisition declares, but a completely different sin. During the Cold War, determinations as to who was 'good' and who was 'evil' depended on the time and place. At that time in the Third World it was the Western countries, above all the United States, that were the enslaving powers, violating weaker countries and societies. But Kapuściński did commit a sin against his own profession, even if he did not fully realize it. Could he have been unaware of committing it? I think he could have, and for a long time at that. He did not grow up in the liberal culture of the Western world, where there is open debate about objectivity and bias in the media, about conflicts of interest and independence. Certain questions might not have occurred to him. Throughout his youth and middle age he was a commit-ted reporter, an idealist who grew up in a Promethean, Romantic tradition, fighting for socialism or promoting the idea abroad; a reporter and man of his era, who identified with the ideals of peoples who were trying to gain their liberty – from Western bondage – and who saw the world in black and white. Moreover, he believed that way of seeing was perfectly appropriate.

By co-operating with intelligence, it was he himself whom he harmed the most, as he came to realize many years after his involvement ended. When *Shah of Shahs* came out in America in the mid-1980s, it was Kapuściński himself, without pressure from anyone – this is my conjecture – who removed the passages about the key role of the CIA in deposing Iranian prime minister Mosaddegh in 1953. Earlier I presented several hypotheses as to why he did it; here I offer only the most significant one. If his own biography included an episode of co-operation with the intelli-gence service of a Soviet bloc country, it would have been an unwise move, in Cold War–era America, to accuse the American intelligence agency of a political crime. Kapuściński could not know whether the CIA had in its files a profile of him – a correspondent from communist Poland, possibly an intelligence agent – a profile analogous to the one he himself had compiled in Mexico on the editor of *Reader's Digest*. (It would not be surprising, in fact, if that man had profiled Kapuściński.) Not knowing whether the CIA had ever taken an interest in him, he preferred not to take the risk. As a former collaborator – no matter how insignificant – he had to deal with the fact that if he made accusations about the CIA in a book published in America, the agency might strike back. And knock him out. How would this have affected his credibility in the United States, what would have been the fate of his books or his subsequent career, if the CIA had leaked to the press the information that the author of *Shah of Shahs*, the denouncer of the CIA's covert operation in Iran, was once in the pay of a rival – communist – intelligence service?

I have tried to determine whether the CIA holds any material on Kapuściński. Thomas Blanton, director of the National Security Archive, who has often fought battles with the agency for declassification of its documents, tells me I shouldn't waste my time and energy. The CIA does not provide information about people and never answers questions about specific individuals. In addition, the CIA has won several precedent-setting cases, in which attempts had been made, based on legislation concerning access to information, to force the agency to confirm or deny information about the existence in its archives of documents on specific individuals. It refuses even to issue a negative answer, such as, 'We have nothing on Kapuściński' – regardless of whether they have something or not.

40

Legends 5: The Price of Greatness

Is it really because he could be publicly pilloried for co-operating with PRL intelligence that in the last few years of his life he is so fearful, so often sad and downcast for a man who has achieved such great success at home and abroad?

Apart from Kapuściński, it is hard to name a writer or thinker from Poland (Zygmunt Bauman perhaps? Stanisław Lem?) who can boast that his books are on sale in as many countries, or published in as many languages. Every day the postman brings him letters from all over the world: invitations to give readings, attend conferences, run workshops, or give interviews. He is awarded honorary doctorates and prestigious prizes; he is a juror, commentator and mentor. Often, however, perhaps too often, friends get the impression that he is less pleased about all the honours paid to him by his readers and by the literary experts, and more horrified by 'those dreadful chaps': the proponents of lustration and decommunization, who are busy searching through the biographies of public figures for evidence of co-operation with the PRL's special services.

Words from the beginning of my journey through Rysiek's life return: despite the world fame that should have made him feel self-confident, there was something oppressing him. I could see it in his eyes, in his step – that smile, that softness.

He expressed his anxiety in a poem written in the final years of his life:

> What should I really have done, said no?
> I said yes,
> And then it began, all this tumbling down and down.
>
> What is there to say?[1]

As I approach the end of this account, I begin to think he was crushed by fear – and not merely of revelations of his co-operation with the intelligence service. It was about far more than that.

Wiktor Osiatyński suggests the following explanation: 'Rysiek produced great work. However, in order for this work to come into existence, he also had to create himself, his own image. In the mid–1980s in America I observed at close hand how he learned that a writer has to build his own image to achieve success. He put a great deal of work and effort into it – it was hard for him, especially at the start, but he passed that exam with flying colours.'

'What sort of image of himself did he create for the world?' I ask.

'The image of a fearless war reporter. How far he consciously created it I do not know, but that was the picture that came out of this creative effort.'

'Also the image of a man who knew in person all the major figures in the most recent history of the countries he wrote about: Che Guevara, Lumumba, Idi Amin?'

'Yes, he reckoned that without this legend no one would want to listen to and read a reporter, a writer from faraway Poland. Later on he created the image of a thinker. Paradoxically, when he died and could no longer create this image, it went on creating itself spontaneously, carrying Rysiek higher and higher.'

'He created a legend about himself in which there are a lot of beautiful, impressive and sometimes blood-chilling tales, but quite often, unfortunately, they are "embellished",' I say.

'That is the price he paid for his greatness,' replies Osiatyński. 'Usually it was the price of minor inaccuracies, sometimes even confabulations. In time it changed into the price of fear that it would all come out and sully the image he had worked so hard to create.

'I will sell you for nothing an idea for the title of your book: "Kapuściński – the price of greatness". If we look at Kapuściński's life story in this way, then all the confabulations, pacts with the authorities in the PRL era and co-operation with intelligence – subordinating everything, even family life, to success – will sound much milder and, to my mind, fairer.'

41

Maestro Kapu

'Herodotus finally has a worthy companion.'

Jaime Abello shows me one of the e-mails which were sent to the Ibero-American New Journalism Foundation in Cartagena, Colombia, when Kapu – as everyone here calls Kapuściński – died.

'Evidently God demanded to know what's really happening in the world, so he summoned the best man to his presence,' says another.

'You're sure to be chatting with people like yourself, living in those territories conquered by grannies and aunties who are expert story-tellers,' says a third, referring to the Latin American world as depicted by García Márquez.

Many of the letters – I counted 144 of them – have come from people who took part in Kapuściński's workshops; even more are from those who did not get into the workshops, though they wanted to. These people express the most regret that they will never be able to meet the master.

I arrive at the foundation almost a year after his death. It occupies a few small rooms in a tenement house in the charming colonial old town area. On the walls are photographs of its famous founder and president, Gabriel García Márquez, who established it in his favourite city. He and a group of his friends decided to do something to improve the poor state, as he saw it, of journalism in Latin America. The main idea was to train a new generation of print reporters to be aware of the mission of the profession.

In 1995 workshops were started up, run by the cream of the profession from both Americas and Europe. These included Alma Guillermoprieto and Jon Lee Anderson (both connected with the *New Yorker*), Horacio Verbitsky and Tomás Eloy Martínez from Argentina, Clovis Rossi from Brazil, Sergio Ramírez from Nicaragua and Joaquín Estefania from Spain. In recent years the star of the workshops was Kapuściński.

'Usually about 100 to 120 journalists apply for the workshops with the other top professionals. There would be 180 to 200 applications for Kapu's workshops,' says Abello, who manages the foundation on a daily basis. Eventually a group of fifteen is selected to take part in the workshops.

★   ★   ★

Although listed among the masters suggested by García Márquez long ago, Kapuściński ended up at the foundation by a roundabout route. In 2000 he visited Bogotá at the invitation of Maruja Pachón, heroine of García Márquez's reportage-novel *News of a Kidnapping*. In the early 1990s Maruja, then a journalist, was kidnapped by drugs baron Pablo Escobar, who was trying to force the Colombian government to renounce the policy of extraditing criminals like him to the United States. Maruja spent six months in captivity, and now runs the Luis Carlos Galán Institute for Development of Democracy (named after her brother-in-law, a politician murdered by Escobar). The Institute runs social programmes and supports the development of local groups in the Colombian interior.

Kapuściński fell in love with Cartagena. He was not always keen to go when he was invited to various conferences and lectures. Public events dragged him away from the most important task, which was writing; and therefore in the final years of his life he more often refused than accepted invitations, though even so he did a lot of travelling. With the foundation in Cartagena it was different: the thought of going to another workshop in one of the Latin American countries – a region that fascinated him and which he loved – brought relief at times of doubt, nervousness and fear, the feeling that he could break away and forget everything for a while. Apart from that, it was García Márquez's foundation that was inviting him, and Kapuściński cared about his friendship with the Nobel laureate, the most famous writer in the region and in the Spanish language.

Jaime and Kapu established that in a few months' time, in March 2001, he would run his first workshops in Mexico City.

In the foundation's archive I review the application letters to get a sense of what the reporters were looking for in Kapuściński's workshops.

'I have used up all the strength needed to write good reportage,' wrote an applicant from Venezuela. 'I'm suffering from "dehydration of the imagination". My dream is that meeting Mr Kapuściński will be a source of inspiration.'

Another one says: 'Kapuściński is a journalist who tells about great events from the point of view of HUMANITY. In his books he has deflated the significance of governments, armies, and big business, and given a voice to the ordinary people, the ordinary soldier, who, though he doesn't understand why he has to kill, does his duty, even with a certain degree of satisfaction.'

The principle of the workshops is that each participant brings his own piece of reportage. Everyone reads each text, and during the sessions they analyse them together: the choice of topic, interviewees, language and method.

Sandra La Fuente from Caracas, whom I met through Kapuściński, says that in fact the most important things were not the conversations about the craft at all – everyone had to work on that alone. 'Kapu showed me the sense of practising this profession.'

I understand what she has in mind after looking through a record of discussions held during the workshops. The reporters ask about everything: about his war experiences, about how he puts up with the loneliness, how he deals with fear, and whether objectivity really exists.

Someone asked why he thinks journalism is not a profession for cynics. This question was an allusion to the title of a Spanish book, never published in Polish (or in English), titled *Los cínicos no sirven para este oficio* (Cynics Are No Good for this Job); it is a record of Kapuściński's meetings with foreign reporters. 'I don't believe,' replied Kapu,

> that a real journalist can be a cynic, and I've known a lot of journalists. Our professional success relies on other people. Our interlocutors can unerringly tell the difference between a reporter who asks about matters which are of deep concern to him personally, and one who has only come to get a story and rush off again. Without empathy it is impossible to share the joys and sufferings of the people we write about. Only at the level of more profound interpersonal relations can we find good material for our writing.

Jaime García Márquez, younger brother of the writer and the foundation's number two, spreads his hands when I ask for his help in getting a meeting with Gabo, as everyone here calls Gabriel García Márquez.

'Gabito never talks about or writes memoirs of his deceased friends.' (From another source I hear that his state of health does not allow him to give interviews.) But the writer's brother is in no doubt that, besides mutual admiration for each other's literary achievements, Kapu and Gabo had good 'political chemistry'.

Both were fascinated by the topic of power – especially the absolute kind. At roughly the same time as Kapu was writing *The Emperor*, Gabo published *The Autumn of the Patriarch*. When Gabo was planning to write a novel about Simón Bolívar (*The General in His Labyrinth*), Kapu was conquering the world with *Shah of Shahs*. Did they ever argue over their views about Fidel Castro, with whom García Márquez has been friendly for more than thirty years? We shall never know. Kapuściński, who never wrote a full-length article about Castro – with the exception of analyses for the PAP's Special Bulletin – did make a few critical public remarks about the Cuban leader; at parties accompanying the workshops in Mexico City, he called Castro one of the world's few remaining representatives of authoritarian power and said he belonged to the past.

Kapu and Gabo met in 1970, when Kapuściński was working as the PAP correspondent in Mexico City. *One Hundred Years of Solitude* had not yet been translated into Polish, and Gabo, who was only just becoming a giant of Latin American fiction, was still better known as a reportage writer.

'I have always regarded him as a friend, as someone with whom I have a perfect understanding,' wrote Kapuściński, remembering their joint workshops in Mexico City. He called Gabo 'a classic of reportage' and claimed that 'however much one admires his novels, García Márquez's greatness lies in his journalistic articles from which the later literature grew'.

Gabo arrived deliberately late for Kapu's first workshops in Mexico City to avoid drawing attention to himself. All in vain – as soon as he appeared, everyone stood up to greet him: 'Master . . .' To which Gabo said, 'The real master is here,' and pointed to Kapuściński. After that he sat with the audience to stress that Kapu had one more pupil.

Jaime Abello once conducted the following experiment: While on his own with each of them in turn, he asked the same question: 'What is the best route to good journalism?' Both independently gave the same answer: via poetry. Why? Because more than any other literary form, it forces one to aim for conciseness and aptness of expression. Kapu also added history, which he had studied at university. He believed that a journalist is a sort of historian, who writes about the present day.

It is hard to believe that at Kapu's meetings with a group of ambitious journalists there was never once a clash, and that the master experienced a sheer idyll full of compliments, as everyone here says, wanting to remember nothing but good things about Kapu. I share my intuition with Jon Lee Anderson and discover that merely inviting Kapuściński to the workshops as a master of journalism stirred some controversy. No one from the foundation in Cartagena will officially confirm this fact.

The issue is not the literary excellence of Kapuściński's books – everyone agrees about that – but rather the tasks of a foundation which is meant to be contributing to raising the standards of journalism in Latin America. One set of standards that demand development, improvement and the goal of perfection involves accuracy of information, credibility, attention to detail, and also book-keeping – the checking and rechecking of doubtful facts. It is no secret to anyone – and certainly not at the foundation – that in Kapuściński's books the factual precision is not exemplary. In which case, should he be invited as a master of the profession? Perhaps he should be at some sort of literary workshops instead?

Factual accuracy and faithfulness to reality are a topic of debate during the workshops in Mexico City. In the course of the discussion, García Márquez poses a provocative question: 'Does a journalist have the right to "paint in" a tear on the sad old woman featured in his report, which in reality she did not actually shed? "Paint it in" for a stronger literary effect?'

'That is a betrayal of journalism,' replies Graciela Mochkofsky, from Argentina. 'A writer may do that, a journalist absolutely cannot. He's not allowed to correct reality.'

Graciela is seconded by a colleague from Colombia, Juanita León.

'But I think,' says García Márquez in reply, 'a journalist does have the right to "paint in" that tear. Better to reflect the atmosphere of the moment, the state of mind of the person being described. Where's the betrayal in that?'

And smiling, he turns to Kapuściński: 'You tell lies sometimes too, don't you, Ryszard?'

Kapuściński laughs. He doesn't utter a single word. The workshop participants can tell perfectly what the answer is.

Graciela thinks Kapuściński was not greatly concerned about the issue of the 'truth' in reportage: 'He was more interested in creating a new literature, a new genre, new narrative forms; realism and descriptive precision, as journalists understand it, were in the background.'

Some of the workshop participants are disappointed: each has brought one of his or her own articles, which all of them were to read and then jointly discuss, but Kapu, who has received all the texts in advance, has not read a single one. This makes a bad impression on the workshop audience – they do not know the real reason for the master's lack of preparation. They do not know that Kapu is tired, overcome by weakness and brought down by old age, or that he really is trying to read their articles, but sadly discovers in the course of his attempts that he does not understand Spanish as well as he once did. It is thirty years since he left his post as a correspondent in Latin America; he has returned several times since then and has also travelled to Spain, but only for short periods. He can still speak Spanish, but feature articles and the literary vocabulary prove an insuperable obstacle. And so he proposes a plan B to the workshop participants: each of them is to describe one fundamental problem he or she struggles with in his or her professional life. Then there will be an exchange of comments and experiences – a debate.

'Kapu didn't want to say anything about himself, though' – I hear this comment from three of the participants: Graciela, Boris Muñoz from Venezuela and Julio Villanueva from Peru.

The Mexico City workshops are coming to an end, it is the final day, and Kapu has not yet told the young reporters anything about himself, not a word – he has simply moderated the discussions. Julio and Boris refuse to speak anymore, and ask the master to take the floor. After a pause for thought, Kapu agrees. He talks sketchily about his trips to Africa, about covering armed conflict, and a little about his wartime childhood, also about how *The Emperor* came into being.

Boris: 'It felt as if he was jealously guarding his secrets, personal and literary.' Graciela and Julio feel the same way. Just before leaving, Julio conducts an interview with Kapuściński, but he will not even discover what books the master is planning to write. That, too, is a secret.

'Just before the end of the workshops,' says Graciela, 'once he had finally told us something about himself, I asked if he regretted anything in life, if he had ever missed out on anything important by being away from home for so many years, far from his wife and daughter.'

'Why do women always ask that question?' replied Kapuściński tetchily.

'I am a man,' offers one of the journalists, 'and I'm interested in the answer to that question too.'

Half offended, Kapuściński angrily leaves the room. The workshops are over.

The foundation published a record of Kapuściński's three workshops and the conferences accompanying them in a booklet called *Los cinco sentidos del periodista* (The Journalist's Five Senses) – to be, to see, to hear, to empathize, to think. In the contract, which Jaime Abello shows me, Kapuściński makes clear that the book must be given away, and not sold ('My agent in Switzerland would be jealous,' he joked).

It is a sort of summing up by Kapuściński of the journalist's profession (in the course of the series of workshops and public panels, he did in fact say something about himself and the occupation of journalist). He admits to being inspired by the French school of social history known as Annales – a way of thinking based on building an image of the whole out of details and extracting 'long lasting' elements.

He outlines the reporting tradition with which he identifies: Balzac, Goethe, Orwell, Malaparte, Chatwin, Baudrillard, García Márquez. He talks about the reporter's mission as an 'interpreter of cultures', encountering 'the Other', and the threats of globalization – themes familiar from his books, articles and interviews.

In a section about the dilemmas of the profession the journalists ask, among other things, how to deal with censorship. Kapu tells them about toying with the censor in the days of the PRL, but he sees the main threat nowadays in a different type of censorship: the conflict between the truth and the interests of the media owners, including the fact that the media have taken up residence close to power and have ceased to be critical.

'Here there is no single piece of good advice. You have to fight and negotiate to remain faithful to our professional mission.'

One more confession: Kapu does not believe in objectivity. Formal objectivity in conflict situations can even result in disinformation. The greatest reporters, such as Orwell or García Márquez, always practised 'journalism with intent', which 'fights for a cause'. (In other words, to the end of his life he never changes his mind about this!)

At the foundation's headquarters in Cartagena, I peruse the workshop participants' feedback forms, commenting on Kapuściński. Not a single appraisal is negative, and only two comments are lukewarm: 'Good work'; 'OK'. The rest are in this spirit: 'This is Ryszard Kapuściński. There's nothing more to be said.' Or 'At last I can say the word "master" without the slightest hesitation'.

The Colombian journalist Oscar Escamilla took to heart Kapu's lessons about building up bigger images from details, and in the introduction to *Los cincos sentidos del periodista* he wrote:

> I noticed his small feet – and I wasn't the only one who did. Someone later said to me that he would never have imagined that a man who had spent such a large part of his life travelling the world could have such small feet.[1]

42

Unwritten Books

He typed out the title page: 'Ryszard Kapuściński, *Amin*, Czytelnik 1983'.

> In the morning I went to the market, thinking maybe I'll find some fish.
> The street was empty, but suddenly I saw a green Land Rover appear in
> it, which disappeared shortly after. At the last moment, once it had
> already overtaken me, I noticed Amin at the wheel.[1]

That was to be the start of one of the books he never wrote.

He left behind several unfinished projects and unwritten volumes. He
had been nursing some of the ideas for years, but had then dropped them
for more urgent ones. But there were also books he never stopped thinking
about, writing them in his mind, and also in exercise books, on notepads
and on loose sheets of paper.

1.

The book about the Ugandan dictator Idi Amin was meant to be the third
volume, after *The Emperor* and *Shah of Shahs*, of a triptych about the mechanisms of power.

Years later, Kapuściński told how he had been laid up with cerebral
malaria in hospital in Kampala, when he saw Amin among a group of officers who had come to tour the newly opened clinic. How he could have
known, in 1962, half-conscious with malarial fever, that the 'jovial clown,
a great big fellow' was Amin – an unknown figure at the time – remains a
mystery. (I think this is just another legend.)

In the period from 1971 to 1979, Idi Amin slaughtered – according to
various estimates – from 150,000 to 300,000 people.

According to Kapuściński, Amin was:

Psychologically immature, a sort of big, cruel child, unstable, impetuous,
volatile. In the morning he could be cheerful, in the evening he could fall
into rage or depression. He was quickly bored, would leap up from his chair
and leave the room. He had racing thoughts, spoke chaotically and didn't

finish his sentences. However, in his wildness and madness, he acted logically and consistently.

About fifteen years after the unfortunate trip during which he fell ill with malaria, Kapuściński again visits Uganda. It is the zenith of Amin's violent insanity. Journalists are not admitted to the police state that he rules, and Kapuściński is probably issued a Ugandan visa by mistake in neighbouring Ethiopia.

As soon as he arrives at the airport he notices he is being tailed. Silent, broad-shouldered gentlemen in uniforms and dark glasses never abandon him for a moment. He stays at the Hotel Stanley, as he usually has done on past trips to Kampala. The gentlemen in dark glasses are right behind him. When he goes into the bar and sits down at a table, the gentlemen in dark glasses sit at the next table. They don't ask questions. They just watch.

On the morning of 24 December 1977 Kapuściński goes to the market. It is Christmas Eve and, in keeping with Polish tradition, he wants to buy fish for dinner. Suddenly a green Land Rover comes speeding down the empty street in the city centre. At the last moment he notices the driver – Amin, it was Amin. In the opening paragraphs of the unfinished book he writes:

> He raced along, crossed a junction (in spite of a red light) and waved at someone (whom? there wasn't a soul in sight). I could have sworn I heard his laughter, still loud as it faded into the distance. Only some time later a column of vehicles came slowly down that same street, in the same direction – some covered jeeps with bodyguards, their barrels aimed at gates, trees, windows and the sky, and in the middle of the column Amin's shiny Citroën-Maserati (and sprawled on the back seat the massive figure of an officer, on display for an assassin's murderous shot).[2]

At the sight of the column Kapuściński does not bat an eyelid, but just keeps on walking as before, no faster, no slower. At moments like these, the iron principle applies: do not draw attention to yourself, just blend into the landscape. The gunmen drive off without stopping or firing a shot.

He goes to the Kisenyi district, the former heart of Kampala. Once, he recalls, there was life here: trading, drinking and amusement all night long. Now Kisenyi is gloomy, suspicious and aggressive. You can get a stone in the face, you can get knifed.

He meets a white missionary called Father Eusebio. Kapuściński invites him to dinner – after all, it is Christmas Eve – but the missionary does not reply.

> He smiles and makes a gesture from which I cannot tell if he will come or not, and suddenly disappears. White people prefer not to gather in

groups – a group arouses suspicion. They've gathered together – what for? They're standing there talking – about what? Where have they been, who was there, what did they talk about, how long did it last? Names. Precise statements. Who they were laughing at. What they decided. Where who went afterwards. With whom. By what means.[3]

In his handwritten notes, plans and sketches for the book, Kapuściński writes that *Amin* will be a book not just about a man but also about a situation; Amin is a man and a situation all in one. It also involves a climate of universal mendacity and all-embracing fear. The lying, notes Kapuściński, depends on total reversal of the truth. The truth cannot be just a little twisted, it must be completely reversed. For example, Amin murders people connected with his enemy Milton Obote, and announces that Obote himself has murdered them in order to compromise Amin.

Kapuściński looks for the key to the character study of the tyrant–butcher, the tyrant–clown, the tyrant–child. He consults the works of philosophers and psychologists. It looks like the makings of a treatise on stupidity. (Once he knows he will never write the book about Amin, he includes some of these comments in the *Lapidaria*). Here is a sample from the notes:

> Popper makes an incisive comment on the topic of ignorance. Ignorance, he writes, is not just a simple lack of knowledge, but an ATTITUDE, an attitude of refusal, an attitude of dissent against accepting knowledge. The fool REFUSES to know . . .
>
> The fool has pre-set opinions about everything which, as they never change, make it seem as if he was born with them, as if he drank them in with his mother's milk . . .
>
> Here, however, another variety of fool appears – the cunning fool, who sees secret forces everywhere, levers and springs ('there's something hiding behind it', 'there's something in it' etc.).[4]

A fool of this type, a fool who saw conspiracies everywhere but was at the same time able to calculate, act logically and effectively – to gain and keep his own power – that was Amin.

In February 1988 Kapuściński receives a letter from Kampala. The sender is Piotr Zeydler, a Polish émigré who works in Uganda but whose permanent home is in Switzerland. From the American weekly *Time*, Zeydler has learned that Kapuściński is planning to write a book about Amin, so he's come up with the idea of inviting the writer to Kampala. He offers him a place to stay and any help he needs, and warns him of the risks involved.

He reminds Kapuściński that there is a sort of civil war going on in Uganda, and also that the AIDS epidemic is spreading like wildfire. He reassures him that the sexual restraint recommended by the government is providing protection against the disease (though in those years it is not yet clear if it is possible to be infected with AIDS through mosquito bites, and there are plenty of mosquitoes in Uganda).

They set a date for his arrival: 25 May 1988.

Is Uganda an unlucky place for him? A few days after arriving, Kapuściński notes:

> Something like a mild attack of malaria. I lie in bed until noon. Then I write up my notes and read. At seven pm, when the sky fades and dusk falls, a loud, intense, very insistent concert of crickets suddenly begins.[5]

He spends a lot of time in the library, where – as it turns out – there are some properly bound annual volumes of newspapers from the period of Amin's governments. Almost 100 percent of his notes from the trip are excerpts from the press and from books; there is a fat, green-covered spiral notebook full of them.

For instance, a note derived from Henry Kyemba's book, *State of Blood*:

> If Amin took a liking to a woman, he murdered her husband or fiancé . . .
> Amin took money from the state treasury and kept his pockets stuffed with it. Then he handed it out to whomsoever he wished.[6]

William Pike, founder and editor-in-chief of the newspaper *New Vision*, shows him places in Kampala connected with the figure of Amin. The North Korean embassy is now housed in the building from which Amin ran his coup d'état. Thanks to his press card from a socialist country, Kapuściński manages to get inside and poke around for a while, under the watchful eye of some Korean security agents.

Years later he told an interviewer:

> Lots of books have been written about Amin, but no good ones that deal with the actual phenomenon of Amin. There's a simple reason why I never wrote my own. I had only just started to make a few drafts, when perestroika began in the Soviet Union. The reporting journalist in me won the day – I dropped Amin and raced east to gather material for *Imperium*.[7]

His friends recall that he was indeed urged to write the book about the collapsing Soviet empire. At first he hadn't been keen on this idea. One reason he held back was that he was busy working on the book about Amin. The argument was won by the potential success in the West of a book about the fall of communism, written by a reporter from Eastern

Europe who by then was already famous. Who, if not someone from the region, for example Kapuściński, should be telling people in the West about the collapsing empire?

Wasn't it a pity to abandon so many years of work on Amin?

'It's a pity, but I don't know if I'll have time, if I'll ever manage to fit him into my demanding schedule', he said in August 2003,[8] just before Amin died in exile in Saudi Arabia.

2.

On 25 May 2000, Kapuściński lands in Lima. He doesn't recognize the city where he briefly lived thirty-two years ago. At the time, he shut himself away in a hotel room for two weeks and translated the diary of Che Guevara, who had been executed a few months earlier.

Many years later, he got down to work on the book about Latin America which he had been talking about since the 1970s. In 1998, when he published his summing up of Africa, *The Shadow of the Sun*, he announced that he would devote the next volume to the Latin American world.

After Kapuściński's death I received an e-mail from Ignacio Ramonet of *Le Monde Diplomatique*, asking if Ryszard had left behind any unfinished passages of this new book, or if he had started writing it at all. While Kapuściński was still alive, Ramonet had said, 'The world is waiting for this book.'

It was going to be called *Fiesta* (he also considered the title *Flight of Birds*). On an A4 sheet of paper he wrote out the idea for the book: it would be the most essay-like of all his books to date. It would contain elements of reportage, but only to serve as a starting point for broader anthropological reflection. There would be three basic themes: the realities of the continent, the mix of cultures – the uniting of both Americas – and the 'global context'.

But first: the journey. What sort of continent is it nowadays? How has it changed? What do the people live on?

It is his first head-on encounter for years. He does not recognize Lima, he does not recognize a world which he thought he knew extremely well, and where he spent almost five years as a PAP correspondent. The aristocracy and wealthy bourgeoisie have disappeared from the centre of Lima, built according to models of colonial architecture; the richer people have moved to smart districts far from the centre. In his travel diary for 31 May 2000, he notes:

> Their former houses and mansions now stand empty, shut up and decaying, often with broken windows.
>
> Only thirty years ago old gentlemen were strolling along these streets, exchanging bows, and dropping in at cafés which were like the cafés in

Vienna or Barcelona. Nowadays these streets belong to the young Peruvians, to the Andean people dressed identically in jeans and trainers, eating hamburgers, chips and ice cream on sticks. They come here in crowds, and clearly being here in this place is for them a form of enno-blement – their grandfathers would never have dared to cross the thresh-old of the old city! But now it is all open to them!

It is curious that all the shops selling Peruvian folklore have vanished from the old town – these people have not brought it with them, they have left it in the Andes and cut themselves off in favour of chewing gum and Coca Cola.[9]

As ever, Kapuściński takes notice of the poor:

Friday, 2 June 2000. Here (in Peru) El Pobre [the poor man] is like another person, living in a different world . . . It is better to dissociate yourself from *El Pobre, pobreza* [poverty] is like an infectious disease, a social form of AIDS, something people talk about with reluctance and disgust.[10]

Keywords, obsession words, in the diary include 'hybrid', 'syncretism', and '-*mezcla*' (mixture).

Apart from his observations, he records certain reflections and generali-zations heralded in the synopsis of the book:

Latin America offers a model for future world civilization.

This is where modernity began (the arrival of Columbus) – this is where the twenty-first century is beginning. This is the century for presenting a wealth and diversity of different cultures, visions and atti-tudes. At the centre of the wealth of cultures is the fiesta of the title – a festival. A festival means joy because of the harvest, a festival means joy because of a soccer team's victory, a festival means sheer fun.[11]

As always in his writing, there are some adventures, too. In Peru on 9 June 2000 he goes on a 'suicidal' – as he notes afterwards – trip to Alto Andino. The means of transport is a dilapidated off-road Toyota, so dirty that it is impossible to tell its colour. At one point the car drives down what appears to be a vertical wall:

There is total silence in the car . . . I'm feeling nauseous. We are driving along a rough track, a shelf in the wall. The bends are hidden. Terror. It's impossible to turn around. The engine stops. We can't get out. Bald tyres. Worn brakes. Going back is even worse . . . I cling to the car, but it makes no sense . . . God, let me live a little longer. Why do I have to

die now? And here of all places! Somewhere at the bottom of this
Barranca [ravine]! I was trying not to look. But no way – the tighter I
closed my eyes, the greater the temptation to open them and stare into
the abyss . . .

We have to take some extra people to weight the car down. Otherwise
we might slip off. Some stone-like figures come to life. They get in,
grateful that we're picking them up, that we're taking them with us to our
death.[12]

He asks questions about yesterday's and today's Peru. His interviewees are
academics, clergy and social workers. One of the topics is the criminal
guerrilla group the Shining Path.

The provinces – the universities were a school of frustration. The students
could not go back to the countryside, but they had no chance of social
advance, because the level of teaching was low. They gave them a totalitarian ideology, which explained everything. This sort of ideology has a
religious dimension. Like Hitler, Stalin – the leader is a sort of god. This
is the mentality of Jehovah's Witnesses . . . Abimael Guzman [the Shining
Path's ideologue] is a Maoist. He had no love for Peru, just a desire for
war against Peruvian society.[13]

Before landing in Bolivia, Kapuściński is worried about how he will
cope with the altitude. The airport at El Alto, where he lands, is situated at
over 4,000 metres above sea-level. Some people suffer badly from altitude
sickness, soroche. They feel sick, vomit and have hallucinations. It can also
cause pulmonary or cerebral oedema.

The officer spent a long time studying the list of countries whose citizens
do not require a visa to enter Bolivia. (Here I often come across the question: 'Is Poland a communist country?')[14]

In Bolivia he is interested in the new ethnic movements – one of the
leaders, Evo Morales, will become president five years later – but even more
in the culture of the Andean peoples.

The Andean world is a world of silence, a world of few words. You have
to listen carefully to each of these words, and imagine what lies hidden
behind them. There must be a space between them to be filled in by our
imagination.[15]

Then Paraguay. In a town called Encarnación, as he passes a small hotel,
the Polish priests who are acting as his guides tell him a local legend.

Apparently Dr Mengele, the torturer from Auschwitz, was in hiding here, and a female Mossad agent who was on his trail, was killed.

After almost two months of travelling, Kapuściński is tired. More and more of the excerpts have no date. The notes are perfunctory. He promises to have done with the exhausting journeys.

The final stage is São Paulo, Brazil. His attention is caught by the following information in a newspaper: 'Supranational corporations are opening their own banks in our country'. The conclusion:

> The element of US penetration in Latin America. The era of armed intervention and *golpe de estado* [coups d'état] is over. Nowadays we have not just velvet revolutions, we also have velvet expansion (the world is becoming civilized – partly!)[16]

He is surprised by one of his discoveries:

> My major topic was mass movements of the wronged and the humiliated who were fighting for dignity and the right to a better life, but the wronged and humiliated aren't fighting for anything nowadays, they are just trying to adapt, to tear off the little piece they manage to finagle, to dig out for themselves as comfortable, warm and private a niche as possible, and to look out of it, to right and to left, to see what else they might be able to wangle for themselves here.[17]

A year later, after a visit to Mexico City, he clearly changes his mind. He is impressed by the entry of Subcomandante Marcos's rebels into the capital. He prophesies the awakening of ethnic America. He discerns a new wave of protests by the wronged and the humiliated, which he calls 'the spring of the Latino peoples'. He is brimming with optimism, because now the battle is (usually) being fought without the bloodshed which he witnessed when he first came to this continent in the 1960s.

Something on the continent has ended, and something new has begun.

> This topic of mine is finished. Because it was the drama of power, and power is no longer going through dramas, at most it is going through fear that its bank accounts will be discovered and that it will go to prison.[18]

He sets Latin America aside for later.

3.
First the planning and the logistics.

When is the best time to go to the Trobriand Islands?

How do you get there? Can it be done by plane, or only by ship?

Where can you stay?

What security measures should you take?

What medicines and inoculations do you need?

Can you drink the water there?

In July 2004 he finishes writing *Travels with Herodotus* and starts musing on a new book. He regarded Herodotus as the first reporter, his progenitor. The ancient historian was meant to be a mirror for his own experiences as a reporter, traveller and researcher of Otherness. In this same role he now casts his next hero, the famous Polish anthropologist Bronisław Malinowski. *Travels with Malinowski*? This book, too, is intended to embody in the form of reportage the positive obsession of his final years – the need for an 'encounter with the Other' that is marked by respect and understanding ('otherwise we shall all kill each other, and there are six billion of us!' he would doggedly repeat in many interviews). Both books are, to some extent, about himself.

Less than a year later, he asks a friend from Gdańsk how to get to the Trobriand Islands, where Malinowski conducted his research. She replies that the days of the PRL are over, when Polish ships used to sail the world's seas and oceans. The friend establishes that now they only transport goods to Hamburg and Rotterdam and to ports on the Mediterranean, whence the goods travel on huge container ships, to Singapore for example. Only from there do they finally go to Australia. No one knows anything about sea voyages to Papua New Guinea.

There is a chance that the people from POL-Euro and Polfracht (offshoots of Polish Ocean Lines) could assist Kapuściński with the journey, but first they would like to know more about his plans.

The idea falls apart. It is hard to establish anything for certain, and Kapuściński has doubts whether he could cope with such a long journey.

At the same time another friend, Jola Wolski (who has been living in Australia for years) conducts e-mail correspondence on Kapuściński's behalf to work out a journey in Malinowski's footsteps. A friend of hers in Sydney establishes that there are only two flights a week (on Tuesdays and Sundays) from Port Moresby to Losuia, and only two places where one can stay on the islands, 'modest but comfortable'. He writes about difficulties with flight connections and possible delays, and advises how to make a ticket reservation. He also advises checking the web site of the World Health Organization to see if you should take anti-malaria drugs before travelling to the Trobriands. Kapuściński replies that his wife, who is a doctor, has advised caution, long trousers, long sleeves and mosquito repellent.

Kapuściński considers making the journey in September, October or November 2005, and is counting on friends to advise him which time of year is the most suitable. The plan collapses in ruins, however, because of a hip complaint and the dreadful pain that accompanies it. He cannot sit for long and must spend time lying down.

Meanwhile, there's something he can do at home: get on with the reading. He reads the works of the acclaimed American anthropologist Clifford Geertz, as well as books about Geertz (and, on 30 October 2006, Geertz dies at the age of eighty).

He wonders 'how to construct a scholarly text based on one's own, personal, biographical experiences, to be at once a pilgrim and a cartographer, both friendly and dispassionate. Because anthropology is embroiled with the issue of encountering the Other'.

Finally, there is the hero of the story himself, Malinowski:

Malinowski is a man with an exceptionally well-developed ability to adapt and a highly developed capacity to empathize. On the one hand a romantic, on the other a rigorous scholar.

Malinowski embodies ethnography relying on immersion.

Knowledge is only possible through 'total immersion'. For that you need a 'sense of vocation'. Immersion in the dark recesses of one's own 'self'. The capacity to lead a polymorphic life . . .

Reporting, surveying – is an act of violence (at a symbolic level) – violating the integrity of my interlocutor. Emersion.[19]

He makes a simulation of the journey: in a file entitled 'The Trobriand Islands (Journey)' is a sort of run-through of the connections, travel times and prices. Warsaw to Frankfurt (1 hr 45 mins), Frankfurt to Singapore (12 hrs), Singapore to Cairns, Australia (7 hrs 50 mins). Then the journey to Papua New Guinea: from Cairns to Port Moresby, then to Losuia on Kiriwina, the biggest of the Trobriand Islands. The approximate price of the flights in both directions (in April–May 2006) is 8,866 zloty (approximately £1,530 in autumn 2006). Another simulation, to Australia and from there to the islands, runs over 12,000 zloty (more than £2,000). On-site some Polish missionaries, Pallotine Fathers, would be helping him (there are four names).

This is the last note he makes on 'the Malinowski case':

Nowadays, however, it is not a description of isolated peoples that is needed and possible, but an increase in the possibility for dialogue between people of varying interests and views shut in a world of never-ending mutual connections, a world containing a whole range of ever more interwoven (?) differences. 'There' and 'here' are less and less sharply defined. You have to struggle with the realities in a world which has changed its nature again.[20]

During his preparations for the long journey, he makes notes and drafts poems about old age, pain and death. He senses that he will never go. Planning the journey is a way of escaping from depression and from nagging thoughts about the end.

43

No Strength to Furnish the Face

This is the end of the journey. I go back to its beginning: less than a year after Rysiek's death, when I enter his kingdom in the loft. I am to write an article for the newspaper about this study, or rather, something about its late inhabitant.

The most conspicuous thing is the books. There are books everywhere. There are press cuttings everywhere. There are exercise books, notebooks and notepads everywhere.

To the left of the entrance is the guest area: a small table and some low armchairs. People would sit here and chat for hours. He would lie on a sofa when his back hurt after prolonged writing – increasingly often during the last two years, when his bad hip kept him from sitting for long periods.

At the right of the entrance, in the depths, stands the desk. There is an Erica typewriter covered with a cloth, and a photograph in a clip frame, depicting his hands as he was writing a dedication to someone in a book – the words aren't clear and might be in Spanish. There are two lamps, a standard lamp and an anglepoise that gives light from above. There are hundreds of ballpoint pens in mugs, erasers, sticky tape, and coloured slips of paper for marking passages in books. There are various notes – in pocketbooks and on loose sheets of paper.

One of the final notes reads:

23.12.06: The reporter turns into a PATIENT who is going into hospital for an abdominal operation. *Don't complain.*[1]

There is a list of people he has to call before going into hospital – fourteen names.

On the desk extension there is a cloth-covered laptop, which he learned to use for writing but which he never liked. 'No one has ever written a great book on a computer!' he once argued quite seriously with his friends' daughter, Dorota.

'But Rysiek, what are you saying? So many great writers write on computers nowadays,' she told him. 'He gave me such a telling-off that I cried.' It was Dorota who recommended someone who taught him how to use this modern invention – without much success.

It is the second computer he ever bought in his life. The first one, he suspected, was stolen by a photographer who accompanied a foreign reporter conducting an interview, and who was left on his own in the room for quite a long time 'to take pictures of the master's study'. After that visit, the laptop vanished into thin air, as did the photographer, hired via the Internet.

I have been here dozens of times before, but only now do I establish the geography of the cavernous study in the loft, full of nooks and crannies. The living quarters are on the floor below, but the real kingdom is up here.

Facing the entrance is a table where the reading matter needed for his current book in progress always lay. Because, he contended, the main thing involved in writing is reading ('for every single page that you write, read a hundred' – for years he had been drumming this into young reporters' heads).

'It's all just as he left it when he went to hospital,' says Alicja.

Under the table is an impressive collection of dozens of books about Latin America. Several years earlier, when he set about writing his summation of Latin America, these books were on top of the table. He would walk around them, highlighting quotations and inserting Post-it notes – until one day *Herodotus* shoved them under the table. After *Travels with Herodotus*, the small table became a complete mess.

He continued to dream of writing that book – the notes from the journey to Peru, Bolivia, Brazil and Colombia left on the desk testify to the fact that this idea had taken up permanent residence in his mind. But this plan was not immediate enough for the Latin American books to return to the table where earlier the African materials had been lying while he was writing *The Shadow of the Sun*, and the books about antiquity when he was working on *Travels with Herodotus*.

Whereas on the little table, the one to the left of the entrance, which I call the tea table – where he received friends and acquaintances – he left the reading matter on anthropology, about rituals on Pacific islands. Preparations for *Travels with Malinowski*.

On the shelves above the desk are all sorts of literature: philosophy, religion, history (mainly ancient and medieval), civilizations, anthropology. Further on: literary theory, modern political philosophy, and art history. Here we unexpectedly come upon the entrance to a kitchenette, where he made tea and coffee; further on is a small bathroom. Hanging there are some chest expanders and rubber rings for squeezing in the hands; on the floor are one-kilo dumb-bells and a 17.5 kilo weight!

Next to the steps leading to a mezzanine (where there is a storeroom with all the foreign editions of *The Emperor, Shah of Shahs, The Shadow of the Sun*, etc.) are books about Pińsk and Polesie, along with classics of reportage and travel writing. Further on, there are dictionaries and encyclopaedias, including Britannica.

And everywhere there is poetry, strewn about the entire kingdom. One might find collections by Joseph Brodsky (his portrait is pinned to a wooden post with files on it, full of notes, cuttings and quotations), Tadeusz Różewicz, Czesław Miłosz and W. H. Auden, or read stanzas by Wisława Szymborska or Anna Świrszczyńska pinned to the wall. Somewhere in there is a brief letter from Edward Stachura, Mexico City, 14 January 1975: 'Best Wishes for the New Year and several dozen to follow, if they don't blow up our planet'.

The scattered poets and poetry (and prose, too, which he changed into poetry by cutting out or underlining a passage, a quote, or an aphorism) say the most about the absent ruler of this kingdom. Without them it is a library – impressive, but just a library. The poems, quotes and aphorisms are the soul of this place. And many of its elements can only be described by poetry.

For example, on a shelf under the window lies a jumble of souvenirs and gadgets. What isn't to be found here?

A piece of charoite – a purple stone with a note attached: the only deposit discovered to date is on the River Chara (a tributary of the Lena in Siberia).

A pipe for drinking yerba maté.

Some old coins from the PRL era and several from countries whose alphabet I do not recognize.

A tiny picture of the Buddha.

A little car from Cartagena (they give them away at the best hotels in this city on the shores of the Caribbean.)

A Solidarity badge.

A Lenin badge.

Figurines of little angels (gold and white – on the window-sill above the small shelf).

Some mascots: a squirrel, a little goat, a rose, and two small metal elephants.

Some rifle cartridges.

Some clay vessels, a figurine from India and a thousand other treasures.

What immediately comes to mind is a poem by Leopold Staff:

O, fairy-tale poetry of a small boy's pocket,
Where more priceless wonders lie hidden
Than on the sea-bed, whole treasuries of assorted jumble:
Pebbles, bits of string, pieces of glass, rusty pens
And coloured crayons, where landscapes only seen in dreams
Lie sleeping, in a hundred colours but never painted.[2]

The landscapes of Latin America. Of the islands of Oceania. Of his hometown, Pińsk.

On the desk there is a piece of paper with a handwritten note – like a self-commentary on the 'small boy's pocket' that lies scattered on the shelf and the window-sill: 'Studies of child psychology are studies of human psychology. In actual fact, only in very few people does it change with age. Most of us remain children inside to the very end – except with more and more wrinkled skin.'

And how am I to describe the globe in the upper part of the loft? Luckily it describes itself. Each continent, with no state borders, displays one or more words or phrases.

North America: community.

South America: trust.

Eurasia has many words: inquiring nature, openness, joy, friendship, sympathy, hope.

Australia has no words.

Africa: LOVE.

He often said that writing is torment, and that more than talent it requires passion, perseverance and concentration.

Now, on a cork board on the door, I find a quotation from the diary of Kazimierz Brandys, which he often paraphrased in many ways:

> I know many people who despite excellent promise, like full-fat, well-cultured milk, have curdled or never set. I think the reason is an incapacity for inner concentration on their vocation. It demands an effort. A terrible effort.

Other notes on the same theme:

> In the morning at breakfast don't think about anything except that you'll go to your studio where the stretched canvases are waiting (Miłosz).

> Not every day can bring prey, but every day must be a hunting day (Ernst Jünger).

Effort, planning, discipline. Also frustration that time is running out. If I had to pinpoint the dominant impression from this tour of the loft's nooks and crannies, I would say: a sense of time running out. Being in a hurry, trying not to lose a single hour. Old age is catching up, there is no time for nonsense. There is still so much to read and think about, to write and to relate.

Another lesson from touring the study is that fame is not just the laurels, it also involves dread, constant anxiety. There are quotes underlined in red in Mircea Eliade's diary, *Fragments d'un journal*, which he left on his desk (next to the typewriter):

> Whole days spent in writing one page. . . .
>
> I stay at my desk for seven or eight hours, but I work effectively for only three or four. For the rest, I transcribe, daydream, or read. . .
>
> Letters, letters! . . . The day before yesterday I wrote five, yesterday nine, and today I'm on the sixth already.[3]

Why did Eliade never write novels? The answer is there too:

> [W]ere I an excellent novelist, it would still be a great pity to spend my time writing novels. There have been, are, or will be at least a thousand great novelists in the world, whereas, at the present time, I am the only person capable of writing 'Shamanism' and the others . . .
>
> As is the case with any prolific author, I carry within me several books that will never be written.[4]

Time is running out, so one must write at speed. More quotes and aphorisms from the wall:

> After sixty he began to hurry up (Parandowski on Petrarch).[5]

> L. N. Tolstoy said that he did not have much longer to live, but a great deal that he would still like to say and do. He is in a hurry and works without cease (Alexei Suvorin, Diary).[6]

A page torn from a book by the sixteenth-century Polish poet and writer Mikołaj Rej:

> Nothing is dearer to man than time, and he must guard every hour not to let it go by licentiously, not to let that noble jewel, the time of his life, flow by like a leaf on water, abjectly and needlessly in vain.[7]

The dumb-bells and expander were meant to extend time.

'I try to keep fit,' he said with some pride before his final illness. 'I go to the gym and I even have my own trainer.'[8]

A note on a loose sheet of paper says: 'Perform hundreds of activities a day that demand movement – in movement there is life'. In a clip frame on the wall there is a poem by Anna Świrszczyńska (written out by hand) about the 'wisely trained body' – a creature 'for whom concentration and discipline are fitting'.[9]

And – on rather a sour note – a bitter quotation from Eliade's diary: 'My best books will be written by someone else'.

Whence the bitterness in such a successful writer?

On 5 October 2005 *Gazeta Wyborcza* carries an article titled 'Nobel comes on Thursday'. Here is an extract:

> Who will get the Nobel Prize for literature? After decades of indulging novelists, playwrights and poets, will a representative of criticism, literary theory, philosophy or non-fiction be rewarded? Ryszard Kapuściński is being mentioned among the candidates.[10]

Rumours about the Nobel Prize have persistently cropped up before now, and will do so again a year from now. It is said he has a strong lobby on the Nobel jury, that it is only a matter of time and he will finally get the world's most prestigious literary prize.

In October 2006, three months before his death, he notes: 'This morning there was a call from Professor Noszczyk, to say: "I'm disappointed that you didn't get the Nobel Prize." ' Not a word about his own reaction, though it could have been similar to the answer he gave to an almost identical phone call I made a year earlier: 'And a good thing too! It'd be a nightmare, I'd never be left in peace.' The tone of his voice, however, said quite the opposite. What writer wouldn't want to be a Nobel laureate?

'When I called him,' recalls Wiktor Osiatyński, 'and said "What a pity", he tried to play down the significance of the Nobel. He said there are other prizes that matter too, which he had been generously awarded all over the world.'

'He very much wanted to win the Nobel Prize, and at the same time he was extremely afraid of it,' says Jerzy Nowak.

It is a recurring motif: conversations about the Nobel Prize, one of his obsessions during the final years of his life.

The best books will be written by someone else. This is not just about prizes, or even about writing, but about time, which he no longer has. The passage of time. Suffering. They do not make you wiser, they do not 'ennoble', and so what?

Before the reporter turns into a patient, he notes:

Old age means progressive stiffening – of the muscles and the mindset. A man sinks into himself, and grows weaker, so do his connections with his surroundings, with the world. This goes on for some time until the stiffening is total, and the connections are entirely gone for ever.

I am pleased when a younger man complains of tiredness and old age. 'Oh, I don't think I'm doing that badly yet!'

Old age means fear of being alone. Now I understand why Aunt Oleńka was so keen to go into an old people's home.[11]

12 October 2005, when his bad hip was making itself felt:

Take small steps.
First – one, two.
And pause to rest.
Switch off.
Then the next one.
And pause.

How many times did he repeat, with quiet despair: 'A reporter with no legs? That's the end.' Because of this fear, when he started having trouble with his circulation years earlier, he gave up smoking.

Illness is sticky (it's a spider). It sucks in everything around it. It ensnares, entangles and finishes you off.[12]

Alicja:

In 1994 he had a stroke. He came down from upstairs into the house where we were already living – he had his study upstairs, with his books and records, and he spent days on end up there. He said: 'Listen, there's something wrong with my hand, I can't hit any of the right keys.' And I could hear he was talking strangely. He lay down, and I saw him lying there, staring at his hand, and he started to cry. Not long before, a younger friend of his had died of brain cancer, a man he liked, who was also a journalist. 'No,' I told him, 'what you've got are the symptoms of an injury to the left cerebral hemisphere.' It was Friday evening, I started calling the neurologists I knew, and they all told me to take him to hospital at once. 'I'm not going to hospital at the weekend! I'm not going to lie in an empty hospital, in a cold corridor! I'm not going anywhere!'

I hung on with him until Monday, giving him relaxant drugs, and first thing on Monday I called an old trainee of mine who is head of the neurological clinic on Banach Street. 'Rysiek, we're going to Banach Street, Hubert will examine you.' And Rysiek said: 'Then why are you packing my pyjamas? I'm not staying in hospital.' I said: 'All right, we'll go without your pyjamas.' I secretly put the pyjamas in my bag and we left. Professor Hubert Kwieciński did a brain scan, confirmed a cerebral embolism and decided it should be dissolved immediately.

'I'm not staying in hospital,' declared Rysiek. 'I'm due at a meeting in Berlin.'

'Then your wife will call and tell them you can't go because you are ill,' Professor Kwieciński tried to explain.

'And what will she say? That I've had a stroke! They'll write me off, everyone will write me off – Kapuściński has lost his mind, he's useless, he'll never write again, you can't count on it.'

To which the professor calmly said: 'Your wife will call and say you had a minor car crash and are lying down for a few days just to make sure nothing is broken.'

So he stayed put. They dissolved the embolism and put him back on his feet, and I took him home. I had the quiet satisfaction of having got my way.

At home he told me he had been invited to the Congress of Polonia in Australia and was going. For pity's sake, I pleaded.

And off he went. The neurologist's explanations didn't help. He went all round Australia and came back happy.

In 2005 he needed a hip operation. He couldn't walk. He refused to have the operation, but agreed to rehab. Twice a week for a year and a half I took him to Bielany for exercises. He had a tough time sitting in the car, I had a Tico with hard seats, so we bought a Nissan Micra because it would be soft and comfortable. He used to have an hour's rehab while I got all my errands done – the post office, the pharmacy, the shops.

I got him out of a lot of illnesses, but I didn't succeed with this one. Maybe there was something I neglected?[13]

Did he look for God? Did God feature in his life at all?

'My family home was very Catholic,' he told the Dominican father Tomasz Dostatni. 'During the war I was an altar boy. When the priest says *Our Father* during mass I am not able to say it in Polish, I say: *Pater Noster, qui es in caelis: sanctificetur Nomen tuum. Adveniat regnum tuum. Fiat voluntas tua, sicut in caelo et in terra. Panem nostrum quotidianum da nobis hodie . . .* And I can go on like that to the end.'

'There is one more topic left for us to talk about,' says Father Dostatni. 'A very personal and dramatic one. Because you have had several brushes with death in your life.'

'It is not pleasant. In those situations I always prayed. And I failed to stick to my pledges. I always prayed to the Virgin Mary. And I said: "If you save me now, I swear I'll never get myself into another fix like this one." And of course I didn't keep the oath. I am a serial oath-breaker. But whenever anything happens, I start praying again.'

Some of his friends are surprised by this conversation (a lengthy excerpt appears in *Gazeta Wyborcza* after Kapuściński's death). Rysiek and the Church? Rysiek and faith? This is an unfamiliar side of their friend.

About a dozen years earlier a Catalan journalist asked him directly: 'Are you a Catholic?'

'I was brought up in the Catholic faith. In Poland, just as in Iran, religion is a fundamental component of the national tradition. The roots of this lie in the days when the Church was the only keystone of the collective identity, and provided an outlet for dissatisfaction aimed at the political authorities. In a cultural sense I regard myself as a Catholic, though I am not a believer.'

His close friend from Barcelona, Agata Orzeszek, witnessed this conversation. She claims Kapuściński gave a different reply, the gist of it being, 'I do not feel tied to the Church as an institution, I do not prostrate myself in church, but I am a believer.'

'Did you ever talk about faith, about God?' I ask her.

'Often. It was always clear to me that Rysiek was a believer. He didn't have to say it – you can sense things like that. I used to tease him, saying that for me it was impossible to understand how you could be a communist and a believer all at once. Then he would calmly explain to me that it was completely understandable, and there was no contradiction. Both Christianity and Marxism, he said, arise out of concern for the poor, and speak up for those who have no voice, and one of the values central to them is justice. Christ was a rebel against some powerful authorities.'

'So it is faith in the style of liberation theology?'

'Exactly.'

If he happened to be near a church and mass was being said at the time, he was capable of going up for communion without confession. It posed no problem for him.

On 9 September 2006 he writes:

> There are energetic
> dynamic days
> and there are others –
> washed-out
> impotent (then the bones ache,
> the heart is weaker
> the legs are wobbly)

Some days, he doesn't want to get out of bed. He takes anti-depressants. He gets up and tries to find the remains of life in himself.

Anything at all can make him fly off the handle. He is capable of hurling abuse at the cloak-room attendant who hands him his coat too slowly at the Bookseller's Club.

Ever weaker, he flies to Italy. The journey is torture, but also provides an impetus for life. That same day, he finds out that Polish public television is preparing a programme exposing him and a few other journalists and writers (he doesn't know the details) involved in co-operation with the intelligence service in the PRL. He is afraid.

He wants to run away from this fear, and Italy, where he is beloved, is one of the best places for a temporary escape. High-school pupils and college students from the Bolzano area greet him with enthusiasm and adoration, and look up to him like a guru, a sage. When a schoolgirl named Anna recites one of his poems for him, he cannot hide his emotion:

> Only those clad in sackcloth
> are able to take upon themselves
> the suffering of another
> to share his pain[14]

A record of those meetings is published after his death.

> Okęcie airport, Friday, 13 October 2006
> – the most important thing is to get back into the rhythm of work. The rhythm is something that brings things together, makes the whole coherent, and above all forces you to take the next step, and the next.
> Caffè Greco – Mickiewicz, Norwid and Miłosz all used to go there; the six greatest Italian specialists in Polish studies are going to read their translations.[15]

And from the Italian notes, 22 October 2006:

> There comes a moment in life when we can no longer take in new faces. This is to do with the fact that Jarek [Mikołajewski] calls: a charming couple have arrived – he is a film director with a very lovely wife. Will you come and join us for coffee? But right now I'm sitting here engrossed in Rilke. No, I'm not coming. Because I can't anymore. Because somehow I'd have to refurnish, furnish my own face. Smile, be friendly and so on – but I no longer have the desire or the strength.[16]

It is hard to believe that this is the man who once hung this aphorism on his door: 'Enthusiasm makes the world go round.'

★   ★   ★

Once the end is near, he won't talk about it. When it was far away, he was happy to – as soon as he reached forty, he was always bringing up the subject of dying in conversation. He used to collect statistics relating to the tendency of journalists to be short-lived; he established that their average life expectancy was about sixty. Whenever he heard that one had died, he would repeat with resignation, 'There you are – the statistics are confirmed.'

Years earlier, when he bought a raincoat, he said it was the last one he would ever get. It was the same when he bought a Volkswagen – 'that's the last car ever'. Indeed it was: he bought it a quarter of a century before his death.

Before his final Christmas holiday, he suggests to his closest friend: 'You know what, Jurek, we must think about what to do if something were to happen to one of us.' He senses he will be the first to go.

But immediately afterward he sets about planning his tour of Oceania. Making preparations for the next book or the next journey is the best medicine for depression, for coming to terms with the end.

'It will be very hard for me,' he tells another good friend, Andrzej Lubowski, 'because I don't know much about the world of Oceania. It's a long way off, I'll have to spend at least a few months living there. And before that, look, I have to read all this.' (Here he points at a pile of books in various languages.) 'Unless I digest all that, there's no point in going.'

'How will you get there? Have you the strength for it?' asks his friend.

'In April 2006,' recalls Lubowski, 'at a grand ball at the Waldorf Astoria in New York he received the Kościuszko Foundation award. At one point a beautiful tall girl asked him to dance. He smiled a little awkwardly, and a little disarmingly, and to my surprise he went onto the dance floor. Next day I asked him how he coped with it. "I couldn't refuse. I've gradually learned to live with pain," he said. And added quietly, with that timid smile of his, "I know I'm dying, but I so very much want to get to the place I don't know." That Oceania again.'

Alicja gives Agata Orzeszek a final message from him: 'Rysiek said he won't do the interview – you know, the one he promised someone.'

'Only later did I realize that this was his farewell,' Orzeszek tells me.

Wiktor Osiatyński does not say goodbye to his friend: he suspects his stories about a serious illness are just another fit of hypochondria. 'He was always dying of something, then he'd leap up, grab a suitcase and be off to the other end of the world. So when he really did die, I couldn't believe it.'

According to Alicja:

On 13 December I was invited to my clinic to celebrate St Nicholas Day. I said to Rysiek – he was so wretched, lying there, feeling ill, and he had no appetite – 'Rysiek, I'm not making any dinner. They serve home-cooked meals just round the corner on Krzywicki Street, they're very tasty. Go there,' I said, 'take a walk.' 'I haven't the strength,' he said. I insisted: 'Go for a walk.' He did. I came back from the party, and he said: 'The food was awful today, too salty, I told them off.' Now I knew. 'You've got something wrong with your digestive tract,' I said. 'It's not just the leg.'

The next day I did an ultrasound. A tumour on the pancreas.

I couldn't forgive myself for discovering it so late. But afterwards the surgeons told me pancreatic cancer doesn't show any symptoms for ages. It could have been developing for a year. They operated. But after the operation he had a heart attack.

And that was it.[17]

The end of the journey has come. The reporter goes to hospital for an abdominal operation.

A note from his desk:

Crossed out: 'Start a diary'.

Below: 'Bodil wants me to write a diary (a journal). I think so – otherwise, why else would she have sent me a blank notebook from France?'

He doesn't write the diary. Just a few little notes, comments on who came to visit, less often brief thoughts:[18]

Wednesday, 3 January 2007:

First thing today I had a series of pre-op tests. The general result is favourable. The hospital is efficient and well-organized. The people are friendly and sympathetic . . .

I asked [Professor Wojciech Noszczyk] what my operation will involve. 'Strictly speaking,' he said, 'we don't know anything until we open up the abdomen. Only then can we see what's going on in there . . .'

The crisis came in the evening. I suddenly felt myself getting weaker, flying downwards, into a dark fog . . .

Friday, 5 January 2007:

Today I was fitted with an extra-intestinal feeding pump. At noon I had a dehydration crisis: crisis = dehydration = I get weaker, I feel as if my remaining strength has slipped away, I'm falling into an abyss and a black fog is enveloping me.

A terrible feeling of helplessness, I'm losing touch with the world, with the light, with my surroundings, with reality, it's all drifting away, disappearing.

The nurse puts me on an IV drip: slowly I come back to life, to strength. I can see again, but I still can't hear.

Every minute it gets better – I feel like crying for joy . . .

How we fail to appreciate the mechanical aspect of human nature! Until finally plugged into various tubes, containers, wires and clocks a man sees that he has become nothing but a cog, and often a minor one, in this great world of machines.

He is not capable of writing, just a few sentences at a time, a few notes. He cannot read, just a little – *Pan Tadeusz*, the greatest epic in the Polish language. He has had enough of hospital and wants to go home to his study in the loft, his kingdom of learned volumes and poetry.

> How could you
> leave me like this
> o mysterious force
> known as life![19]

Herodotus is losing his strength, his enthusiasm, his childlike optimism. Everything is drifting away, disappearing. How is he to travel in this state, how is he to open up to an encounter with the world, with the Other? How can he live without discovering something new? Hadn't he better be going now? *Navigare necesse est, vivere non est necesse*: sailing is a necessity – life is not a necessity. Yet another aphorism from the loft wall.

Let others do the sailing. He has blazed enough trails. He has left behind enough compasses, maps and warnings about what to take on the journey.

August 2008 – January 2010
Dąbrowa Leśna – Buenos Aires – New York – Kampala – Dąbrowa Leśna

Notes

Introduction: The Smile

1 Ryszard Kapuściński, *Shah of Shahs*, trans. William R. Brand and Katarzyna Mroczkowska-Brand, London: Penguin, 2006, 4.
2 Ibid., 14.

1 Daguerreotypes

1 Ryszard Kapuściński, 'Suffering and Guilt', in *I Wrote Stone: The Selected Poetry of Ryszard Kapuściński*, trans. Diana Kuprel and Marek Kusiba, Emeryville, Canada: Biblioasis, 2007, 68.
2 Ryszard Kapuściński, 'Dałem głos ubogim' (I Gave a Voice to the Poor), in *Rozmowy z młodzieżą* (Conversations with Young People), Kraków: SIW Znak, 2008.
3 Artur Domosławski, 'Kamyki, szkiełka i tysiąc innych skarbów' (Pebbles, Pieces of Glass and a Thousand Other Treasures), *Gazeta Wyborcza*, 24 December 2007.

2 Pińsk: The Beginning

1 'Człowiek z bagna' (Man from the Marshes), interview with Ryszard Kapuściński by Barbara N. Łopieńska, *Przekrój*, 13 July 2003.
2 Ibid.
3 'Słów kilka o Pińsku' (A Few Words about Pińsk), booklet, Marshal Piłsudski High School: Tourist Circle, 1936.
4 'Człowiek z bagna'.
5 *Piński Przegląd Diecezjalny*, 17 September 1930.
6 Ibid., 16 October 1930.
7 *Dwutygodnik Kresowy* 1, 1938.
8 Azriel Shohat, 'Under Polish Rule 1921–1939', ch. 3 in *History of the Jews of Pinsk 1881–1941*, http://www.jewishgen.org/Yizkor/Pinsk1/Pine11_050.html.
9 Ibid.
10 Ryszard Kapuściński, 'Dobre wychowanie dzieci chrześcijańskich' (Good Manners for Christian Children), quoted in Artur Domosławski, 'Hycle w Arkadii' (Dog Catchers in Arcadia), *Gazeta Wyborcza*, 21 January 2008.

11 Nahum Boneh (Mular), 'The Holocaust and the Revolt', trans. G. Eliasberg and Kibbutz Beth-Zera, in *Pinsk: The Story of the Jews of Pinsk, 1506–1942*, vol. 1, part 2, ed. Wolf Zeev Rabinowitsch, Tel Aviv: Association of the Jews of Pinsk in Israel, 1977, p. 145.
12 Ibid.
13 Ryszard Kapuściński, *The Soccer War*, trans. William Brand, London: Granta Books, 2007, 133–4.

3 War

1 Ryszard Kapuściński, 'Ćwiczenia pamięci' (Exercises of Memory), in *Busz po polsku* (The Polish Bush), Warsaw: Czytelnik, 2009, 5–7.
2 Ryszard Kapuściński, *Imperium*, trans. Klara Glowczewska, London: Granta Books, 2007, 4.
3 Kapuściński, *Busz po polsku*, 8.
4 Ibid., 13–14.
5 Kapuściński, *Imperium*, 4–5.
6 Ibid., 9.
7 Ibid., 10.
8 Ibid., 15–16.
9 Kapuściński, *Busz po polsku*, 9.
10 Ibid., 10–11.
11 Ryszard Kapuściński, *Travels with Herodotus*, trans. Klara Glowczewska, London: Penguin, 2008, 34.
12 Kapuściński, *Busz po polsku*, 11.
13 Ibid., 12–13.

4 Legends 1: His Father and Katyń

1 Ryszard Kapuściński, *Imperium*, trans. Klara Glowczewska, London: Granta Books, 2007, 8.
2 'Człowiek z bagna' (Man from the Marshes), interview with Ryszard Kapuściński by Barbara N. Łopieńska, *Przekrój*, 13 July 2003.

5 Inspired by Poetry, Storming Heaven

1 Ryszard Kapuściński, *Lapidarium II*, Warsaw: Czytelnik, 1996.
2 Ryszard Kapuściński, 'Uzdrowienie' (The Healing), *Dziś i Jutro*, 14 August 1949.
3 Ryszard Kapuściński, *Bóg rani miłością* (God Wounds with Love), extract in *Rzeczpospolita*, 3 March 2007.
4 'Dyskusja o poezji w gimnazjum im. Staszica w Warszawie' (Debate about Poetry Held at Staszic High School in Warsaw), *Odrodzenie*, 5 March 1950.
5 Ryszard Kapuściński, 'W sprawie obowiązań' (On Obligations), ibid.

6 Lapidarium 1: The Poet

1 'Pisanie wierszy jest dla mnie luksusem' (Writing Poetry is a Luxury for Me), Ryszard Kapuściński in conversation with Jarosław Mikołajewski, *Gazeta Wyborcza*, 21 February 2006.
2 Claudio Magris, *Corriere della Sera*, 24 December 2004.

7 On the Construction Site of Socialism

1 Ryszard Kapuściński, *Travels with Herodotus*, trans. Klara Glowczewska, London: Penguin Books, 2008, 4.
2 Ryszard Kapuściński, *Busz po polsku* (The Polish Bush), Warsaw: Czytelnik, 2009, 80.
3 Ryszard Kapuściński, *Shah of Shahs*, trans. William R. Brand and Katarzyna Mroczkowska-Brand, London: Penguin, 2006, 149.
4 Zbigniew Herbert, 'Prologue', *The Collected Poems 1956–98*, trans. and ed. Alissa Valles, New York: Ecco, 2007.
5 Jacek Kuroń and Jacek Żakowski, *PRL dla początkujących* (The PRL for Beginners), Wrocław: Wydawnictwo Dolnośląskie, 1995.
6 Ibid.
7 Stefan Kieniewicz, 'Z rozmyślań dziejopisa czasów porozbiorowych' (From the Thoughts of a Chronicler of the Post-Partition Era), *Kwartalnik Historii Nauki i Techniki* 2, 1980.
8 Akta studenta Ryszarda Kapuścińskiego (Ryszard Kapuściński's Student Documents), WH 19900, Warsaw University Archive.
9 Kuroń and Żakowski, *PRL dla początkujących*.
10 Ryszard Kapuściński and Zygmunt Korta, 'W oparciu o doświadczenia Komsomołu . . .' (Based on the Experiences of the Komsomol), *Sztandar Młodych*, 22 August 1950.
11 Ibid.
12 Kapuściński, *Shah of Shahs*, 141, 143.

9 On the Construction Site of Socialism, *Continued*

1 Application to the District Party Organization at Warsaw University History Faculty, in Leszek Żebrowski, ' "Chcę partyjnie żyć, pracować i walczyć" czyli o Ryszardzie Kapuścińskim inaczej' ('I Want to Live, Work and Fight for the Party', or, A Different View of Ryszard Kapuściński), *Nasz Dziennik*, 16 June 2009.
2 Bronisław Geremek's recommendation, ibid.
3 Ryszard Kapuściński, *Lapidarium*, Warsaw: Czytelnik, 1990.
4 Statements by Ryszard Kapuściński in Beata Nowacka and Zygmunt Ziątek, *Ryszard Kapuściński. Biografia pisarza* (Ryszard Kapuściński, Biography of a Writer), Kraków: SIW Znak, 2008.
5 Statements by Wiktor Woroszylski in Anna Bikont and Joanna Szczęsna, *Lawina i kamienie. Pisarze wobec komunizmu* (Avalanche and Stones: Writers' Attitudes to Communism), Warsaw: Prószyński i S-ka, 2006.
6 Statements by Tadeusz Konwicki, ibid.
7 Ryszard Kapuściński, *Travels with Herodotus*, trans. Klara Glowczewska, London: Penguin Books, 2008, 8.

8 Wojciech Borsuk, ed., *Był taki dziennik. „Sztandar Młodych"* (Once There Was a Newspaper, *Sztandar Młodych*), Warsaw: Wydawnictwo Nowy Świat, 2006.

9 Ryszard Kapuściński, 'Nasze dni' (Our Days), extract from 'Droga prowadzi naprzód' (The Road Leads Forward), *Sztandar Młodych*, 12 August 1950.

10 Ryszard Kapuściński, 'Łamiąc stare niesłuszne normy' (Breaking the Old, Incorrect Norms), *Sztandar Młodych*, 31 August 1950.

11 Ryszard Kapuściński, 'II Światowy Kongres Obrońców Pokoju' (Second Defenders of Peace Congress), *Sztandar Młodych*, 18 November 1950.

12 Kapuściński, *Lapidarium*.

10 Alicja, Maminek, Zojka

1 Statements by Alicja Kapuścińska in 'Mąż reporter' (My Husband the Reporter), interview with Alicja Kapuścińska by Teresa Torańska and Artur Domosławski, *Gazeta Wyborcza*, 19 January 2009.

11 '56: Revolution All Over Again

1 Ryszard Kapuściński, *Shah of Shahs*, trans. William R. Brand and Katarzyna Mroczkowska-Brand, London: Penguin Books, 2006, 104.

2 Ryszard Kapuściński, *Travels with Herodotus*, trans. Klara Glowczewska, London: Penguin Books, 2008, 9.

3 Ibid., 8.

4 'Debate within the Polish Writers' Union', in Anna Bikont and Joanna Szczęsna, *Lawina i kamienie. Pisarze wobec komunizmu* (Avalanche and Stones: Writers' Attitudes to Communism), Warsaw: Prószyński i S-ka, 2006.

5 Mieczysław Jastrun, 'Epoka' (Epoch), in *Gorący popiół* (Burning Ash), Warsaw: PIW, 1956.

6 Witold Dąbrowski, in Jacek Kuroń and Jacek Żakowski, *PRL dla początkujących* (The PRL for Beginners), Wrocław: Wydawnictwo Dolnośląskie, 1995.

7 Jacek Kuroń, in ibid.

8 Ibid.

9 Kapuściński, *Shah of Shahs*, 103.

10 Ryszard Kapuściński, 'W połowie drogi' (Halfway Down the Road), *Sztandar Młodych*, 26–27 November 1955.

11 Kapuściński, *Shah of Shahs*, 138.

12 Ryszard Kapuściński and R. Rywanowicz, 'Niespełnione zadania. Po łódzkim plenum ZMP' (Unfulfilled Tasks: After the Łódź Plenum of the ZMP), *Sztandar Młodych*, 29 March 1955.

13 Ryszard Kapuściński, 'Walka, spór i „rzeczy drobne" ' (Fighting, Arguing and 'Petty Things'), *Walka Młodych* 3, 1956.

14 Kapuściński, *Shah of Shahs*, 143–4.

15 Wojciech Adamiecki, 'Nie podam ci ręki' (I Will Not Shake Your Hand), statement in 'Odszedł dziennikarz wieku' (The Journalist of the Century Has Passed Away), *Press* 2, 2007.

16 Adam Ważyk, 'Poemat dla dorosłych' (A Poem for Adults), in *Mówię do swojego ciała* (Talking to My Body), Kraków: Colonel Press, 2002. (This translation by Antonia Lloyd-Jones.)

17 Remigiusz Szczęsnowicz, 'Wspomnień czar' (The Charm of Memories), in

Wojciech Borsuk, ed., *Był taki dziennik. „Sztandar Młodych"* (Once There Was a Newspaper, *Sztandar Młodych*), Warsaw: Wydawnictwo Nowy Świat, 2006.

18 Ryszard Kapuściński, 'To też jest prawda o Nowej Hucie' (This Is Also the Truth about Nowa Huta), *Sztandar Młodych*, 30 September 1955.

19 'Komunikat o wypadkach w Poznaniu' (Message about Events in Poznań), *Sztandar Młodych*, 29 June 1959.

20 Jacek Kuroń, in Kuroń and Żakowski, *PRL dla początkujących*.

21 Ryszard Kapuściński, 'Poszukiwanie klucza' (Looking for the Key), *Sztandar Młodych*, 13 February 1956.

22 Ryszard Kapuściński, 'O demokracji robotniczej' (On Workers' Democracy), *Sztandar Młodych*, 29-30 September 1956.

23 Statement by Hanna Świda-Ziemba, in Bikont and Szczęsna, *Lawina i kamienie*.

24 Statement by Adam Michnik, ibid.

25 Statement by Artur Starewicz, in materials from the session of the CC Press Office held on 14 September 1957, Archiwum Akt Nowych (Archive of New Documents), Zespół KC PZPR 237/XIX-144.

26 Ryszard Kapuściński and Krzysztof Kąkolewski, 'Metryka naszego urodzenia' (Our Birth Certificate), *Sztandar Młodych*, 20–22 April 1957.

27 Kapuściński, *Shah of Shahs*, 139–40.

28 Kapuściński and Kąkolewski, 'Metryka naszego urodzenia'.

12   The Third World: A Clash and a Beginning

1 Ryszard Kapuściński, *Podróże z Herodotem* ('Travels With Herodotus'), SIW Znak, Kraków, 2004, 38.

2 Ryszard Kapuściński, 'Co się nie udało Kolumbowi . . .' (What Columbus Failed to Do . . .), *Sztandar Młodych*, 24 January 1957.

3 Ryszard Kapuściński, 'Na lotnisku' (At the Airport), *Sztandar Młodych*, 24 June 1955.

4 Ryszard Kapuściński, 'Gorzki smak wody' (The Bitter Taste of Water), *Sztandar Młodych*, 28 January 1957.

5 Kapuściński, *Travels with Herodotus*, trans. Klara Glowczewska, London: Penguin Books, 2008, 20.

6 Kapuściński, 'Gorzki smak wody'.

7 Ryszard Kapuściński, 'Fatamorgana egzotyki' (The Mirage of the Exotic'), *Sztandar Młodych*, 20 February 1957.

8 Ryszard Kapuściński, 'Okrzyk Napoleona' (Napoleon's Shout), *Sztandar Młodych*, 8 March 1957.

9 Ryszard Kapuściński, 'How Many More Worlds?', in *I Wrote Stone: The Selected Poetry of Ryszard Kapuściński*, trans. Diana Kuprel and Marek Kusiba, Emeryville, Canada: Biblioasis, 2007, 31.

10 Kapuściński and Kąkolewski, 'Metryka naszego urodzenia' (Our Birth Certificate), *Sztandar Młodych*, 20–22 April 1957.

13   In 'Rakowski's Gang'

1 Ryszard Kapuściński, *Busz po polsku* (The Polish Bush), Warsaw: Czytelnik, 2009, 80–1.

2 Wiesław Władyka, *„Polityka" i jej ludzie* (*Polityka* and Its People), Warsaw: Polityka, 2007.

3 Ibid.
4 Ryszard Kapuściński, *Travels with Herodotus*, trans. Klara Glowczewska, London: Penguin Books, 2008, 73.
5 Ryszard Kapuściński, *The Soccer War*, trans. William Brand, London: Granta Books, 2007, 20–1.
6 Ryszard Kapuściński, 'Bojkot na ołtarzu' (Boycott on the Altar), *Polityka* 9, 1960.
7 Ibid.
8 Ryszard Kapuściński, 'Stracony dla Forda' (Lost for Ford), *Polityka* 18, 1960.
9 Ryszard Kapuściński, 'Zaproszenie do Afryki' (Invitation to Africa), *Polityka* 44, 1960.
10 Kapuściński, *The Soccer War*, 21.
11 Ibid., 40.
12 Ryszard Kapuściński, 'List z Afryki' (Letter from Africa), *Polityka* 6, 1961.
13 Ryszard Kapuściński, 'Kongo z bliska' (Congo Close Up), *Polityka* 12, 1961.
14 Kapuściński, *The Soccer War*, 68.
15 Ibid., p. 62.

14   Legends 2: Sentenced to Death by Firing Squad

1 Bożena Dudko, ed., *Podróże z Ryszardem Kapuścińskim* (Travels with Ryszard Kapuściński), Kraków: SIW Znak, 2007.
2 Jaroslav Bouček, 'Do Nitra Konga. Pravda Kapuścinského a Pravda Boučka' (Into the Heart of Congo: Kapuściński's Truth and Bouček's Truth), in *Cestování Čechů a Poláků v 19. a 20. století* (Czech and Polish Travels in the 19th and 20th Centuries), Prague: AAV ČR, 2008.
3 Ibid.
4 'Czeterokrotnie rozstrzelany' (Executed by Firing Squad Four Times), Ryszard Kapuściński in conversation with Wojciech Giełżyński, *Ekspres Reporterów* 6, 1978.
5 'Gdzieś kryje się większa racja . . .' (Greater Rationale Lies Hidden Somewhere), Ryszard Kapuściński in conversation with Andrzej Kantowicz, *Kultura* 31, 1976.

15   In 'Rakowski's Gang', Continued

1 Ryszard Kapuściński, 'Kongo z bliska' (Congo Close Up), *Polityka* 12, 1961.
2 Mieczysław F. Rakowski, *Dzienniki polityczne 1958–1962* (Political Diaries 1958–1962), Warsaw: Iskry, 1999.
3 Wiesław Władyka, *„Polityka" i jej ludzie* (*Polityka* and Its People), Warsaw: Polityka, 2007.
4 Ryszard Kapuściński, *Busz po polsku* (The Polish Bush), Warsaw: Czytelnik, 2009, 51.
5 Ibid., 77.
6 Ibid., 52.
7 Ryszard Kapuściński, 'Uprowadzenie Elżbiety' (The Abduction of Elżbieta) in *Busz po polsku*, vol. 3 of *Dzieła wybrane Ryszarda Kapuścińskiego* (The Selected Works of Ryszard Kapuściński), Warsaw: Agora, 2008.
8 Małgorzata Szejnert, 'Postscriptum. Busz po 46 latach' (Postscript: The Bush 46 Years On), in ibid.
9 Kapuściński, *Busz po polsku*, 42.

10 Ibid., 85.
11 Ryszard Kapuściński, 'Dalszy ciąg dramatu (List do redakcji tygodnika *Polityka*)' (The Drama Continues: Letter to the Editors of *Polityka*), *Polityka* 46, 1961.
12 Ibid.
13 'List B. Drozdowskiego' (Letter by Bohdan Drozdowski [to the editors of *Polityka*]), *Polityka* 47, 1961.
14 'Odpowiedź redakcji' (Reply from the Editors [of *Polityka* to Bohdan Drozdowski's letter]), *Polityka* 47, 1961.
15 Julian Przyboś, reply to a survey titled 'Inspiracja czy plagiat' (Inspiration or Plagiarism?), *Współczesność* 2, 1962.
16 Kapuściński, *Busz po polsku*, 84–8.

16 Life in Africa

1 Ryszard Kapuściński, *The Shadow of the Sun*, trans. Klara Glowczewska, London: Penguin Books, 2002, 38.
2 Ryszard Kapuściński, *The Soccer War*, trans. William Brand, London: Granta Books, 2007, 16.
3 Kapuściński, *The Shadow of the Sun*, 83.
4 Ibid., 62.

17 Objects of Fascination: The African Icons

1 Frantz Fanon, *The Wretched of the Earth*, trans. Richard Philcox, New York: Grove Press, 2004, 50–2.
2 Ibid., 81.
3 Ryszard Kapuściński, 'Elita władzy' (The Ruling Élite), *Polityka* 8, 1964.
4 Ryszard Kapuściński, 'Bar wzięty' (A Popular Bar), *Polityka* 20, 1961.
5 Ryszard Kapuściński, *The Soccer War*, trans. William Brand, London: Granta Books, 2007, 25.
6 Ibid., 49.

18 Life in Africa, Continued

1 Statements by Alicja Kapuścińska in 'Mąż reporter' (My Husband the Reporter), interview with Alicja Kapuścińska by Teresa Torańska and Artur Domosławski, *Gazeta Wyborcza*, 19 January 2009.
2 Ryszard Kapuściński, Letters to Jerzy and Izabella Nowak, Kampala, October 1962.
3 Ibid.
4 Ibid.
5 Ryszard Kapuściński, Letter to Jerzy and Izabella Nowak, Nairobi, n.d. (probably November or December 1963).
6 Ryszard Kapuściński, 'Nairobi, Korespondencja z Kenii' (Nairobi: Correspondence from Kenya), PAP Special Bulletin, Weekly Supplement 491, 25 November 1963.
7 Ryszard Kapuściński, 'Pierwszy polski dziennikarz w Republice Zanzibaru' (First Polish Journalist in the Republic of Zanzibar), *Trybuna Ludu* 18, 1964.

8 Ibid.

9 Ryszard Kapuściński, 'Nigeria przed i po przewrocie' (Nigeria Before and After the Coup), PAP Special Bulletin, Weekly Supplement 719, 7 February 1966.

10 Ryszard Kapuściński, 'Sytuacja w Nigerii – do wiadomości redakcji' (The Situation in Nigeria – Information for the Editors), PAP Special Bulletin, Weekly Supplement 715, 24 January 1966.

11 Ryszard Kapuściński, Letter to Jerzy Nowak, Lagos, 29 September 1965.

12 Ibid.

13 Ryszard Kapuściński, Letter to Jerzy Nowak, Lagos, 6 January 1966.

14 Ibid.

15 Ibid.

16 Ryszard Kapuściński, *The Soccer War*, trans. William Brand, London: Granta Books, 2007, 137.

17 Ryszard Kapuściński, Letter to Jerzy Nowak, Lagos, 29 September 1965.

18 Ryszard Kapuściński, Letter to Jerzy Nowak, Lagos, 6 January 1966.

19 Ryszard Kapuściński, *Gdyby cała Afryka . . .* (If Only the Whole of Africa . . .), Warsaw: Czytelnik, 1971.

20 Ryszard Kapuściński, Postcard to Jerzy Nowak, Addis Ababa, 16 November 1993.

19   In the Corridors of Power

1 Mieczysław F. Rakowski, *Dzienniki polityczne 1963–1966* (Political Diaries 1963–1966), Warsaw: Iskry, 1999.

2 Ryszard Kapuściński, Letter to Jerzy Nowak, Mexico City, 15 December 1969.

3 Mieczysław F. Rakowski, *Dzienniki polityczne 1984–1986* (Political Diaries 1984–1986), Warsaw: Iskry, 2005.

4 Ryszard Kapuściński, Letter to Jerzy Nowak, Mexico City, 15 December 1969.

20   Lapidarium 3: The Reporter as Politician

1 Ryszard Kapuściński, *Kirgiz schodzi z konia* (The Kyrgyz Dismounts), Warsaw: Czytelnik, 2007.

21   On the Trail of Che Guevara

1 Ryszard Kapuściński, 'Ostry kryzys w Ameryce Łacińskiej' (Acute Crisis in Latin America), *Życie Warsawy* 30, 1969, and 'Fala konfliktów i walk w krajach Ameryki Łacińskiej' (Wave of Conflict and Fighting in the Latin American Countries), *Trybuna Ludu* 82, 1970.

2 Ryszard Kapuściński, 'Ostre napięcia w Chile' (Acute Tensions in Chile), *Trybuna Ludu*, 10 May 1968.

3 Ryszard Kapuściński, Letter to Jerzy Nowak, Rio de Janeiro, 4 November 1968.

4 Ryszard Kapuściński, 'Od tłumacza' (Translator's Preface), in Ernesto 'Che' Guevara, *Dziennik z Boliwii* (The Bolivian Diary), Warsaw: Książka i Wiedza, 1969.

5 Ryszard Kapuściński, 'KP Chile wzywa do udaremnienia zamachu stanu' (The Chilean CP Calls for the Prevention of the Coup d'État), *Trybuna Ludu*, 14 May 1968.

23 On the Trail of Che Guevara, Continued

1 Ryszard Kapuściński, Letter to Jerzy and Izabella Nowak, Rio de Janeiro, 4 November 1968.
2 Ibid.
3 Ibid.
4 Ibid.
5 Ryszard Kapuściński, Letter to Jerzy and Izabella Nowak, Mexico City, 22 September 1971.
6 Ryszard Kapuściński, Letter to Jerzy and Izabella Nowak, Mexico City, 15 December 1969.
7 Kapuściński, Letter, 22 September 1971.
8 Ryszard Kapuściński, 'Relacja polskiego korespondenta z walk Hondurasu z Salwadorem' (A Polish Correspondent's Account of the Fight between Honduras and El Salvador), *Życie Warszawy* 171, 1969.
9 Ryszard Kapuściński, 'Pierwsza autentyczna rewolucja' (First Authentic Revolution), *Polityka* 42, 1970.
10 Ryszard Kapuściński, 'Emigranci kubańscy w USA przygotowują nową awanturę przeciw Kubie?' (Are Cuban Emigrés in the USA Preparing a New Fight against Cuba?), *Trybuna Ludu* 125, 1970.
11 Ryszard Kapuściński, 'W sobotę – ostateczny wybór prezydenta Chile' (On Saturday – The Final Vote for the President of Chile), *Trybuna Ludu* 292, 1970.
12 Ryszard Kapuściński, 'Kandydat lewicy S. Allende prezydentem Chile' (Left-wing Candidate S. Allende Is President of Chile), *Trybuna Ludu* 297, 1970.
13 'Wiosna ludów latynoskich' (The Latin American Spring of Nations'), interview with Ryszard Kapuściński by Artur Domosławski, *Gazeta Wyborcza*, 7 April 2001.

24 Objects of Fascination: The Latin American Icons

1 Ryszard Kapuściński, *Chrystus z karabinem na ramieniu* (Christ with a Rifle on His Shoulder), Warsaw: Czytelnik, 1976.
2 Ibid.
3 Ryszard Kapuściński, 'Radykalizacja duchowieństwa latynoamerykańskiego' (The Radicalization of the Latin American Clergy), *Trybuna Ludu* 216, 1970.

25 On the Trail of Che Guevara, Continued Further

1 Ryszard Kapuściński, 'Dr Héctor Cuadra o problemie porywania diplomatów' (Dr Héctor Cuadra on the Problem of the Kidnapping of Diplomats), PAP Special Bulletin, Weekly Supplement 84, 23 May 1970.
2 Ibid.
3 'Z tamtego świata. Z Ryszardem Kapuścińskim rozmawia Jacek Syski' (From the Other World. Jacek Syski in conversation with Ryszard Kapuściński), Literatura, 22 July 1976.
4 Ryszard Kapuściński, *Dlaczego zginął Karl von Spreti* (Why Karl von Spreti Died), Warsaw: Czytelnik, 2010, 20–2.

5 Ryszard Kapuściński, 'Pierwsze oceny wizyty Fidela Castro w Chile' (First Appraisals of Fidel Castro's Visit to Chile), PAP Special Bulletin, Weekly Supplement 1306, 11 November 1971.

6 Ibid.

7 Wiktor Osiatyński, 'Zamki z piasku' (Castles Made of Sand), *Odra* 7–8, 1980.

8 Ryszard Kapuściński, Letter to Jerzy and Izabella Nowak, Mexico City, 19 February 1972.

26 Zojka's Escapes

1 Statements by Alicja Kapuścińska in 'Mąż reporter' (My Husband the Reporter), interview with Alicja Kapuścińska by Teresa Torańska and Artur Domosławski, *Gazeta Wyborcza*, 19 January 2009.

2 Ibid.

3 Ibid.

4 Ibid.

5 'Mój tata Ryszard Kapuściński' (My Dad Ryszard Kapuściński), interview with René Maisner by Bartosz Marzec, *Rzeczpospolita*, 21 January 2008, and 'Z René Maisner rozmawia Liliana Śnieg-Czaplewska' (Liliana Śnieg-Czaplewska in Conversation with René Maisner), *Gala* 5, 2009.

27 A Committed Reporter, a Black-and-White World

1 Ryszard Kapuściński, 'Rozmowy o wojnie w Etiopii' (Conversations about the War in Ethiopia), *Sztandar Młodych*, 31 August 1977.

2 'Czterokrotnie rozstrzelany' (Executed by Firing Squad Four Times), interview with Ryszard Kapuściński by Wojciech Giełżyński, *Ekspres Reporterów* 6, 1978.

3 Interview with Ryszard Kapuściński for Mexican journal *La Jornada*, reprinted in *El Espectador*, 3 January 1988.

4 'Z tamtego świata' (From the Other World), interview with Ryszard Kapuściński by Jacek Syski, *Literatura*, 22 July 1976.

5 Ibid.

6 'Gdzieś kryje się większa racja . . .' (The Greater Rationale Lies Hidden Somewhere . . .), interview with Ryszard Kapuściński by Andrzej Kantowicz, *Kultura* 31, 1976.

7 'Czterokrotnie rozstrzelany'.

8 Ryszard Kapuściński, *Gdyby cała Afryka . . .* (If Only the Whole of Africa . . .), Warsaw: Czytelnik, 1971.

9 'Serdecznie witamy w Polsce cesarza Haile Selassie I' (We Warmly Welcome the Emperor Haile Selassie I to Poland), *Trybuna Ludu*, 17 September 1964.

10 'Toast Edwarda Ochaba' (Edward Ochab's Toast [in honour of the Emperor Haile Selassie I]), *Trybuna Ludu*, 18 September 1964.

11 'Wizyta przywódcy Etiopii w Polsce. Henryk Jabłoński, Mengistu Haile Mariam' (Visit of the Ethiopian Leader to Poland: Henryk Jabłoński, Mengistu Haile Mariam), *Trybuna Ludu*, 11 December 1978.

12 Ryszard Kapuściński, 'W Etiopii nasila się coraz bardziej terrorystyczna działalność sił prawicy' (Terrorist Activity of Right-Wing Forces Continues to Intensify in Ethiopia), *Życie Warszawy* 276, 1976.

13 'W drodze' (On the Road), interview with Ryszard Kapuściński by Teresa Krzemień, *Kultura*, 19 November 1978.
14 'Czterokrotnie rozstrzelany'.
15 Ryszard Kapuściński, 'Sytuacja w Angoli (nie do przedrukowania w prasie)' (The Situation in Angola, Not for Reprint in the Press), PAP Special Bulletin, Weekly Supplement 1700, 16 October 1975.
16 'Rozmowa z Sekretarzem Generalnym KC Komunistycznej Partii Chile tow. Luisem Corvalanem' (A Conversation with Secretary General of the Central Committee of the Chilean Communist Party, Comrade Luis Corvalan), conducted by Ryszard Kapuściński and Walery Namiotkiewicz, *Nowe Drogi* 1, 1973.
17 'Czterokrotnie rozstrzelany'.
18 Ryszard Kapuściński, 'Velasco Ibarra zostaje dyktatorem' (Velasco Ibarra Becomes Dictator), PAP Special Bulletin 7633, 16 July 1970.

28   Christ with a Rifle in a Czech Comedy at the Emperor's Court

1 Ryszard Kapuściński, *The Emperor*, trans. William R. Brand and Katarzyna Mroczkowska-Brand, Penguin, 2006, 39.
2 Ibid., 86.
3 Ibid., 90.
4 Ibid., 86.
5 Ibid.
6 Ibid., 49.
7 Barbara N. Łopieńska, 'Ulica Brzeska' (Brzeska Street), in *Łapa w łapę i inne reportaże* (Hand in Hand and Other Reports), Warsaw: Iskry, 2004.
8 Kapuściński, *The Emperor*, 47.
9 Ibid., 94.
10 Ibid.
11 'Z tamtego świata' (From the Other World), interview with Ryszard Kapuściński by Jacek Syski, *Literatura*, 22 July 1976.
12 Andrzej Pawluczuk, 'Świat na stadionie' (The World at the Stadium), *Kontrasty* 4, 1979.
13 Kapuściński, *The Emperor*, 52.
14 Ibid., 35.
15 Ibid., 32.
16 Ibid., 36.
17 Ibid., 125.
18 Ibid., 54.
19 Ibid., 7.
20 Ibid., 5.
21 Ibid., 129–30.
22 Józef Tejchma, *W kręgu nadziei i rozczarowań* (In the Circle of Hopes and Disappointments), Warsaw: Wydawnictwo Projekt, 2002.
23 Kapuściński, *The Emperor*, 108–9.
24 Ibid., 120.

29 On Love and Other Demons

1 Ryszard Kapuściński, *Lapidarium III*, Warsaw: Czytelnik, 1997.
2 Statements by Alicja Kapuścińska in 'Mąż reporter' (My Husband the Reporter), interview with Alicja Kapuścińska by Teresa Torańska and Artur Domosławski, *Gazeta Wyborcza*, 19 January 2009.
3 Ibid.
4 Ryszard Frelek, Statement in 'Odszedł dziennikarz wieku' (The Journalist of the Century Has Passed Away), *Press* 2, 2007.
5 Ryszard Kapuściński, 'Fin de siècle' in *Wiersze zebrane* (Collected Poems), *Dzieła wybrane Ryszarda Kapuścińskiego* (Collected Works of Ryszard Kapuściński), vol. 10, Warsaw: Agora, 2008.
6 Ryszard Kapuściński, *Another Day of Life*, trans. William R. Brand and Katarzyna Mroczkowska-Brand, London: Penguin Books, 2001, 52–3.
7 Ryszard Kapuściński, *The Shadow of the Sun*, trans. Klara Glowczewska, London: Penguin Books, 2002, 76–7.
8 Ryszard Kapuściński, *Travels with Herodotus*, trans. Klara Glowczewska, London: Penguin Books, 2008, 13.
9 Kapuściński, 'Odkąd jesteś' (Ever Since You), in *Wiersze zebrane*.
10 Statements by Alicja Kapuścińska in 'Mąż reporter'.

30 The Final Revolution, the Final Coup

1 Statement by Ryszard Kapuściński in *Kto tu wpuścił dziennikarzy. 20 lat później* (Who Let the Journalists in Here? 20 Years Later), Warsaw: Rosner i Wspólnicy, 2005.
2 Timothy Garton Ash, *The Polish Revolution: Solidarity*, New York: Charles Scribner's Sons, 1984, 32.
3 Statement by Kapuściński, in *Kto tu wpuścił dziennikarzy*.
4 Ibid.
5 Ibid.
6 Ryszard Kapuściński, *Shah of Shahs*, trans. William R. Brand and Katarzyna Mroczkowska-Brand, London: Penguin Books, 2006, 115–16.
7 Ibid., 111.
8 Statement by Kapuściński in *Kto tu wpuścił dziennikarzy*.
9 Ibid.
10 Ibid.
11 Ibid.
12 Ibid.
13 Ibid.
14 Ibid.
15 Ibid.
16 Ibid.
17 Ibid.
18 Ryszard Kapuściński, 'Notatki z Wybrzeża' (Notes from the Coast), *Kultura* 37, 1980.
19 Ibid.
20 Ibid.
21 Ibid.

22 Statement by Kapuściński in *Kto tu wpuścił dziennikarzy*.
23 'Wyjście z kostiumu' (Coming out of Costume), interview with Ryszard Kapuściński by Zbigniew Miazga, *Sztandar Ludu*, 11 March 1981.
24 Statement by Ryszard Kapuściński in 'Etos klasy robotniczej' (The Ethos of the Working Class), *Miesięcznik Literacki* 4, 1981.
25 Ryszard Piekarowicz, unpublished diary.
26 Ibid.
27 Jerzy Urban, Letter to Mariusz Szczygieł, *Gazeta Wyborcza*, 29 January 2007.
28 Jerzy Urban, Statement at the Government Spokesman's Press Conference, in Beata Nowacka and Zygmunt Ziątek, *Ryszard Kapuściński. Biografia pisarza* (Ryszard Kapuściński: Biography of a Writer), Kraków: SIW Znak, 2008.
29 Statement by Kapuściński in *Kto tu wpuścił dziennikarzy*.
30 Ibid.
31 Ryszard Kapuściński, Letter to Jerzy Nowak, Warsaw, n.d. (first half of 1982).
32 Ryszard Kapuściński, Letter to Jerzy Nowak, Warsaw, 4 November 1982.
33 Ryszard Kapuściński, Letter to Jerzy Nowak, Warsaw, n.d.

31 Worth More Than a Thousand Grizzled Journofantasists

1 Ryszard Kapuściński, *Lapidarium*, Warsaw: Czytelnik, 1990.
2 William Brand, 'Prawnik zażądał notarialnych poświadczeń' (The Lawyer Requested Notarized Certificates), in Bożena Dudko, ed., *Podróże z Ryszardem Kapuścińskim* (Travels with Ryszard Kapuściński), Kraków: SIW Znak, 2007.
3 Ibid.
4 Peter Prescott, 'His Clement Highness', *Newsweek*, 11 April 1983, 76.
5 Salman Rushdie in 'Christmas Books', *Sunday Times*, 11 December 1983, p. 39.
6 David Wise and Thomas B. Ross, *The Invisible Government*, New York: Random House, 1964, 110–13, quoted in Ryszard Kapuściński, *Szachinszach*, Warsaw: Czytelnik, 1997.
7 Brand, 'Prawnik zażądał notarialnych poświadczeń'.
8 Salman Rushdie, 'Reporting a Nightmare', *Guardian*, 13 February 1987, 15.
9 Joe Queenan, 'A Pole Apart', *Wall Street Journal*, 25 April 1991.
10 Adam Hochschild, 'Magic Journalism', *New York Review of Books*, 3 November 1994.
11 Statement by Antoni Libera in 'Oskarżał Zachód o nędzę świata' (He Blamed the West for World Poverty), *Dziennik*, 26–27 January 2008.
12 Kapuściński, *Lapidarium*.
13 Ryszard Kapuściński, Letter to Jerzy and Izabella Nowak, Philadelphia, 21 February 1988.
14 Kapuściński, *Lapidarium*.
15 Ryszard Kapuściński, *Lapidarium II*, Warsaw: Czytelnik, 1996.

32 Lapidarium 4: Why Did Kapuściński Have No Critics in Poland?

1 Ryszard Kapuściński, *Lapidarium II*, Warsaw: Czytelnik, 1996.
2 Artur Domosławski, *Ameryka zbuntowana* (Rebellious America), Warsaw: Świat Książki, 2007, 239.

33 The Reporter Amends Reality, or, Critics of All Nations, Unite!

1 Harold G. Marcus, 'Prejudice and Ignorance in Reviewing Books about Africa: The Strange Case of Ryszard Kapuściński's *The Emperor*', *History in Africa* 17, 1990, 373–8.

2 Ibid.

3 Ryszard Kapuściński, *Shah of Shahs*, trans. William R. Brand and Katarzyna Mroczkowska-Brand, London: Penguin Books, 2006, 24.

4 Ibid., 117.

5 'Czeterokrotnie rozstrzelany' (Executed by Firing Squad Four Times), Ryszard Kapuściński in conversation with Wojciech Giełżyński, *Ekspres Reporterów* 6, 1978.

6 Ryszard Kapuściński, *Lapidarium III*, Warsaw: Czytelnik, 1997.

7 Ibid.; quotation from Susannah Clapp retranslated from Polish.

8 Kapuściński, *Lapidarium III*.

9 Ryszard Kapuściński, *Chrystus z karabinem na ramieniu* (Christ with a Rifle on His Shoulder), Warsaw: Czytelnik, 1976.

10 Ibid.

11 Ibid.

12 Ryszard Kapuściński, *The Shadow of the Sun*, trans. Klara Glowczewska, London: Penguin Books, 2002, 152.

13 Ibid., 145.

14 John Ryle, 'At Play in the Bush of Ghosts: Tropical Baroque, African Reality and the Work of Ryszard Kapuściński', *Times Literary Supplement*, 27 July 2001.

15 Lluís Albert Chillón Asensio, *Literatura y periodismo. Una tradición de relaciones promiscuas* (Literature and Journalism, a Tradition of Promiscuous Relationships), Bellaterra: Universidad Autónoma de Barcelona, 1999.

16 Ryszard Kapuściński, *Autoportret reportera* (Self-portrait of a Reporter), Kraków: SIW Znak, 2003.

17 Wojciech Jagielski, *The Night Wanderers*, trans. Antonia Lloyd-Jones, New York: Seven Stories, 2012.

18 'Bez litości' (No Mercy), interview with Wojciech Jagielski by Andrzej Skworz, *Press* 11, 2009.

19 Ryszard Kapuściński, *Lapidarium*. Warsaw: Czytelnik, 1990.

35 Our Friend Rysiek

1 Ryszard Kapuściński, Letter to Jerzy and Izabella Nowak, Mexico City, 19 February 1972.

2 Ryszard Kapuściński, Letter to Izabella Nowak, Mexico City, 15 December 1969.

3 Ryszard Kapuściński, Letter to Jerzy and Izabella Nowak, Mexico City, 11 February 1970.

4 Ryszard Kapuściński, 'Takie sobie zwrotki na urodziny Dorotki' in Witold Bereś and Krzysztof Burnetko, *Kapuściński: nie ogarniam świata* (Kapuściński: I Cannot Embrace the World), Warsaw: Świat Książki, 2007.

5 Ryszard Kapuściński, 'Why Did the World', in *I Wrote Stone: The Selected Poetry of Ryszard Kapuściński*, trans. Diana Kuprel and Marek Kusiba, Emeryville, Canada: Biblioasis, 2007, 52.

36   Where to from Socialism?

1   Ryszard Kapuściński, *Imperium*, trans. Klara Glowczewska, London, Granta Books, 2007, 84–5.
2   Ibid., 202.
3   Ibid., 215–6.
4   Ryszard Kapuściński, *Lapidarium*, Warsaw: Czytelnik, 1990.
5   Ryszard Kapuściński, 'A Note', in *I Wrote Stone: The Selected Poetry of Ryszard Kapuściński*, trans. Diana Kuprel and Marek Kusiba, Emeryville, Canada: Biblioasis, 2007, 47.
6   Kapuściński, *Lapidarium*.
7   Ibid.
8   Ibid.
9   Ryszard Kapuściński, Letter to Jerzy Nowak, 4 May 1991.
10 Ryszard Kapuściński, *Lapidarium II*, Warsaw: Czytelnik, 1996.
11 Ibid.
12 Ibid.
13 'Dziennikarz wieku 1999' (Journalist of the Century 1999), *Press*, www.press.pl.

37   Lapidarium 5: Was Kapuściński a Thinker?

1   Ryszard Kapuściński, *The Shadow of the Sun*, trans. Klara Glowczewska, London: Penguin Books, 2002, 83.
2   Ryszard Kapuściński, *Lapidarium II*, Warsaw: Czytelnik, 1996.
3   Ryszard Kapuściński, *Shah of Shahs*, trans. William R. Brand and Katarzyna Mroczkowska-Brand, London: Penguin Books, 2006, 109.
4   Kapuściński, *Lapidarium II*.
5   Kapuściński, *The Shadow of the Sun*, 229–30.
6   'Nasz kruchy świat' (Our Fragile World), interview with Ryszard Kapuściński by Artur Domosławski and Aleksander Kaczorowski, *Gazeta Wyborcza*, 28 September 2001.
7   Ryszard Kapuściński, *Lapidarium V*, Warsaw: Czytelnik, 2002.
8   Ibid.
9   Ryszard Kapuściński, *The Other*, trans. Antonia Lloyd-Jones, London: Verso Books, 2008, 92.
10 'Reporter to taki zwiadowca' (A Reporter Is Like a Scout), interview with Ryszard Kapuściński by Marek Radziwon, *Gazeta Wyborcza*, 29 September 2005.

38   Where to from Socialism? Continued

1   Ryszard Kapuściński, *Lapidarium III*, Warsaw: Czytelnik, 1997.
2   Ryszard Kapuściński, *Lapidarium IV*, Warsaw: Czytelnik, 2000.
3   Ryszard Kapuściński, *Lapidarium V*, Warsaw: Czytelnik, 2002.
4   Ibid.
5   Ryszard Kapuściński, *The Shadow of the Sun*, trans. Klara Glowczewska, London: Penguin Books, 2002, 228.
6   'Wiosna ludów latynoskich' (The Springtime of the Latino Peoples), interview with Ryszard Kapuściński by Artur Domosławski, *Gazeta Wyborcza*, 7 April 2001.

7 Andrzej Pawluczuk, 'Reporter ginącego świata. Opowieść o Ryszardzie Kapuścińskim' (Reporter of a Dying World: A Tale about Ryszard Kapuściński), http://www.kapuscinski.info/page/zyciorys/15.

8 'Nasz kruchy świat' (Our Fragile World), interview with Ryszard Kapuściński by Artur Domosławski and Aleksander Kaczorowski, *Gazeta Wyborcza*, 28 September 2001.

9 Ibid.

10 Ibid.

11 Ernest Skalski, 'Zero tolerancji' (Zero Tolerance), *Gazeta Wyborcza*, 3 October 2001.

12 'Ciszej z tymi werblami' (Stop Banging the Drums), interview with Ryszard Kapuściński by Artur Domosławski, *Gazeta Wyborcza*, 24 December 2002.

13 Ryszard Kapuściński, *Lapidarium*, Warsaw: Czytelnik, 1990.

39   The File

1 Ian Traynor, 'Famed Polish Writer Outed as "Spy" in Anti-communist Purge', *The Guardian*, 22 May 2007, 19.

2 Paolo Rumiz and Andrea Tarquini, 'Accuse postume a Kapuscinski: "Era una spia di Varsavia" ' (Kapuściński Posthumously Accused: 'He Was a Spy for Warsaw'), *la Repubblica*, 22 May 2007 (retranslated from Polish).

3 File for Operational Contact Known as 'The Poet', Instytut Pamięci Narodowej (Institute of National Remembrance) BU 001043/255.

4 Author's note: After leaving Mexico, Sobieski went to work for the Central Committee's Foreign Department, run by Frelek, and often used to meet Kapuściński there.

5 Igor Ryciak, 'Kontakt 11630/I' (Contact 11630/I), *Newsweek Polska*, 27 May 2007.

6 John Stockwell, *In Search of Enemies: A CIA Story*, New York: W.W. Norton, 1978, 101.

40   Legends 5: The Price of Greatness

1 Ryszard Kapuściński: 'Właściwie co miałem zrobić . . .' (What Should I Really Have Done . . .), in *Wiersze zebrane* (Collected Poems), *Dzieła wybrane Ryszarda Kapuścińskiego t. 10* (Collected Works of Ryszard Kapuściński), vol. 10, Warsaw: Agora, 2008.

41   Maestro Kapu

1 Oscar Escamilla, 'Retrato de un encuentro' (Portrait of a Meeting) in Ryszard Kapuściński, *Los cincos sentidos del periodista* (The Journalist's Five Senses), Bogotá: Fundación Nuevo Periodismo Latinoamericano, 2004.

42   Unwritten Books

1 Ryszard Kapuściński, Notes for unwritten books, in Artur Domosławski, 'Hycle w Arkadii' (Dog Catchers in Arcadia), *Gazeta Wyborcza*, 21 January 2008.

2 Ibid.
3 Ibid.
4 Ibid.
5 Ibid.
6 Ibid.
7 'Czarny Ląd i czarne karty' (The Dark Continent and Dark Pages), interview with Ryszard Kapuściński by Wojciech Jagielski, *Gazeta Wyborcza*, 23 August 2003.
8 Ibid.
9 Kapuściński, Notes, in Domosławski, Hycle w Arkadii.
10 Ibid.
11 Ibid.
12 Ibid.
13 Ibid.
14 Ibid.
15 Ibid.
16 Ibid.
17 Ibid.
18 Ibid.
19 Ibid.
20 Ibid.

43   No Strength to Furnish the Face

1 Ryszard Kapuściński, Notes, in Artur Domosławski, 'Kamyki, szkiełka i tysiąc innych skarbów' (Pebbles, Pieces of Glass and a Thousand Other Treasures), *Gazeta Wyborcza*, 24 December 2007.
2 Leopold Staff, 'Kieszeń' (The Pocket), in *Poezje zebrane* (Collected Poems), Warsaw: PIW, 1967.
3 Mircea Eliade, *Journal I, 1945–1955*, trans. Mac Linscott Ricketts, Chicago: University of Chicago Press, 1990, 182–6 .
4 Mircea Eliade, *Journal II*, trans. Fred H. Johnson Jr, Chicago: University of Chicago Press, 1989, 13–16.
5 Jan Parandowski, *Petrarka* (Petrarch), Warsaw: Czytelnik, 1956.
6 Alexei Suvorin, *Dnievnik* (Diary), Moscow: Novosti, 1992.
7 Mikołaj Rej, *Żywot człowieka poczciwego* (The Life of the Honest Man), Wrocław: Ossolineum, 1956.
8 Kapuściński, Notes, in Domosławski, 'Kamyki, szkiełka'.
9 Anna Świrszczyńska, *Mówię do swego ciała* (Talking to My Body), Kraków: Colonel Press, 2002.
10 Konrad Godlewski, 'Nobel przychodzi w czwartek' (Nobel Comes on Thursday), *Gazeta Wyborcza*, 5 October 2005.
11 Kapuściński, Notes, in Domosławski, 'Kamyki, szkiełka'.
12 Ibid.
13 Statements by Alicja Kapuścińska in 'Mąż reporter' (My Husband the Reporter), interview with Alicja Kapuścińska by Teresa Torańska and Artur Domosławski, *Gazeta Wyborcza*, 19 January 2009.
14 Ryszard Kapuściński, 'Suffering and Guilt', in *I Wrote Stone: The Selected Poetry of Ryszard Kapuściński*, trans. Diana Kuprel and Marek Kusiba, Emeryville, Canada: Biblioasis, 2007, 68.

15 Kapuściński, Notes, in Domosławski, 'Kamyki, szkiełka'.
16 Ibid.
17 Alicja Kapuścińska, in 'Mąż reporter'.
18 Ryszard Kapuściński, 'Zapiski szpitalne' (Hospital Jottings), in Jarosław Mikołajewski, *Sentymentalny portret Ryszarda Kapuścińskiego* (A Sentimental Portrait of Ryszard Kapuściński), Kraków: Wydawnictwo Literackie, 2008.
19 Ibid.

Index